# Bloom's Period Studies

BLOOM'S PERIOD STUDIES

# American Naturalism

Edited and with an introduction by
## Harold Bloom
Sterling Professor of the Humanities
Yale University

CHELSEA HOUSE
PUBLISHERS
A Haights Cross Communications Company
Philadelphia

©2004 by Chelsea House Publishers, a subsidiary of
Haights Cross Communications.

A Haights Cross Communications ◀▔ Company

Introduction © 2004 by Harold Bloom.

Printed and bound in the United States of America.
10  9  8  7  6  5  4  3  2  1


Library of Congress Cataloging-in-Publication Data applied for.

  ISBN: 0-7910-7897-3


Chelsea House Publishers
1974 Sproul Road, Suite 400
Broomall, PA 19008-0914

http://www.chelseahouse.com

Contributing Editor: Jesse Zuba

Cover designed by Keith Trego

Cover: Courtesy of the Library of Congress

Layout by EJB Publishing Services

# Contents

# Editor's Note

My Introduction begins with interpretations of Stephen Crane's *The Red Badge of Courage* and of his three best stories: "The Open Boat", "The Blue Hotel", and "The Bride Comes to Yellow Sky". I follow my account of Crane with critical meditations upon Kate Chopin's *The Awakening*, and Edith Wharton's *Ethan Frome* and *The Custom of the Country*, before concluding with the masterpiece of American Naturalism, Theodore Dreiser's *An American Tragedy*.

The most aggressive of our Naturalist novelists, Frank Norris, exalts the Romanticism of Zola, accurately pointing to its phantasmagoria, and proceeds to persuasively redefine Naturalism as being anything but "an inner circle of realism."

In the most celebrated critical essay on American Naturalism, Lionel Trilling centers upon the later Dreiser, after which Philip Rahv emphasizes the movement's decline in the rise of a different mode in John Dos Passos.

Malcolm Cowley praises the Naturalists, despite their faults, for their exuberant responses to the vitality of American urban life, after which Donald Pizer broods upon the achievements of Norris, Dreiser, and Crane.

Henry James's brilliant metaphor, "the house of fiction," prompts an illuminating excursus by the critic Richard Poirier, who contrasts Edith Wharton's *The House of Mirth* to Dreiser's *Sister Carrie*, and finds in Dreiser the Emersonian drive to build a world out of the self.

Farrell's *Studs Lonigan* is read by Ann Douglas as a warning to "discipline our perception," while Harold Kaplan finds in Dreiser's *Sister Carrie* an allegory of a system that requires a revolution.

Zola's influence upon our literary Naturalism is investigated by Richard Lehan, in relation to Norris and to Dreiser.

Michael Fabre studies Richard Wright's effort to get beyond Naturalism, while Philip Fisher subtly traces the visionary contours of Dreiser's Chicago.

Frank Norris insisted that: "We don't want literature, we want life," a slogan that Michael Davitt Bell shows to be self-defeating, after which Donald Pizer returns, to bring us up to date on Naturalism's survival in Norman Mailer and Robert Stone.

Kate Chopin and Edith Wharton are contrasted by Barbara Hochman, while Donna M. Campbell places Jack London between Dreiser and Crane as three "rescuers" of "fallen women."

HAROLD BLOOM

# Introduction

## Stephen Crane

Stephen Crane's contribution to the canon of American literature is fairly slight in bulk: one classic short novel, three vivid stories, and two or three ironic lyrics. *The Red Badge of Courage*; "The Open Boat," "The Blue Hotel," and "The Bride Comes to Yellow Sky"; "War is Kind" and "A Man Adrift on a Slim Spar"—a single small volume can hold them all. Crane was dead at twenty-eight, after a frantic life, but a longer existence probably would not have enhanced his achievement. He was an exemplary American writer, flaring in the forehead of the morning sky and vanishing in the high noon of our evening land. An original, if not quite a Great Original, he prophesied Hemingway and our other journalist-novelists and still seems a forerunner of much to come.

*The Red Badge of Courage* is Crane's undoubted masterwork. Each time I reread it, I am surprised afresh, particularly by the book's originality, which requires a reader's act of recovery because Crane's novel has been so influential. To write about battle in English, since Crane, is to be shadowed by Crane. Yet Crane, who later saw warfare in Cuba and between the Greeks and the Turks in his work as a correspondent, had experienced no fighting when he wrote *The Red Badge of Courage*. There is no actual experience that informs Crane's version of the Battle of Chancellorsville, one of the most terrible carnages of the American Civil War. Yet anyone who has gone through warfare, from the time of the novel's publication (1895) until now, has testified to Crane's uncanny accuracy at the representation of battle. *The Red Badge of Courage* is an impressionist's triumph, in the particular sense that

1

"impressionist" had in the literature of the nineties, a Paterian sense that went back to the emphasis upon *seeing* in Carlyle, Emerson, and Ruskin. Conrad and Henry James, both of whom befriended Crane, had their own relation to the impressionist mode, and each realized that Crane was a pure or natural impressionist, indeed the only one, according to Conrad.

Pater, deftly countering Matthew Arnold, stated the credo of literary impressionism:

> The first step towards seeing one's object as it really is, is to know one's impression as it really is, to discriminate it, to realize it distinctly.

Pater's "object" is a work of art, verbal or visual, but the critic here has stated Stephen Crane's quest to see the object of experience as it is, to know one's impression of it, and to realize that impression in narrative fiction. Scholarly arguments as to whether and to what degree *The Red Badge of Courage* is naturalistic, symbolist, or impressionist, can be set aside quickly. Joyce's *Ulysses* is both naturalistic and symbolist within the general perspective of the Paterian or impressionistic "epiphany" or privileged moment, but juxtapose the *Red Badge* to *Ulysses* and Crane is scarcely naturalistic or symbolist in comparison. Crane is altogether an impressionist, in his "vivid impressionistic description of action on that woodland battlefield," as Conrad phrased it, or, again in Conrad's wording, in "the imaginative analysis of his own temperament tried by the emotions of a battlefield."

If Crane's impressionism had a single literary origin, as to some extent is almost inevitable, Kipling is that likely forerunner. The puzzles of literary ancestry are most ironical here, since Kipling's precursor was Mark Twain. Hemingway's famous observation that all modern American literature comes out of one book, *Huckleberry Finn*, is only true of Crane, the indubitable beginning of our modern literature, insofar as Crane took from Kipling precisely what the author of *The Light That Failed* and *Kim* owed to Twain. Michael Fried's association of Crane with the painter Eakins is peculiarly persuasive, since Crane's visual impressionism is so oddly American, without much resembling Whistler's. Crane is almost the archetype of the writer as a child of experience, yet I think this tends to mean that then there are a few strong artistic precursors, rather than a tradition that makes itself available. Associate Crane with Kipling and Eakins, on the way to, but still a distance from, Conrad and the French Postimpressionists, and you probably have stationed him accurately enough.

II

*The Red Badge of Courage* is necessarily a story about fear. Crane's Young Soldier, again as Conrad noted, "dreads not danger but fear itself.... In this he stands for the symbol of all untried men." Henry Fleming, as eventually we come to know the Young Soldier, moves ironically from a dangerous self-doubt to what may be an even more dangerous dignity. This is the novel's famous yet perhaps equivocal conclusion:

> For a time this pursuing recollection of the tattered man took all elation from the youth's veins. He saw his vivid error, and he was afraid that it would stand before him all his life. He took no share in the chatter of his comrades, nor did he look at them or know them, save when he felt sudden suspicion that they were seeing his thoughts and scrutinizing each detail of the scene with the tattered soldier.
>
> Yet gradually he mustered force to put the sin at a distance. And at last his eyes seemed to open to some new ways. He found that he could look back upon the brass and bombast of his earlier gospels and see them truly. He was gleeful when he discovered that he now despised them.
>
> With this conviction came a store of assurance. He felt a quiet manhood, nonassertive but of sturdy and strong blood. He knew that he would no more quail before his guides wherever they should point. He had been to touch the great death, and found that, after all, it was but the great death. He was a man.
>
> So it came to pass that as he trudged from the place of blood and wrath his soul changed. He came from hot plowshares to prospects of clover tranquilly, and it was as if hot plowshares were not. Scars faded as flowers.
>
> It rained. The procession of weary soldiers became a bedraggled train, despondent and muttering, marching with churning effort in a trough of liquid brown mud under a low, wretched sky. Yet the youth smiled, for he saw that the world was a world for him, though many discovered it to be made of oaths and walking sticks. He had rid himself of the red sickness of battle. The sultry nightmare was in the past. He had been an animal blistered and sweating in the heat and pain of war. He turned now with a lover's thirst to images of tranquil skies, fresh meadows, cool brooks—an existence of soft and eternal peace.

Over the river a golden ray of sun came through the hosts of leaden rain clouds.

More Hemingway than Hemingway are these very American sentences: "He had been to touch the great death, and found that, after all, it was but the great death. He was a man." Is the irony of that dialectical enough to suffice? In context, the power of the irony is beyond question, since Crane's prose is strong enough to bear rephrasing as: "He had been to touch the great fear, and found that, after all, it was still the great fear. He was not yet a man." Crane's saving nuance is that the fear of being afraid dehumanizes, while accepting one's own mortality bestows upon one the association with others that grants the dignity of the human. How does Crane's prose find the strength to sustain a vision that primary and normative? The answer, I suspect, is the Bible and Bunyan, both of them being deeply at work in this unbelieving son of a Methodist minister: "He came from hot plowshares to prospects of clover tranquilly, and it was as if hot plowshares were not." The great trope of Isaiah is assimilated in the homely and unassuming manner of Bunyan, and we see the Young Soldier, Henry Fleming, as an American Pilgrim, anticipating when both sides of the Civil War "shall beat their swords into plowshares, and their spears into pruning hooks."

III

Crane's accurate apprehension of the phantasmagoria that is battle has been compared to Tolstoy's. There is something to such a parallel, perhaps because Tolstoy even more massively is a biblical writer. What is uniquely Crane's, what parts him from all prior visionaries of warfare, is difficult to define, but is of the highest importance for establishing his astonishing originality. Many examples night be chosen, but I give the death of the color sergeant from the conclusion of chapter 19:

Over the field went the scurrying mass. It was a handful of men splattered into the faces of the enemy. Toward it instantly sprang the yellow tongues. A vast quantity of blue smoke hung before them. A nighty banging made ears valueless.

The youth ran like a madman to reach the woods before a bullet could discover him. He ducked his head low, like a football player. In his haste his eyes almost closed, and the scene was a wild blur. Pulsating saliva stood at the corners of his mouth.

Within him, as he hurled himself forward, was born a love, a despairing fondness for this flag which was near him. It was a creation of beauty and invulnerability. It was a goddess, radiant, that bended its form with an imperious gesture to him. It was a woman, red and white, hating and loving, that called him with the voice of his hopes. Because no harm could come to it he endowed it with power. He kept near, as if it could be a saver of lives, and an imploring cry went from his mind.

In the mad scramble he was aware that the color sergeant flinched suddenly, as if struck by a bludgeon. He faltered, and then became motionless, save for his quivering knees.

He made a spring and a clutch at the pole. At the same instant his friend grabbed it from the other side. They jerked at it, stout and furious, but the color sergeant was dead, and the corpse would not relinquish its trust. For a moment there was a grim encounter. The dead man, swinging with bended back, seemed to be obstinately tugging, in ludicrous and awful ways, for the possession of the flag.

It was past in an instant of time. They wrenched the flag furiously from the dead man, and, as they turned again, the corpse swayed forward with bowed head. One arm swung high, and the curved hand fell with heavy protest on the friend's unheeding shoulder.

In the "wild blur" of this phantasmagoria, there are two images of pathos, the flag and the corpse of the color sergeant. Are they not to some degree assimilated to one another, so that the corpse becomes a flagpole, and the flag a corpse? Yet so dialectical is the interplay of Crane's biblical irony that the assimilation, however incomplete, itself constitutes a figure of doubt as to the normative intensities of patriotism and group solidarity that the scene exemplifies, both in the consciousness of Henry Fleming and in that of the rapt reader. The "despairing fondness" for the flag is both a Platonic and a Freudian Eros, but finally more Freudian. It possesses "invulnerability" for which the soldier under fire has that Platonic desire for what he himself does not possess and quite desperately needs, but it manifests even more a Freudian sense of the ambivalence both of and towards the woman as object of the drive, at once a radiant goddess sexually bending her form though imperiously, yet also a woman, red and white, hating and loving, destroying and healing.

The corpse of the color sergeant, an emblem of devotion to the flag and the group even beyond death, nevertheless keeps Fleming and his friend from the possibility of survival as men, compelling them to clutch and jerk at the pole, stout and furious. Life-in-death incarnate, the corpse obstinately tugs for the staff of its lost life. Homer surely would have appreciated the extraordinary closing gesture, as the corpse sways forward, head bowed but arm swung high for a final stroke, as "the curved hand fell with heavy protest on the friend's unheeding shoulder."

Crane is hardly the American Homer; Walt Whitman occupies that place forever. Still, *The Red Badge of Courage* is certainly the most Homeric prose narrative ever written by an American. One wants to salute it with Whitman's most Homeric trope, when he says of the grass:

And now it seems to me the beautiful uncut hair of graves.

Stephen Crane's primary contribution to American literature remains his Civil War novel, *The Red Badge of Courage*. Yet his talents were diverse: a handful of his experimental poems continue to be vibrant, and his three finest stories are perpetually rewarding for lovers of that genre.

A war correspondent by enthusiastic profession, Stephen Crane was the Hemingway of his era, always in pursuit of material for his narrative art. "The Open Boat" is directly founded upon Crane's own experience, while "The Blue Hotel" and "The Bride Comes to Yellow Sky" reflect his travels in the American West. Crane's death, from tuberculosis at age twenty-eight, was an extraordinary loss for American letters, and his three great stories examined in this brief volume can be regarded as the most promising of his works.

"The Open Boat" intended, as Crane said, to be "after the fact," but is very different from "Stephen Crane's Own Story," his journalistic account of surviving the sinking of the *Commodore*, a cargo ship bearing arms for the Cuban rebels against Spain in January 1897. Much admired by Joseph Conrad, "The Open Boat" so handles reality as to render it phantasmagoric. The four survivors of the *Commodore* find themselves floating off a coast that absurdly declines to observe them. Even when people on shore waved to them, it is without recognition of the survivors' predicament. Compelled to make an unaided run to land, the boat is swamped in the icy water, and Crane swims ashore with the greatest difficulty. "The Open Boat" concludes with a sentence that memorializes the complex nature of the ordeal:

When it came night, the white waves paced to and fro in the moonlight, and the wind brought the sound of the great sea's voice to the men on shore, and they felt that they could then be interpreters.

One thinks of Melville and Conrad as interpreters of the mirror of the sea; if Stephen Crane is of their visionary company, it can only be in an outsider's sense. What Crane conveys is the incomprehensibility of the sea when seen from a land-perspective. When I think of "The Open Boat," what I recall first is the frustrated helplessness of the survivors in the boat, who cannot communicate to those on shore the precariousness and desperation of shipwreck. Crane, neither a moralist like Conrad nor a Gnostic rebel like Melville, cannot quite reveal his interpretation to us.

"The Bride Comes to Yellow Sky" is a genial comedy, yet it also turns upon the absurdity of non-recognition. Scratchy Wilson, the story's insane and alcoholic gunman, cannot take in the enormous change that Jack Potter, town marshal of Yellow Sky, stands before him not only unarmed but accompanied by his new bride:

> "Well," said Wilson at last, slowly, "I s'pose it's all off now."
>
> "It's all off if you say so, Scratchy. You know I didn't make the trouble." Potter lifted his valise.
>
> "Well, I 'low it's off, Jack," said Wilson. He was looking at the ground. "Married!" He was not a student of chivalry; it was merely that in the presence of this foreign condition he was a simple child of the earlier plains. He picked up his starboard revolver, and placing both weapons in their holsters, he went away. His feet made funnel-shaped tracks in the heavy sand.

As in "The Open Boat," Crane relies upon a total clash of incongruities. Sea and land are as far apart as marriage and Scratchy Wilson, who knows only that part of his world has ended forever. Crane acts as interpreter, and yet keeps his distance from the absurd gap that is very nearly beyond interpretation.

Crane worked very hard writing "The Blue Hotel," his masterpiece of narrative. The Swede is a kind of culmination for Crane: an authentically unpleasant character, whose reality is so persuasive as to become oppressive. Lured by the myth of the West, the Swede attempts to incarnate its code, but individuates himself instead as a bully and an interloper. His fight with young Scully is a false victory, isolating him totally, until he provokes the gambler into murdering him. The rest is irony:

The corpse of the Swede, alone in the saloon, had its eyes fixed upon a dreadful legend that dwelt a-top of the cash machine: "This registers the amount of the purchase."

Yet has the Swede purchased death or been tricked into it? Crane's final irony is to reveal that young Scully *has* been cheating at cards, thus rightly provoking the Swede to combat. Is the Easterner correct when he ends the story by asserting that five men, himself included, pragmatically murdered the Swede? I think that the reader decides differently. The Swede, and the myth of the West, are the only culprits.

## THE AWAKENING

There are several intrinsic affinities between Walt Whitman's poetry and *The Awakening*, which I will explore here. However, there is an ironical extrinsic similarity that I mention first, doubtless at some risk of giving offense. Whitman's poetry is now much written about by academic critics who care only for the homoerotic Walt; the poetry, to them, is of interest only insofar as it represents the poet's undoubted desires. Similarly, Kate Chopin's *The Awakening* is now a favorite work of feminist critics, who find in it a forerunner of Liberation. I regard all this with amiable irony, since so much of Whitman's best poetry is quite overtly autoerotic while Edna Pontellier's awakening is to her own "shifting, treacherous, fickle deeps," not so much of her soul (as Chopin carefully adds) but of her body. If *The Awakening* is a breakthrough, it is as the subtle female version of the self-gratification slyly celebrated by Goethe (in *Faust, Part Two*) and openly sung by Walt Whitman.

Though *The Awakening* follows in the path of Flaubert's *Madame Bovary*, it shares little with that formidable precursor. Emma Bovary indeed awakens, belatedly and tragically, but the narcissistic Edna singly drifts from one mode of reverie to another, until she drowns herself in the sea, which for her as for Whitman represents night and the mother, death and the inmost self. Far from being a rebel, moved by sympathy with victims of societal oppression, Edna is even more isolated at the end than before. It is a very peculiar academic fashion that has transformed Edna into any kind of a feminist heroine. The protagonist of *The Awakening* is her own victim, unless one agrees with Kathleen Margaret Lane's assertion that: "Edna awakens to the horrible knowledge that she can never, because she is female, be her own person." Late 19th-century Creole society was not Afghanistan under the rule of the Taliban or Iran under the Ayatollah Khomeini. Chopin shows it as having something of a hothouse atmosphere, but that alas does seem the only possible context for Edna, who in fact loves no one—not her children, husband, friends, or lovers—and whose awakening is only to the ecstasies of self-gratification.

The influence of Whitman is pervasive throughout *The Awakening*, and suggests that Chopin was deeply immersed in *Leaves of Grass*, particularly in the *Sea-Drift* poems, and in the *Lilacs* elegy for Lincoln. Gouvernail, the benign bachelor who is one of the guests at Edna's birthday party, had appeared earlier in Chopin's short story, "A Respectable Woman," where he recites part of Section 21 of *Song of Myself*: "Night of south winds—night of the large few stars!/Still nodding night—." The entire passage could serve as an epigraph for *The Awakening*.

> Press close bare-bosom'd night—press close magnetic
> nourishing night!
> Night of south winds—night of the few large stars!
> Still nodding night—mad naked summer night.

This is the model for the ecstatic rebirth of Edna's self, a narcissistic self-investment that awards Edna a new ego. Had Edna been able to see that her awakening was to a passion for herself, then her suicide perhaps could have been avoided. Chopin, a very uneven stylist, nevertheless was erotically subtler than most of her critics have been. Edna emulates Whitman by falling in love with her own body: "observing closely, as if it were something she saw for the first time, the fine, firm quality and texture of her flesh." This stems from Whitman's grand proclamation: "If I worship one thing more than another it shall be the spread of my own body, or any part of it." When Edna awakens to self, she hears the voice of the sea, and experiences its Whitmanesque embrace: "The touch of the sea is sensuous, enfolding the body in its soft, close embrace." When the naked Edna enters the mothering sea for a last time, we hear an echo of the undulating serpentine death that Whitman welcomes in *When Lilacs Last in the Dooryard Bloom'd*: "The foamy wavelets curled up to her white feet and coiled like serpents about her ankles." Is this indeed a chant of Women's Liberation, or a siren song of a Whitmanesque Love-Death?

EDITH WHARTON

The most formidable figure in all Wallace Stevens's marvelous roster of fabulistic caricatures is that grand reductionist, "Mrs. Alfred Uruguay":

> So what said the others and the sun went down
> And, in the brown blues of evening, the lady said,
> In the donkey's ear, "I fear that elegance
> Must struggle like the rest." She climbed until
> The moonlight in her lap, mewing her velvet,
> And her dress were one and she said, "I have said no
> To everything, in order to get at myself.
> I have wiped away moonlight like mud. Your innocent ear
> And I, if I rode naked, are what remain."

Not for a moment do I suggest that this is an imaginary portrait of the formidable novelist Mrs. Edith Wharton, for Edith Wharton was more than a reductionist. Rather, Stevens's Mrs. Uruguay is a fierce reductionist out of old New York society as Wharton herself might have represented such a personage, and sometimes did. By "reductionist" I mean an adept in practicing what might be called "the reductive fallacy," which is the incessant translation of: "Tell me what she or he is *really* like," as: "Tell me the very worst thing you can, about her or him, which is in any way true or accurate."

Wharton's most savage portrait of such a reductionist is Undine Spragg in *The Custom of the Country*, which is likely to seem, some day, Wharton's strongest achievement, though I find it rather an unpleasant novel to reread. Undine Spragg (marvelous name! but then, Wharton's names are always superb) is not quite of the eminence of Thackeray's Becky Sharp, but she has an antithetical greatness about her that R. W. B. Lewis, Wharton's biographer, shrewdly traces to Wharton's dialectical self-knowledge:

> But the most of Edith Wharton is revealed, quite startlingly, in the characterization of Undine Spragg. No one (except possibly Ethan Frome) would at first glance seem more remote from Edith Wharton than Undine: a crude, unlettered, humorless, artificial, but exceedingly beautiful creature, with the most minimal moral intuitions and virtually no talent whatever for normal human affection. Undine did, undoubtedly, stand for everything in the new American female that Edith despised and

recoiled from. But the matter, as it turns out, is much more interesting than that.

There are smaller and larger telltale similarities. As a child Undine, like Edith, enjoyed dressing up in her mother's best finery and "playing lady" before a mirror. Moffatt addresses her by Edith's youthful nickname, "Puss." Edith's long yearning for psychological freedom is queerly reflected in Undine's discovery that each of her marriages is no more than another mode of imprisonment; and Undine's creator allows more than a hint that the young woman is as much a victim as an aggressor amid the assorted snobberies, tedium, and fossilized rules of conduct of American and, even more, French high society. Above all, Undine suggests what Edith Wharton might have been like if, by some dreadful miracle, all her best and most lovable and redeeming features had been suddenly cut away.

So imagined, we see in Undine Spragg how Edith sometimes appeared to the view of the harried and aging Henry James: demanding, imperious, devastating, resolutely indifferent to the needs of others; something like an irresistible force of nature. James's image of Edith as a cyclone is borrowed (Minnie Cadwalader Jones probably showed her the letter) to describe the uproar Undine caused on one occasion, when "everything had gone down before her, as towns and villages went down before one of the tornadoes of her native state." Marvell thinks of his young bride as an eagle, and one has the decided impression of a number of men carried off seriatim, "struggling in her talons." No character Edith Wharton ever invented more closely resembles that bird of prey by which James, Sturgis, and others so often, and only half-jokingly, portrayed Edith herself. Undine Spragg is, so to say, a dark Angel of Devastation: Edith Wharton's antiself; and like all anti-selves, a figure that explains much about its opposite.

To Lewis's fine characterization of Undine Spragg and Edith Wharton as "demanding, imperious, devastating ... an irresistible force of nature" (all qualities also of Mrs. Alfred Uruguay) I would add only "darkly reductive" for Undine and (sometimes) "ironically reductive" for Wharton. That ironic reductiveness can mar her strength at representation, as it does in the concluding vision of Undine in *The Custom of the Country:*

There was a noise of motors backing and advancing in the court, and she heard the first voices on the stairs. She turned to give herself a last look in the glass, saw the blaze of her rubies, the glitter of her hair, and remembered the brilliant names on her list.

But under all the dazzle a tiny black cloud remained. She had learned that there was something she could never get, something that neither beauty nor influence nor millions could ever buy for her. She could never be an Ambassador's wife; and as she advanced to welcome her first guests she said to herself that it was the one part she was really made for.

Undine has just been told by her first, fourth, and final husband, Elmer Moffatt, a Kansas billionaire, that he could not have become Ambassador to England, because: "They won't have divorced Ambassadresses." To Undine, it is "as if the rule had been invented to humiliate her." In some curious sense, Wharton revenges herself upon her antithetical self, Undine, in a mode more reductive than even the formidable Undine deserves. We hear the voice of old New York speaking through Wharton's satisfaction that there was something Undine could never buy, and we remember Mrs. Uruguay's satisfaction in having wiped away moonlight like mud. Not that Undine is other than a false moonlight, but rather that she has force, drive, and desire, and a cold splendor, and our imaginations wish to hear her final note as a grand villain should be heard, holding on in wicked glory.

In 1911, two years before *The Custom of the Country* was published, Wharton brought out the short novel that seems her most American story, the New England tragedy *Ethan Frome*. I would guess that it is now her most widely read book, and is likely to remain so. Certainly *Ethan Frome* is Wharton's only fiction to have become part of the American mythology, though it is hardly an early-twentieth-century *Scarlet Letter*. Relentless and stripped, *Ethan Frome* is tragedy not as Hawthorne wrote it, but in the mode of pain and of a reductive moral sadism, akin perhaps to Robert Penn Warren's harshness toward his protagonists, particularly in *World Enough and Time*. The book's aesthetic fascination, for me, centers in Wharton's audacity in touching the limits of a reader's capacity at absorbing really extreme suffering, when that suffering is bleak, intolerable, and in a clear sense unnecessary. Wharton's astonishing authority here is to render such pain with purity and economy, while making it seem inevitable, as much in the nature of things and of psyches as in the social customs of its place and time.

R. W. B. Lewis praises *Ethan Frome* as "a classic of the realistic genre"; doubtless it is, and yet literary "realism" is itself intensely metaphorical, as Lewis keenly knows. *Ethan Frome* is so charged in its representation of reality as to be frequently phantasmagoric in effect. Its terrible vividness estranges it subtly from mere naturalism, and makes its pain just bearable. Presumably Edith Wharton would not have said: "Ethan Frome—that is myself," and yet he is more his author than Undine Spragg was to be. Like Wharton, Ethan has an immense capacity for suffering, and an overwhelming sense of reality; indeed like Edith Wharton, he has too strong a sense of what was to be the Freudian reality principle.

Though an exact contemporary of Freud, Edith Wharton showed no interest in him, but she became an emphatic Nietzschean, and *Ethan Frome* manifests both a Nietzschean perspectivism, and an ascetic intensity that I suspect goes back to a reading of Schopenhauer, Nietzsche's precursor. What fails in Ethan, and in his beloved Mattie, is precisely what Schopenhauer urged us to overcome: the Will to Live, though suicide was hardly a Schopenhauerian solution. In her introduction to *Ethan Frome*, Wharton states a narrative principle that sounds more like Balzac, Browning, or James, but that actually reflects the Nietzsche of *The Genealogy of Morals:*

> Each of my chroniclers contributes to the narrative *just so much as he or she is capable of understanding* of what, to them, is a complicated and mysterious case; and only the narrator of the tale has scope enough to see it all, to resolve it back into simplicity, and to put it in its rightful place among his larger categories.

But does Wharton's narrator have scope enough to see all of the tale that is *Ethan Frome?* Why is the narrator's view more than only another view, and a simplifying one at that? Wharton's introduction memorably calls her protagonists "these figures, my *granite outcroppings;* but half-emerged from the soil, and scarcely more articulate." Yet her narrator (whatever her intentions) lacks the imagination to empathize with granite outcroppings who are also men and women:

> Though Harmon Gow developed the tale as far as his mental and moral reach permitted there were perceptible gaps between his facts, and I had the sense that the deeper meaning of the story was in the gaps. But one phrase stuck in my memory and served as the nucleus about which I grouped my subsequent inferences: "Guess he's been in Starkfield too many winters."

Before my own time there was up I had learned to know what that meant. Yet I had come in the degenerate day of trolley, bicycle and rural delivery, when communication was easy between the scattered mountain villages, and the bigger towns in the valleys, such as Bettsbridge and Shadd's Falls, had libraries, theatres and Y.M.C.A. halls to which the youth of the hills could descend for recreation. But when winter shut down on Starkfield, and the village lay under a sheet of snow perpetually renewed from the pale skies, I began to see what life there—or rather its negation—must have been in Ethan Frome's young manhood.

I had been sent up by my employers on a job connected with the big power-house at Corbury Junction, and a long-drawn carpenters' strike had so delayed the work that I found myself anchored at Starkfield—the nearest habitable spot—for the best part of the winter. I chafed at first, and then, under the hypnotising effect of routine, gradually began to find a grim satisfaction in the life. During the early part of my stay I had been struck by the contrast between the vitality of the climate and the deadness of the community. Day by day, after the December snows were over, a blazing blue sky poured down torrents of light and air on the white landscape, which gave them back in an intenser glitter. One would have supposed that such an atmosphere must quicken the emotions as well as the blood; but it seemed to produce no change except that of retarding still more the sluggish pulse of Starkfield. When I had been there a little longer, and had seen this phase of crystal clearness followed by long stretches of sunless cold; when the storms of February had pitched their white tents about the devoted village and the wild cavalry of March winds had charged down to their support; I began to understand why Starkfield emerged from its six months' siege like a starved garrison capitulating without quarter. Twenty years earlier the means of resistance must have been far fewer, and the enemy in command of almost all the lines of access between the beleaguered villages; and, considering these things, I felt the sinister force of Harmon's phrase: "Most of the smart ones get away." But if that were the case, how could any combination of obstacles have hindered the flight of a man like Ethan Frome?

The narrator's "mental and moral reach" is not in question, but his vision has acute limitations. Winter indeed is the cultural issue, but *Ethan Frome* is not exactly Ursula K. LeGuin's *The Left Hand of Darkness.* It is not a "combination of obstacles" that hindered the flight of Ethan Frome, but a terrible fatalism which is a crucial part of Edith Wharton's Emersonian heritage. Certainly the narrator is right to express the contrast between the winter sublimity of: "a blazing blue sky poured down torrents of light and air on the white landscape, which gave them back in an intenser glitter," and the inability of the local population to give back more than sunken apathy. But Frome, as the narrator says on the novel's first page, is himself a ruined version of the American Sublime: "the most striking figure in Starkfield ... his great height ... the careless powerful look he had ... something bleak and unapproachable in his face." Ethan Frome is an Ahab who lacks Moby-Dick, self-lamed rather than wounded by the white whale, and by the whiteness of the whale. Not the whiteness of Starkfield but an inner whiteness or blankness has crippled Ethan Frome, perhaps the whiteness that goes through American tradition "from Edwards to Emerson" and on through Wharton to Wallace Stevens contemplating the beach world lit by the glare of the Northern Lights in "The Auroras of Autumn":

> Here, being visible is being white,
> Is being of the solid of white, the accomplishment
> Of an extremist in an exercise ...
>
> The season changes. A cold wind chills the beach.
> The long lines of it grow longer, emptier,
> A darkness gathers though it does not fall
>
> And the whiteness grows less vivid on the wall.
> The man who is walking turns blankly on the sand.
> He observes how the north is always enlarging the change,
>
> With its frigid brilliances, its blue-red sweeps
> And gusts of great enkindlings, its polar green,
> The color of ice and fire and solitude.

That, though with a more sublime eloquence, is the visionary world of *Ethan Frome*, a world where the will is impotent, and tragedy is always circumstantial. The experiential puzzle of *Ethan Frome* is ultimately also its aesthetic strength: we do not question the joint decision of Ethan and Mattie to immolate themselves, even though it is pragmatically outrageous and psychologically quite impossible. But the novel's apparent realism is a mask for its actual fatalistic mode, and truly it is a northern romance, akin even to *Wuthering Heights*. A visionary ethos dominates Ethan and Mattie, and would have dominated Edith Wharton herself, had she not battled against it with her powerful gift for social reductiveness. We can wonder whether even *The Age of Innocence*, with its Jamesian renunciations in the mode of *The Portrait of a Lady*, compensates us for what Wharton might have written, had she gone on with her own version of the American romance tradition of Hawthorne and Melville.

### AN AMERICAN TRAGEDY

The phrase that haunts Dreiser criticism is Lionel Trilling's "reality in America," implying as it does that *An American Tragedy* (1925) represents a rather drab projection of a dead-level naturalistic vision. More than sixty years later, novelistic reality in America extends rather widely, from Norman Mailer's not un-Dreiserian *The Executioner's Song* all the way to Thomas Pynchon's phantasmagoria in *The Crying of Lot 49*. Reality in America in the Age of Reagan included Iran-Contragate, Jim and Tammy Bakker, and Modern Language Association conventions with scheduled seminars such as "Lesbian Approaches to Franz Kafka." Not even Pynchon could rival such inventions, and at this time Dreiser is in danger of seeming drabber than ever.

Irving Howe, writing in the midsixties, at a time of rising social protest, praised *An American Tragedy* for its grasp of the realities of American institutions:

> Dreiser published *An American Tragedy* in 1925. By then he was fifty-four years old, an established writer with his own fixed and hard-won ways, who had written three first-rate novels: *Sister Carrie, Jennie Gerhardt* and *The Financier*. These books are crowded with exact observation—observation worked closely into the grain of narrative—about the customs and class structure of American society in the phase of early finance capitalism. No other novelist has absorbed into his work as much knowledge as Dreiser had about American institutions: the mechanisms of business, the stifling rhythms of the factory, the inner hierarchy of a large hotel, the chicaneries of city politics, the status arrangements of rulers and ruled. For the most part Dreiser's characters are defined through their relationships to these

institutions. They writhe and suffer to win a foothold in the slippery social world or to break out of the limits of established social norms. They exhaust themselves to gain success, they destroy themselves in acts of impulsive deviancy. But whatever their individual lot, they all act out the drama of determinism—which, in Dreiser's handling, is not at all the sort of listless fatality that hostile critics would make it seem, but is rather a fierce struggle by human beings to discover the harsh limits of what is possible to them and thereby perhaps to enlarge those limits by an inch or two. That mostly they fail is Dreiser's tribute to reality.

That is rugged and sincere criticism, yet it repeats Dreiser's own tendency to identify reality with existent institutions, and to assume that reality is entirely social in its nature. "The harsh limits of what is possible" meant to Heraclitus (and Freud) a reminder that character is fate. Tragedy in America aesthetically can manifest the American difference, but that difference is hardly a naive social determinism. If *An American Tragedy* indeed is a tragedy, it requires something more than Howe asserts for Dreiser. Clyde Griffiths would have to have something in him that cannot be defined entirely through his relationships to social institutions. Howe, knowing that poor Clyde is rather puny, insists that Dreiser "nevertheless manages to make the consequences of Clyde's mediocrity, if not the mediocrity itself, seem tragic." Like Dreiser, Howe is a master of pathos, but the tragic cannot be a matter of pathos alone. It demands ethos (and Clyde has no character) and at least a touch of logos (and Clyde has no mind to speak of). I think we must defend *An American Tragedy* as a masterpiece of pathos alone, and I suggest we think of the book as *An American Suffering* or *An American Passion*. It then will require much less defense, and Dreiser's aesthetic permanence would not be questioned by critics who believe that the aesthetic is, after all, at least partly a matter of perception and of cognition.

Robert Penn Warren's homage to Dreiser shrewdly sought to defend *An American Tragedy* as a "root tragedy," naturalistic with the proverbial vengeance, "grounded in the essential human condition." Since Warren is a dualist who rejects transcendence, his view of Clyde is Cartesian: "A mechanism with a consciousness." It would seem that "root tragedy" is strong pathos, which returns us to the Passion of Clyde as Dreiser's true subject. That *An American Tragedy* has an authentic aesthetic dignity I do not doubt; rereading it is both a depressing and an engrossing experience. But I am persuaded that the critical defense of Dreiser, like that of Eugene O'Neill and indeed most serious American drama, depends upon restoring a sense of the aesthetics of suffering, which means of a sharing without transcendence or redemption.

In tragedy, the protagonist joins a beyond, which is a sharing with some sense of the Sublime. What Hart Crane nobly called "the visionary company of love" chooses its members, generally at very great cost. Clyde joins nothing, and would never have been capable of joining himself to anything, which is to repeat, in another range, Philip Fisher's insight as to Clyde's "defective membership" in any realm whatsoever. Pathos is universal, but it does not provide membership. That is the one certain principle of Dreiser's vision, maintaining itself into the moment before dying:

And then in the dark of this midwinter morning—the final moment—with the guards coming, first to slit his right trouser leg for the metal plate and then going to draw the curtains before the cells: "It is time, I fear. Courage, my son." It was the Reverend McMillan—now accompanied by the Reverend Gibson, who, seeing the prison guards approaching, was then addressing Clyde.

And Clyde now getting up from his cot, on which, beside the Reverend McMillan, he had been listening to the reading of John, 14, 15, 16: "Let not your heart be troubled. Ye believe in God—believe also in me." And then the final walk with the Reverend McMillan on his right hand and the Reverend Gibson on his left—the guards front and rear. But with, instead of the customary prayers, the Reverend McMillan announcing: "Humble yourselves under the mighty hand of God that He may exalt you in due time. Cast all your care upon Him for He careth for you. Be at peace. Wise and righteous are His ways, who hath called us into His eternal glory by Christ Jesus, after that we have suffered a little. I am the way, the truth and the life—no man cometh unto the Father but by me."

But various voices—as Clyde entered the first door to cross to the chair room, calling: "Good-by, Clyde." And Clyde, with enough earthly thought and strength to reply: "Good-by, all." But his voice sounding so strange and weak, even to himself, so far distant as though it emanated from another being walking alongside of him, and not from himself. And his feet were walking, but automatically, it seemed. And he was conscious of that familiar shuffle—shuffle—as they pushed him on and on toward that door. Now it was here; now it was being opened.

There it was—at last—the chair he had so often seen in his dreams—that he so dreaded—to which he was now compelled to go. He was being pushed toward that—into that—on—on—through the door which was now open—to receive him—but which was as quickly closed again on all the earthly life he had ever known.

The enormous power of this is not necessarily literary or imaginative; Dreiser, like Poe, had the uncanny quality of being able to tap into our common nightmares. Compulsiveness dominates us here, but we cannot help seeing that Clyde cannot even join himself in these final moments. Like every crucial transition in Clyde's life, this is another mechanical operation of the spirit. The passion of Clyde embraces everything in us that is untouched by the will and the intellect. Dreiser is almost the unique instance in high literature of an author lived by forces he could not understand, forces that strongly did the writing for him.

FRANK NORRIS

# Zola as a Romantic Writer[4]

It is curious to notice how persistently M. Zola is misunderstood. How strangely he is misinterpreted even by those who conscientiously admire the novels of the "man of the iron pen." For most people Naturalism has a vague meaning. It is a sort of inner circle of realism—a kind of diametric opposite of romanticism, a theory of fiction wherein things are represented "as they really are," inexorably, with the truthfulness of a camera. This idea can be shown to be far from right, that Naturalism, as understood by Zola, is but a form of romanticism after all.

Observe the methods employed by the novelists who profess and call themselves "realists"—Mr. Howells, for instance. Howells's characters live across the street from us, they are "on our block." We know all about them, about their affairs, and the story of their lives. One can go even further. We ourselves are Mr. Howells's characters, so long as we are well behaved and ordinary and bourgeois, so long as we are not adventurous or not rich or not unconventional. If we are otherwise, if things commence to happen to us, if we kill a man or two, or get mixed up in a tragic affair, or do something on a large scale, such as the amassing of enormous wealth or power or fame, Mr. Howells cuts our acquaintance at once. He will none of us if we are out of the usual.

This is the real Realism. It is the smaller details of every-day life, things that are likely to happen between lunch and supper, small passions, restricted

From *The Literary Criticism of Frank Norris*, ed. Donald Pizer. © 1964 by Donald Pizer.

emotions, dramas of the reception-room, tragedies of an afternoon call, crises involving cups of tea. Every one will admit there is no romance here. The novel is interesting—which is after all the main point—but it is the commonplace tale of commonplace people made into a novel of far more than commonplace charm. Mr. Howells is not uninteresting; he is simply not romantic. But that Zola should be quoted as a realist, and as a realist of realists, is a strange perversion.

Reflect a moment upon his choice of subject and character and episode. The Rougon-Macquart live in a world of their own; they are not of our lives any more than are the Don Juans, the Jean Valjeans, the Gil Blases, the Marmions, or the Ivanhoes. We, the bourgeois, the commonplace, the ordinary, have no part nor lot in the *Rougon-Macquart*, in *Lourdes*, or in *Rome*; it is not our world, not because our social position is different, but because we are *ordinary*. To be noted of M. Zola we must leave the rank and the file, either run to the forefront of the marching world, or fall by the roadway; we must separate ourselves; we must become individual, unique. The naturalist takes no note of common people, common in so far as their interests, their lives, and the things that occur in them are common, are ordinary. Terrible things must happen to the characters of the naturalistic tale. They must be twisted from the ordinary, wrenched out from the quiet, uneventful round of every-day life, and flung into the throes of a vast and terrible drama that works itself out in unleashed passions, in blood, and in sudden death. The world of M. Zola is a world of big things; the enormous, the formidable, the terrible, is what counts; no teacup tragedies here. Here Nana holds her monstrous orgies, and dies horribly, her face distorted to a frightful mask; Etienne Lantier, carried away by the strike of coal miners of *Le Voreux*, (the strike that is almost war), is involved in the vast and fearful catastrophe that comes as a climax of the great drama; Claude Lantier, disappointed, disillusioned, acknowledging the futility of his art after a life of effort, hangs himself to his huge easel; Jacques Lantier, haunted by an hereditary insanity, all his natural desires hideously distorted, cuts the throat of the girl he loves, and is ground to pieces under the wheels of his own locomotive; Jean Macquart, soldier and tiller of the fields, is drawn into the war of 1870, passes through the terrible scenes of Sedan and the Siege of Paris only to bayonet to death his truest friend and sworn brother-at-arms in the streets of the burning capital.[5]

Everything is extraordinary, imaginative, grotesque even, with a vague note of terror quivering throughout like the vibration of an ominous and low-pitched diapason. It is all romantic, at times unmistakably so, as in *Le Rêve* or *Rome*, closely resembling the work of the greatest of all modern romanticists, Hugo. We have the same huge dramas, the same enormous scenic effects, the same love of the extraordinary, the vast, the monstrous, and the tragic.

Naturalism is a form of romanticism, not an inner circle of realism. Where, is the realism in the *Rougon-Macquart?* Are such things likely to happen between lunch and supper? That Zola's work is not purely romantic as was Hugo's, lies chiefly in the choice of Milieu. These great, terrible dramas no longer happen among the personnel of a feudal and Renaissance nobility, those who are in the fore-front of the marching world, but among the lower—almost the lowest—classes; those who have been thrust or wrenched from the ranks, who are falling by the roadway. This is not romanticism—this drama of the people, working itself out in blood and ordure. It is not realism. It is a school by itself, unique, somber, powerful beyond words. It is naturalism.

### NOTES

4. *Wave*, XV, (June 27, 1896), 3.
5. The novels referred to are, in order, *Nana, Germinal, L'Oeuvre, La Bête Humaine,* and *La Débâcle.*

# Reality in America

## I

It is possible to say of V.L. Parrington that with his *Main Currents in American Thought* he has had an influence on our conception of American culture which is not equaled by that of any other writer of the last two decades. His ideas are now the accepted ones wherever the college course in American literature is given by a teacher who conceives himself to be opposed to the genteel and the academic and in alliance with the vigorous and the actual. And whenever the liberal historian of America finds occasion to take account of the national literature, as nowadays he feels it proper to do, it is Parrington who is his standard and guide. Parrington's ideas are the more firmly established because they do not have to be imposed—the teacher or the critic who presents them is likely to find that his task is merely to make articulate for his audience what it has always believed, for Parrington formulated in a classic way the suppositions about our culture which are held by the American middle class so far as that class is at all liberal in its social thought and so far as it begins to understand that literature has anything to do with society.

Parrington was not a great mind; he was not a precise thinker or, except when measured by the low eminences that were about him, an impressive one. Separate Parrington from his informing idea of the economic and social

---

From *The Liberal Imagination: Essays on Literature and Society,* © 1978 by Diana Trilling and James Trilling.

determination of thought and what is left is a simple intelligence, notable for its generosity and enthusiasm but certainly not for its accuracy or originality. Take him even with his idea and he is, once its direction is established, rather too predictable to be continuously interesting; and, indeed, what we dignify with the name of economic and social determinism amounts in his use of it to not much more than the demonstration that most writers incline to stick to their own social class. But his best virtue was real and important—he had what we like to think of as the saving salt of the American mind, the lively sense of the practical, workaday world, of the welter of ordinary undistinguished things and people, of the tangible, quirky, unrefined elements of life. He knew what so many literary historians do not know, that emotions and ideas are the sparks that fly when the mind meets difficulties.

Yet he had after all but a limited sense of what constitutes a difficulty. Whenever he was confronted with a work of art that was complex, personal and not literal, that was not, as it were, a public document, Parrington was at a loss. Difficulties that were complicated by personality or that were expressed in the language of successful art did not seem quite real to him and he was inclined to treat them as aberrations, which is one way of saying what everybody admits, that the weakest part of Parrington's talent was his aesthetic judgment. His admirers and disciples like to imply that his errors of aesthetic judgment are merely lapses of taste, but this is not so. Despite such mistakes as his notorious praise of Cabell, to whom in a remarkable passage he compares Melville, Parrington's taste was by no means bad. His errors are the errors of understanding which arise from his assumptions about the nature of reality.

Parrington does not often deal with abstract philosophical ideas, but whenever he approaches a work of art we are made aware of the metaphysics on which his aesthetics is based. There exists, he believes, a thing called *reality*; it is one and immutable, it is wholly external, it is irreducible. Men's minds may waver, but reality is always reliable, always the same, always easily to be known. And the artist's relation to reality he conceives as a simple one. Reality being fixed and given, the artist has but to let it pass through him, he is the lens in the first diagram of an elementary book on optics: Fig. 1, Reality; Fig. 2, Artist; Fig. 1ʹ, Work of Art. Figs. 1 and 1ʹ are normally in virtual correspondence with each other. Sometimes the artist spoils this ideal relation by "turning away from" reality. This results in certain fantastic works, unreal and ultimately useless. It does not occur to Parrington that there is any other relation possible between the artist and reality than this passage of reality through the transparent artist; he meets evidence of imagination and creativeness with a settled hostility the expression of which suggests that he regards them as the natural enemies of democracy.

In this view of things, reality, although it is always reliable, is always rather sober-sided, even grim. Parrington, a genial and enthusiastic man, can understand how the generosity of man's hopes and desires may leap beyond reality; he admires will in the degree that he suspects mind. To an excess of desire and energy which blinds a man to the limitations of reality he can indeed be very tender. This is one of the many meanings he gives to *romance* or *romanticism*, and in spite of himself it appeals to something in his own nature. The praise of Cabell is Parrington's response not only to Cabell's elegance—for Parrington loved elegance—but also to Cabell's insistence on the part which a beneficent self-deception may and even should play in the disappointing fact-bound life of man, particularly in the private and erotic part of his life.[1]

The second volume of *Main Currents* is called *The Romantic Revolution in America* and it is natural to expect that the word romantic should appear in it frequently. So it does, more frequently than one can count, and seldom with the same meaning, seldom with the sense that the word, although scandalously vague as it has been used by the literary historians, is still full of complicated but not wholly pointless ideas, that it involves many contrary but definable things; all too often Parrington uses the word romantic with the word romance close at hand, meaning *a* romance, in the sense that *Graustark* or *Treasure Island* is a romance, as though it signified chiefly a gay disregard of the limitations of everyday fact. Romance is refusing to heed the counsels of experience (p. iii); it is ebullience (p. iv); it is utopianism (p. iv); it is individualism (p. vi); it is self-deception (p. 59)—"romantic faith ... in the beneficent processes of trade and industry" (as held, we inevitably ask, by the romantic Adam Smith?); it is the love of the picturesque (p. 49); it is the dislike of innovation (p. 50) but also the love of change (p. iv); it is the sentimental (p. 192); it is patriotism, and then it is cheap (p. 235). It may be used to denote what is not classical, but chiefly it means that which ignores reality (pp. ix, 136, 143, 147, and *passim*); it is not critical (pp. 225, 235), although in speaking of Cooper and Melville, Parrington admits that criticism can sometimes spring from romanticism.

Whenever a man with whose ideas he disagrees wins from Parrington a reluctant measure of respect, the word romantic is likely to appear. He does not admire Henry Clay, yet something in Clay is not to be despised—his romanticism, although Clay's romanticism is made equivalent with his inability to "come to grips with reality." Romanticism is thus, in most of its significations, the venial sin of *Main Currents;* like carnal passion in the *Inferno,* it evokes not blame but tender sorrow. But it can also be the great and saving virtue which Parrington recognizes. It is ascribed to the transcendental reformers he so much admires; it is said to mark two of his most cherished heroes, Jefferson and Emerson: "they were both romantics and their idealism was only a different expression of a common spirit." Parrington held, we may say, at least two different views of romanticism which suggest two different views of reality. Sometimes he speaks of reality in an honorific way, meaning the substantial stuff of life, the ineluctable facts with which the mind must cope, but sometimes he speaks of it pejoratively and means the world of established social forms; and he speaks of realism in two ways: sometimes as the power of dealing intelligently with fact, sometimes as a cold and conservative resistance to idealism.

Just as for Parrington there is a saving grace and a venial sin, there is also a deadly sin, and this is turning away from reality, not in the excess of generous feeling, but in what he believes to be a deficiency of feeling, as with Hawthorne, or out of what amounts to sinful pride, as with Henry James. He tells us that there was too much realism in Hawthorne to allow him to give his faith to the transcendental reformers: "he was too much of a realist to change fashions in creeds"; "he remained cold to the revolutionary criticism that was eager to pull down the old temples to make room for nobler." It is this cold realism, keeping Hawthorne apart from his enthusiastic contemporaries, that alienates Parrington's sympathy—"Eager souls, mystics and revolutionaries, may propose to refashion the world in accordance with their dreams; but evil remains, and so long as it lurks in the secret places of the heart, utopia is only the shadow of a dream. And so while the Concord thinkers were proclaiming man to be the indubitable child of God, Hawthorne was critically examining the question of evil as it appeared in the light of his own experience. It was the central fascinating problem of his intellectual life, and in pursuit of a solution he probed curiously into the hidden, furtive recesses of the soul." Parrington's disapproval of the enterprise is unmistakable.

Now we might wonder whether Hawthorne's questioning of the naïve and often eccentric faiths of the transcendental reformers was not, on the face of it, a public service. But Parrington implies that it contributes nothing to democracy, and even that it stands in the way of the realization of democracy. If democracy depends wholly on a fighting faith, I suppose he is right. Yet society is after all something that exists at the moment as well as in the future, and if one man wants to probe curiously into the hidden furtive recesses of the contemporary soul, a broad democracy and especially one devoted to reality should allow him to do so without despising him. If what Hawthorne did was certainly nothing to build a party on, we ought perhaps to forgive him when we remember that he was only one man and that the future of mankind did not depend upon him alone. But this very fact serves only to irritate Parrington; he is put out by Hawthorne's loneliness and believes that part of Hawthorne's insufficiency as a writer comes from his failure to get around and meet people. Hawthorne could not, he tells us, establish contact with the "Yankee reality," and was scarcely aware of the "substantial world of Puritan reality that Samuel Sewall knew."

To turn from reality might mean to turn to romance, but Parrington tells us that Hawthorne was romantic "only in a narrow and very special sense." He was not interested in the world of, as it were, practical romance, in the Salem of the clipper ships; from this he turned away to create "a romance of ethics." This is not an illuminating phrase but it is a catching one, and it might be taken to mean that Hawthorne was in the tradition of, say, Shakespeare; but we quickly learn that, no, Hawthorne had entered a barren field, for although he himself lived in the present and had all the future to mold, he preferred to find many of his subjects in the past. We learn too that his romance of ethics is not admirable because it requires the hard, fine pressing of ideas, and we are told that "a romantic uninterested in adventure and afraid of sex is likely to become somewhat graveled for matter." In short, Hawthorne's mind was a thin one, and Parrington puts in evidence his use of allegory and symbol and the very severity and precision of his art to prove that he suffered from a sadly limited intellect, for so much fancy and so much art could scarcely be needed unless the writer were trying to exploit to the utmost the few poor ideas that he had.

Hawthorne, then, was "forever dealing with shadows, and he knew that he was dealing with shadows." Perhaps so, but shadows are also part of reality and one would not want a world without shadows, it would not even be a "real" world. But we must get beyond Parrington's metaphor. The fact is that Hawthorne was dealing beautifully with realities, with substantial things. The man who could raise those brilliant and serious doubts about the nature and possibility of moral perfection, the man who could keep himself aloof from the "Yankee reality" and who could dissent from the orthodoxies of dissent and tell us so much about the nature of moral zeal, is of course dealing exactly with reality.

Parrington's characteristic weakness as a historian is suggested by the title of his famous book, for the culture of a nation is not truly figured in the image of the current. A culture is not a flow, nor even a confluence; the form of its existence is struggle, or at least debate—it is nothing if not a dialectic. And in any culture there are likely to be certain artists who contain a large part of the dialectic within themselves, their meaning and power lying in their contradictions; they contain within themselves, it may be said, the very essence of the culture, and the sign of this is that they do not submit to serve the ends of any one ideological group or tendency. It is a significant circumstance of American culture, and one which is susceptible of explanation, that an unusually large proportion of its notable writers of the nineteenth century were such repositories of the dialectic of their times— they contained both the yes and the no of their culture, and by that token they were prophetic of the future. Parrington said that he had not set up shop as a literary critic; but if a literary critic is simply a reader who has the ability to understand literature and to convey to others what he understands, it is not exactly a matter of free choice whether or not a cultural historian shall be a literary critic, nor is it open to him to let his virtuous political and social opinions do duty for percipience. To throw out Poe because he cannot be conveniently fitted into a theory of American culture, to speak of him as a biological sport and as a mind apart from the main current, to find his gloom to be merely personal and eccentric, "only the atrabilious wretchedness of a dipsomaniac," as Hawthorne's was "no more than the skeptical questioning of life by a nature that knew no fierce storms," to judge Melville's response to American life to be less noble than that of Bryant or of Greeley, to speak of Henry James as an escapist, as an artist similar to Whistler, a man characteristically afraid of stress—this is not merely to be mistaken in aesthetic judgment; rather it is to examine without attention and from the point of view of a limited and essentially arrogant conception of reality the documents which are in some respects the most suggestive testimony to what America was and is, and of course to get no answer from them.

Parrington lies twenty years behind us, and in the intervening time there has developed a body of opinion which is aware of his inadequacies and of the inadequacies of his coadjutors and disciples, who make up what might be called the literary academicism of liberalism. Yet Parrington still stands at the center of American thought about American culture because, as I say, he expresses the chronic American belief that there exists an opposition between reality and mind and that one must enlist oneself in the party of reality.

## II

This belief in the incompatibility of mind and reality is exemplified by the doctrinaire indulgence which liberal intellectuals have always displayed toward Theodore Dreiser, an indulgence which becomes the worthier of remark when it is contrasted with the liberal severity toward Henry James, Dreiser and James: with that juxtaposition we are immediately at the dark and bloody crossroads where literature and politics meet. One does not go there gladly, but nowadays it is not exactly a matter of free choice whether one does or does not go. As for the particular juxtaposition itself, it is inevitable and it has at the present moment far more significance than the juxtaposition which once used to be made between James and Whitman. It is not hard to contrive factitious oppositions between James and Whitman, but the real difference between them is the difference between the moral mind, with its awareness of tragedy, irony, and multitudinous distinctions, and the transcendental mind, with its passionate sense of the oneness of multiplicity. James and Whitman are unlike not in quality but in kind, and in their very opposition they serve to complement each other. But the difference between James and Dreiser is not of kind, for both men addressed themselves to virtually the same social and moral fact. The difference here is one of quality, and perhaps nothing is more typical of American liberalism than the way it has responded to the respective qualities of the two men.

Few critics, I suppose, no matter what their political disposition, have ever been wholly blind to James's great gifts, or even to the grandiose moral intention of these gifts. And few critics have ever been wholly blind to Dreiser's great faults. But by liberal critics James is traditionally put to the ultimate question: of what use, of what actual political use, are his gifts and their intention? Granted that James was devoted to an extraordinary moral perceptiveness, granted too that moral perceptiveness has something to do with politics and the social life, of what possible practical value in our world of impending disaster can James's work be? And James's style, his characters, his subjects, and even his own social origin and the manner of his personal life are adduced to show that his work cannot endure the question. To James no quarter is given by American criticism in its political and liberal aspect. But in the same degree that liberal criticism is moved by political considerations to treat James with severity, it treats Dreiser with the most sympathetic indulgence. Dreiser's literary faults, it gives us to understand, are essentially social and political virtues. It was Parrington who established the formula for the liberal criticism of Dreiser by calling him a "peasant": when Dreiser thinks stupidly, it is because he has the slow stubbornness of a peasant; when he writes badly, it is because he is impatient of the sterile literary gentility of the bourgeoisie. It is as if wit, and flexibility of mind, and perception, and knowledge were to be equated with aristocracy and political reaction, while dullness and stupidity must naturally suggest a virtuous democracy, as in the old plays.

The liberal judgment of Dreiser and James goes back of politics, goes back to the cultural assumptions that make politics. We are still haunted by a kind of political fear of the intellect which Tocqueville observed in us more than a century ago. American intellectuals, when they are being consciously American or political, are remarkably quick to suggest that an art which is marked by perception and knowledge, although all very well in its way, can never get us through gross dangers and difficulties. And their misgivings become the more intense when intellect works in art as it ideally should, when its processes are vivacious and interesting and brilliant. It is then that we like to confront it with the gross dangers and difficulties and to challenge it to save us at once from disaster. When intellect in art is awkward or dull we do not put it to the test of ultimate or immediate practicality. No liberal critic asks the question of Dreiser whether *his* moral preoccupations are going to be useful in confronting the disasters that threaten us. And it is a judgment on the proper nature of mind, rather than any actual political meaning that might be drawn from the works of the two men, which accounts for the unequal justice they have received from the progressive critics. If it could be conclusively demonstrated—by, say, documents in James's handwriting—that James explicitly intended his books to be understood as pleas for co-operatives, labor unions, better housing, and more equitable taxation, the American critic in his liberal and progressive character would still be worried by James because his work shows so many of the electric qualities of mind. And if something like the opposite were proved of Dreiser, it would be brushed aside—as his doctrinaire anti-Semitism has in fact been brushed aside—because his books have the awkwardness, the chaos, the heaviness which we associate with "reality." In the American metaphysic, reality is always material reality, hard, resistant, unformed, impenetrable, and unpleasant. And that mind is alone felt to be trustworthy which most resembles this reality by most nearly reproducing the sensations it affords.

In *The Rise of American Civilization*, Professor Beard uses a significant phrase when, in the course of an ironic account of James's career, he implies that we have the clue to the irrelevance of that career when we know that James was "a whole generation removed from the odors of the shop." Of a piece with this, and in itself even more significant, is the comment which Granville Hicks makes in *The Great Tradition* when he deals with James's stories about artists and remarks that such artists as James portrays, so concerned for their art and their integrity in art, do not really exist: "After all, who has ever known such artists? Where are the Hugh Verekers, the Mark Ambients, the Neil Paradays, the Overts, Limberts, Dencombes, Delavoys?" This question, as Mr. Hicks admits, had occurred to James himself, but what answer had James given to it? "If the life about us for the last thirty years refused warrant for these examples," he said in the preface to volume XII of the New York Edition, "then so much the worse for that life...."

There are decencies that in the name of the general self-respect we must take for granted, there's a rudimentary intellectual honor to which we must, in the interest of civilization, at least pretend." And to this Mr. Hicks, shocked beyond argument, makes this reply, which would be astonishing had we not heard it before: "But this is the purest romanticism, this writing about what ought to be rather than what is!"

The "odors of the shop" are real, and to those who breathe them they guarantee a sense of vitality from which James is debarred. The idea of intellectual honor is not real, and to that chimera James was devoted. He betrayed the reality of what is in the interests of what ought to be. Dare we trust him? The question, we remember, is asked by men who themselves have elaborate transactions with what ought to be. Professor Beard spoke in the name of a growing, developing, and improving America. Mr. Hicks, when he wrote *The Great Tradition*, was in general sympathy with a nominally radical movement. But James's own transaction with what ought to be is suspect because it is carried on through what I have called the electrical qualities of mind, through a complex and rapid imagination and with a kind of authoritative immediacy. Mr. Hicks knows that Dreiser is "clumsy" and "stupid" and "bewildered" and "crude in his statement of materialistic monism"; he knows that Dreiser in his personal life—which is in point because James's personal life is always supposed to be so much in point—was not quite emancipated from "his boyhood longing for crass material success," showing "again and again a desire for the ostentatious luxury of the successful business man." But Dreiser is to be accepted and forgiven because his faults are the sad, lovable, honorable faults of reality itself, or of America itself—huge, inchoate, struggling toward expression, caught between the dream of raw power and the dream of morality.

"The liability in what Santayana called the genteel tradition was due to its being the product of mind apart from experience. Dreiser gave us the stuff of our common experience, not as it was hoped to be by any idealizing theorist, but as it actually was in its crudity." The author of this statement certainly cannot be accused of any lack of feeling for mind as Henry James represents it; nor can Mr. Matthiessen be thought of as a follower of Parrington—indeed, in the preface to *American Renaissance* he has framed one of the sharpest and most cogent criticisms of Parrington's method. Yet Mr. Matthiessen, writing in the *New York Times Book Review* about Dreiser's posthumous novel, *The Bulwark*, accepts the liberal cliché which opposes crude experience to mind and establishes Dreiser's value by implying that the mind which Dreiser's crude experience is presumed to confront and refute is the mind of gentility.

This implied amalgamation of mind with gentility is the rationale of the long indulgence of Dreiser, which is extended even to the style of his prose. Everyone is aware that Dreiser's prose style is full of roughness and ungainliness, and the critics who admire Dreiser tell us it does not matter. Of course it does not matter. No reader with a right sense of style would suppose that it does matter, and he might even find it a virtue. But it has been taken for granted that the ungainliness of Dreiser's style is the only possible objection to be made to it, and that whoever finds in it any fault at all wants a prettified genteel style (and is objecting to the ungainliness of reality itself). For instance, Edwin Berry Burgum, in a leaflet on Dreiser put out by the Book Find Club, tells us that Dreiser was one of those who used—or, as Mr. Burgum says, utilized—"the diction of the Middle West, pretty much as it was spoken, rich in colloquialism and frank in the simplicity and directness of the pioneer tradition," and that this diction took the place of "the literary English, formal and bookish, of New England provincialism that was closer to the aristocratic spirit of the mother country than to the tang of everyday life in the new West." This is mere fantasy. Hawthorne, Thoreau, and Emerson were for the most part remarkably colloquial—they wrote, that is, much as they spoke; their prose was specifically American in quality, and, except for occasional lapses, quite direct and simple. It is Dreiser who lacks the sense of colloquial diction—that of the Middle West or any other. If we are to talk of bookishness, it is Dreiser who is bookish; he is precisely literary in the bad sense; he is full of flowers of rhetoric and shines with paste gems; at hundreds of points his diction is not only genteel but fancy. It is he who speaks of "a scene more distingué than this," or of a woman "artistic in form and feature," or of a man who, although "strong, reserved, aggressive, with an air of wealth and experience, was *soidisant* and not particularly eager to stay at home." Colloquialism held no real charm for him and his natural tendency is always toward the "fine":

> ... Moralists come and go; religionists fulminate and declare the pronouncements of God as to this; but Aphrodite still reigns. Embowered in the festal depths of the spring, set above her altars of porphyry, chalcedony, ivory and gold, see her smile the smile that is at once the texture and essence of delight, the glory and despair of the world! Dream on, oh Buddha, asleep on your lotus leaf, of an undisturbed Nirvana! Sweat, oh Jesus, your last agonizing drops over an unregenerate world! In the forests of Pan still ring the cries of the worshippers of Aphrodite! From her altars the incense of adoration ever rises! And see, the new red grapes dripping where votive hands new-press them!

Charles Jackson, the novelist, telling us in the same leaflet that Dreiser's style does not matter, remarks on how much still comes to us when we have lost by translation the stylistic brillance of Thomas Mann or the Russians or Balzac. He is in part right. And he is right too when he says that a certain kind of conscious, supervised artistry is not appropriate to the novel of large dimensions. Yet the fact is that the great novelists have usually written very good prose, and what comes through even a bad translation is exactly the power of mind that made the well-hung sentence of the original text. In literature style is so little the mere clothing of thought—need it be insisted on at this late date?—that we may say that from the earth of the novelist's prose spring his characters, his ideas, and even his story itself.[2]

To the extent that Dreiser's style is defensible, his thought is also defensible. That is, when he thinks like a novelist, he is worth following—when by means of his rough and ungainly but no doubt cumulatively effective style he creates rough, ungainly, but effective characters and events. But when he thinks like, as we say, a philosopher, he is likely to be not only foolish but vulgar. He thinks as the modern crowd thinks when it decides to think: religion and morality are nonsense, "religionists" and moralists are fakes, tradition is a fraud, what is man but matter and impulses, mysterious "chemisms," what value has life anyway? "What, cooking, eating, coition, job holding, growing, aging, losing, winning, in so changeful and passing a scene as this, important? Bunk! It is some form of titillating illusion with about as much import to the superior forces that bring it all about as the functions and gyrations of a fly. No more. And maybe less." Thus Dreiser at sixty. And yet there is for him always the vaulgarly saving suspicion that maybe, when all is said and done, there is Something Behind It All. It is much to the point of his intellectual vulgarity that Dreiser's anti-Semitism was not merely a social prejudice but an idea, a way of dealing with difficulties.

No one, I suppose, has ever represented Dreiser as a masterly intellect. It is even commonplace to say that his ideas are inconsistent or inadequate. But once that admission has been made, his ideas are hustled out of sight while his "reality" and great brooding pity are spoken of. (His pity is to be questioned: pity is to be judged by kind, not amount, and Dreiser's pity— *Jennie Gerhardt* provides the only exception—is either destructive of its object or it is self-pity.) Why has no liberal critic ever brought Dreiser's ideas to the bar of political practicality, asking what use is to be made of Dreiser's dim, awkward speculation, of his self-justification, of his lust for "beauty" and "sex" and "living" and "life itself," and of the showy nihilism which always seems to him so grand a gesture in the direction of profundity? We live, understandably enough, with the sense of urgency; our clock, like

Baudelaire's, has had the hands removed and bears the legend, "It is later than you think." But with us it is always a little too late for mind, yet never too late for honest stupidity; always a little too late for understanding, never too late for righteous, bewildered wrath; always too late for thought, never too late for naïve moralizing. We seem to like to condemn our finest but not our worst qualities by pitting them against the exigency of time.

But sometimes time is not quite so exigent as to justify all our own exigency, and in the case of Dreiser time has allowed his deficiencies to reach their logical, and fatal, conclusion. In *The Bulwark* Dreiser's characteristic ideas come full circle, and the simple, didactic life history of Solon Barnes, a Quaker business man, affirms a simple Christian faith, and a kind of practical mysticism, and the virtues of self-abnegation and self-restraint, and the belief in and submission to the hidden purposes of higher powers, those "superior forces that bring it all about"—once, in Dreiser's opinion, so brutally indifferent, now somehow benign. This is not the first occasion on which Dreiser has shown a tenderness toward religion and a responsiveness to mysticism. *Jennie Gerhardt* and the figure of the Reverend Duncan McMillan in *An American Tragedy* are forecasts of the avowals of *The Bulwark*, and Dreiser's lively interest in power of any sort led him to take account of the power implicit in the cruder forms of mystical performance. Yet these rifts in his nearly monolithic materialism cannot quite prepare us for the blank pietism of *The Bulwark*, not after we have remembered how salient in Dreiser's work has been the long surly rage against the "religionists" and the "moralists," the men who have presumed to believe that life can be given any law at all and who have dared to suppose that will or mind or faith can shape the savage and beautiful entity that Dreiser liked to call "life itself." Now for Dreiser the law may indeed be given, and it is wholly simple—the safe conduct of the personal life requires only that we follow the Inner Light according to the regimen of the Society of Friends, or according to some other godly rule. And now the smiling Aphrodite set above her altars of porphyry, chalcedony, ivory, and gold is quite forgotten, and we are told that the sad joy of cosmic acceptance goes hand in hand with sexual abstinence.

Dreiser's mood of "acceptance" in the last years of his life is not, as a personal experience, to be submitted to the tests of intellectual validity. It consists of a sensation of cosmic understanding, of an overarching sense of unity with the world in its apparent evil as well as in its obvious good. It is no more to be quarreled with, or reasoned with, than love itself—indeed, it is a kind of love, not so much of the world as of oneself in the world. Perhaps it is either the cessation of desire or the perfect balance of desires. It is what used often to be meant by "peace," and up through the nineteenth century a good many people understood its meaning. If it was Dreiser's own emotion at the end of his life, who would not be happy that he had achieved it? I am not even sure that our civilization would not be the better for more of us knowing and desiring this emotion of grave felicity. Yet granting the personal validity of the emotion, Dreiser's exposition of it fails, and is, moreover, offensive. Mr. Matthiessen has warned us of the attack that will be made on the doctrine of *The Bulwark* by "those who believe that any renewal of Christianity marks a new 'failure of nerve.' " But Dreiser's religious avowal is not a failure of nerve—it is a failure of mind and heart. We have only to set his book beside any work in which mind and heart are made to serve religion to know this at once. Ivan Karamazov's giving back his ticket of admission to the "harmony" of the universe suggests that *The Bulwark* is not morally adequate, for we dare not, as its hero does, blandly "accept" the suffering of others; and the Book of Job tells us that it does not include enough in its exploration of the problem of evil, and is not stern enough. I have said that Dreiser's religious affirmation was offensive; the offense lies in the vulgar ease of its formulation, as well as in the comfortable untroubled way in which Dreiser moved from nihilism to pietism.[3]

*The Bulwark* is the fruit of Dreiser's old age, but if we speak of it as a failure of thought and feeling, we cannot suppose that with age Dreiser weakened in mind and heart. The weakness was always there. And in a sense it is not Dreiser who failed but a whole way of dealing with ideas, a way in which we have all been in some degree involved. Our liberal, progressive culture tolerated Dreiser's vulgar materialism with its huge negation, its simple cry of "Bunk!," feeling that perhaps it was not quite intellectually adequate but certainly very *strong*, certainly very *real*. And now, almost as a natural consequence, it has been given, and is not unwilling to take, Dreiser's pietistic religion in all its inadequacy.

Dreiser, of course, was firmer than the intellectual culture that accepted him. He *meant* his ideas, at least so far as a man can mean ideas who is incapable of following them to their consequences. But we, when it came to his ideas, talked about his great brooding pity and shrugged the ideas off. We are still doing it. Robert Elias, the biographer of Dreiser, tells us that "it is part of the logic of [Dreiser's] life that he should have completed *The Bulwark* at the same time that he joined the Communists." Just what kind of logic this is we learn from Mr. Elias's further statement. "When he supported left-wing movements and finally, last year, joined the Communist Party, he did so not because he had examined the details of the party line and found them satisfactory, but because he agreed with a general program that represented a means for establishing his cherished goal of greater equality among men." Whether or not Dreiser was following the logic of his own life, he was certainly following the logic of the liberal criticism that accepted him so undiscriminatingly as one of the great, significant expressions of its spirit. This is the liberal criticism, in the direct line of Parrington, which establishes the social responsibility of the writer and then goes on to say that, apart from his duty of resembling reality as much as possible, he is not really responsible for anything, not even for his ideas. The scope of reality being what it is, ideas are held to be mere "details," and, what is more, to be details which, if attended to, have the effect of diminishing reality. But ideals are different from ideas; in the liberal criticism which descends from Parrington ideals consort happily with reality and they urge us to deal impatiently with ideas— a "cherished goal" forbids that we stop to consider how we reach it, or if we may not destroy it in trying to reach it the wrong way.

## NOTES

1. See, for example, how Parrington accounts for the "idealizing mind"—Melville's— by the discrepancy between "a wife in her morning kimono" and "the Helen of his dreams." Vol. II, p. 259.

2. The latest defense of Dreiser's style, that in the chapter on Dreiser in the *Literary History of the United States*, is worth noting: "Forgetful of the integrity and power of Dreiser's whole work, many critics have been distracted into a condemnation of his style. He was, like Twain and Whitman, an organic artist; he wrote what he knew—what he was. His many colloquialisms were part of the coinage of his time, and his sentimental and romantic passages were written in the language of the educational system and the popular literature of his formative years. In his style, as in his material, he was a child of his time, of his class. Self-educated, a type or model of the artist of plebeian origin in America, his language, like his subject matter, is not marked by internal inconsistencies." No doubt Dreiser was an organic artist in the sense that he wrote what he knew and what he was, but so, I suppose, is every artist; the question for criticism comes down to *what* he knew and *what* he was. That he was a child of his time and class is also true, but this can be said of everyone without exception; the question for criticism is how he transcended the imposed limitations of his time and class. As for the defense made on the ground of his particular class, it can only be said that liberal thought has come to a strange pass when it assumes that a plebeian origin is accountable for a writer's faults through all his intellectual life.

3. This case and comfortableness seem to mark contemporary religious conversions. Religion nowadays has the appearance of what the ideal modern house has been called, "a machine for living," and seemingly one makes up one's mind to acquire and use it not with spiritual struggle but only with a growing sense of its practicability and convenience. Compare *The Seven Storey Mountain*, which Monsignor Sheen calls "a twentieth-century form of the *Confessions* of St. Augustine," with the old, the as it were original, *Confessions* of St. Augustine.

PHILIP RAHV

# Notes on the Decline of Naturalism

Quite a few protests have been aired in recent years against the sway of the naturalist method in fiction. It is charged that this method treats material in a manner so flat and external as to inhibit the search for value and meaning, and that in any case, whatever its past record, it is now exhausted. Dissimilar as they are, both the work of Franz Kafka and the works of the surrealist school are frequently cited as examples of release from the routines of naturalist realism, from its endless book-keeping of existence. Supporting this indictment are mostly those writers of the younger group who are devoted to experimentation and who look to symbolism, the fable, and the myth.

The younger writers are stirred by the ambition to create a new type of imaginative prose into which the recognizably real enters as one component rather than as the total substance. They want to break the novel of its objective habits; some want to introduce into it philosophical ideas; others are not so much drawn to expressing ideas as to expressing the motley strivings of the inner self—dreams, visions, and fantasies. Manifestly the failure of the political movement in the literature of the past decade has resulted in a revival of religio-esthetic attitudes. The young men of letters are once again watching their own image in the mirror and listening to inner promptings. Theirs is a program calling for the adoption of techniques of planned derangement as a means of cracking open the certified structure of

From *Image and Idea.* © 1949 by Philip Rahv.

reality and turning loose its latent energies. And surely one cannot dispose of such a program merely by uncovering the element of mystification in it. For the truth is that the artist of the avant-garde has never hesitated to lay hold of the instruments of mystification when it suited his purpose, especially in an age such as ours, when the life about him belies more and more the rational ideals of the cultural tradition.

It has been remarked that in the long run the issue between naturalism and its opponents resolves itself into a philosophical dispute concerning the nature of reality. Obviously those who reject naturalism in philosophy will also object to its namesake in literature. But it seems to me that when faced with a problem such as that of naturalist fiction, the critic will do well not to mix in ontological maneuvres. From the standpoint of critical method it is impermissible to replace a concrete literary analysis with arguments derived from some general theory of the real. For it is plainly a case of the critic not being able to afford metaphysical commitments if he is to apply himself without preconceived ideas to the works of art that constitute his material. The art-object is from first to last the one certain datum at his disposal; and in succumbing to metaphysical leanings—either of the spiritualist or materialist variety—he runs the risk of freezing his insights in some kind of ideational schema the relevance of which to the task in hand is hardly more than speculative. The act of critical evaluation is best performed in a state of *ideal aloofness* from abstract systems. Its practitioner is not concerned with making up his mind about the ultimate character of reality but with observing and measuring its actual proportions and combinations within a given form. The presence of the real affects him directly, with an immediate force contingent upon the degree of interest, concreteness, and intensity in the impression of life conveyed by the literary artist. The philosopher can take such impressions or leave them, but luckily the critic has no such choice.

Imaginative writing cannot include fixed and systematic definitions of reality without violating its own existential character. Yet in any imaginative effort that which we mean by the real remains the basic criterion of viability, the crucial test of relevance, even if its specific features can hardly be determined in advance but must be *felt anew* in each given instance. And so far as the medium of fiction is concerned, one cannot but agree with Henry James that it gains its "air of reality"—which he considers to be its "supreme virtue"—through "its immense and exquisite correspondence with life." Note that James's formulation allows both for analogical and realistic techniques of representation. He speaks not of copies or reports or transcripts of life but of relations of equivalence, of a "correspondence" which he identifies with the "illusion of life." The ability to produce this illusion he regards as the storyteller's inalienable gift, "the merit on which all other merits ... helplessly and submissively depend." This insight is of an elementary nature and scarcely peculiar to James alone, but it seems that its truth has been lost on some of our recent catch-as-catch-can innovators in the writing of fiction.

It is intrinsically from this point of view that one can criticise the imitations of Kafka that have been turning up of late as being one-sided and even inept. Perhaps Kafka is too idiosyncratic a genius to serve as a model for others, but still it is easy to see where his imitators go wrong. It is necessary to say to them: To know how to take apart the recognizable world is not enough, is in fact merely a way of letting oneself go and of striving for originality at all costs. But originality of this sort is nothing more than a professional mannerism of the avant-garde. The genuine innovator is always trying to make us actually experience his creative contradictions. He therefore employs means that are subtler and more complex: *at the very same time that he takes the world apart he puts it together again.* For to proceed otherwise is to dissipate rather than alter our sense of reality, to weaken and compromise rather than change in any significant fashion our feeling of relatedness to the world. After all, what impressed us most in Kafka is precisely this power of his to achieve a simultaneity of contrary effects, to fit the known into the unknown, the actual into the mythic and vice versa, to combine within one framework a conscientiously empirical account of the visibly real with a dreamlike and magical dissolution of it. In this paradox lies the pathos of his approach to human existence.

A modern poetess has written that the power of the visible derives from the invisible; but the reverse of this formula is also true. Thus the visible and the invisible might be said to stand to each other in an ironic relation of inner dependence and of mutual skepticism mixed with solicitude. It is a superb form of doubletalk; and if we are accustomed to its exclusion from naturalistic writing, it is all the more disappointing to find that the newly-evolved 'fantastic' style of the experimentalists likewise excludes it. But there is another consideration, of a more formal nature. It seems to me a profound error to conceive of reality as merely a species of material that the fiction-writer can either use or dispense with as he sees fit. It is a species of material, of course, and something else besides: it also functions as the *discipline of fiction*, much in the same sense that syllablic structure functions as the discipline of verse. This seeming identity of the formal and substantial means of narrative-prose is due, I think, to the altogether free and open character of the medium, which prevents it from developing such distinctly technical controls as poetry has acquired. Hence even the dream, when told in a story, must partake of some of the qualities of the real.

Whereas the surrealist represents man as immured in dreams, the naturalist represents him in a continuous waking state of prosaic daily living, in effect as never dreaming. But both the surrealist and the naturalist go to extremes in simplifying the human condition. J. M. Synge once said that the artist displays at once the difficulty and the triumph of his art when picturing the dreamer leaning out to reality or the man of real life lifted out of it. "In all the poets," he wrote, and this test is by no means limited to poetry alone, "the greatest have both these elements, that is they are supremely engrossed with life, and yet with the wildness of their fancy they are always passing out of what is simple and plain."

The old egocentric formula, "Man's fate is his character" has been altered by the novelists of the naturalist school to read, "Man's fate is his environment." (Zola, the organizer and champion of the school, drew his ideas from physiology and medicine, but in later years his disciples cast the natural sciences aside in favor of the social sciences.) To the naturalist, human behavior is a function of its social environment; the individual is the live register of its qualities; he exists in it as animals exist in nature.[1] Due to this emphasis the naturalist mode has evolved historically in two main directions. On the one hand it has tended towards passive documentation (milieu-panoramas, local-color stories, reportorial studies of a given region or industry, etc.), and on the other towards the exposure of socio-economic conditions (muckraking). American fiction of the past decade teems with examples of both tendencies, usually in combination. The work of James T. Farrell, for instance, is mostly a genre-record, the material of which is in its very nature operative in producing social feeling, while such novels as *The Grapes of Wrath* and *Native Son* are exposure-literature, as is the greater part of the fiction of social protest. Dos Passos' triology, *U. S. A.*, is thoroughly political in intention but has the tone and gloss of the methodical genre-painter in the page by page texture of its prose.

I know of no hard and fast rules that can be used to distinguish the naturalist method from the methods of realism generally. It is certainly incorrect to say that the difference is marked by the relative density of detail. Henry James observes in his essay *The Art of Fiction* that it is above all "solidity of specification" that makes for the illusion of life—the air of reality—in a novel; and the truth of this dictum is borne out by the practice of the foremost modern innovators in this medium, such as Proust, Joyce, and Kafka. It is not, then, primarily the means employed to establish verisimilitude that fix the naturalist imprint upon a work of fiction. A more conclusive test, to my mind, is its treatment of the relation of character to background. I would classify as naturalistic that type of realism in which the individual is portrayed not merely as subordinate to his background but as wholly determined by it—that type of realism, in other words, in which the environment displaces its inhabitants in the role of the hero. Theodore Dreiser, for example, comes as close as any American writer to plotting the careers of his characters strictly within a determinative process. The financier Frank Cowperwood masters his world and emerges as its hero, while the "little man" Clyde Griffiths is the victim whom it grinds to pieces; yet hero and victim alike are essentially implements of environmental force, the carriers of its contradictions upon whom it stamps success or failure—not entirely at will, to be sure, for people are marked biologically from birth—but with sufficient autonomy to shape their fate.

In such a closed world there is patently no room for the singular, the unique, for anything in fact which cannot be represented plausibly as the product of a particular social and historical complex. Of necessity the naturalist must deal with experience almost exclusively in terms of the broadly typical. He analyses characters in such a way as to reduce them to standard types. His method of construction is that of accretion and enumeration rather than of analysis or storytelling; and this is so because the quantitative development of themes, the massing of detail and specification, serves his purpose best. He builds his structures out of literal fact and precisely documented circumstance, thus severely limiting the variety of creative means at the disposal of the artist.

This quasi-scientific approach not only permits but, in theory at least, actually prescribes a neutral attitude in the sphere of values. In practice, however, most naturalists are not sufficiently detached or logical to stay put in such an ultra-objective position. Their detractors are wrong in denying them a moral content; the most that can be said is that theirs is strictly functional morality, bare of any elements of gratuity or transcendence and devoid of the sense of personal freedom.[2] Clearly such a perspective allows for very little self-awareness on the part of characters. It also removes the possibility of a tragic resolution of experience. The world of naturalist fiction is much too big, too inert, too hardened by social habit and material necessity, to allow for that tenacious self-assertion of the human by means of which tragedy justifies and ennobles its protagonists. The only grandeur naturalism knows is the grandeur of its own methodological achievement in making available a vast inventory of minutely described phenomena, in assembling an enormous quantity of data and arranging them in a rough figuration of reality. *Les Rougon-Macquart* stands to this day as the most imposing monument to this achievement.

But in the main it is the pure naturalist—that monstrous offspring of the logic of a method—that I have been describing here. Actually no such literary animal exists. Life always triumphs over methods, over formulas and theories. There is scarcely a single novelist of any importance wearing the badge of naturalism who is all of a piece, who fails to compensate in some way for what we miss in his fundamental conception. Let us call the roll of the leading names among the French and American naturalists and see wherein each is saved.

The Goncourts, it is true, come off rather badly, but even so, to quote a French critic, they manage "to escape from the crude painting of the naked truth by their impressionistic mobility" and, one might add, by their mobile intelligence. Zola's case does not rest solely on our judgment of his naturalist dogmas. There are entire volumes by him—the best, I think, is *Germinal*— and parts of volumes besides, in which his naturalism, fed by an epic imagination, takes on a mythic cast. Thomas Mann associates him with Wagner in a common drive toward an epic mythicism:

> They belong together. The kinship of spirit, method, and aims is most striking. This lies not only in the ambition to achieve size, the propensity to the grandiose and the lavish; nor is it the Homeric leitmotiv alone that is common to them; it is first and foremost a special kind of naturalism, which develops into the mythical.... In Zola's epic ... the characters themselves are raised up to a plane above that of every day. And is that Astarte of the Second Empire, called Nana, not symbol and myth?" (*The Sufferings and Greatness of Richard Wagner*).

Zola's prose, though not controlled by an artistic conscience, overcomes our resistance through sheer positiveness and expressive energy—qualities engendered by his novelistic ardor and avidity for recreating life in all its multiple forms.[3] As for Huysmans, even in his naturalist period he was more concerned with style than with subject-matter. Maupassant is a naturalist mainly by alliance, i.e. by virtue of his official membership in the School of Médan; actually he follows a line of his own, which takes off from naturalism never to return to it. There are few militant naturalists among latter-day French writers. Jules Romains is sometimes spoken of as one, but the truth is that he is an epigone of all literary doctrines, including his own. Dreiser is still unsurpassed so far as American naturalism goes, though just at present he may well be the least readable. He has traits that make for survival—a Balzacian grip on the machinery of money and power; a prosiness so primary in texture that if taken in bulk it affects us as a kind of poetry of the commonplace and ill-favored; and an emphatic eroticism which is the real climate of existence in his fictions—Eros hovering over the shambles. Sinclair Lewis was never a novelist in the proper sense that Zola and Dreiser are novelists, and, given his gift for exhaustive reporting, naturalism did him more good than harm by providing him with a ready literary technique. In Farrell's chronicles there is an underlying moral code which, despite his explicit rejection of the Church, seems to me indisputably orthodox and Catholic; and his Studs Lonigan—a product of those unsightly urban neighborhoods where youth prowls and fights to live up to the folk-ideal of the "regular guy"—is no mere character but an archetype, an eponymous hero of the street-myths that prevail in our big cities. The naturalism of Dos Passos is most completely manifested in *U.S.A.*, tagged by the critics as a "collective" novel recording the "decline of our business civilization." But what distinguishes Dos Passos from other novelists of the same political animus is a sense of justice so pure as to be almost instinctive as well as a deeply elegiac feeling for the intimate features of American life and for its precipitant moments. Also, *U.S.A.* is one of the very few naturalist novels in which there is a controlled use of language, in which a major effect is produced by the interplay between story and style. It is necessary to add, however, that the faults of Dos Passos' work have been obscured by its vivid contemporaneity and vital political appeal. In the future, I think, it will be seen more clearly than now that it dramatizes social symptoms rather than lives and that it fails to preserve the integrity of personal experience. As for Faulkner, Hemingway, and Caldwell, I do not quite see on what grounds some critics and literary historians include them in the naturalist school. I should think that Faulkner is exempted by his prodigious inventiveness and fantastic humor. Hemingway is a realist on one level, in his attempts to catch the "real thing, the sequence of motion and fact which made the emotion": but he is also subjective, given to self-portraiture and to playing games with his ego; there is very little study of background in his work, a minimum of documentation. In his best novels Caldwell is a writer of rural abandon—and comedy. His *Tobacco Road* is a sociological area only in patches; most of it is exotic landscape.

It is not hard to demonstrate the weakness of the naturalist method by abstracting it, first, from the uses to which individual authors put it and, second, from its function in the history of modern literature. The traditionalist critics judge it much too one-sidedly in professing to see in its rise nothing but spiritual loss—an invasion of the arcanum of art by arid scientific ideas. The point is that this scientific bias of naturalism was

historically productive of contradictory results. Its effect was certainly
depressive insofar as it brought mechanistic notions and procedures into
writing. But it should be kept in mind that it also enlivened and, in fact,
revolutionized writing by liquidating the last assets of "romance" in fiction
and by purging it once and for all of the idealism of the "beautiful lie"—of
the long-standing inhibitions against dealing with the underside of life, with
those inescapable day-by-day actualities traditionally regarded as too
"sordid" and "ugly" for inclusion within an aesthetic framework. If it were
not for the service thus rendered in vastly increasing the store of literary
material, it is doubtful whether such works as *Ulysses* and even *Remembrance
of Things Past* could have been written. This is not clearly understood in the
English speaking countries, where naturalism, never quite forming itself into
a "movement," was at most only an extreme emphasis in the general onset of
realistic fiction and drama. One must study, rather, the Continental writers
of the last quarter of 19th Century in order to grasp its historical role. In
discussing the German naturalist school of the 1880's, the historian Hans
Naumann has this to say, for instance:

> Generally it can be said that to its early exponents the doctrine of
> naturalism held quite as many diverse and confusing meanings as
> the doctrine of expressionism seemed to hold in the period just
> past. Imaginative writers who at bottom were pure idealists
> united with the dry-as-dust advocates of a philistine natural-
> scientific program on the one hand and with the shameless
> exploiters of erotic themes on the other. All met under the banner
> of naturalism—friends today and enemies tomorrow.... But there
> was an element of historical necessity in all this. The fact is that
> the time had come for an assult, executed with glowing
> enthusiasm, against the epigones ... that it was finally possible to
> fling aside with disdain and anger the pretty falsehoods of life and
> art (*Die Deutshce Dichtung der Gegenwart, Stuttgart*, 1930, p. 144).

And he adds that the naturalism of certain writers consisted simply in their
"speaking honestly of things that had heretofore been suppressed."

But to establish the historical credit of naturalism is not to refute the
charges that have been brought against it in recent years. For whatever its
past accomplishments, it cannot be denied that its present condition is one
of utter debility. What was once a means of treating material truthfully has
been turned, through a long process of depreciation, into a mere convention

of truthfulness, devoid of any significant or even clearly definable literary purpose or design. The spirit of discovery has withdrawn from naturalism; it has now become the common denominator of realism, available in like measure to the producers of literature and to the producers of kitsch. One might sum up the objections to it simply by saying that it is no longer possible to use this method *without taking reality for granted*. This means that it has lost the power to cope with the ever-growing element of the problematical in modern life, which is precisely the element that is magnetizing the imagination of the true artists of our epoch. Such artists are no longer content merely to question particular habits or situations or even institutions; it is reality itself which they bring into question. Reality to them is like that "open wound" of which Kierkegaard speaks in his *Journals:* "A healthy open wound; sometimes it is healthier to keep a wound open; sometimes it is worse when it closes."

There are also certain long-range factors that make for the decline of naturalism. One such factor is the growth of psychological science and, particularly, of psychoanalysis. Through the influence of psychology literature recovers its inwardness, devising such forms as the interior monologue, which combines the naturalistic in its minute description of the mental process with the anti-naturalistic in its disclosure of the subjective and the irrational. Still another factor is the tendency of naturalism, as Thomas Mann observes in his remarks on Zola, to turn into the mythic through sheer immersion in the typical. This dialectical negation of the typical is apparent in a work like *Ulysses*, where "the myth of the *Odyssey*," to quote from Harry Levin's study of Joyce, "is superimposed upon the map of Dublin" because only a myth could "lend shape or meaning to a slice of life so broad and banal." And from a social-historical point of view this much can be said, that naturalism cannot hope to survive the world of 19th century science and industry of which it is the product. For what is the crisis of reality in contemporary art if not at bottom the crisis of the dissolution of this familiar world? Naturalism, which exhausted itself in taking an inventory of this world while it was still relatively stable, cannot possibly do justice to the phenomena of its disruption.

One must protest, however, against the easy assumption of some avant-gardist writers that to finish with naturalism is the same as finishing with the principle of realism generally. It is one thing to dissect the real, to penetrate beneath its faceless surface and transpose it into terms of symbol and image; but the attempt to be done with it altogether is sheer regression or escape. Of the principle of realism it can be said that it is the most valuable acquisition of the modern mind. It has taught literature how to take in, how to grasp and encompass, the ordinary facts of human existence; and I mean this in the simplest sense conceivable. Least of all can the novelist dispense with it, as his medium knows of no other principle of coherence. In Gide's *Les Faux-Monnayeurs* there is a famous passage in which the novelist Edouard enumerates the faults of the naturalist school. "The great defect of that school is that it always cuts a slice of life in the same direction: in time, lengthwise. Why not in breadth? Or in depth? As for me, I should like not to cut at all. Please understand: I should like to put everything into my novel." "But I thought," his interlocutor remarks, "that you want to abandon reality." Yes, replies Edouard, "my novelist wants to abandon it; but I shall continually bring him back to it. In fact that will be the subject; the struggle between the facts presented by reality and the ideal reality."

## Notes

1. Balzac, to whom naturalism is enormously indebted, explains in his preface to the *Comédie Humaine* that the idea of that work came to him in consequence of a "comparison between the human and animal kingdoms." "Does not society," he asks, "make of man, in accordance with the environment in which he lives and moves, as many different kinds of man as there are different zoological species? ... There have, therefore, existed and always will exist social species, just as there are zoological species."

Zola argues along the same lines: "All things hang together: it is necessary to start from the determination of inanimate bodies in order to arrive at the determination of living beings; and since savants like Claude Bernard demonstrate now that fixed laws govern the human body, we can easily proclaim ... the hour in which the laws of thought and passion will be formulated in their turn. A like determination will govern the stones of the roadway and the brain of man.... We have experimental chemistry and medicine and physiology, and later on an experimental novel. It is an inevitable evolution." (*The Experimental Novel*)

2. Chekhov remarks in one of his stories that "the sense of personal freedom is the chief constituent of creative genius."

3. Moreover, it should be evident that Zola's many faults are not rectified but merely inverted in much of the writing—so languidly allusive and decorative—of the literary generations that turned their backs on him.

MALCOLM COWLEY

# Naturalism in American Literature

I

Naturalism appeared thirty years later in American literature than it did in Europe and it was never quite the same movement. Like European naturalism it was inspired by Darwin's theory of evolution and kept repeating the doctrine that men, being part of the animal kingdom, were subject to natural laws. But theories and doctrines were not the heart of it. The American naturalists turned to Europe; they read—or read about—Darwin, they studied Spencer and borrowed methods from Zola because they were rebelling against an intolerable situation at home. What bound them together into a school or movement was this native rebellion and not the nature of the help that, like rebels in all ages, they summoned from abroad.

They began writing during the 1890's, when American literature was under the timid but tyrannical rule of what afterward came to be known as the genteel tradition. It was also called Puritanism by its enemies, but that was a mistake on the part of writers with only a stereotyped notion of American history. The original Puritans were not in the least genteel. They believed in the real existence of evil, which they denounced in terms that would have shocked William Dean Howells and the polite readers of the *Century Magazine*. The great New England writers, descendants of the Puritans, were moralists overburdened with scruples; but they were never

From *Evolutionary Thought in America* ed. Stow Persons. © 1950 by Yale University Press.

mealymouthed in the fashion of their successors. Gentility—or "ideality" or "decency," to mention two favorite words of the genteel writers—was something that developed chiefly in New York and the Middle West and had its flowering after the Civil War.

Essentially it was an effort to abolish the various evils and vulgarities in American society by never speaking about them. It was a theory that divided the world into two parts, as Sunday was divided from the days of the week or the right side from the wrong side of the railroad tracks. On one side was religion; on the other, business. On one side was the divine in human beings; on the other, everything animal. On one side was art; on the other, life. On one side were women, clergymen, and university professors, all guardians of art and the ideal; on the other side were men in general, immersed in their practical affairs. On one side were the church and the school; on the other side were the saloon, the livery stable, and other low haunts where men gathered to talk politics, swap stories, and remember their wartime adventures with the yellow girls in New Orleans. In America during the late nineteenth century culture was set against daily living, theory against practice, highbrow against lowbrow; and the same division could be found even in the language itself—for one side spoke a sort of bloodless literary English, while the other had a speech that was not American but Amurrkn, ugly and businesslike, sometimes picturesque but not yet a literary idiom.

The whole territory of literature was thought to lie on the right side of the railroad tracks, in the chiefly feminine realm of beauty, art, religion, culture, and the ideal. Novels had to be written with pure heroines and happy endings in order to flatter the self-esteem of female readers. Magazines were edited so as not to disturb the minds of young girls or call forth protests from angry mothers. Frank Norris said of American magazines in 1895:

> They are safe as a graveyard, decorous as a church, as devoid of immorality as an epitaph.... They adorn the center table. They do not "call a blush to the cheek of the young." They can be placed—oh, crowning virtue, oh, supreme encomium—they can be "safely" placed in the hands of any young girl the country over. ... It is the "young girl" and the family center table that determine the standard of the American short story.

Meanwhile there were new men appearing year by year—Frank Norris was one of them—who would not write for the young girl or the center table and could not express themselves without breaking the rules of the genteel editors.

These new men, who would be the first American naturalists, were all in some way disadvantaged when judged by the social and literary standards then prevailing. They were not of the Atlantic seaboard, or not of the old stock, or not educated in the right schools, or not members of the Protestant churches, or not sufficiently respectable in their persons or in their family backgrounds. They were in rebellion against the genteel tradition because, like writers from the beginning of time, they had an urgent need for telling the truth about themselves, and because there was no existing medium in which they were privileged to tell it.

## II

Instinctively the new writers began a search for older allies. There were a few of these to be found in America, but not enough of them to serve as the basis of a new literary movement. For most of their support the rebels had to look eastward across the Atlantic.

They were especially attracted by the English evolutionary scientists and pamphleteers. Most of the young writers read the works of this whole English group, beginning with Darwin, whose observations were too rigorously set forth to please their slipshod literary tastes. They could not find much to use in Darwin's books, except his picture of natural selection operating through the struggle for life; most of their Darwinism was acquired at second hand. Huxley they seem to have read with less veneration but more interest, chiefly because of his arguments against the Bible as revealed truth and because of his long war with the Protestant clergy. Young writers, feeling that the churches were part of a vast conspiracy to keep them silent, believed that Huxley was fighting their battle. It was Herbert Spencer, however, who deeply affected their thinking. Spencer's American popularity during the last half of the nineteenth century is something without parallel in the history of philosophic writing. From 1860 to 1903 his books had a sale of 368,755 copies in the authorized editions, not counting the many editions that appeared without his consent. In the memoirs of many famous Americans born in the 1860's and 1870's, one finds the reading of Spencer mentioned as an event that changed the course of their lives. Said John R. Commons, speaking of his father's cronies, "Every one of them in that eastern section of Indiana was a Republican living on the battle cries of the Civil War, and every one was a follower of Herbert Spencer.... I was brought up on Hoosierism, Republicanism, Presbyterianism and Spencerism."

What was a family inheritance for Commons was a personal discovery for most of the young writers who belonged to the same generation. Hamlin

Garland, when he was starving in Boston on three or four dollars a week, managed to borrow Spencer's books from the public library. After a five-cent breakfast of coffee and two doughnuts, he went "with eager haste," so he says, to Spencer's Synthetic Philosophy. Edgar Lee Masters read Spencer in Illinois, at the age of nineteen. Jack London read him in the little room in Oakland, Calif., where he was teaching himself to write. He says of his autobiographical hero, Martin Eden, that he opened Spencer's *First Principles* in bed, hoping that the book would put him to sleep after algebra and physics and an attempt at a sonnet. "Morning found him still reading. It was impossible for him to sleep. Nor did he write that day. He lay on the bed till his body grew tired, when he tried the hard floor, reading on his back, the book held in the air above him, or changing from side to side. He slept that night, and did his writing next morning, and then the book tempted him and he fell reading all afternoon, oblivious to everything." Theodore Dreiser read Huxley and Spencer in Pittsburgh, when he was working as a young reporter on the *Dispatch*. He tells us in *A Book about Myself* that the discovery of Spencer's *First Principles* "quite blew me, intellectually, to bits." And he goes on to say:

> Hitherto, until I had read Huxley, I had some lingering filaments of Catholicism trailing about me, faith in the existence of Christ, the soundness of his moral and sociologic deductions, the brotherhood of man. But on reading *Science and Hebrew Tradition* and *Science and Christian Tradition*, and finding both the Old and New Testaments to be not compendiums of revealed truth but mere records of religious experiences, and very erroneous ones at that, and then taking up *First Principles* and discovering all I deemed substantial—man's place in nature, his importance in the universe, this too, too solid earth, man's very identity save as an infinitesimal speck of energy or a "suspended equation" drawn or blown here and there by larger forces in which he moved quite unconsciously as an atom—all questioned and dissolved into other and less understandable things, I was completely thrown down in my conceptions or non-conceptions of life.

Not many of Spencer's readers were left with this impression of being confused and "completely thrown down." There were many more who valued him because he fitted together the pieces of a universal scheme that had been shattered by their earlier loss of faith in Christian dogmas. Garland, for example, found that "the universe took on order and harmony" as he considered Spencer's theory of the evolution of music or painting or sculpture. "It was thrilling, it was joyful," he says, "to perceive that everything moved from the simple to the complex—how the bow-string became the harp and the egg the chicken." Spencer's chief value, for the generation of writers who studied him, was that he gave them another unified world picture to replace the Christian synthesis. In that early age of specialization, he was the only great lay scholar with the courage to expound a synthetic philosophy. Many young men worshiped him not merely as a teacher but as a religious prophet. "To give up Spencer," said Jack London's autobiographical hero, "would be equivalent to a navigator throwing the compass and chronometer overboard." Later, when he heard a California judge disparaging Spencer, the hero burst into a rage. "To hear that great and noble man's name upon your lips," he shouted, "is like finding a dewdrop in a cesspool." In his quieter way, Edwin Arlington Robinson was almost as loyal to the synthetic philosopher. He said in a letter written in 1898 to one of his Harvard friends:

> Professor James's book is entertaining and full of good things; but his attitude toward Spencer makes me think of a dream my father once had. He dreamed he met a dog. The dog annoyed him, so he struck him with a stick. Then the dog doubled in size and my father struck him again with the same result. So the thing went on till the universe was pretty much all dog. When my father awoke, he was, or rather had been, halfway down the dog's throat.

But Spencer, enormous as he seemed, was no guide to young writers in the specific problems of their craft; nor was he a model to which they could point as justification for their dealing frankly with the world around them. In fiction and poetry they had to find other allies and, once again, most of them were transatlantic.

There were, for example, the English eighteenth-century classics, which could always be cited in arguments for honest realism. *Roxana, or the Fortunate Mistress* was one of Howells' favorites. "Did you ever read Defoe's 'Roxana'?" he said in a letter to his friend Samuel Clemens. "If not, then read it, not merely for some of the deepest insights into the lying, suffering, sinning, well-meaning human soul, but the best and most natural English that a book was ever written in." Still, he was more than a little worried by the effect that novels like *Roxana* and even scenes from Shakespeare might have on public morals. "I hope the time will come," he said in an essay written not long after his letter to Clemens, "when the beast-man will be so far submerged and tamed in us that the memory of him in literature will be left to perish; that what is lewd and ribald in the great poets shall be kept out of such editions as are meant for public reading." But this was only a pious wish, and perhaps not wholly sincere. General readers could still buy Defoe and Fielding and Smollett in unexpurgated volumes printed in England.

They could also buy translations of living Continental writers, sometimes in paper-bound reprints that sold for as little as ten cents a copy. Turgeniev and Tolstoy both had a following among literary people, and Tolstoy, because of his reputation for frankness, even had a popular sale. Ibsen was not often played, but he was widely discussed. There was a complete translation of Balzac, which stood on the shelves of the larger public libraries, and there were many editions of his separate novels. Zola also had a large public here and an extensive underground influence, in spite of the fact that he was seldom mentioned in the critical journals without being sweepingly condemned. "I read everything of Zola's that I can lay hands on," Howells confessed in a letter to John Hay. "But I have to hide the books from the children!" Theodore Dreiser tells us in his memoirs that when he was working as a reporter on the St. Louis *Republic*, in 1893, the city editor kept advising him "to imitate Zola's vivid description of the drab and the gross and the horrible, if I could—assuming that I had read him," Dreiser added, "which I had not, but I did not say so."

By that time, however, he had gained a fairly definite notion of Zola's methods at second hand. Two of his colleagues on the St. Louis *Globe-Democrat*, where he had worked the preceding year, had written a novel in the Zola manner. It was about a young and very beautiful actress named Theo, who was the mistress of a French newspaper man. Though deeply in love with her, the hero was unfaithful on at least one occasion; and this, Dreiser said when he retold the story in his memoirs, "brought about a Zolaesque scene in which she spanked another actress with a hairbrush. There was treacherous plotting on the part of somebody with regard to a local murder, which brought about the arrest and conviction of the newspaper man for something he knew nothing about. This entailed a great struggle on the part of Theo to save him, which resulted in her failure and his death on the guillotine. A priest figured in it in some way, grim, jesuitical."

This novel, which never found a publisher, must have been one of the earliest attempts to write in the manner of the French naturalists. Dreiser read it in manuscript and was greatly impressed, though he also wondered why his friends found it necessary to deal with French, not American, life when they wished to write in terms of fact. He didn't read Zola till much later in his career, so he tells us; but he discovered Balzac in 1894, when he was a reporter in Pittsburgh. "It was for me," he says, "a literary revolution. Not only for the brilliant and incisive manner with which Balzac grasped life and invented themes whereby to present it, but for the fact that the types he handled with most enthusiasm and skill—the brooding, seeking, ambitious beginners in life's social, political, artistic and commercial affairs (Rastignac, Raphael, de Rubempré, Bianchon)—were, I thought, so much like myself." Doors had opened in his mind. "Coming out of the library this day," he says, "and day after day thereafter, the while I rendered as little reportorial service as was consistent with even a show of effort, I marveled at the physical similarity of the two cities"—Pittsburgh and Paris—"as I conceived it, at the chance for pictures here as well as there. American pictures here, as opposed to French pictures there."

This experience of Dreiser's brings to light a curious phenomenon connected with the whole stream of foreign influence. Not only did the rebels of Dreiser's generation learn technical methods from the European naturalists, and find examples of frankness that supported them in their struggle with the genteel tradition; they also were inspired by Europeans to write about American scenes. They had to read European books in order to discover their own natures, and travel in imagination through European cities before they gained courage to describe their own backgrounds. Hamlin Garland, who was the most dogmatically American of them all, and the most vehemently opposed to the imitation of foreign masters, was at the same time a disciple of Ibsen, Tolstoy, and the French Impressionist painters. "In my poor, blundering fashion," he said long afterward, "I was standing for all forms of art which expressed, more or less adequately, the America I knew.... Ibsen's method, alien as his material actually appeared, pointed the way to a new and more authentic American drama. 'If we must imitate, let us imitate those who represent the truth and not those who uphold conventions,' was my argument."

### III

Meanwhile there were a very few living American authors whose work seemed to represent the truth and could therefore serve as models to the new generation. There was Whitman, still living meanly in his little house in Camden and still saying over and over again that American books should deal with American life. There were the local-color novelists, scores of them, each studying the folkways of his native or deliberately chosen territory. Garland thought that they represented a national movement, but the truth was that they dealt with a very few sections of the country: chiefly New England, the Southern Highlands, Louisiana, or California.

There were, however, three local writers from the Middle West who described their respective backgrounds with less sentiment and decorum than those from other sections. Edward Eggleston, of southern Indiana, had published *The Hoosier Schoolmaster* in 1871, at a time when there were no American models for that sort of homely writing; his inspiration for the book, he said, was a translation of Taine's lectures on *Art in the Netherlands*, in which he first encountered the thesis that an artist should work courageously with the materials he finds in his own environment. Edgar Watson Howe, of Kansas, had failed to find a publisher for his *Story of a Country Town* and had printed it at his own expense in 1883. It was the first novel to suggest that there was narrowness, frustration, and sexual hypocrisy in Midwestern lives. Joseph Kirkland, of Illinois, had read *The Hoosier Schoolmaster* and had wondered whether a similar background couldn't be presented more honestly than in Eggleston's book; in 1885 he published *Zury, the Meanest Man in Spring County*. Later he said to Garland, who greatly admired his novel, "Why shouldn't our prairie country have its novelists as well as England or France or Norway? Our characters will not be peasants, but our fiction can be close to the soil." Kirkland recognized the imperfections of his pioneer work; "I began too late," he said.

All these early realists began too late in their lives, and with insufficient preparation. Eggleston, whose books were popular in Scandinavia, was the only one who became a professional man of letters, and that was only after he had abandoned fiction for lecturing on American history. Kirkland was a lawyer who wrote in his spare time. Ed Howe was a newspaper editor. "When I quit the newspaper," he wrote to Garland, "I will write my best book, but I am successful at newspaper work and afraid to give it up." He never quit the newspaper or wrote another book as good as *The Story of a Country Town*. Men like Howe had no assurance that they could earn a living merely by writing novels; no assurance that there was any large public for the sort of truth they had to tell. Their few honest books pointed toward a road that they were unable to follow. But meanwhile, as a model for young writers, there was also William Dean Howells, who, for all his timidity, was trying to present the American world that lay before his eyes. Howells was the real patron and precursor of naturalism in America.

Frank Norris, in one of his magazine pieces, "A Lost Story," described the old schoolmaster as he appeared to the literary rebels of 1898. "He was," Norris said, speaking of an imaginary character named Trevor, but undoubtedly thinking of Howells, "a short, rotund man, rubicund as to face, bourgeois as to clothes and surroundings, jovial in manner, indulging even in slang. One might easily set him down as a retired groceryman—wholesale, perhaps, but none the less a groceryman. Yet touch him upon the subject of his profession, and the *bonhomie* lapsed away from him at once." And Norris continued,

> This elderly man of letters, who had seen the rise and fall of a dozen schools, was above the influence of fads, and he whose books were among the classics even before his death was infallible in his judgments of the work of the younger writers. All the stages of their evolution were known to him—all their mistakes, all their successes. He understood; and a story by one of them, a poem, a novel, that bore the stamp of his approval, was "sterling."

But the public, in 1898, had lost its taste for sterling. It had ceased to buy Howells' novels, let alone those of the young men he kept recommending in his many critical articles. Instead it was buying the romances of F. Hopkinson Smith and Kate Douglas Wiggin, brassy sentiment covered with a thin silver wash.

## IV

Norris had dressed in tails to spend his first evening at the Howells'; he liked to be the dandy when he had money for good clothes. He was a big, engaging young man of twenty-eight with prematurely gray hair and a wide cupid's-bow mouth that curled into consciously boyish smiles. Unlike the other naturalists, he had been the rather spoiled child of a wealthy family; and he had formed a high opinion of himself that kept him from feeling professional jealousy and therefore permitted him to have a high opinion of others. Howells liked him so much at their first meeting that he consented to read the manuscript of the Zolaesque novel that his visitor had lately finished after working on it at intervals for four years. It was called *McTeague* and it was the story of an unlicensed San Francisco dentist who had murdered his miserly wife. A few evenings later Norris came back to hear the master's judgment. This time he was received by Howells in lounging slippers and they sat for a long time by the open fire talking about the novel. It wouldn't be popular, Howells said, but he gave it the stamp of his approval; it was sterling.

Most of the magazines were shocked by *McTeague* when it was published in February, 1899. The *Independent* called it a dangerous book that had "no moral, esthetical or artistic reason for being." The *Bookman* condemned it as "the unexpected revival of realism in its most unendurable form." Other critics were incensed by a page in *McTeague* that described a little boy wetting his pants; they said that Norris had mentioned the unmentionable. There was much in the book that worried Howells, too, but he reviewed it with something close to enthusiasm. It prompted him to raise a serious question in the weekly column he was writing for *Literature*. The question was "whether we shall abandon the old-fashioned American ideal"—to which Howells himself had always clung—"of a novel as something which may be read by all ages and sexes, for the European notion of it as something fit only for age and experience, and for men rather than women; whether we shall keep to the bonds of the provincial proprieties, or shall include within the imperial territory of our fiction the passions and motives of the savage world which underlies as well as environs civilization." Howells did not try to answer the question; but he did say with a sense of prophecy, "The time may come at last when we are to invade and control Europe in literature. I do not say that it has come, but if it has we may have to employ European means and methods."

*McTeague* was not the first novel in the manner of the French naturalists to be written in the United States, for there must have been others that remained in manuscript, like the wicked book by Dreiser's two St. Louis friends. It was not even the first naturalistic novel to be published here, for Stephen Crane's *Maggie, a Girl of the Streets* had been issued by D. Appleton & Company in 1896, after being privately printed in 1893. But *Maggie*, though it dealt with poverty and prostitution from a naturalistic point of view, was not so much American as metropolitan; it was an episode that might have taken place in any of the world's large cities. *McTeague* was localized; it was the first novel that applied Zola's massive technique, his objective approach and his taste for the grotesquely common to a setting that everyone recognized as American.

Today it has lost its power to shock, but it retains more vitality and clear-sightedness than any of Norris' later novels. The others, even *The Octopus*, are full of romantic situations in the taste of the time; we read them today as period pieces. And the author himself, when we follow his career in Franklin Walker's biography, arouses a good deal of affectionate amusement mingled with our respect for what he achieved. He was a giant who never grew up. He never got over his dependence on his strong-minded mother; every illness sent him scurrying home to her apron strings. Harry Thurston Peck, the editor of the *Bookman*, said of Norris in a letter, "The author of the terrible 'McTeague' is a pleasant, cultivated young gentleman, inclined to be obstreperous—and humorless—in arguments on realism, but in every other respect a very pleasant boy." He also thought that his face suggested "photographs of Hawthorne or of some classic actor." Another observer thought that he resembled "an old-time tragedian ... Edwin Booth, perhaps." The truth was that Norris' writing was full of stage effects and that he never lost the actor's habit of looking at himself admiringly in the successive roles he played: the art student, the French dandy with sideburns and a cane, the fraternity brother, the breezy Westerner, the man about town, the Anglo-Saxon imperialist and explorer, the romantic lover, the struggling writer, the great novelist. Yes, even the last was a role; for his letters give the impression that Norris stood back and applauded himself as the author of books on big themes that he chose for their bigness, no matter how foreign they might be to his own experience.

About the time that *McTeague* appeared, he was getting launched on the biggest theme of all. "Tell Burgess I'm full of ginger and red pepper," he said in a letter, "and am getting ready to stand up on my hind legs and yell *big*." At the end of March, 1899, he wrote to Howells thanking him for his review of *McTeague*. "I have the idea of another novel or rather series of novels buzzing in my head these days," he added. "I think there is a chance for somebody to do some great work with the West and California as a background, and which will be at the same time thoroughly American. My idea is to write three novels around the one subject of *Wheat*. First, a story of California (the producer), second, a story of Chicago (the distributor), third, a story of Europe (the consumer) and in each keep to the idea of this huge Niagara of wheat rolling from West to East. I think a big epic trilogy *could* be made out of such a subject, that at the same time would be modern and distinctly American. The idea is so big that it frightens me at times but I have about made up my mind to have a try at it." He was in fact already working on his plans, and early in April he went to California in a search for characters, incidents, and local color.

The first volume of the trilogy was published just two years later, in April, 1901. *The Octopus* was on all counts his most ambitious novel, the most carefully composed, the broadest and most colorful in its background, the closest in its theme to great historical events. It was written after a period of sudden booms and depressions, when big business was swallowing little businesses and millions of individuals felt themselves the victims of impersonal corporations or uncontrollable forces. Norris gave expression to their sense of injustice and bewilderment; and he also introduced new technical methods, especially in his collective treatment of the California ranchers. His chapters on the barn dance and the rabbit hunt were almost the first portrayals in American fiction of a group that exulted and suffered as one man. *The Octopus*, in one of his favorite phrases, was a book "as big as all outdoors"; but its bigness was achieved at the expense of many strained effects and more concessions than he had made in *McTeague* to the bad taste of the day. At the end it declined into muzzy sentiments and fine writing. There is one long passage describing a dinner given by a railroad tycoon, with ortolan patties and Londonderry pheasants served at the exact moment when Mrs. Hooven, robbed of her home by the railroad, was dying of starvation in a vacant lot—one passage of twenty pages that belongs in an old-fashioned servant girls' weekly.

Howells admired *The Octopus* with reservations; after the comparatively unpretentious honesty of *McTeague*, he seems to have felt that it made too many compromises. But there were still more compromises in the second volume of the trilogy, *The Pit*, which appeared in January, 1903, after being serialized in the *Saturday Evening Post*. With its effort to romanticize the big gambler on the Chicago Board of Trade, and with its secondary plot about the wife who discovers that she really loves him after being tempted to run away with a freshwater esthete, who in turn is merely funny instead of being the sinister figure that Norris tried to present, it becomes a provincial melodrama rather than a second canto in the epic of the wheat. *The Pit* seems to indicate that the author had made his peace with genteel society. Perhaps the indication is false, for Norris was dissatisfied with this latest work. Perhaps the next book would have been better; but he died suddenly of peritonitis in the autumn of 1902, before *The Pit* was published and before he had even begun to collect material for the third volume of his trilogy.

It is easy now to see the faults of his work. He was a borrower of literary effects; he took those he needed wherever he found them, in Kipling, Stevenson, Tolstoy, Zola, or Maupassant. He depended on instinct rather than intelligence for his choice of borrowings, since he always thought viscerally, with his heart and bowels instead of his brain. In that respect he resembled the first Roosevelt; and Henry Adams' judgment on the President applies to the novelist equally: "We are timid and conventional, all of us, except T. R., and he has no mind." But T. R. was often timid and conventional in politics, for all his bluster, just as Norris was often conventional in writing his big dramatic scenes and timid in his moral judgments. One remembers how Presley, the poet in *The Octopus* who often speaks for the author, sets out to rescue the penniless Hooven family, finds that the daughter has become a prostitute and runs away from her in sick terror, feeling that with her first step into sin she has passed beyond all human help. Norris' moral rebellion, like T. R.'s political rebellion, stayed within the limits of what was then good form.

He had no feeling for any but the most obvious social values; I think it was Henry James who said that Norris' pictures of Chicago society would have been good satires if he had known they were satires. He was proud of not writing careful prose. He didn't live long enough to learn many subtleties of character or the use in portraying them of many shades between black and white. Yet it may be that his faults and failures helped to keep him close to a public that had missed the ironies in Henry B. Fuller's work and felt that Stephen Crane was cold, European and possibly corrupt. They were the faults of his time and they contributed, in their way, to his timely influence on American writing. His great virtues were also of a sort that the public could learn to respect: freshness, narrative vigor, a marvelous eye for the life around him and courage to portray it in its drama and violence, besides the ability to construct his novels like Zola's in massive blocks. During a literary career of only six years, he managed to impress his personality, some of his particular virtues, and many of his shortcomings on the whole naturalistic school that would follow him.

V

After half a century we can look back in an objective or naturalistic spirit at the work of the writers inspired by Dreiser and Norris. We can describe their principles, note how these were modified in practice and reach some sort of judgment on their achievements.

Naturalism in literature has been defined by Oscar Cargill as pessimistic determinism, and the definition is true so far as it goes. The naturalists were all determinists in that they believed in the omnipotence of natural forces. They were pessimists in that they believed in the absolute incapacity of men and women to shape their own destinies. They regarded the individual as merely "a pawn on a chessboard"; the phrase recurs time and again in their novels. They felt that he could not achieve happiness by any conscious decision and that he received no earthly or heavenly reward for acting morally; man was, in Dreiser's words, "the victim of forces over which he has no control."

In some of his moods, Frank Norris carried this magnification of forces and minification of persons to an even greater extreme. "Men were nothings, mere animalculae, mere ephemerides that fluttered and fell and were forgotten between dawn and dusk," he said in the next-to-last chapter of *The Octopus*. "Men were naught, life was naught; FORCE only existed—FORCE that brought men into the world, FORCE that made the wheat grow, FORCE that garnered it from the soil to give place to the succeeding crop."

But Norris, like several other naturalists, was able to combine this romantic pessimism about individuals with romantic optimism about the future of mankind. "The individual suffers, but the race goes on," he said at the very end of the novel. "Annixter dies, but in a far distant corner of the world a thousand lives are saved. The larger view always and through all shams, all wickednesses, discovers the Truth that will, in the end, prevail, and all things, surely, inevitably, resistlessly work together for good." This was, in its magniloquent way, a form of the belief in universal progress announced by Herbert Spencer, but it was also mingled with native or Emersonian idealism, and it helped to make naturalism more palatable to Norris' first American readers.

Zola had also declared his belief in human perfectibility, in what he called "a constant march toward truth"; and it was from Zola rather than Spencer or any native sources that Norris had borrowed most of his literary doctrines. Zola described himself as "a positivist, an evolutionist, a materialist." In his working notes, which Norris of course had never seen, but which one might say that he divined from the published text of the novels, Zola had indicated some of his aims as a writer. He would march through the world observing human behavior as if he were observing the forms of animal life. "Study men as simple elements and note the reactions," he said. And again, "What matters most to me is to be purely naturalistic, purely physiological. Instead of having principles (royalism, Catholicism) I shall have laws (heredity, atavism)." And yet again, "Balzac says that he wishes to paint men, women and things. I count men and women as the same, while admitting their natural differences, and *subject men and women to things.*" In that last phrase, which Zola underlined, he expressed the central naturalistic doctrine: that men and women are part of nature and subject to the same indifferent laws.

The principal laws, for Zola, were those of heredity, which he assumed to be as universal and unchanging as the second law of thermodynamics. He fixed upon the hereditary weakness of the Rougon-Macquart family as a theme that would bind together his vast series of novels. Suicide, alcoholism, prostitution, and insanity were all to be explained as the result of the same hereditary taint. "Vice and virtue," he said, "are products like vitriol and sugar." Norris offered the same explanation for the brutality of McTeague. "Below the fine fabric of all that was good in him," Norris said, "ran the foul stream of hereditary evil, like a sewer. The vices and sins of his father and of his father's father, to the third and fourth and five hundredth generation, tainted him. The evil of an entire race flowed in his veins. Why should it be? He did not desire it. Was he to blame?" Others of the naturalistic school, and

Norris himself in his later novels, placed more emphasis on environmental forces. When Stephen Crane sent a copy of *Maggie* to the Reverend Thomas Dixon, he wrote on the flyleaf: "It is inevitable that this book will greatly shock you, but continue, pray, with great courage to the end, for it tries to show that environment is a tremendous thing and often shapes lives regardlessly. If I could prove that theory, I would make room in Heaven for all sorts of souls (notably an occasional street girl) who are not confidently expected to be there by many excellent people." Maggie, the victim of environment, was no more to blame for her transgressions than McTeague, the victim of hereditary evil. Nobody was to blame in this world where men and women are subject to the laws of things.

A favorite theme in naturalistic fiction is that of the beast within. As the result of some crisis—usually a fight, a shipwreck, or an expedition into the Arctic—the veneer of civilization drops or is stripped away and we are faced with "the primal instinct of the brute struggling for its life and for the life of its young." The phrase is Norris', but it might have been written by any of the early naturalists. When evolution is treated in their novels, it almost always takes the opposite form of devolution or degeneration. It is seldom that the hero evolves toward a superhuman nature, as in Nietzsche's dream; instead he sinks backward toward the beasts. Zola set the fashion in *L'Assommoir* and *La Bête humaine* and Norris followed him closely in the novel he wrote during his year at Harvard, *Vandover and the Brute*. Through yielding to his lower instincts, Vandover loses his humanity; he tears off his clothes, paddles up and down the room on his hands and feet and snarls like a dog.

A still earlier story, *Lauth*, was written at the University of California after Norris had listened to the lectures of Professor Joseph Le Conte, the famous evolutionist. The action takes place in medieval Paris, where Lauth, a student at the Sorbonne, is mortally wounded in a brawl. A doctor brings him back to life by pumping blood into his veins, but the soul had left the body and does not return. Without it, Lauth sinks back rapidly through the various stages of evolution: he is an ape, then a dog, then finally "a horrible shapeless mass lying upon the floor. It lived, but lived not as do the animals or the trees, but as the protozoa, the jellyfish, and those strange lowest forms of existence wherein the line between vegetable and animal cannot be drawn." That might have been taken as a logical limit to the process of devolution; but Jack London, who was two parts naturalist, if he was also one part socialist and three parts hack journalist, tried to carry the process even further, into the realm of inanimate nature. Here, for example, is the description of a fight in *Martin Eden*:

Then they fell upon each other, like young bulls, in all the glory of youth, with naked fists, with hatred, with desire to hurt, to maim, to destroy. All the painful, thousand years' gains of man in his upward climb through creation were lost. Only the electric light remained, a milestone on the path of the great human adventure. Martin and Cheese-Face were two savages, of the stone age, of the squatting place and the tree refuge. They sank lower and lower into the muddy abyss, back into the dregs of the raw beginnings of life, striving blindly and chemically, as atoms strive, as the star-dust of the heavens strives, colliding, recoiling and colliding again and eternally again.

It was more than a metaphor when London said that men were atoms and star dust; it was the central drift of his philosophy. Instead of moving from the simple to the complex, as Herbert Spencer tells us that everything does in this world, the naturalists kept moving from the complex to the simple, by a continual process of reduction. They spoke of the nation as "the tribe," and a moment later the tribe became a pack. Civilized man became a barbarian or a savage, the savage became a brute and the brute was reduced to its chemical elements. "Study men as simple elements," Zola had said; and many years later Dreiser followed his advice by presenting love as a form of electromagnetism and success in life as a question of chemical compounds; thus he said of his brother Paul that he was "one of those great Falstaffian souls who, for lack of a little iron or sodium or carbon dioxide in his chemical compost, was not able to bestride the world like a Colossus."

There was a tendency in almost all the naturalistic writers to identify social laws with biological or physical laws. For Jack London, the driving force behind human events was always biology—"I mean," says his autobiographical hero, Martin Eden, "the real interpretative biology, from the ground up, from the laboratory and the test tube and the vitalized inorganic right on up to the widest esthetic and social generalizations." London believed that such biological principles as natural selection and the survival of the fittest were also the laws of human society. Thomas Hardy often spoke as if men's destinies were shaped by the physical sciences. He liked to say that his characters were doomed by the stars in their courses; but actually they were doomed by human conflicts or by the still Puritan conventions of middle-class England. Norris fell into the same confusion between the physical and the social world when he pictured the wheat as "a huge Niagara ... flowing from West to East." In his novels wheat was not a grain improved by men from various wild grasses and grown by men to meet human needs; it was an abstract and elemental force like gravity. "I corner the wheat!" says Jadwin, the hero of *The Pit*. "Great heavens, it is the wheat that has cornered me." Later, when he is ruined by the new grain that floods the market, Jadwin thinks to himself,

> The Wheat had grown itself: demand and supply, these were the two great laws that the Wheat obeyed. Almost blasphemous in his effrontery, he had tampered with these laws, and roused a Titan. He had laid his puny human grasp upon Creation and the very earth herself, the great mother, feeling the touch of the cobweb that the human insect had spun, had stirred at last in her sleep and sent her omnipotence moving through the grooves of the world, to find and crush the disturber of her appointed courses.

Just as the wheat had grown itself, so, in the first volume of Norris' trilogy, the Pacific and Southwestern Railroad had built itself. This octopus that held a state in its tentacles was beyond human control. Even Shelgrim, the president of the railroad, was merely the agent of a superhuman force. At the end of the novel he gives a lecture to Presley which overwhelms the poet and leaves him feeling that it rang "with the clear reverberation of truth." "You are dealing with forces," Shelgrim says, "when you speak of Wheat and the Railroads, not with men. There is the Wheat, the supply. It must be carried to the People. There is the demand. The Wheat is one force, the Railroad, another, and there is the law that governs them—supply and demand. Men have little to do with the whole business." If the two forces came into conflict—if the employees of the railroad massacred the wheat ranchers and robbed them of their land—then Presley should "blame conditions, not men."

The effect of naturalism as a doctrine is to subtract from literature the whole notion of human responsibility. "Not men" is its constant echo. If naturalistic stories had tragic endings, these were not to be explained by human wills in conflict with each other or with fate; they were the blind result of conditions, forces, physical laws, or nature herself. "There was no malevolence in Nature," Presley reflects after meeting the railroad president. "Colossal indifference only, a vast trend toward appointed goals. Nature was, then, a gigantic engine, a vast, cyclopean power, huge, terrible, a leviathan with a heart of steel, knowing no compunction, no forgiveness, no tolerance; crushing out the human atom standing in its way, with nirvanic calm." Stephen Crane had already expressed the same attitude toward nature in a sharper image and in cleaner prose. When the four shipwrecked men in *The Open Boat* are drifting close to the beach but are unable to land because of the breakers, they stare at a windmill that is like "a giant standing with its back to the plight of the ants. It represented in a degree, to the correspondent, the serenity of nature amid the struggles of the individual—nature in the wind, and nature in the visions of men. She did not seem cruel to him, then, nor beneficent, nor treacherous, nor wise. But she was indifferent, flatly indifferent."

These ideas about nature, science, and destiny led to the recurrent use of words and phrases by which early naturalistic fiction can be identified. "The irony of fate" and "the pity of it" are two of the phrases; "pawns of circumstance" is another. The words that appear time and again are "primitive," "primordial" (often coupled with "slime"), "prehensile," "apelike," "wolflike," "brute" and "brutal," "savage," "driving," "conquering," "blood" (often as an adjective), "master" and "slave" (also as adjectives), "instinct" (which is usually "blind"), "ancestor," "huge," "cyclopean," "shapeless," "abyss," "biological," "chemic" and "chemism," "hypocrisy," "taboo," "unmoral." Time and again we read that "The race is to the swift and the battle to the strong." Time and again we are told about "the law of claw and fang," "the struggle for existence," "the blood of his Viking ancestors," and "the foul stream of hereditary evil." "The veneer of civilization" is always being "stripped away," or else it "drops away in an instant." The characters in early naturalistic novels "lose all resemblance to humanity," reverting to "the abysmal brute." But when they "clash together like naked savages," or even like atoms and star dust, it is always the hero who "proves himself the stronger"; and spurning his prostrate adversary he strides forward to seize "his mate, his female." "Was he to blame?" the author asks his readers; and always he answers, "Conditions, not men, were at fault."

## VI

All these characteristics of the earlier American naturalists might have been deduced from their original faith in Darwinian evolution and in the need for applying biological and physical laws to human affairs. But they had other characteristics that were more closely connected with American life in their own day.

The last decade of the nineteenth century, when they started their literary careers, was an age of contrasts and sudden changes. In spite of financial panics, the country was growing richer, but not at a uniform rate for all sections: the South was hopelessly impoverished and rural New England was returning to wilderness. Cities were gaining in population, partly at the expense of the Eastern farms, industry was thriving at the expense of agriculture, and independent factories were being combined into or destroyed by the trusts. It was an age of high interest rates, high but uncertain profits, low wages and widespread unemployment. It was an age when labor unions were being broken, when immigrants were pouring through Ellis Island to people the new slums and when the new American baronage was building its magnificently ugly chateaux. "America," to quote again from Dreiser's memoirs, "was just entering upon the most lurid phase of that vast, splendid, most lawless and most savage period in which the great financiers were plotting and conniving at the enslavement of the people and belaboring each other." Meanwhile the ordinary citizen found it difficult to plan his future and even began to suspect that he was, in a favorite naturalistic phrase, "the plaything of forces beyond human control."

The American faith that was preached in the pulpits and daily reasserted on editorial pages had lost its connection with American life. It was not only an intolerable limitation on American writing, as all the rebel authors had learned; it also had to be disregarded by anyone who hoped to rise in the business world and by anyone who, having failed to rise, wanted to understand the reasons for his failure. In its simplest terms, the American faith was that things were getting better year by year, that the individual could solve his problems by moving, usually westward, and that virtue was rewarded with wealth, the greatest virtue with the greatest wealth. Those were the doctrines of the editorial page; but reporters who worked for the same newspaper looked around them and decided that wealth was more often the fruit of selfishness and fraud, whereas the admirable persons in their world—the kind, the philosophic, the honest, and the open-eyed—were usually failures by business standards. Most of the early naturalistic writers, including Stephen Crane, Harold Frederic, David Graham Phillips, and Dreiser, were professional newspaper men; while the others either worked for short periods as reporters or wrote series of newspaper articles. All were more or less affected by the moral atmosphere of the city room; and the fact is important, since the newspaper men of the 1890's and 1900's were a special class or type. "Never," says Dreiser, speaking of his colleagues on the Pittsburgh *Dispatch*, "had I encountered more intelligent or helpful or companionable albeit more cynical men than I met here"; and the observation leads to general remarks about the reporters he had known:

One can always talk to a newspaper man, I think, with the full confidence that one is talking to a man who is at least free of moralistic mush. Nearly everything in connection with those trashy romances of justice, truth, mercy, patriotism, public profession of all sorts, is already and forever gone if they have been in the business for any length of time. The religionist is seen by them for what he is: a swallower of romance or a masquerader looking to profit and preferment. Of the politician, they know or believe but one thing: that he is out for himself.

Essentially the attitude forced upon newspaper men as they interviewed politicians, evangelists, and convicted criminals was the same as the attitude they derived or might have derived from popular books on evolution. Reading and experience led to the same convictions: that Christianity was a sham, that all moral professions were false, that there was nothing real in the world but force and, for themselves, no respectable role to play except that of detached observers gathering the facts and printing as many of them as their publishers would permit. They drank, whored, talked shop, and dreamed about writing cynical books. "Most of these young men," Dreiser says, "looked upon life as a fierce, grim struggle in which no quarter was either given or taken, and in which all men laid traps, lied, squandered, erred through illusion: a conclusion with which I now most heartily agree." His novels one after another would be based on what he had learned in his newspaper days.

In writing their novels, most of the naturalists pictured themselves as expressing a judgment of life that was scientific, dispassionate, and, to borrow one of their phrases, completely unmoral; but a better word for their attitude would be "rebellious." Try as they would, they could not remain merely observers. They had to revolt against the moral standards of their time; and the revolt involved them more or less consciously in the effort to impose new standards that would be closer to what they regarded as natural laws. Their books are full of little essays or sermons addressed to the reader; in fact they suggest a naturalistic system of ethics complete with its vices and virtues. Among the vices those most often mentioned are hypocrisy, intolerance, conventionality, and unwillingness to acknowledge the truth. Among the virtues perhaps the first is strength, which is presented as both a physiological and a moral quality; it implies the courage to be strong in spite of social restraints. A second virtue is naturalness, that is, the quality of acting in accordance with one's nature and physical instincts. Dreiser's Jennie Gerhardt was among the first of the purely natural heroines in American literature, but she had many descendants. A third virtue is complete candor about the world and oneself; a fourth is pity for others; and a fifth is tolerance, especially of moral rebellion and economic failure. Most of the characters presented sympathetically in naturalistic novels are either the victors over moral codes which they defy (like Cowperwood in *The Financier* and Susan Lenox in the novel by David Graham Phillips about her fall and rise) or else victims of the economic struggle, paupers and drunkards with infinitely more wisdom than the respectable citizens who avoid them. A great deal of naturalistic writing, including the early poems of Edwin Arlington Robinson, is an eloquent hymn to loneliness and failure as the destiny, in America, of most superior men.

There are other qualities of American naturalism that are derived not so much from historical conditions as from the example of the two novelists whom the younger men regarded as leaders or precursors. Norris first and Dreiser after him fixed the patterns that the others would follow.

Both men were romantic by taste and temperament. Although Norris was a disciple of Zola's, his other favorite authors belonged in one way or another to the romantic school; they included Froissart, Scott, Dickens, Dumas, Hugo, Kipling, and Stevenson. Zola was no stranger in that company, Norris said; on one occasion he called him "the very head of the Romanticists."

> Terrible things must happen [he wrote], to the characters of the naturalistic tale. They must be twisted from the ordinary, wrenched from the quiet, uneventful round of everyday life and flung into the throes of a vast and terrible drama that works itself out in unleashed passions, in blood and sudden death.... Everything is extraordinary, imaginative, grotesque even, with a vague note of terror quivering throughout like the vibration of an ominous and low-pitched diapason.

Norris himself wished to practice naturalism as a form of romance, instead of taking up what he described as "the harsh, loveless, colorless, blunt tool called Realism." Dreiser in his autobiographical writings often refers to his own romantic temper. "For all my modest repute as a realist," he says, "I seem, to my self-analyzing eyes, somewhat more of a romanticist." He speaks of himself in his youth as "a creature of slow and uncertain response to anything practical, having an eye to color, romance, beauty. I was but a half-baked poet, romancer, dreamer." The other American naturalists were also romancers and dreamers in their fashion, groping among facts for the extraordinary and even the grotesque. They believed that men were subject to natural forces, but they felt those forces were best displayed when they led to unlimited wealth, utter squalor, collective orgies, blood, and sudden death.

Among the romantic qualities they tried to achieve was "bigness" in its double reference to size and intensity. They wanted to display "big"—that is, intense—emotions against a physically large background. Bigness was the virtue that Norris most admired in Zola's novels. "The world of M. Zola," he said, "is a world of big things; the enormous, the formidable, the terrible, is what counts; no teacup tragedies here." In his own novels, Norris looked for big themes; after his trilogy on Wheat, he planned to write a still bigger trilogy on the three days' battle of Gettysburg, with one novel devoted to the events of each day. The whole notion of writing trilogies instead of separate novels came to be connected with the naturalistic movement, although it was also adopted by the historical romancers. Before Norris there had been only one planned trilogy in serious American fiction: *The Littlepage Manuscripts*, written by James Fenimore Cooper a few years before his death; it traces the story of a New York state landowning family through a hundred years and three generations. After Norris there were dozens of trilogies, with a few tetralogies and pentalogies: to mention some of the better known, there were Dreiser's trilogy on the career of a financier, T. S. Stribling's trilogy on the rise of a poor-white family, Dos Passos' trilogy on the United States from 1900 to 1930, James T. Farrell's trilogy on Studs Lonigan and Eugene O'Neill's trilogy of plays, *Mourning Becomes Electra*. Later O'Neill set to work on a trilogy of trilogies, on a theme that he planned to treat in nine full-length plays. Farrell wrote a tetralogy about the boyhood of Danny O'Neill and then attacked another theme that would require several volumes, the young manhood of Bernard Clare. Trilogies expanded into whole cycles of novels somehow related in theme. Thus, after the success of *The Jungle*, which had dealt with the meat-packing industry in Chicago, Upton Sinclair wrote novels on other cities (Denver, Boston) and other industries (oil, coal, whisky, automobiles); finally he settled on a character, Lanny Budd, whose adventures were as endless as those of Tarzan or Superman. Sinclair Lewis dealt one after another with various trades and professions: real estate, medicine, divinity, social service, hotel management, and the stage; there was no limit to the subjects he could treat, so long as his readers' patience was equal to his own.

With their eyes continually on vast projects, the American naturalists were careless about the details of their work and indifferent to the materials they were using; often their trilogies resembled great steel-structural buildings faced with cinder blocks and covered with cracked stucco ornaments. Sometimes the buildings remained unfinished. Norris set this pattern, too, when he died before he could start his third novel on the Wheat. Dreiser worked for years on *The Stoic*, which was to be the sequel to

*The Financier* and *The Titan;* but he was never satisfied with the various endings he tried, and the book had to be completed by others after his death. O'Neill stopped work on his trilogy of trilogies. Lewis never wrote his novel on labor unions, although he spent months or years gathering material for it and spoke of it as his most ambitious work. In their effort to achieve bigness at any cost, the naturalists were likely to undertake projects that went beyond their physical or imaginative powers, or in which they discovered too late that they weren't interested.

Meanwhile they worked ahead in a delirium of production, like factories trying to set new records. To understand their achievements in speed and bulk one has to compare their output with that of an average novelist. There is of course no average novelist, but there are scores of men and women who earn their livings by writing novels, and many of them try to publish one book each year. If they spend four months planning and gathering material for the book, another four months writing the first draft (at the rate of about a thousand words a day), and the last four months in revision, they are at least not unusual. Very few of the naturalists would have been satisfied with that modest rate of production. Harold Frederic wrote as much as 4,000 words a day and often sent his manuscripts to the printer without corrections. At least he paused between novels to carry on his work as a foreign correspondent; but Jack London, who wrote only 1,000 words a day, tried to fulfill that quota six days a week and fifty-two weeks a year; he allowed himself no extra time for planning or revision. He wrote fifty books in seventeen years, and didn't pretend that all of them were his best writing. "I have no unfinished stories," he told an interviewer five years before his death. "Invariably I complete every one I start. If it's good, I sign it and send it out. If it isn't good, I sign it and send it out." David Graham Phillips finished his first novel in 1901 and published sixteen others before his death in 1911, in addition to the articles he wrote for muckraking magazines. He left behind him the manuscripts of six novels (including the two-volume *Susan Lenox*) that were published posthumously. Upton Sinclair set a record in the early days when he was writing half-dime novels for boys. He kept three secretaries busy; two of them would be transcribing their notes while the third was taking dictation. By this method he once wrote 18,000 words in a day. He gained a fluency that helped him later when he was writing serious books, but he also acquired a contempt for style that made them painful to read, except in their French translations. Almost all the naturalists read better in translation; that is one of the reasons for their international popularity as compared with the smaller audience that some of them found at home.

The naturalistic writers of all countries preferred an objective or scientific approach to their material As early as 1864 the brothers Goncourt had written in their journal, "The novel of today is made with documents narrated or selected from nature, just as history is based on written documents." A few years later Zola defined the novel as a scientific experiment; its purpose, he said in rather involved language, was to demonstrate the behavior of given characters in a given situation. Still later Norris advanced the doctrine "that no one could be a writer until he could regard life and people, and the world in general, from the objective point of view—until he could remain detached, outside, maintain the unswerving attitude of the observer." The naturalists as a group not only based their work on current scientific theories, but tried to copy scientific methods in planning their novels. They were writers who believed, or claimed to believe, that they could deliberately choose a subject for their work instead of being chosen by a subject; that they could go about collecting characters as a biologist collected specimens; and that their fictional account of such characters could be as accurate and true to the facts as the report of an experiment in the laboratory.

It was largely this faith in objectivity that led them to write about penniless people in the slums, whom they regarded as "outside" or alien subjects for observation. Some of them began with a feeling of contempt for the masses. Norris during his college years used to speak of "the canaille" and often wished for the day when all radicals could be "drowned on one raft." Later this pure contempt developed into a contemptuous interest, and he began to spend his afternoons on Polk Street, in San Francisco, observing with a detached eye the actions of what he now called "the people." The minds of the people, he thought, were simpler than those of persons in his own world; essentially these human beings were animals, "the creatures of habit, the playthings of forces," and therefore they were ideal subjects for a naturalistic novel. Some of the other naturalists revealed the same rather godlike attitude toward workingmen. Nevertheless they wrote about them, a bold step at a time when most novels dealt only with ladies, gentlemen, and faithful retainers; and often their contemptuous interest was gradually transformed into sympathy.

Their objective point of view toward their material was sometimes a pretense that deceived themselves before it deceived others. From the outside world they chose the subjects that mirrored their own conflicts and obsessions. Crane, we remember, said his purpose in writing *Maggie* was to show "that environment is a tremendous thing and often shapes lives regardlessly." Yet, on the subjective level, the novel also revealed an obsessive notion about the blamelessness of prostitutes that affected his career from beginning to end; it caused a series of scandals, involved him in a feud with the vice squad in Manhattan and finally led him to marry the madam of a bawdy house in Jacksonville. Norris's first novel, *Vandover and the Brute*, is an apparently objective study of degeneration, but it also mirrors the struggles of the author with his intensely Puritan conscience; Vandover is Norris himself. He had drifted into some mild dissipations and pictured them as leading to failure and insanity. Dreiser in *Sister Carrie*, was telling a story based on the adventures of one of his own sisters; that explains why Carrie Meeber in the novel is "Sister" Carrie, even though her relatives disappear after the first few pages. "My mind was a blank except for the name," Dreiser said when explaining how he came to write the novel. "I had no idea who or what she was to be. I have often thought that there was something mystic about it, as if I were being used, like a medium." In a sense he was being used by his memories, which had become subconscious. There was nothing mystic to Upton Sinclair about his fierce emotion in writing *The Jungle*; he knew from the beginning that he was telling his own story. "I wrote with tears and anguish," he says in his memoirs,

> pouring into the pages all that pain which life had meant to me. Externally, the story had to do with a family of stockyards workers, but internally it was the story of my own family. Did I wish to know how the poor suffered in Chicago? I had only to recall the previous winter in a cabin, when we had only cotton blankets, and cowered shivering in our separate beds.... Our little boy was down with pneumonia that winter, and nearly died, and the grief of that went into the book.

Indeed, there is personal grief and fury and bewilderment in all the most impressive naturalistic novels. They are at their best, not when they are scientific or objective, in accordance with their own theories, but when they are least naturalistic, most personal and lyrical.

If we follow William James and divide writers into the two categories of the tough and the tender-minded, then most of the naturalists are tender-minded. The sense of moral fitness is strong in them; they believe in their hearts that nature *should* be kind, that virtue *should* be rewarded on earth, that men *should* control their own destinies. More than other writers, they are wounded by ugliness and injustice, but they will not close their eyes to either; indeed, they often give the impression of seeking out ugliness and injustice in order to be wounded again and again. They have hardly a trace of the cynicism that is often charged against them. It is the quietly realistic or classical writers who are likely to be cynics, in the sense of holding a low opinion of life and human beings; that low estimate is so deeply ingrained in them that they never bother to insist on it—for why should they try to make converts in such a hopeless world? The naturalists are always trying to convert others and themselves, and sometimes they build up new illusions simply to enjoy the pain of stripping them away. It is their feeling of fascinated revulsion toward their subject matter that makes some of the naturalists hard to read; they seem to be flogging themselves and their audience like a band of penitentes.

## VII

So far I have been trying to present the positive characteristics of a movement in American letters, but naturalism can also be defined in terms of what it is not. Thus, to begin a list of negations, it is not journalism in the bad sense, merely sensational or entertaining or written merely to sell. It has to be honest by definition, and honesty in literature is a hard quality to achieve, one that requires more courage and concentration than journalists can profitably devote to writing a novel. Even when an author holds all the naturalistic doctrines, his books have to reach a certain level of observation and intensity before they deserve to be called naturalistic. Jack London held the doctrines and wrote fifty books, but only three or four of them reached the required level. David Graham Phillips reached it only once, in *Susan Lenox*, if he reached it then.

Literary naturalism is not the sort of doctrine that can be officially sponsored and taught in the public schools. It depends for too many of its effects on shocking the sensibilities of its readers and smashing their illusions. It always becomes a threat to the self-esteem of the propertied classes. *Babbitt*, for example, is naturalistic in its hostile treatment of American businessmen. When Sinclair Lewis defended Babbittry in a later novel, *The Prodigal Parents*, his work had ceased to be naturalistic.

For a third negative statement, naturalism is not what we have learned to call literature "in depth." It is concerned with human behavior and with explanations for that behavior in terms of heredity or environment. It presents the exterior world, often in striking visual images; but unlike the work of Henry James or Sherwood Anderson or William Faulkner—to mention only three writers in other traditions—it does not try to explore the world within. Faulkner's method is sometimes described as "subjective naturalism," but the phrase is self-contradictory, almost as if one spoke of "subjective biology" or "subjective physics."

Naturalism does not deal primarily with individuals in themselves, but rather with social groups or settings or movements, or with individuals like Babbitt and Studs Lonigan who are regarded as being typical of a group. The naturalistic writer tries not to identify himself with any of his characters, although he doesn't always succeed; in general his aim is to present them almost as if they were laboratory specimens. They are seldom depicted as being capable of moral decisions. This fact makes it easy to distinguish between the early naturalists and some of their contemporaries like Robert Herrick and Edith Wharton who also tried to write without optimistic illusions. Herrick and Wharton, however, dealt with individuals who possessed some degree of moral freedom; and often the plots of their novels hinge on a conscious decision by one of the characters. Hemingway, another author whose work is wrongly described as naturalistic, writes stories that reveal some moral quality, usually stoicism or the courage of a frightened man.

Many naturalistic works are valuable historical documents, but the authors in general have little sense of history. They present each situation as if it had no historical antecedents, and their characters might be men and women created yesterday morning, so few signs do they show of having roots in the past. "Science" for naturalistic writers usually means laboratory science, and not the study of human institutions or patterns of thought that persist through generations.

With a few exceptions they have no faith in reform, whether it be the reform of an individual by his own decision or the reform of society by reasoned courses of action. The changes they depict are the result of laws and forces and tendencies beyond human control. That is the great difference between the naturalists and the proletarian or Marxian novelists of the 1930's. The proletarian writers—who were seldom proletarians in private life—believed that men acting together could make a new world. But they borrowed the objective and exterior technique of the naturalists, which was unsuited to their essentially religious purpose. In the beginning of each book they portrayed a group of factory workers as the slaves of economic conditions, "the creatures of habit, the playthings of forces"; then later they portrayed the conversion of one or more workers to Marxism. But conversion is a psychological, not a biological, phenomenon, and it could not be explained purely in terms of conditions or forces. When the conversion took place, there was a shift from the outer to the inner world, and the novel broke in two.

It was not at all extraordinary for naturalism to change into religious Marxism in the middle of a novel, since it has always shown a tendency to dissolve into something else. On the record, literary naturalism does not seem to be a doctrine or attitude to which men are likely to cling through their whole lives. It is always being transformed into satire, symbolism, lyrical autobiography, utopian socialism, Communism, Catholicism, Buddhism, Freudian psychology, hack journalism or the mere assembling of facts. So far there is not in American literature a single instance in which a writer has remained a naturalist from beginning to end of a long career; even Dreiser before his death became a strange mixture of Communist and mystic. There are, however, a great many works that are predominantly naturalistic; and the time has come to list them in order to give the basis for my generalities.

I should say that those works, in fiction, were *Maggie* and *George's Mother* by Stephen Crane, with many of his short stories; *The Damnation of Theron Ware* by Harold Frederic; *Vandover*, *McTeague* and *The Octopus* (but not *The Pit*) by Frank Norris; *The Call of the Wild*, which is a sort of naturalistic Aesop's fable, besides *The Sea Wolf* and *Martin Eden* by Jack London; *The Jungle* by Upton Sinclair, as far as the page where Jurgis is converted to socialism; *Susan Lenox* by David Graham Phillips; all of Dreiser's novels except *The Bulwark* which has a religious ending written at the close of his life; all the serious novels of Sinclair Lewis between *Main Street* (1920) and *Dodsworth* (1929), but none he wrote afterward; Dos Passos' *Manhattan Transfer* and *U.S.A.*; James T. Farrell's work in general, but especially *Studs Lonigan*; Richard Wright's *Native Son*; and most of John Steinbeck's novels, including *In Dubious Battle* and all but the hortatory passages in *The Grapes of Wrath*. In poetry there is Robinson's early verse (*The Children of the Night*) and there is Edgar Lee Masters' *Spoon River Anthology*. In the drama there are the early plays of Eugene O'Neill, from *Beyond the Horizon* to *Desire under the Elms*. Among essays there are H. L. Mencken's *Prejudices* and Joseph Wood Krutch's *The Modern Temper*, which is the most coherent statement of the naturalistic position. There are other naturalists in all fields, especially fiction, and other naturalistic books by several of the authors I have mentioned; but these are the works by which the school is likely to be remembered and judged.

And what shall we say in judgment?—since judge we must, after this long essay in definition. Is naturalism true or false in its premises and good or bad in its effect on American literature? Its results have been good, I think, in so far as it has forced its adherents to stand in opposition to American orthodoxy. Honest writing in this country, the only sort worth bothering about, has almost always been the work of an opposition, chiefly because the leveling and unifying elements in our culture have been so strong that a man who accepts orthodox judgments is in danger of losing his literary personality. Catullus and Villon might be able to write their poems here; with their irregular lives they wouldn't run the risk of being corrupted by the standards of right-thinking people. But Virgil, the friend of Augustus, the official writer who shaped the myth of the Roman state—Virgil would be a dubious figure as an American poet. He would be tempted to soften his values in order to become a prophet for the masses. The American myth of universal cheap luxuries, tiled bathrooms, and service with a smile would not provide him with the basis for an epic poem.

The naturalists, standing in opposition, have been writers of independent and strongly marked personalities. They have fought for the right to speak their minds and have won a measure of freedom for themselves and others. Yet it has to be charged against them that their opposition often takes the form of cheapening what they write about; of always looking for the lowdown or the payoff, that is, for the meanest explanation of everything they describe. There is a tendency in literary naturalism—as distinguished from philosophical naturalism, which is not my subject—always to explain the complex in terms of the simple: society in terms of self, man in terms of his animal inheritance, and the organic in terms of the inorganic. The result is that something is omitted at each stage in this process of reduction. To say that man is a beast of prey or a collection of chemical compounds omits most of man's special nature; it is a metaphor, not a scientific statement.

This scientific weakness of naturalism involves a still greater literary weakness, for it leads to a conception of man that makes it impossible for naturalistic authors to write in the tragic spirit. They can write about crimes, suicides, disasters, the terrifying, and the grotesque; but even the most powerful of their novels and plays are case histories rather than tragedies in the classical sense. Tragedy is an affirmation of man's importance; it is "the imitation of noble actions," in Aristotle's phrase; and the naturalists are unable to believe in human nobility. "We write no tragedies today," said Joseph Wood Krutch in his early book, *The Modern Temper,* which might better have been called "The Naturalistic Temper." "If the plays and novels of today deal with littler people and less mighty emotions it is not because we have become interested in commonplace souls and their unglamorous adventures but because we have come, willy-nilly, to see the soul of man as commonplace and its emotions as mean." But Krutch was speaking only for those who shared the naturalistic point of view. There are other doctrines held by modern writers that make it possible to endow their characters with human dignity. Tragic novels and plays have been written in these years by Christians, Communists, humanists, and even by existentialists, all of whom believe in different fashions and degrees that men can shape their own fates.

For the naturalists, however, men are "human insects" whose brief lives are completely determined by society or nature. The individual is crushed in a moment if he resists; and his struggle, instead of being tragic, is merely pitiful or ironic, as if we had seen a mountan stir itself to overwhelm a fly. Irony is a literary effect used time and again by all the naturalistic writers. For Stephen Crane it is the central effect on which almost all his plots depend: thus, in *The Red Badge of Courage* the boy makes himself a hero by running away. In *A Mystery of Heroism* a soldier risks his life to bring a bucket of water to his comrades, and the water is spilled. In *The Monster* a Negro stableman is so badly burned in rescuing a child that he becomes a faceless horror; and the child's father, a physician, loses his practice as a reward for sheltering the stableman. The irony in Dreiser's novels depends on the contrast between conventional morality and the situations he describes: Carrie Meeber loses her virtue and succeeds in her career; Jennie Gerhardt is a kept woman with higher principles than any respectable wife. In Sinclair Lewis the irony is reduced to an obsessive and irritating trick of style; if he wants to say that a speech was dull and stupid, he has to call it "the culminating glory of the dinner" and then, to make sure that we catch the point, explain that it was delivered by Mrs. Adelaide Tarr Gimmitch, "known throughout the country as 'the Unkies' Girl.'" The reader, seeing the name of Gimmitch, is supposed to smile a superior smile. There is something superior and ultimately tiresome in the attitude of many naturalists toward the events they describe. Irony—like pity, its companion—is a spectator's emotion, and it sets a space between ourselves and the characters in the novel. They suffer, but their cries reach us faintly, like those of dying strangers we cannot hope to save.

There is nothing in the fundamental principles of naturalism that requires a novel to be written in hasty or hackneyed prose. Flaubert, the most careful stylist of his age, was the predecessor and guide of the French naturalists. Among the naturalistic writers of all countries who wrote with a feeling for language were the brothers Goncourt, Ibsen, Hardy, and Stephen Crane. But it was Norris, not Crane, who set the standards for naturalistic fiction in the United States, and Norris had no respect for style. "What pleased me most in your review of 'McTeague,'" he said in a letter to Isaac Marcosson, "was 'disdaining all pretensions to style.' It is precisely what I try most to avoid. I detest 'fine writing,' 'rhetoric,' 'elegant English'— tommyrot. Who cares for fine style! Tell your yarn and let your style go to the devil. We don't want literature, we want life." Yet the truth was that Norris' novels were full of fine writing and lace-curtain English. "Untouched, unassailable, undefiled," he said of the wheat, "that mighty world force, that nourisher of nations, wrapped in Nirvanic calm, indifferent to the human swarm, gigantic, resistless, moved onward in its appointed grooves." He never learned to present his ideas in their own clothes or none at all; it was easier to dress them in borrowed plush; easier to make all his calms Nirvanic and all his grooves appointed.

Yet Norris wrote better prose than most of his successors among the American naturalists. With a few exceptions like Dos Passos and Steinbeck, they have all used language as a blunt instrument; they write as if they were swinging shillelaghs. O'Neill is a great dramatist, but he has never had an ear for the speech of living persons. Lewis used to have an ear, but now listens only to himself. He keeps being arch and ironical about his characters until we want to snarl at him, "Quit patronizing those people! Maybe they'd have something to say if you'd only let them talk." Farrell writes well when he is excited or angry, but most of the time he makes his readers trudge through vacant lots in a South Chicago smog. Dreiser is the worst writer of all, but in some ways the least objectionable; there is something native to himself in his misuse, of the language, so that we come to cherish it as a sign of authenticity, like the tool marks on Shaker furniture. Most of the others simply use the oldest and easiest phrase.

But although the naturalists as a group are men of defective hearing, they almost all have keen eyes for new material. Their interest in themes that others regarded as too unpleasant or illbred has immensely broadened the scope of American fiction. Moreover, they have had enough vitality and courage to be exhilarated by the American life of their own times. From the beginning they have exulted in the wealth and ugliness of American cities, the splendor of the mansions and the squalor of the tenements. They compared Pittsburgh to Paris and New York to imperial Rome. Frank Norris thought that his own San Francisco was the ideal city for storytellers; "Things happen in San Francisco," he said. Dreiser remarked of Chicago, "It is given to some cities, as to some lands, to suggest romance, and to me Chicago did that hourly.... Florence in its best days must have been something like this to young Florentines, or Venice to the young Venetians." The naturalists for all their faults were embarked on a bolder venture than those other writers whose imaginations can absorb nothing but legends already treated in other books, prepared and predigested food. They tried to seize the life around them, and at their best they transformed it into new archetypes of human experience. Just as Cooper had shaped the legend of the frontier and Mark Twain the legend of the Mississippi, so the naturalists have been shaping the harsher legends of an urban and industrial age.

DONALD PIZER

# Late Nineteenth-Century American Naturalism

Most literary critics and historians who attempt definitions are aware of the dangers and advantages inherent in this enterprise. But few, I believe, recognize that many literary genres and modes have their barriers of established terms and ideas to overcome or outflank. The writer who seeks to define tragedy usually finds that his definition takes shape around such traditional guideposts as the tragic hero, the tragic flaw, recognition and catharsis, and so on. American naturalism, as a concept, has two such channelled approaches to its definition. The first is that since naturalism comes after realism, and since it seems to take literature in the same direction as realism, it is primarily an "extension" or continuation of realism—only a little different. The second almost inevitable approach involves this difference. The major distinction between realism and naturalism, most critics agree, is the particular philosophical orientation of the naturalists. A traditional and widely accepted concept of American naturalism, therefore, is that it is essentially realism infused with a pessimistic determinism. Richard Chase argues that American naturalism is realism with a "necessitarian ideology," and George J. Becker (defining all naturalism, including American) considers it as "no more than an emphatic and explicit philosophical position taken by some realists," the position being a "pessimistic materialistic determinism."[1] The common belief is that the naturalists were like the realists in their fidelity to the details of

From *Realism and Naturalism in Nineteenth-Century American Literature.* © 1966 by Donald Pizer.

contemporary life, but that they depicted everyday life with a greater sense of the role of such causal forces as heredity and environment in determining behavior and belief.

This traditional approach to naturalism through realism and through philosophical determinism is historically justifiable and has served a useful purpose, but it has also handicapped thinking both about the movement as a whole and about individual works within the movement. It has resulted in much condescension toward those writers who are supposed to be naturalists yet whose fictional sensationalism (an aspect of romanticism) and moral ambiguity (a quality inconsistent with the absolutes of determinism) appear to make their work flawed specimens of the mode.

I would like, therefore, to propose a modified definition of late nineteenth-century American naturalism.[2] For the time being, let this be a working definition, to be amplified and made more concrete by the illustrations from which it has been drawn. I suggest that the naturalistic novel usually contains two tensions or contradictions, and that the two in conjunction comprise both an interpretation of experience and a particular aesthetic recreation of experience. In other words, the two constitute the theme and form of the naturalistic novel. The first tension is that between the subject matter of the naturalistic novel and the concept of man which emerges from this subject matter. The naturalist populates his novel primarily from the lower middle class or the lower class. His characters are the poor, the uneducated, the unsophisticated. His fictional world is that of the commonplace and unheroic in which life would seem to be chiefly the dull round of daily existence, as we ourselves usually conceive of our lives. But the naturalist discovers in this world those qualities of man usually associated with the heroic or adventurous, such as acts of violence and passion which involve sexual adventure or bodily strength and which culminate in desperate moments and violent death. A naturalistic novel is thus an extension of realism only in the sense that both modes often deal with the local and contemporary. The naturalist, however, discovers in this material the extraordinary and excessive in human nature.

The second tension involves the theme of the naturalistic novel. The naturalist often describes his characters as though they are conditioned and controlled by environment, heredity, instinct, or chance. But he also suggests a compensating humanistic value in his characters or their fates which affirms the significance of the individual and of his life. The tension here is that between the naturalist's desire to represent in fiction the new, discomforting truths which he has found in the ideas and life of his late nineteenth-century world, and also his desire to find some meaning in experience which reasserts the validity of the human enterprise. The naturalist appears to say that although the individual may be a cipher in a world made amoral by man's lack of responsibility for his fate, the imagination refuses to accept this formula as the total meaning of life and so seeks a new basis for man's sense of his own dignity and importance.

The naturalistic novel is therefore not so superficial or reductive as it implicitly appears to be in its conventional definition. It involves a belief that life on its lowest levels is not so simple as it seems to be from higher levels. It suggests that even the least significant human being can feel and strive powerfully and can suffer the extraordinary consequences of his emotions, and that no range of human experience is free of the moral complexities and ambiguities which Milton set his fallen angels to debating.[3] Naturalism reflects an affirmative ethical conception of life, for it asserts the value of all life by endowing the lowest character with emotion and defeat and with moral ambiguity, no matter how poor or ignoble he may seem. The naturalistic novel derives much of its aesthetic effect from these contrasts. It involves us in the experience of a life both commonplace and extraordinary, both familiar and strange, both simple and complex. It pleases us with its sensationalism without affronting our sense of probability. It discovers the "romance of the commonplace," as Frank Norris put it. Thus, the melodramatic sensationalism and moral "confusion" which are often attacked in the naturalistic novel should really be incorporated into a normative definition of the mode and be recognized as its essential constituents.

The three novels which I have chosen to illustrate this definition, and also to suggest the possible range of variation within it, are Frank Norris's *McTeague* (1899), Theodore Dreiser's *Sister Carrie* (1900), and Stephen Crane's *The Red Badge of Courage* (1895). These works are important novels by the three leading late nineteenth-century American naturalists, and each novel has frequently been read as a key example of its author's values and his fictional form. A definition drawn from these three novels will not be applicable to all late nineteenth-century naturalistic fiction. But, given the significance of these writers and of these novels, it would, I believe, be a useful introduction to this major movement in American literary history.

ii

A good deal of *McTeague* is devoted to depicting the routine, ordered world of Polk Street, the lower middle class service street in San Francisco on which McTeague practices and lives. The life of Polk Street enters the novel in two ways—through set pieces describing street activities or the daily lives of the central characters in relation to the life of the street, and through constant incidental allusion to its activities and inhabitants. Norris dramatically establishes Polk Street as above all a life of the repetitious and constant. The street exists as a source of the ordered and the routine in McTeague's life, as a world where the harness shop, the grocery, and the car conductors' coffee joint are always available in their set roles, where the children go to school at the same time each day, followed by the shop clerks coming to work, and so on. McTeague is settled and content in this life, and we recognize that his inner needs and outer world are in harmony.

A central theme in Norris's work is that beneath the surface of our placid, everyday lives there is turbulence, that the romance of the extraordinary is not limited to the distant in time and place but can be found "in the brownstone house on the corner and in the office building downtown."[4] Norris therefore used the incident which had stimulated him to write the novel, a vicious murder in a San Francisco kindergarten, as a controlling paradox in *McTeague* as in scene after scene he introduces the sensational into the commonplace activities and setting of Polk Street. So we have such incidents as McTeague grossly kissing the anesthetized Trina in his dental parlor, or the nearly murderous fight between Marcus and McTeague at the picnic. Some of the best moments in the novel powerfully unite these two streams of the commonplace and the extraordinary. In one such moment the frightened and incoherent Trina, having just found Maria's corpse with its cut throat and its blood soaked clothes, rushes out into the everyday routine of Polk Street and has difficulty convincing the butcher's boy that something is wrong or even convincing herself that it is not improper "to make a disturbance and create a scene in the street."[5]

Norris believed that the source of this violence beneath the surface placidity of life is the presence in all men of animal qualities which have played a major role in man's evolutionary development but which are now frequently atavistic and destructive.[6] Norris's theme is that man's racial atavism (particularly his brute sexual desires) and man's individual family heritage (alcoholic degeneracy in McTeague's case) can combine as a force toward reversion, toward a return to the emotions and instincts of man's animal past. McTeague is in one sense a "special case" of reversion, since his atavistic brutality is in part caused by his degenerate parents. He is also, however, any man caught up in the net of sex, and in this second aspect of man's inherited animal nature Norris introduces a tragic element into McTeague's fall, an element which contributes to the novel's thematic tension.

In describing the courtship of Trina and McTeague, Norris is at pains to stress their overt sexual innocence yet intuitive sexuality. The woman in Trina "was not yet awakened; she was yet, as one might say, without sex." [20] For McTeague, Trina is his "first experience. With her the feminine element suddenly entered his little world. It was not only her that he saw and felt, it was the woman, the whole sex, an entire new humanity...." [23] Despite their innocence and lack of experience, both react intuitively and atavistically— McTeague desiring to seize and possess her, she instinctively withdrawing yet desiring to be conquered.

The most important sexual encounter between McTeague and Trina occurs at the B Street Station where McTeague for a second time proposes. When Trina hesitates, he seizes her "in his enormous arms, crushing down her struggle with his immense strength. Then Trina gave up, all in an instant, turning her head to his. They kissed each other, grossly, full in the mouth." [72] Within the literary conventions of the day, this kiss symbolizes Trina's sexual submission. At this moment the strands in the web of sexual determinism begin the pull taut, for "the instant she allowed him to kiss her, he thought less of her. She was not so desirable, after all." [73] McTeague senses this diminution along with a dim awareness "that this must be so, that it belonged to the changeless order of things—the man desiring the woman only for what she withholds; the woman worshipping the man for that which she yields up to him. With each concession gained the man's desire cools; with every surrender made the woman's adoration increases." [73] Norris is concerned in this second meeting not with a special flaw in McTeague or Trina but with a sexual determinism affecting all men. The possessive sexual desire of the man aroused by the first woman he experiences sensually, the instinctive desire of the woman for sexual submission responding to the first man who assaults her—these are the atavistic animal forces which bring Trina and McTeague together.

A major theme in *McTeague* is therefore that of the sexual tragedy of man and woman. Caught up by drives and instincts beyond their control or comprehension, they mate by chance. In *McTeague* sex is that which comes to all men and women, disrupting their lives and placing them in relationships which the sanctity of marriage cannot prevent from ending in chaos and destruction. Norris does not tell the old tale of the fallen fornicator, as he does in *Vandover and the Brute*, but rather reaches out toward the unexplored ground of the human dilemma of sexual attraction.

The tension between this deterministic aspect of *McTeague* and its humanistic element does not lie in McTeague as a fully developed tragic figure. Rather, it is contained in the theme that man can seldom escape the violence inherent in his own nature, that man's attempt to achieve an ordered world is constantly thwarted by man himself. Norris devotes much attention to the element of order in the details of McTeague's life not only because of his belief in the romance of the commonplace but because the destruction of that order is the source of the tragic quality in McTeague's fall and of our own compassionate involvement with him despite his grotesqueness. Norris carefully documents McTeague's life as a dentist and as an inhabitant of Polk Street because the habitual tasks and minor successes of this life represent the order and stability which McTeague requires. In the course of the novel we begin to feel compassion for him as he becomes a victim of Trina's avarice and as we recognize that his emerging brutality is at least partly the result of the destruction of his world. When McTeague learns that he can no longer practice dentistry, his reaction is that of a man whose life is emptied of all meaning. In a scene of considerable power Trina comes upon him sitting in his dental chair, "looking stupidly out of the window, across the roofs opposite, with an unseeing gaze, his red hands lying idly in his lap." [229] We are never completely one with McTeague; his brute strength and dull mind put us off. But because he is trapped in the universal net of sex, and because we recognize the poignancy of the loss of his world, we respond to him ultimately as a human being in distress, as a figure of some significance despite his limitations—as a man, in short, whose fall contains elements of the tragic.

For *McTeague* is in part a tragic novel. True, McTeague neither bears full responsibility for his fate nor is he in any sense noble or profound. He is rather like Gervaise in *L'Assommoir*: they are both poor creatures who want above all a place to rest and be content, yet who are brought low by their needs and desires. There is a sense of common humanity in McTeague's fall, and that quality is perhaps the modern residue of the tragic theme, since we are no longer certain of man's transcendent nobility or of the reality of major responsibility for our fates. The theme of *McTeague* is not that drunkenness leads to a tragic fall, but that tragedy is inherent in the human situation given man's animal past and the possibility that he will be dominated by that past in particular circumstances. Norris does not deny the strength of man's past or present animality, but neither does he deny the poignancy of the fall of even such a gross symbol of this animality as McTeague. It is out of this tension that much of the meaning and power of the novel arises.

iii

Even more than Norris, Theodore Dreiser creates a sense of the solidity of life. His early novels in particular affirm that we cannot escape the impact of physical reality and that this fact is one of the few that man may know with certainty. So the several worlds of Carrie—her sister's working class existence, her life with Drouet in Chicago and with Hurstwood in New York—achieve a sense of massiveness both in their painstaking documentation and in their inescapable effect on Carrie. The effect on us, however, is not only to enforce a sense of the importance of clothes, of furniture, of how much one owes the grocer and of exactly how much one earns and spends—the impact, too, is of normalcy, of the steady pace of life, since life does indeed seem to be measured out in coffee spoons. Dreiser's ability to capture the tangible commonplace of everyday existence powerfully suggests that the commonplace and everyday are the essence of experience, particularly since he returns again and again to the unexciting details of the furnishings of an apartment or the contents of a meal. Moreover, Dreiser's dispassionate tone contributes to this effect. He is, indeed, something of an ironist. He frequently sets events or beliefs in ironic juxtaposition, as when Carrie is worried that Hurstwood will discover that she and Drouet are unmarried though she herself is unaware that Hurstwood *is* married. But Dreiser's irony differs from Crane's intense and pervasive ironic vision of life, a vision which colors every incident or observation in Crane's work with the implication that things are not what they seem. Dreiser's plodding, graceless paragraphs imply the opposite—that the concrete world he so seriously details is real and discernible and that nothing can shake or undermine it.

Dreiser's central theme in *Sister Carrie*, however, sets forth the idea— Lionel Trilling to the contrary[7]—that the physically real is not the only reality and that men seek something in life beyond it. His theme is that those of a finer, more intense, more emotional nature who desire to break out of their normal solid world—whether it be a Carrie oppressed by the dull repetitiousness and crudity of her sister's home, or a Hurstwood jaded by the middle class trivialities of his family—that when such as these strive to discover a life approximate to their natures they introduce into their lives the violent and the extraordinary. Carrie leaves her sister's flat for two illicit alliances, attracted to each man principally by the opportunities he offers for a better life. Drouet and Hurstwood represent to her not so much wealth or sexual attraction as an appeal to something intangibly richer and fuller in herself. She is drawn to each in turn, and then finally to Ames, because each appeals to some quality in her temperament which she finds unfulfilled in her life of the moment. Dreiser's depiction of her almost asexual relations with all of these men represents less his capitulation to contemporary publishing restrictions (although some of this is present) than his desire that the three characters reflect the upward course of Carrie's discovery and realization of her inner nature. Finally, Carrie's career on the stage symbolizes both the emotional intensity she is capable of bringing to life and the fact that she requires the intrinsically extraordinary and exciting world of the theatre to call forth and embody her emotional depth.

Hurstwood also introduces the sensational into his life by reaching out beyond his established world. For him, the extraordinary arises from his attempt to gain and then hold Carrie, since she represents to him his last opportunity to grasp life fully and intensely. We follow him as he breaks the seemingly set mold of his life by his theft and by his elopement. His participation in the violence of the street car strike is his final attempt to recover his fortunes (and Carrie) in New York. With Carrie gone, he sinks still further and eventually commits suicide.

Hurstwood's suicide can be explored as a typical example of Dreiser's combination of the concretely commonplace and the sensational. It takes place in a cheap Bowery hotel. Hurstwood's method is to turn on the gas, not resolutely but hesitantly, and then to say weakly, "'What's the use?'" as he "stretched himself to rest."[8] Dreiser thus submerges an inherently sensational event in the trivial and unemotional. He not only "takes the edge off" the extraordinariness of the event by his full and detached elaboration of its commonplace setting but also casts it in the imagery of enervation and rest. This scene is in one sense a special instance, since Hurstwood seeks death as a refuge. But Dreiser's total effect as a novelist is often similar to the effect produced by this scene as he dramatizes throughout *Sister Carrie* the solidity and therefore seeming normalcy of experience and yet its underlying extraordinariness if man seeks beyond the routine. His principal aesthetic impact, however, is different from that of Norris, who appears to combine the sensational and commonplace much as Dreiser does. Norris's effect is basically that of dramatic sensationalism, of the excitement of violence and sudden death. Dreiser's effect is more thematic and less scenic because he colors the sensational with the same emotional stolidity with which he characterizes all experience. It is not only that the sensational and extraordinary exist in our commonplace lives, Dreiser appears to say, but that they are so pervasive and implicit in our experience that their very texture differs little from the ordinary course of events. Thus, such potentially exciting and dramatically sensational moments in Dreiser's fiction as the seduction of Jennie Gerhardt or the imprisonment of Frank Cowperwood have an almost listless dullness compared to Norris's treatment of parallel events in his fiction.

Carrie, like many of Dreiser's characters, has her life shaped by chance and need. Chance involves her with Drouet and later plays a large role in

Hurstwood's theft and therefore in her own departure with him. Her needs are of two kinds—first to attain the tangible objects and social symbols of comfort and beauty which she sees all around her in Chicago and New York, and then to be loved. Of the major forces in her life, it is primarily her desire for objects that furnish a sense of physical and mental well-being—for fine clothing and furniture and attractive apartments and satisfactory food—which determines much of her life. As she gains more of these, her fear of returning to poverty and crudity—to her sister's condition—impels her to seek even more vigorously. Much of the concrete world that Dreiser fills in so exhaustively in *Sister Carrie* thus exists as a determining force in Carrie's life, first moving her to escape it, as in her encounters with working-class Chicago, and then to reach out for it, as when Drouet takes her to a good restaurant and buys her some fashionable clothes and so introduces into her imagination the possibility of making these a part of her life.

But Carrie's response to her needs is only one side of her nature. She also possesses a quality which is intrinsic to her being, though its external shape (a Drouet, a dress seen on the street) is determined by accidental circumstance. For in this his first novel Dreiser endows Carrie with the same capacity to wonder and to dream which he felt so strongly in himself. It is this ability to dream about the nature of oneself and one's fate and of where one is going and how one will get there and to wonder whether happiness is real and possible or only an illusion—it is this capacity which ultimately questions the reality and meaning of the seemingly solid and plain world in which we find ourselves.

This "dream" quality underlies the most striking symbol in the novel, the rocking chair. Occasionally the rocking chair has been interpreted as principally a symbol of circularity because Carrie rocks on her first night in Chicago and again at the novel's close in her New York apartment.[9] It is suggested that Dreiser means to imply that nothing really has happened to Carrie, that although her outer circumstances have changed, she is essentially the same both morally and spiritually. The symbol does indeed function partly in this way, but its primary emphasis is not the negative one of nothing changed and therefore nothing gained or learned. Its stress is rather the positive idea that Carrie continues to have the ability to wonder about herself and her future, that her imaginative response to life has not been dulled by experience. Although she has not achieved the happiness that she thought accompanied the life she desired and which she now has, she will continue to search. Perhaps Ames represents the next, higher step in this quest, Dreiser implies. But in any case, she possesses this inner force, a force which is essentially bold and free. Although it brings her worry and loneliness—the rocking chair symbolizes these as well—it is an element in her which Dreiser finds estimable and moving. She will always be the dreamer, Dreiser says, and though her dreams take an earthly shape controlled by her world, and though she is judged immoral by the world because she violates its conventions in pursuit of her dreams, she has for Dreiser—and for us, I believe—meaning and significance and stature because of her capacity to rock and dream, to question life and to pursue it. Thus Carrie seeks to fulfill each new venture and gain each new object as though these were the only realities of life, and yet by her very dissatisfaction and questioning of what she has gained to imply the greater reality of the mind and spirit that dreams and wonders. The rocking chair goes nowhere, but it moves, and in that paradox lies Dreiser's involvement with Carrie and his ability to communicate the intensity and nature of her quest. For in his mind, too, the world is both solid and unknowable, and man is ever pursuing and never finding.

iv

The Red Badge of Courage also embodies a different combination of the sensational and commonplace than that found in McTeague. Whereas Norris demonstrates that the violent and the extraordinary are present in seemingly dull and commonplace lives, Crane, even more than Dreiser, is intent on revealing the commonplace nature of the seemingly exceptional. In The Red Badge Henry Fleming is a raw, untried country youth who seeks the romance and glory of war but who finds that his romantic, chivalric preconceptions of battle are false. Soldiers and generals do not strike heroic poses; the dead are not borne home triumphantly on their shields but fester where they have fallen; and courage is not a conscious striving for an ideal mode of behavior but a temporary delirium derived from animal fury and social pride or fear. A wounded officer worries about the cleanliness of his uniform; a soldier sweats and labors at his arms "like a laborer in a foundry";[10] and mere chance determines rewards and punishments—the death of a Conklin, the red badge of a Fleming. War to Crane is like life itself in its injustice, in its mixing of the ludicrous and the momentarily exhilarating, in its self-deceptions, and in its acceptance of appearances for realities. Much of Crane's imagery in the novel is therefore consciously and pointedly antiheroic, not only in his obviously satirical use of conventional chivalric imagery in unheroic situations (a soldier bearing a rumor comes "waving his [shirt] banner-like" and adopting "the important air of a herald in red and gold" [238]) but also more subtly in his use of machine and animal imagery to deflate potentially heroic moments.

Crane's desire to devalue the heroic in war stems in part from his stance as an ironist reacting against a literary and cultural tradition of idealized courage and chivalry. But another major element in his desire to reduce war to the commonplace arises from his casting of Fleming's experiences in the form of a "life" or initiation allegory. Henry Fleming is the universal youth who leaves home unaware of himself or the world. His participation in battle is his introduction to life as for the first time he tests himself and his preconceptions of experience against experience itself. He emerges at the end of the battle not entirely self-perceptive or firm-willed—Crane is too much the ironist for such a reversal—but rather as one who has encountered some of the strengths and some of the failings of himself and others. Crane implies that although Fleming may again run from battle and although he will no doubt always have the human capacity to rationalize his weaknesses, he is at least no longer the innocent.

If *The Red Badge* is viewed in this way—that is, as an antiheroic allegory of "life"—it becomes clear that Crane is representing in his own fashion the naturalistic belief in the interpenetration of the commonplace and the sensational. All life, Crane appears to be saying, is a struggle, a constant sea of violence in which we inevitably immerse ourselves and in which we test our beliefs and our values. War is an appropriate allegorical symbol of this test, for to Crane violence is the very essence of life, not in the broad Darwinian sense of a struggle for existence or the survival of the fittest, but rather in the sense that the proving and testing of oneself, conceived both realistically and symbolically, entails the violent and the deeply emotional, that the finding of oneself occurs best in moments of stress and is itself often an act of violence. To Crane, therefore, war as an allegorical setting for the emergence of youth into knowledge embodies both the violence of this birth and the commonplaces of life which the birth reveals—that men are controlled by the trivial, the accidental, the degradingly unheroic, despite the preservation of such accoutrements of the noble as a red badge or a captured flag. Crane shows us what Norris and Dreiser only suggest, that there is no separation between the sensational and the commonplace, that the two are coexistent in every aspect and range of life. He differs from Norris in kind and from Dreiser in degree in that his essentially ironic imagination leads him to reverse the expected and to find the commonplace in the violent rather than the sensational beneath the trivial. His image of life as an unheroic battle captures in one ironic symbol both his romanticism and his naturalism—or, in less literary terms, his belief that we reveal character in violence but that human character is predominantly fallible and self-deceptive.

Much of Crane's best fiction displays this technique of ironic deflation. In *Maggie*, a young urchin defends the honor of Rum Alley on a heap of gravel; in "The Open Boat," the stalwart oiler suffers an inconsequential and meaningless death; in "The Blue Hotel," the death of the Swede is accompanied by a derisive sign on the cash register; and in "The Bride Comes to Yellow Sky," the long-awaited "chivalric" encounter is thwarted by the bride's appearance. Each of these crucial or significant events has at its core Crane's desire to reduce the violent and extraordinary to the commonplace, a reduction which indicates both his ironic vision of man's romantic pretensions and his belief in the reality of the fusion of the violent and the commonplace in experience.

As was true of Norris and Dreiser, Crane's particular way of combining the sensational and the commonplace is closely related to the second major aspect of his naturalism, the thematic tension or complexity he embodies in his work. *The Red Badge* presents a vision of man as a creature capable of advancing in some areas of knowledge and power but forever imprisoned within the walls of certain inescapable human and social limitations. Crane depicts the similarity between Henry Fleming's "will" and an animal's instinctive response to crisis or danger. He also presents Fleming's discovery that he is enclosed in a "moving box" of "tradition and law" [259] even at those moments when he believes himself capable of rational decision and action—that the opinions and actions of other men control and direct him. Lastly, Crane dramatizes Fleming's realization that although he can project his emotions into natural phenomena and therefore derive comfort from a sense of nature's identification with his desires and needs, nature and man are really two, not one, and nature offers no reliable or useful guide to experience or to action. But, despite Crane's perception of these limitations and inadequacies, he does not paint a totally bleak picture of man in *The Red Badge*. True, Fleming's own sanguine view of himself at the close of the novel—that he is a man—cannot be taken at face value. Fleming's self-evaluations contrast ironically with his motives and actions throughout the novel, and his final estimation of himself represents primarily man's ability to be proud of his public deeds while rationalizing his private failings.

But something has happened to Fleming which Crane values and applauds. Early in the novel Fleming feels at odds with his comrades. He is separated from them by doubts about his behavior under fire and by fear of their knowledge of his doubts. These doubts and fears isolate him from his fellows, and his isolation is intensified by his growing awareness that the repressive power of the "moving box" of his regiment binds him to a group from which he now wishes to escape. Once in battle, however, Fleming becomes "not a man but a member" as he is "welded into a common personality which was dominated by a single desire." [271] The "subtle battle brotherhood" [272] replaces his earlier isolation, and in one sense the rest of the novel is devoted to Fleming's loss and recovery of his feeling of oneness with his fellows. After his initial success in battle, Henry loses this quality as he deserts his comrades and then wanders away from his regiment in actuality and in spirit. His extreme stage of isolation from the regiment and from mankind occurs when he abandons the tattered soldier. After gaining a "red badge" which symbolically reunites him with those soldiers who remained and fought, he returns to his regiment and participates successfully in the last stages of the battle. Here, as everywhere in Crane, there is a deflating irony, for Henry's "red badge" is not a true battle wound. But despite the tainted origin of this symbol of fraternity, its effect on Henry and his fellows is real and significant. He is accepted gladly when he returns, and in his renewed confidence and pride he finds strength and a kind of joy. Crane believed that this feeling of trust and mutual confidence among men is essential, and it is one of the few values he confirms again and again in his fiction. It is this quality which knits together the four men in the open boat and lends them moral strength. And it is the absence of this quality and its replacement by fear and distrust which characterizes the world of "The Blue Hotel" and causes the tragic denouement in that story.

Crane thus points out that courage has primarily a social reality, that it is a quality which exists not absolutely but by virtue of other men's opinions, and that the social unity born of a courageous fellowship may therefore be based on self-deception or on deception of others. He also demonstrates that this bond of fellowship may be destructive and oppressive when it restricts or determines individual choice, as in the "moving box" of the regiment. Fleming, after all, at first stands fast because he is afraid of what his comrades will do or think, and then runs because he feels that the rest of the regiment is deserting as well. But Crane also maintains that in social cohesion man gains both what little power of self-preservation he possesses and a gratifying and necessary sense of acceptance and acknowledgement difficult to attain otherwise. Crane therefore establishes a vital organic relationship between his deflation of the traditional idea of courage and his assertion of the need for and the benefits of social unity. He attacks the conventional heroic ideal by showing that a man's actions in battle are usually determined by his imitation of the actions of others—by the group as a whole. But this presentation of the reality and power of the group also suggests the advantages possible in group unity and group action.

There is, then, a moral ambiguity in Crane's conception of man's relationship with his fellows, an ambiguity which permeates his entire vision of man. Henry Fleming falsely acquires a symbol of group identity, yet this symbol aids him in recovering his group identity and in benefiting the group. Man's involvement with others forces him into psychic compulsion (Henry's running away), yet this involvement is the source of his sense of psychic oneness. Henry is still for the most part self-deceived at the close of the novel, but if he is not the "man" he thinks he has become, he has at least shed some of the innocence of the child. Crane's allegory of life as a battle is thus appropriate for another reason besides its relevance to the violence of discovery. Few battles are clearly or cleanly won or lost, and few soldiers are clearly God's chosen. But men struggle, and in their struggle they learn something about their limitations and capacities and something about the nature of their relations with their fellow men, and this knowledge is rewarding even though they never discover the full significance or direction of the campaign in which they are engaged.

v

The primary goal of the late nineteenth-century American naturalists was not to demonstrate the overwhelming and oppressive reality of the material forces present in our lives. Their attempt, rather, was to represent the intermingling in life of controlling force and individual worth. If they were not always clear in distinguishing between these two qualities in experience, it was partly because they were novelists responding to life's complexities and were not philosophers categorizing experience, and partly because they were sufficiently of our own time to doubt the validity of moral or any other absolutes. The naturalists do not dehumanize man. They rather suggest new or modified areas of value in man while engaged in destroying such old and to them unreal sources of human self-importance as romantic love or moral responsibility or heroism. They are some distance from traditional Christian humanism, but they have not yet reached the despairing emptiness of Joseph Wood Krutch's *The Modern Temper*. One should not deny the bleak view of man inherent in McTeague's or Hurstwood's decline or in Fleming's self-deceptions, but neither should one forget that to the naturalists man's weaknesses and limited knowledge and thwarted desires were still sources of compassion and worth as well as aspects of the human condition to be more forth-rightly acknowledged than writers had done in the past.

Nor is naturalism simply a piling on of unselective blocks of documentation. A successful naturalistic novel is like any successful work of art in that it embodies a cogent relationship between its form (its particular combination of the commonplace and sensational) and its theme (its particular tension between the individually significant and the deterministic). There is a major difference, within general similarities, between Norris's discovery of the sensational in the commonplace and Crane's dramatization of the triviality of the sensational. This variation derives principally from the differing thematic tension in the two novels. Norris wishes to demonstrate the tragic destruction of McTeague's commonplace world by the violence inherent in all life, whereas Crane wishes to dramatize Fleming's violent initiation into the commonplace nature of the heroic. Norris and Crane occupy positions in American naturalism analogous to that of Wordsworth and Byron in English romanticism. Like the poetry of the two earlier figures, their fiction expresses strikingly individual and contrasting visions of experience, yet does so within a body of shared intellectual and literary assumptions belonging to their common historical and literary moment. The naturalistic novel is thus no different from any other major literary genre in its complex intermingling of form and theme, in its reflection of an author's individual temperament and experience within large generic similarities, and—at its best—in its thematic depth and importance. We have done a disservice to the late nineteenth-century American naturalists by our earlier simplistic conception of their art.

### NOTES

1. Richard Chase, *The American Novel and Its Tradition* (Garden City, N.Y., 1957), p. 186 n; George J. Becker, "Modern Realism as a Literary Movement," in *Documents of Modern Literary Realism*, ed. George J. Becker (Princeton, 1963), p. 35. See also the definitions by Lars Ahnebrink, *The Beginnings of Naturalism in American Fiction* (Cambridge, Mass., 1950), pp. vi–vii; Malcolm Cowley, "A Natural History of American Naturalism." *Documents*, pp. 429–30; and Philip Rahv, "Notes on the Decline of Naturalism," *Documents*, pp. 583–84.

2. The discussion of naturalism in the next two paragraphs resembles in several ways that by Charles C. Walcutt in his *American Literary Naturalism, A Divided Stream* (Minneapolis, 1956), pp. 3–29. In general, I accept Walcutt's analysis of naturalism's philosophical and literary ambivalences. I believe, however, that his discussion of the naturalists' divided view of nature and of their maintenance of the idea of free will by implicitly encouraging their readers to social action are ways of describing these ambivalences historically and socially—by source and effect—rather than as they function withint the naturalistic novel itself.

3. Erich Auerbach's *Mimesis: The Representation of Reality in Western Literature* (Princeton, 1953) deals with the representation of these ideas in imaginative literature from antiquity to our own day.

4. Frank Norris, "A Plea for Romantic Fiction," *The Literary Criticism of Frank Norris*, ed. Donald Pizer (Austin Texas, 1964), p. 77.

5. *The Complete Edition of Frank Norris* (Garden City, N.Y., 1928), VIII, 269. References to this edition of *McTeague* will hereafter appear in the text.

6. I discuss this aspect of Norris' thought at some length in my "Evolutionary Ethical Dualism in Frank Norris' *Vandover and the Brute* and *McTeague*," PMLA, LXXVI (December, 1961), 522–60.

7. Lionel Trilling, "Reality in America," *The Liberal Imagination* (New York, 1950).

8. Theodore Dreiser, *Sister Carrie* (Modern Library Edition), p. 554.

9. See particularly William A. Freedman, "A Look at Dreiser as Artist: The Motif of Circularity in *Sister Carrie*," *Modern Fiction Studies*, VII (Winter, 1962–63), 384–92.

10. Stephen Crane, *The Red Badge of Courage and Selected Prose and Poetry*, ed. William M. Gibson (New York, 1956), p. 275. References to this edition will appear hereafter in the text.

RICHARD POIRIER

# Panoramic Environment
# and the Anonymity of the Self

Before his close friendship with Edith Wharton, and before he knew very much about her work, James wrote to Howells about the comic proposition that she "belonged" in New York more than he or his works ever could. Talking about his own writings and about hers, he characteristically speaks of fiction as a house among houses, as the building made within already constructed ones. He was responding to Howells's news that an apartment house had been opened in New York City named the *Henry James*:

> Your most kind communication ... in respect to the miraculously-named "uptown" apartment house has at once deeply agitated me and wildly uplifted me. The agitation as I call it, is verily but the tremor, the intensity of hope, of the delirious dream that such a stroke may "bring my books before the public," or do something toward it—coupled with the reassertion of my constant, too constant conviction that no power on earth can ever do that....
>
> The *Henry James*, I opine, will be a terrifically "private" hotel, and will languish like the Lord of Burleigh's wife under the burden of an honour "unto which it was not born." Refined, liveried, "two-toileted," it will have been a short lived, hectic paradox, and will presently have to close in order to reopen as the

From *A World Elsewhere: The Place of Style in American Literature.* © 1966 by Richard Poirier.

Mary Johnston or the Kate Douglas Wiggin or the James Lane
Allen. Best of all as the Edith Wharton.

Ostensibly, James is simply being wry about the relative unpopularity of his
later books compared to Mary Johnston's *To Have and To Hold* or to Mrs.
Wiggin's children's books, the most famous of which, *Rebecca of Sunnybrook
Farm*, was to appear the next year, or to James Allen's *The Choir Invisible*. And
although he was only beginning to take Edith Wharton seriously—a few
months later he was to read the just published and very un-Jamesian novel
*The Valley of Decision*—James knew when he wrote to Howells in 1902 that
she was then more of a public success for her stories than was he for his
recent popular failure *The Wings of the Dove*.

   But the letter is not merely about popularity. It is also about "building,"
and it is written by a man who was always talking about the *house* of fiction.
He is simply astonished here that his house could conceivably fit into the
environment of New York. As he imagines the building, it creates within
itself an atmosphere altogether alien to anything outside it: refined, liveried,
two-toileted. What houses of fiction do fit into the environment of New
York, of America? James is implying that in novels more popular than his the
created environments in no way challenge the authenticity of what people of
New York or elsewhere ordinarily take their environment to be. The
subservience of such books to the popular consensus is evident in ways only
seemingly contradictory: some pretend to offer intensified versions of life as
it is commonly lived, while others are ostentatiously artificial in the manner
of historical romances. In the one case there is a compliance with reality
simply in the effort faithfully to mirror it, in the other there is the emphatic
admission that it is impossible even to create the *illusion* of an alternative
reality. Historical romances and children's books may give the reader a
glimpse of mysterious, fantastic worlds, but never with the striving nobility
of intention that Santayana, echoing Emerson and predicting Stevens,
ascribed to poetry: "To make us citizens, by anticipation, in the world we
crave." The word "anticipation" eloquently implies that our craving is for
something that has never yet come into existence, that has presently no form
outside the imagination, and can therefore be the effect only of the "poetry"
itself.

   Therein lies the difference between Edith Wharton and Henry
James—in his greater ambition, his confidence in the power of language to
make us citizens in the world we crave, rather than in the world where we
actually live. It is the difference, too, between the two lines in American
literature which, with much criss-crossing, these two writers can be said to

represent. That James and Mrs. Wharton resembled one another in important ways has been a stubborn and, except possibly in Mrs. Wharton's *The Reef*, erroneous assumption, despite what Irving Howe and others have argued to the contrary. It took a recent, very able book, Millicent Bell's *Edith Wharton and Henry James: The Story of Their Friendship*, to make the necessary discriminations. In what each chose to "do" with often similar novelistic circumstances, the two are quite markedly different. Mrs. Wharton herself offered the term "chronicle-novel" to describe her customary manner of doing things, and acknowledged, for contrast, that James "cared only for the elaborate working out on all sides of a central situation." Part of Mrs. Wharton's satisfaction with the simple and sequential ordering of events reflects the fact that her characters are propelled mostly by environmental circumstances external to them. These circumstances were for her not subject to fragmentation or redirection by the exertion of individual needs. There is nothing similarly naturalistic in James, who in eschewing for the most part the conventions of the "chronicle-novel" tried to let the ingredients of events actually reside in the consciousness of his characters. That consciousness often *is* the environment in which his characters contend with their fate. James's grotesquely inclusive later style was designed so that his favorites might indulge in the images and verbal exaggerations necessary to their illusion of freedom, their dream that they create the world they live in. By contrast, the clarity, even to crispness, of Mrs. Wharton's writing indicates a world palpably there in some imposing organization antecedent to anyone's wishes.

But however different from James at his most characteristic, Edith Wharton is heir to the perplexities he confronted and which confused Mark Twain in *Huckleberry Finn*. In so representative a work as *The House of Mirth*, society offers no mode of action, no expression beyond mimicry or silence by which Lily Bart can reveal the best impulses in her nature. Like Mark Twain, Mrs. Wharton succeeds only sporadically in imagining circumstances in which such revelations can easily take place; in both writers, favorable environments are associated with an elusive myth of "natural" life, economically impoverished but emotionally rich, utterly marginal, but, within itself, full of close, familial attachments. Similar difficulties with novelistic environment provide a sort of justification for James's later fiction; they suggest why he chose to create through his style some more hospitable world for not dissimilar heroic figures. His heroes are different from theirs, however, in being aware, self-consciously and initially, that they are risking their freedom of consciousness by efforts to express it through social manners. Theirs is "the tragedy of manners," as Frederick Crews has titled it.

The intriguing quality in Mrs. Wharton and in Dreiser is a phenomenon already noticed in *Huckleberry Finn:* the fascination, apparent in an intensive, detailed rendering, with the environmental forces that destroy what the authors love. They surrender their interest—literally the space they have in their books—to the power which forbids individual fulfillment, so that even sex becomes an aspect of that power rather than an evidence of private involvement or personal society. Edith Wharton and Dreiser will always remain compelling because, anticipating Fitzgerald and still later American novelists, they tacitly admit bedazzlement with the very horrors of the modern scene which obliterate their even more bedazzled heroes. Of course they wrote in "protest," but we read them not for that but because they are more instinctively interested in the panorama that roused in them the energy of protest.

Not even a novelist so consciously protective of his characters' freedom as James could fail to give enormous weight to environmental forces antagonistic to it. The weight is proportionately heavier in Dreiser, Edith Wharton, and Fitzgerald, however, because their heroes are often anxious to surrender themselves to the powers that destroy them. The vision of the Self joining the formative processes of Nature, of the Self believing it can contend for dominance with the forces of Nature, of the Self believing merely that it can define what it is—these notions give way, as literary situations, to an essentially twentieth-century vision of the Self enthralled (and destroyed) by the power and wealth of the City. Norman Mailer's sado-masochistic provocation of the demons of Power is the latest and most self-conscious expression of this phenomenon.

Most American novelists of the late nineteenth and early twentieth centuries *seem* to be saying that environmental forces have so diminished our concept of the self that any latter day projection of it is necessarily a debasement of the possibilities defined by Cooper, Emerson, Whitman, and Mark Twain. But as I've already suggested, this rationalization cannot hide the fact, conspicuous in the proportions and energy of their attention, that these later writers are less interested in worlds defined by the interaction among persons than in a world invulnerable to them. Like Mark Twain in the last two-thirds of *Huckleberry Finn*, their vision often moves panoramically across the massed phenomena of social and economic structures, and it is only within these that they can see the hero at all.

In a curious way, however, this development still carries an Emersonian variation; Emerson is nearly always a hovering presence in American writing, even in the works of Howells, Edith Wharton, and Dreiser. Once the heroes in their novels discover that they are diminished rather than enlarged by efforts to participate in the massed power around them, they also find that they belong to a mysterious brotherhood of souls, a sort of Over-Soul of the lowly in which personal identities are lost and where all share a common destiny. Dreiser's essay "The Myth of Individuality" might be said to adapt Emerson's idea of the Over-Soul to the metropolis, and his admiration for Emerson was implicit much earlier, even in *Sister Carrie*. Fellow feeling of this sort in the face of the impersonality of urban life gets a polite expression, too, in Howells's idea of "complicity," in Mrs. Wharton's idealization, in some of her works, of the sympathetic companionship of the poor and lowly, and in the powerful desire of Faulkner's Isaac McCaslin for "the communal anonymity of brotherhood," providing as it does a source for the political affirmations in *Intruder in the Dust*. The differences among these writers scarcely needs to be mentioned, but they have in common a vision of modern or city "environment" as offering almost no inducement to the human vanity of controlling, much less building, the world one lives in. Howells manages, of course, to suggest a kind of amelioration: the passage of time, as we see in his charming and ignored *Indian Summer*, simply brings into our daily lives a series of helpful distractions from insoluble situations, until by this very process the situations are by-passed.

Again, *Huckleberry Finn*—though Mark Twain is anticipated in this by the Melville of "Bartleby" and *Pierre*—strikes a note that in a few years becomes a momentarily dominant one in American literature: environment becomes force, totally shaping personal relations while remaining unaffected by them. Personal relations come to be little more than inarticulate human huddles, figurations of basic human needs for warmth and tenderness, for food and shelter. "Panoramic environment and the anonymity of the self" is only the most useful titular summary I can give to this aspect of American literature, and many qualifications to it will need to be made by illustrations from *The House of Mirth* and *Sister Carrie*.

II

Mrs. Wharton's life was itself a drama of impulse, impulse that apparently never broke through her personal disciplines or her subscription to public ones. The story of her marriage to an increasingly neurasthenic husband, whom she divorced in 1913, and of the emergence earlier, in 1908 when she was 46, of a passion for Walter Berry, an American lawyer in Paris whom she had known since a year before her marriage, is powerfully told by Mrs. Bell, and her most familiar work, *Ethan Frome*, is a melodrama of the frustrations of love trapped within social and seemingly natural orders. Just as surely as she was a woman with unusual power of personality, she used it to restrain rather than to exercise her feelings. She created a visible image of her personality in the organization of her household. At age eleven she wrote a story on the first page of which was the sentence " 'If only I had known you were going to call, I should have tidied up the drawing-room,' said Mrs. Tompkins." To which young Edith's mother responded with the obviously effective criticism that "Drawing-rooms are always tidy."

Edith Wharton's drawing rooms always were, as her friends ruefully observed, whether in her house in Lenox, Massachusetts, her various apartments in the Rue de Varenne in Paris, or her houses elsewhere in France. Her response to France, even to its landscape, characteristically involved admiration for preordained order and the discipline of impulse: "Every field has a name, a history, a distinct place of its own in the village polity; every blade of grass is there by an old feudal right which has long since dispossessed the worthless and original weed." In France, where she lived for thirty years until her death in Paris in 1937, Mrs. Wharton found the comforting evidence that there existed historical support for the kind of aristocratic life that had all but disappeared, according to *A Backward Glance*, from the New York of her childhood. Daughter of one of the distinguished families of New York City, where she was born in 1862, a descendant of Rhinelanders and Gallatins, she could remark of her fellow expatriot Henry James that "he belonged irrevocably to the old America out of which I also came." Few American writers illustrate more eloquently than she the need in life as well as in novels for some institutional support of feelings otherwise crushed by institutions. The literary consequences of her confused feelings about impulse and order are apparent in the very best of her novels.

*The House of Mirth* was the last of her books written while New York was still her home, and it is a portrayal of life in that city during the closing years of the nineteenth century. Her social background might explain why the book is so mercilessly critical of the commercial forces that had come to dominate the society of New York, but the novel is equally important as literary biography. She tells us that with the writing of *The House of Mirth* she "was turned from the drifting amateur into a professional." Importantly, her ideals of literary professionalism located themselves less in American than in English literature, and in the great European novelists, Balzac, Turgenev, and Flaubert. While she could say that James was "almost the only novelist who has formulated his ideas about his art," and while her achievements as a satirist prepared the way for Sinclair Lewis, who dedicated *Babbitt* to her, the most prevalent influences in her work came from English novelists of manners.

She turned to English novelists for the support of attitudes no longer articulated within the American society she depicts. The result is a precarious mixture of tones, an evidence of discrepancy between the subject of her satire, which is uniquely American and contemporary, and her dependence at certain points on English writers, especially Jane Austen and George Eliot, who never, even in extremity, felt that their values went unrepresented among the dominant forces in the world around them. As a consequence, neither of them used other writers in the way Mrs. Wharton does—as if literature might provide her with the institutional sanctions she could not receive from her own society. In this Mrs. Wharton reveals an American seriousness about literature as an institution that is the foundation for the literary allusiveness so characteristic of American literature from Hawthorne and Melville to T.S. Eliot.

It is of some historical importance that we can hear the accents of Jane Austen and the rhetoric of George Eliot in the pages of this novel. Wherever the wit is most secure, wherever it is least strident and least in anticipation of the satirical style of Sinclair Lewis, it is apt to remind us of Jane Austen. Thus when Miss Stepney brings accusations against the heroine to Miss Bart's guardian, there are recognizably literary encouragements from Jane Austen in the remark that Miss Stepney "was not sufficiently familiar with the classic drama to have recalled in advance how bearers of bad tidings are proverbially received, but she now had a rapid vision of forfeited dinners and reduced wardrobe as a possible consequence of her disinterestedness. To the honor of her sex, however, hatred of Lily prevailed over more personal considerations."

In saying that Mrs. Wharton leaned at such points on an earlier English novelist, I don't mean to suggest that Miss Austen herself felt no corresponding dissatisfactions with her own social and historical environment. The very existence of her novels testifies that she did. If Mrs. Wharton felt, as one of her old friends expressed it, that life in America "unconsciously for all of us began to change from simplicity to vulgarity in the late 'eighties," Jane Austen in the first decade of the same century wrote partly in response to a similar process in England. "It is hard indeed," as Armour Craig points out, "not to use the inevitable 'age of transition' in reflecting on the kind of world" Jane Austen presents, a world where it is becoming difficult "even to provide a homogeneous guest list for a ball." But the forces of disruptive change had to make their way through a texture altogether more resilent and more absorbent, less easily discolored than Mrs. Wharton's.

Jane Austen's was a society at once stronger and more flexible than

anything that New York, even at its most appealing, could allow Edith
Wharton to imagine. Well before the appearance of *The House of Mirth* in
1905, the old conservative families had been replaced by the new ones
enriched through the expansion of business. Lily Bart's career takes her
through the various strata of society, from top to bottom, and the tracing of
her career is coexistent with Mrs. Wharton's panoramic view of the world
that bears down on her. She moves from the Trenors of "Bellomont," who
feel some of the restraints of "old habits," to the Dorsets, who exploit
traditional mores as a disguise for the misconduct eventually paid for by Lily;
from the ferociously social-climbing Brys to the uncritically pleasure-seeking
Gormers, and from there to the outskirts of social acceptability when Lily
becomes a secretary to the latest invader from the Western states, Miss
Hatch of the Hotel Emporium. Mrs. Wharton's description of Lily's stay
with Miss Hatch includes one of the most incisive pictures in our literature
of hotel life in America, reminding us that her preoccupation with
environment was evident, too, in her first book of prose—*A Study of Interior
Decorating*. Though these various elements struggle for power, their essential
qualities blend so easily into one another that there is in this novel actually
no dramatized conflict of class or of social values. There are only conflicts of
economic and social power, in which the outcome is largely determined by
money. Even the efforts of sexual conquest in the book have money as their
primary inducement.

One of Mrs. Wharton's subtly achieved implications is that emotions in
this society are calculated and invested with the coldness of financial
speculation. For anyone as financially impoverished as Lily, the alternative to
calculation is social ruin. "It was seldom," Mrs. Wharton reports in a
metaphor that unites financial with emotional economies, that Lily "could
allow herself the luxury of an impulse." She is therefore not being luxurious
when we see her in Chapter 2 on a train—one of her frequent trips to the
great country houses to which her charm, beauty, and little services win her
invitations—"studying her prey through downcast lashes while she organized
her method of attack." Her prey is Percy Gryce, limited in all things except
prudery, a collection of Americana, and the millions which Lily needs if she
is to secure a place in the New York society where her parents went bankrupt
maintaining even a foothold. As Mrs. Wharton's style would suggest, Lily
can be taken here as only a comic threat to poor Percy, and we have just been
shown in the opening chapter that she is really not studious enough to be a
seductress in so theatrical a vein. She has already acted with the generous
impulsiveness that will make her the "prey" of her proposed victims. While
waiting for the train, she has met Selden, the one man in the book she truly

admires despite his lack of prosperity, and, having accepted an invitation to his rooms for tea, is discovered on leaving by Rosedale, a social-climbing Jewish investor. He is also a gossip, and he promptly catches her in unnecessary and obvious lies about her reasons for being in the building.

Lily's mistake and its consequences justify Mrs. Wharton's claim that in her works "My last page is always latent in my first"—such is the undeflectable force of the social process. At the end of the novel, Lily's hope of becoming active again within society rests with Rosedale, the man who first suspects her deviations from the rules. Having failed with Gryce out of her impulsively expressed wishes to be with Selden; having thoughtlessly accepted what seemed merely the business advice of Gus Trenor, the husband of her best friend, only to discover herself compromised by him; having slipped then to companionship with the Dorsets, where her kindness to the husband is exploited by the wife as a cover for her own amatory adventures, Lily is faced with Rosedale's proposal. He will marry her and give her financial power over her enemies if she will use some letters to Mrs. Dorset that have come into her possession as a way of forcing Mrs. Dorset to withdraw the lies she has been spreading about her. Lily's failure to carry out this blackmail is a matter less of ethics than, once again, of her responding to impulses rather than following the calculated movements that are consonant with the rhythms of her environment. On the way to Mrs. Dorset's she happens past Selden's apartment building and makes, by the sudden decision to visit him, a final grasp for the life of moral refinement which she sees in him and which, by her proposed maneuver, she is about to lose forever for herself. While there, again on an impulse of generous and exalted feeling, she contrives secretly to burn the letters with which she would have implicated Mrs. Dorset and Selden. She seals thereby her social obliteration.

"Obliteration" is not too strong a word to describe how, near the end of the novel, Lily disappears into the mass of New York, again panoramically rendered, into "the thousands of insignificant figures" who watch with her the parade of fashion, in which she herself once took part, along Fifth Avenue. This is the price exacted for those tiny acts of independence, those generous and sympathetic promptings which have set her apart from society in this book even when she is most assiduously trying to join it. To us as to Selden, her attractiveness is "the way in which she detached herself, by a thousand indefinable shades, from the persons who most abounded in her own style." The analogy to Fitzgerald's Gatsby is obvious enough.

Lily's alertness to the possibilities of life is what defeats her by making her deviate from any settled campaign of success. Though she is unfortunately a spendthrift with money, the society of Trenor and Dorset takes its toll of her because she is admirably a spendthrift of emotions. It is thus characteristic that to her drab little friend Gerty she should give the liberal fraction of the money she is about to spend on a dressing case, and that in her treatment of servants she acts like one "long enough in bondage to other people's pleasures to be considerate of those who depend on hers." In Mrs. Wharton's noble phrase, Lily is capable of "those shocks of pity that sometimes decentralize a life." Indeed, in the environment of this book "eccentricity" describes the few natural rather than the many grotesque characters we encounter, much as it defines Melville's Bartleby who, at the very "center" of American financial power, is treated as an intolerable "eccentric" even while his fellow scriveners, Turkey, Nippers, and Ginger Nut are accepted in their Dickensian grotesqueness as merely amusing and convenient fellows to have around Wall Street.

And yet while Mrs. Wharton is a remarkably tough-minded writer, *The House of Mirth* insists on a rather too easy connection between Lily's freedom of impulse and the fact that she is poor and responsive to the poverty of others. The primitivistic assumption that the life of impulse is somehow located in the lower region of society is common enough in literature and notably so in American writers as otherwise different as Dreiser and Faulkner. In Mrs. Wharton's case, the assumption, once recognized as operative in her book, seems a logical consequence of her very rigid satirical view of the high society wherein Lily's career is initially dramatized. In none of the inhabitants of this society, not even in Selden, who likes to be aloof from it, can Mrs. Wharton locate a sustained expression of uncalculated feeling, anything that might create a countermovement to the system of emotional and financial calculation on which the society is built. Lily's financial precariousness lets her see a reflection of her possible destiny in the lives of the poor as well as the rich, and to see it with an intimidated sympathy. One can sense this sympathetic quality in Lily even in the poignant scenes that reveal her incapacity to love Gerty, the person who helps her most unselfishly. Lily recognizes in Gerty's "acquiescence in dinginess" a terrifyingly close approximation of her own situation, were she without the spirit which makes her so attractively full of hope. Gerty has a "moral vision which makes all human suffering so near and insistent that the other aspects of life fade into remoteness."

Even while Mrs. Wharton is perhaps too glib in the connections she makes between lowliness and human warmth, neither she nor her heroine willingly gives up her appetite for the more glamorous possibilities of life. Poverty felt as a threat, no matter what it offers by way of communal feeling, gives to Mrs. Wharton's descriptions of working-class life and the drabness of Lily's surroundings an immediacy comparable to Dreiser's *Sister Carrie*, which appeared five years earlier. Nevertheless there is an increasing emphasis, as such descriptions pile up, on the way spontaneous sympathy and kinship are assets somehow more available to the impoverished than to anyone else in the book. This sentiment accumulates in the next to the last chapter when Lily, having taken her leave of Selden for what will prove the last time, sits in Bryant Park, a deserted and lonely figure. Again, what makes us feel the frailty and smallness of the heroine is the panoramic rendering of her surroundings. The park is located at the relatively unfashionable middle of Fifth Avenue, the most luxurious of the avenues in New York, a kind of gathering place for the unlocated, a passage from the private elegance of the East side to the public show places and tenements of the West. Discovered by Nettie Struther, one of the girls Lily has helped at Gerty's club for young women in distress, she goes to Nettie's apartment, to the warmth of her kitchen, and is there allowed to hold Nettie's newborn baby. In this scene, very nearly at the end of the book, Mrs. Wharton makes an anxious and contrived effort to evoke the kind of human relationship disastrously absent from Lily's life. She is suggesting some positive standard to which the reader and Lily might appeal for an alternative both to the community of dinginess, in which Lily feels condemned, and to the society in which she had hoped to live. It is a society, we now remember with some shock, in which there has been no evidence of children or of childbearing.

The most poignant moment in the scene shows Lily holding Nettie's baby, and its poignancy is of a piece with its metaphoric implications:

> The baby, feeling herself detached from her habitual anchorage, made an instinctive motion of resistance; but the soothing influences of digestion prevailed, and Lily felt the soft weight sink trustfully against her breast. The child's confidence in its safety thrilled her with a sense of warmth and returning life, and she bent over, wondering at the rosy blur of the little face, the empty clearness of the eyes, the vague tendrilly motions of the folding and unfolding fingers. At first the burden in her arms seemed as light as a pink cloud or a heap of down, but as she continued to hold it the weight increased, sinking deeper, and penetrating her with a strange sense of weakness, as though the child entered into her and became a part of herself.

The passage is not making any simple-minded suggestion that Lily would have been happier had she been satisfied with poverty and the common destiny of motherhood. Directing our attention beyond the triviality of such "solutions" is the metaphoric urgency of the passage, its efforts to grasp, like the "folding and unfolding fingers" of the baby, an image of unity and natural kinship. Obvious enough in the last sentence, the intention is implicit in the first: "The baby, feeling itself detached from her habitual anchorage, made an instinctive motion of resistance." The metaphors remind us, by contrast, of the factitious social unities throughout the rest of the novel, of alliances held together by the power of money and by the shared hypocrisies that constitute a standard for the exclusion of Lily. She is soon to die alone in her bed with the drugged illusion that the baby is lying with her, "a gentle penetrating thrill of warmth and pleasure. She settled herself into an easier position, hollowing her arm to pillow the round downy head, and holding her breath lest a sound should disturb the sleeping child." Her tenderness, expending itself at the end on thin air, is an expression of the instinctive compassion that has led to her ruin.

In the society in which Lily has been living, there have not been nor could there be the spontaneous enactments of human solidarity that we witness among Lily, the baby, and Nettie. The contrast is impressed upon us with so little evidence of the author's conscious contrivance that it seems to come from her most inward feeling for her material. Thus we discover, looking back, that Lily's response to Mrs. Dorset and to her schemes was described in nearly the same terms used in the scene with the child: "But compassion, in a moment, got the better of her instinctive recoil from Mrs. Dorset," just as the baby after an "instinctive motion of resistance" surrenders to a desire for warmth and unity. And the metaphoric parallels are further evident in Lily's then thinking of herself as a motherly source of comfort even to her enemy: "it was on Lily's lips to exclaim: 'You poor soul, don't double and turn—come straight to me and we'll find a way out!'"

What is particularly interesting about this novel, and about some of the other works of American literature we have considered, is that the author cannot authenticate her sentiments about compassion and kinship; she cannot give them a positive embodiment in dramatic scenes without going outside the areas of society where the central conflicts of her work have occurred. Instead, she moves into areas tangential to them and occupied by characters mostly anonymous. One implication of the metaphors used to describe such characters is that their sympathy and their recognition of human destinies, other than merely social ones, can be a basis for kinship and community more binding than the power of money. It is here that Mrs. Wharton's admiration for George Eliot seems to have entered as a determining factor in *The House of Mirth*. Lily's sacrificial sympathy for Mrs.

Dorset is much like Dorothea Brooke's in several comparable scenes, especially with Rosamond, at the end of *Middlemarch*.

George Eliot's treatment of personal relations is impassioned by her knowledge of the social fractures in English society that developed on the eve of the Reform Bill of 1832. Of the possible healing unities that are proposed in *Middlemarch*, the tragic inadequacy of the economic and especially the scientific schemes in which the novel abounds are obvious enough. The only dependable social unities that are achieved derive from a kind of Wordsworthean sympathy defined by Ladislaw in his description of a soul "in which knowledge passes instantaneously into feeling, and feeling flashes back as a new organ of knowledge." It is a measure of the difference between the historical situations of the English novelist in 1870 and of the American in 1905 that Mrs. Wharton does not imagine a society in which her heroine can do more than carry out the first part of Ladislaw's prescription. She transforms her knowledge into compassion. But her expression of compassion reveals an ignorance of the nature of her environment that could come only from a beautiful and uncynical nature. Characters like Mrs. Dorset are not motivated by needs and feelings that in George Eliot's moral universe are considered inherently human.

To assume such motivation in the people of *The House of Mirth* is to be admirably and simply a dupe, an innocent. In making Lily what we might call an old-fashioned American who believes that people remain as children in their need for love and sympathy, Mrs. Wharton is not herself in the least an innocent. She knows her heroine well enough to recognize that Lily's unsuspicious nature is in part an expression of ego, the underside of innocence: she has the capacity to think so well of herself that she cannot easily imagine the gross intentions of others with respect to her. Thus when Trenor demands payment of her debts to him he needs to instruct her in the fact that he is not "asking for payment in kind." Her affections will be a proper substitute for his money. All that saves Lily on this occasion is something remaining in Trenor of the social standards whose passing Mrs. Wharton laments in her autobiography. Trenor is prevented from forcing his attentions on Lily, we are told, when "old habits, old restraints, the hand of inherited order, plucked back the bewildered mind which passion had jolted from its ruts."

Even so short a quotation indicates that this moment is one of the weakest in the novel, both in its characterization and in the platitudinous coloration of style, not uncommon in the ladies' magazines for which Mrs. Wharton sometimes wrote. In the scene between Lily and Trenor, Mrs. Wharton tries, quite unsuccessfully I'm afraid, to unite the central areas of social drama in her novel with the standards by which she is most anxious to judge it, standards which she would like to believe are still, if weakly, operative in that society. Her failure at this moment perhaps dissuaded her from any further efforts of the same kind and made it necessary for her to locate analogous standards of human decency in areas uncontaminated by the social forces dominant in the book. At the end, Lily Bart's misery is said to have proceeded from her having been denied an ordering principle for her good impulses. She is without the benefit of those raised, like George Eliot's rural family the Garths, in a community united by memories and customs. "It was indeed miserable to be poor," Lily thinks just before her accidental suicide, and she continues:

> ... to look forward to a shabby, anxious middleage, leading by dreary degrees of economy and self-denial to gradual absorption in the dingy communal existence of the boarding-house. But there was something more miserable still—it was the clutch of solitude at her heart, the sense of being swept like a stray uprooted growth down the heedless current of the years. That was the feeling which possessed her now—the feeling of being something rootless and ephemeral, mere spindrift of the whirling surface of existence, without anything to which the poor little tentacles of self could cling before the awful flood submerged them. And as she looked back she saw that there had never been a time when she had had any real relation to life. Her parents too had been rootless, blown hither and thither on every wind of fashion, without any personal existence to shelter them from its shifting gusts. She herself had grown up without any one spot of earth being dearer to her than another: there was no center of early pieties, of grave endearing traditions, to which her heart could revert and from which it could draw strength for itself and tenderness for others. In whatever form, a slowly-accumulated past lives in the blood—whether in the concrete image of the old house stored with visual memories, or in a conception of the house not built with hands but made up of inherited passions and loyalties—it has the same power of broadening and deepening the individual existence, of attaching it by mysterious links of kinship to all the mighty sum of human striving.

The assumptions in this paragraph are also George Eliot's, whose conservatism is particularly admired by Mrs. Wharton in her review of Leslie

Stephen's *George Eliot:* "a deep reverence for family ties, for the sanctities of tradition, the claims of slowly acquired convictions and slowly formed precedents, is revealed in every page of her books." This particular kind of reverence has since developed into the mythology of the anti-urban and politically conservative literature of the twentieth century. Familiar to readers of Faulkner or Yeats or T. S. Eliot's essays on culture, the mythology invests heavily in Mrs. Wharton's vocabulary: "rootless," "one spot of earth," "early pieties," "inherited passions and loyalties," "traditions," and the mystique of the "house not built by hands but made up of inherited passions and loyalties." Mrs. Wharton's dream of environment is conspicuously different from any she can represent.

Her use of the vocabulary of "tradition" has the ring of platitude. The reason is by now perhaps obvious: the terms as used in *The House of Mirth* are given no nourishing connections to the dramatic substance of the novel. They have their source mostly in the episode of Lily's quite accidental meeting with Nettie Struther, who has not before had any place in the book. There is an air of extemporization precisely at the point where Mrs. Wharton is trying to give us something to carry away, other than a helpless sense of pity and revulsion, from the disasters we have witnessed. What she can give us is merely a vocabulary. Sharing George Eliot's attitude, she is deprived of George Eliot's resources—a society in which there really were "grave and endearing traditions" still in visible and audible form. And because she is a novelist who could not create such a society in her language, she is the more evidently a victim herself of social forces that also defeat her heroine.

Some of the contradictions among critics assessing the illusive role of Selden in this novel result from not fully grasping the literary significance of Mrs. Wharton's dedication to rural traditionalism. Selden has all the intellectual refinements that allows him "a happy air of viewing the show objectively, of having points of contact outside the great gilt cage." But his "points of contact" are essentially to literary and philosophical abstractions and exclude the kinds of contact fatally missing from Lily's life. His "republic of the spirit" is not Mrs. Wharton's ideal community. He is allowed to catch Lily in situations compromising enough to make most men cautious, though not the kind of man Mrs. Wharton characteristically admired in her novels. Selden's feelings are often as calculated as those coming from inside "the great gilt cage." He too judges Lily more by conventional assumptions of propriety than by knowing and trusting her through his affections. When she is most in need of him,. after Mrs. Dorset, in a brilliantly paced scene of social tension, forbids her to return to the yacht, Selden offers her everything but the support of his trust: "The memory of Mrs. Fisher's hints, and the corroboration of his own impressions, while they deepened his pity, also increased his constraint, since, whichever way he sought a free outlet for sympathy, it was blocked by the fear of committing a blunder." He is afraid of precisely those impulses by which Lily continually and sympathetically responds to Mrs. Dorset, with whom Selden has had assignations. These alone make it clear that Mrs. Wharton is not giving us a portrait of masculine sexual incapacity. Selden's somewhat murky characterization is instead a result of her not having found a way, especially at the early stages of the book, to make about him the point that we can make only retrospectively, looking back from the meeting of Lily and Nettie: that he is deficient in a sense of human solidarity and that he knows others not by loving but only by judging them.

The characterization of Selden is an instance of Mrs. Wharton's difficulty in having her standards emanate from within the conflicts she is dramatizing. He is refined, intelligent, and courageously self-consulting within a rigidly conformist environment, but his ways of "knowing" people are essentially cosmopolitan—by the guesswork, the gossip, the categorizing assumptions that substitute for the slowly accumulated intimacy on which Mrs. Wharton places such redeeming value. He is unable, by character and circumstance, to "know" Lily as people of George Eliot's provincial *Middlemarch* can at their best know one another or as Faulkner's characters can know, for example, that one of their number did not commit a crime even though all the apparent evidence indicates that he did. Again, the character in this novel who exercises this kind of knowledge has no place whatever in the major line of action. He belongs instead to Nettie's story, which might be called a pastoral version of Lily's: she became unfortunately involved with a "stylish" man, was left ill and disgraced by him until rescued (with the help of some money from Lily) by Gerty, who is also ready to assist Lily in her distress.

But the difference in Nettie's story, and it has made all the difference, is a character named George. He has known her since childhood and thus with an intimacy that can make him compassionate rather than critical of her later behavior. The vocabulary which Mrs. Wharton gives Nettie confirms once again the relevance to this novel of George Eliot. George Eliot provides the classic image in fiction of a kind of social communion derived, as in later anti-cosmopolitan fiction, from "some center of early pieties ... of grave endearing traditions to which the heart could revert and from which it could draw strength for itself and tenderness for others." Nettie ends her story with the happy news that "when I got back home, George came round and asked me to marry him. At first I thought I couldn't, because we'd been brought up together, and I knew he knew about me. But after awhile I began to see that that made it easier. I never could have told another man, and I'd never have married without telling; but if George cared enough to have me as I was, I didn't see why I shouldn't begin again—and I did."

"And I knew he knew about me"—this compassionate use of knowledge allows us to measure the failure of Selden in his treatment of Lily. He is, we were told earlier, unable to "yield to the growth of an affection which might appeal to pity yet leave the understanding untouched: sympathy would no more delude him than a trick of the eyes, the grace of helplessness than a curve of the cheek." The tone here is partisanly feminine in the suggestion, not sustained by the characterization of Selden in his relationships with women, that he is a sexually unimpassioned man. Here again the basis for some of Mrs. Wharton's attitudes fails to be sufficiently objectified within the fictional world she creates. The trouble with Selden is that he will not allow himself to "know" the heroine through his instincts, his spontaneous affections.

But who *can* know her? Beyond Selden there is only the rhetoric which praises the conditions within which a good way of knowing her might have been fostered by the "grave endearing traditions" not available to anyone except, in some apparently elementary form, to Nettie and her George and to the pitiable Gerty. Mrs. Wharton's difficulty in *The House of Mirth* makes any comparison to the English women novelists with whom she deserves to keep company end with a significant degree of contrast. She is a novelist of manners in a peculiarly American way: she cannot imagine a society, any more than can Emerson or most of the other writers I have considered, in which her values are brought into play at the center of dramatic conflict. Instead of being an aggregate of human relationships, subject to modification in the best interest of its members, society for her as for a majority of American writers becomes an expression of impersonal power, even when that power is being manipulated by some of its victims.

III

Nine years younger than Edith Wharton, and ages behind her in literary and social sophistication, Dreiser wrote *Sister Carrie* out of an instinctive awareness of what Mrs. Wharton would later propose in *The House of Mirth:* that society is composed not of personal relationships extended into historical and communal ones, but that it is made up of forces to which these relationships are irrelevant. At the end of the earlier work, Carrie Meeber, even with the success Lily fails to get, gazes no less yearningly at the same panorama of glittering power: from her chambers at the Waldorf she looks "out upon the old winding procession of carriages rolling up Fifth Avenue." After Carrie's success no less than during Lily's failure there persists what Dreiser calls the never satisfied "strivings of the human heart."

Dreiser belongs "in a very old, a very difficult, a very lonely American tradition," where Alfred Kazin has placed him: "It is no longer 'transcendentalist' but always it seeks to transcend," Kazin writes ... "he does not accept our 'society' as the whole of reality." And he refuses to see very much reality at all in those early pieties, endearing traditions, and family ties promoted by Mrs. Wharton, however ineffectively, as a possible amelioration to the disastrous failures of her heroines. Dreiser's indifference to the saving grace of personal relationships cannot be explained as a deficiency of imagination or experience, though to have any of either means that you do not have all. There was, in fact, considerable warmth within his large, mobile, impoverished family. His father was cold and religiously austere, but Theodore and his brother Paul formed a lifelong attachment and when Dreiser thought of their mother, in *A Book About Myself*, it was of "a magnetic dreamy soul ... beyond or behind so-called good or evil," a woman without much "constructive ability wherewith to make real her dreams." Similarly, it only partly explains his lack of interest in the novelistic intensities of personal relationships to say that he was ignorant of the literary conventions that had endowed them with mythic and symbolic importance. "The costly price of sons and lovers," Emerson called such relationships in "Experience," remarking that he would gladly pay the price *if* this would "introduce me into ... reality." Reality for Emerson, though associated with different forces than for Dreiser, is even more infinitely beyond the measure of merely personal fates.

Dreiser was infatuated primarily by the movements, more often the mere "driftings" of single persons within huge dimensions of impersonal force. Environment in his work becomes synonymous not only with the City as mass but with life itself as energy, the latter phenomenon being especially evident in his later works. He exults, like an awed discoverer of regions where he will probably himself be destroyed, in mapping those forces against which, first in George Eliot, then in Hardy, then in Lawrence, human relatedness of a kind nearly ignored by Dreiser offers the only hope of a personal, as distinguished from an anonymous existence.

Stuart Sherman did not know how right he was fifteen years after *Sister Carrie*, and nearly coincident with the publication of *The "Genius,"* when he announced in "The Barbaric Naturalism of Theodore Dreiser" that "Mr.

Dreiser's field seems curiously outside American society." For Sherman, as for Gertrude Atherton, who said of Dreiser's characters that "not a real American could be found among them with a magnifying glass," American society was a sort of Anglo-Saxon literary club. Necessarily on the outside of this, a product, Sherman was not beneath observing, of the German element of our "mixed population," Dreiser portrayed a "vacuum, from which the obligations of parenthood, marriage, chivalry, and citizenship have been quite withdrawn." The triviality of the judgment is sufficiently indicated by pointing out that the "vacuum" thus described was also created by a writer as impeccably Anglo-Saxon as Emerson when, in the woods, he discovered that "the name of the nearest friend sounds then foreign and accidental: to be brothers, to be acquaintances, master or servant, is then a trifle and a disturbance."

To be "outside American society" is of course to be in the great American literary tradition. It is a tradition, transcendentalism and romanticism being only two aspects of it, in which individuals are characterized less by their relation to one another than by their relation to the conglomerations of power that fill space and that determine the apportionments of time. The conglomerations go under different names: Nature, The City, Society, The Dynamo, The Bomb, The Presidency, and aspects of any one of these may be ascribed to any other. The force that joins people together in Dreiser's world does not manifest itself in marriage, any more than it does in most other American writers. People are instead merged in a common bondage to the humming, souring vistas of the city with their evocations of mysterious promise. Personal attachments, sporadic and "chemic," can take place within such an environment, but they do not compel the interest of Dreiser or his characters. These characters are compelled instead by the non-personal forces that fill the yearning eye with steel and concrete, that manipulate time by the pulsations of manufacture and of money-making.

The time and space of a novel like *Sister Carrie*, or of most of his other novels, is, by comparison to what is given to personal relations, inordinately devoted to the panorama of the City. There is nothing therefore surprising in the way the novel was begun. After exchanging promises with Arthur Henry, with whom Dreiser had worked on the *Toledo Blade*, that they would both write novels, Dreiser merely sat down and put the words of his title at the top of a page without any idea how he was to fill it or succeeding ones. "My mind was a blank," he tells us in *A Book About Myself*, "except for the name. I had no idea who or what she was to be. I have often thought there was something mystic about it, as if I were being used, like a medium." The two words, the blank page, soon to be filled, are symptomatic that so far as character and environment are concerned Dreiser had no intention of creating anything like a Jamesian "house of fiction." The shape of the material was the shape for the most part merely of his recollections. Writing for him obviously did not involve the "building" of a world so much as reporting on one already existent. In fact, the career of Carrie Meeber is in many ways a report of the experience of one of Dreiser's sisters. About the only pattern of disruption in the sequence of reported lives occurs when Dreiser wants to place different kinds of environment in juxtaposition, as when the squalor of the factory where Carrie works is contrasted with the elegance of Fitzgerald and Moy's where the men discuss her. Characteristically, where there is most evidence of concern for presentation, for premeditated organization, there is less care given to the characterization of Carrie than to her environmental situations. It is as if she herself were only part of that environment, a mostly silent figure within the massed, detailed, panoramic globs of language that create it. Environmental force is made altogether more articulate than are any of the characters in the book.

This inarticulateness of persons extends almost as poignantly to Dreiser himself. It is implicit even in his volubility. The floods of language by which he embraces things outside himself are a verbal equivalent to the visual obsessions of his characters. Not until at least his third novel, *The Financier* in 1912, could one sometimes hear in this volubility anything like a firm or authoritative presence of Dreiser himself. In *Sister Carrie* it is impossible to discover him except in disparate fragments. As much as does his heroine or Hurstwood, Dreiser becomes lost to the evoked environments of the book. To reach any assessment of his historical significance as a writer, a question has to be asked this early in his career: who *is* Theodore Dreiser in these pages? At issue is not the fact that he is a different "sounding" person from one page to another. Such transformations are a virtue in most writers and in most people. What is perplexing is that he creates no plastic coherence among the lurid varieties of self-characterization that emerge from his language. His relationship to the reader and to his material is fragmented. His flaccid poetizing, his fatalistic jowl-shaking about sexual compulsions, his verbal endorsements of meretricious glamor side by side with portentously critical assessments of it—the failure of attention to the composite results of these various tones raises questions not answered by the usual attacks on the slovenliness of his style. Granted that he often writes as if language itself were a bore, there remains the mystery of Dreiser's undeniable power over the imagination even of his severest critics.

In one sense, the fractured characterization which Dreiser gives to himself as narrator of *Sister Carrie* is evidence of the integrity of his vision. It is a vision in which character—as a derivative of language and the power of language—is regarded as relatively negligible. In his apparent reluctance to cope with his own fluctuations of voice, Dreiser is in no way protecting himself. Instead, and to an extraordinary degree, he seems not even to care about achieving through language any shaped social identity. To care about doing so would be a concession to the idea, on which most English novels are based, that persons and societies are literally "made" by personal exertion or by the ability to give authoritative shapes to words. Indeed what I find admirable in Dreiser is that he does not in any way compromise himself by subscribing to a bourgeois faith in the reality of language. His essentially religious energy, his personal necessity would not let him adulterate his vision of environment as comprised of chemic, economic, and natural force. He simply cannot permit, for the sake of story or of "literature," those conversational involvements that imply that the self or society is formed by intensities of personal effort. For him, character and society are antecedent to talk; fate has nothing to do with the value of certain words and phrases, with the conflict between people or between a person and his environment.

Correspondingly, the language used by his characters has relatively little to do with creating or sustaining their personal relationships: in their conversations they merely report to each other how external forces are combining or separating their human destinies. Naturally, he is more effective when writing scenes of separation than of meeting, scenes where people can no longer talk rather than scenes where they must talk out of a compulsion of initial attraction. Three such very effective moments reveal Carrie's progress, partly because the breakup, like the formation of relations in Dreiser, is in obedience to accelerations of success or failure. When she leaves her sister and brother-in-law to escape from Wabash Avenue to the "elegance" of life with Drouet she merely absents herself after dinner. She goes into the bathroom, where they cannot disturb her, and writes a little note:

> "Good-bye, Minnie," it read. "I'm not going home. I'm going to stay in Chicago a little while and look for work. Don't worry. I'll be all right."
>
> In the front room Hanson was reading his paper. As usual, she helped Minnie clear away the dishes and straighten up. Then she said:
>
> "I guess I'll stand down at the door a little while." She could scarcely prevent her voice from trembling.
>
> Minnie remembered Hanson's remonstrance.

"Sven doesn't think it looks good to stand down there," she said.

"Doesn't he?" said Carrie. "I won't do it any more after this."

She put on her hat and fidgeted around the table in the little bedroom, wondering where to slip the note. Finally she put it under Minnie's hair-brush.

When she had closed the hall-door, she paused a moment and wondered what they would think. Some thought of the queerness of her deed affected her. She went slowly down the stairs. She looked back up the lighted step, and then affected to stroll up the street. When she reached the corner she quickened her pace.

As she was hurrying away, Hanson came back to his wife.

"Is Carrie down at the door again?" he asked.

"Yes," said Minnie; "she said she wasn't going to do it any more."

He went over to the baby where it was playing on the floor and began to poke his finger at it.

Drouet was on the corner waiting, in good spirits.

"Hello, Carrie," he said, as a sprightly figure of a girl drew near him. "Got here safe, did you? Well, we'll take a car."

She will subsequently leave Drouet for Hurstwood with only slightly more ceremony, occasioned by Drouet's wish that she should stay, and still later, also in the interests of her career, she will leave Hurstwood in a scene not significantly different from the one just quoted. Hurstwood returns to find a note in Carrie's inimitably simple, unapologetic style:

"Dear George," he read, crunching the money in one hand. "I'm going away. I'm not coming back any more. It's no use trying to keep up the flat; I can't do it. I wouldn't mind helping you, if I could, but I can't support us both, and pay the rent. I need what little I make to pay for my clothes. I'm leaving twenty dollars. It's all I have just now. You can do whatever you like with the furniture. I won't want it.—Carrie."

He dropped the note and looked quietly round. Now he knew what he missed. It was the little ornamental clock, which was hers. It had gone from the mantelpiece. He went into the front room, his bedroom, the parlour, lighting the gas as he went. From the chiffoniere had gone the knick-nacks of silver and plate. From the table-top, the lace coverings. He opened the wardrobe—no clothes of hers. He opened the drawers—nothing of hers. Her trunk was gone from its accustomed place. Back in his own room hung his old clothes, just as he had left them. Nothing else was gone.

He stepped into the parlour and stood for a few moments looking vacantly at the floor. The silence grew oppressive. The little flat seemed wonderfully deserted. He wholly forgot that he was hungry, that it was only dinner-time. It seemed later in the night.

Suddenly, he found that the money was still in his hands. There were twenty dollars in all, as she had said. Now he walked back, leaving the lights ablaze, and feeling as if the flat were empty.

"I'll get out of this," he said to himself.

Then the sheer loneliness of his situation rushed upon him in full.

"Left me!" he muttered and repeated, "Left me!"

The place that had been so comfortable, where he had spent so many days of warmth, was now a memory. Something colder and chillier confronted him. He sank down in his chair, resting his chin in his hands—mere sensation, without thought, holding him.

Then something like a bereaved affection and self pity swept over him.

"She needn't have gone away," he said. "I'd have got something."

He sat a long while without rocking, and added quite clearly, out loud: "I tried, didn't I?"

At midnight he was still rocking, staring at the floor.

The circumstances in each of these scenes are, conventionally, among the most dramatically exploitable in literature: the rejection of family, the casting off of one lover and the taking of another, the final collapse of the central relationship of the book and of the heroine. But in each instance Dreiser disdains his dramatic opportunity. No direct confrontation, with its inherent possibilities of conversational drama, is allowed to take place between his people. Instead, his characters reveal their feelings in a manner—notes of departure, soliloquies, primitive interior monologue, all of these in the simplest grammatical structure—that expresses the impossibility or, perhaps one should say, the lack of necessity for dialogue.

The clue to the significance of this pattern is, I think, in the fact that what moves Carrie in each episode, and what therefore moves the plot, is sexual impulse. More accurately, Carrie discovers that her sexual interests are excited by the economic and social power in the men she meets. In his novels, no less than in his autobiographical writing, Dreiser was determined that sex should be recognized as "the controlling and directing force that it is." The distinction which Leslie Stephen made between Fielding and Richardson, letting Fielding represent the truly masculine and Richardson the more feminine way of treating sex, could as easily describe the difference between Dreiser and most American novelists before him. Sexuality, firm and insistent in its pressure, is what ultimately gets communicated by these scenes; the inarticulateness of his characters and yet their strange, indeflectable movement toward or away from one another, even when they are in most respects conspicuously "drifting," gives us the image of truly seduced persons. It was perhaps in reference to this phenomenon that Randolph Bourne, in his review of *The 'Genius,'* observed that Dreiser's "hero is really not Sister Carrie or the Titan or the Genius, but that desire within us that pounds in manifold guise against the iron walls of experience." The "iron walls of experience" might well remind us of Hawthorne's "iron fetters we call reality" though it is here sexual impulse that "pounds against" rather than the "imagination" that merely "lessens" the oppressive surroundings. It is as if sex in Dreiser were almost the only imaginable form of personal interchange since all other contacts have been reduced to the account characters might give of their daily schedules.

Nevertheless, sex in Dreiser does not enrich relationships beyond what they initially were. Sex is merely the instrument of a compulsion to have a relationship, a compulsion excited by a whole complex of inarticulate excitations about the representative glamor of a particular person. Of some autobiographical relevance is Dreiser's admission that he found it "almost affectionately unavoidable to hold three, four—even as many as five and six—women in regard—at one and the same time." His compulsion (and his good luck at escaping its consequences) was the result perhaps of sterility. But on the evidence of his novels he was in any case someone not aware of the emotional responsibilities and convolutions, the whole element of "play" in human relationships which are the mainstay of other novelists. At the end of what in most novels would be very complicated human attachments, his characters simply walk off.

This curious, this very sad and touching sequence by which his people are dispersed into the landscape of the City places Dreiser within that line of American writers who choose not to imagine what I have earlier called a society of alternatives. At the end of *Sister Carrie* nothing has been accumulated from the tangled relationships which hold any two people together, nothing of a personal kind modifies their distress at being in a relationship merely to external force. The novel's last pages, a sort of passing in review of the characters each going his separate way, provide images not so much of isolation as of persons meaningfully related only to the scenery of urban energy or, in Hurstwood's case, indifferently destined for death soon after leaving the anonymous band of brothers auctioned off in the Bowery for money to pay for their beds.

Dreiser's literary characteristics make it predictable that in 1934 he would write an essay called "The Myth of Individuality." He there develops the idea that "man is not living, but is being lived by something which needs not only him but billions like him in order to express itself." There is no contradiction in turning, as he did, from a concept of mechanism to a concept of totality, to what he called "Universe, God, or the Vital Force," quoting in the process Emerson's "Brahma." And Thoreau, he admitted, was of all the philosophers he read the "most illuminative ... of a universal and apparently beneficient control ... however dark and savage its results or expressions may seem to us at times." Matthiessen, who gives a good account of this development, errs, I think, in remarking that Dreiser's discovery of kinship with "such a highly individualistic philosopher fills out the bases of his political beliefs in a way that his hurried pamphleteering often failed to do. He had arrived at the conviction that man cannot find fulfillment except through society. But he had not lost the individual in the mass...."

Insofar as society existed at all for Dreiser, however, it was as impossibly visionary as any imagined by Thoreau. Thoreau's most ecstatic image of "society" comes at the end of *Walden*. It is of men individually disjointed so that they might then join—a nose here, a liver there—in a formative process which is the ex-crementitious flow of Nature, from which emerges "the world and me." Emerson and Thoreau do share with Dreiser a concept of "individuality." But "individuality" for them is quite unrecognizable in Matthiessen's or in the ordinary use of the term. In their works, "individuality" does of course refer to non-conformism, social protest, and a sense of human destiny not satisfied by the opportunities available within the structure of society. Self-affirmation of this sort is only a prelude, however, to a quite different, altogether more "eccentric" kind of individuality wherein Dreiser, Emerson, and Thoreau begin to show important affinities. This is the "individuality" achieved by the surrender of those features which define the individual as a social or psychological entity. "Individuality" becomes indistinguishable, from a social point of view—the point of view of most novelists, let us say—from anonymity. What happens to a man's body or his voice in the Over-Soul or within the movements of Thoreau's Nature is scarcely distinguishable from what happens to him when, in Dreiser, he is "being lived by something which needs not only him but billions like him in order to express itself."

The horror of this formulation ("billions like him") is alleviated only in part by the fact that the "something" to which Dreiser refers is so vague as to be politically harmless, "something" half cosmic, half socialistic. The notion of individuality operative in his works does have a political career and, I would suspect, a predictable one. The fact that Dreiser's Emersonianism had to locate itself in spaces actually filled not by the spirit of Nature but by the spirit of the City, the spirit of the mass yearning for what finance capitalism promised to give it, partly explains his decision to join the Communist Party as a symbolic act of what he liked to think of as "international" solidarity. One reason his novels are of interest now, I think, is for the speculation they excite about the possible connections between his kind of literary imagination (what Lionel Trilling has called the liberal imagination) and political inclinations to the Left, much as in the very different imaginations of Eliot, Pound, or Wyndham Lewis we catch their leanings—or fallings—in the opposite political direction. I am not talking about the political bases for the critical reception of Dreiser, but about the political analogues to the very way in which his novels project reality. Not surprisingly, Dreiser is seldom even considered a "modern" writer he had no interest in individual consciousness, in personal complexity, in those traditional and communal feelings which, according to the pseudo-medical testimony of certain people, run in their blood streams. He had no truck with personal, cultural, or literary "organicism," no concern, finally, even with the absence of an "organic society." These are among the *raison d'être* for the stylistic difficulties of "modern" literature and for the corresponding development of these formal criteria which have dissuaded readers from looking enough at Dreiser to see that he belongs in the strongest tradition of American literature and that in his blatant strangeness he redefines some filaments of that tradition for us.

That creative and shaping force which earlier American writers found in Nature or in the composite man called the Poet is located by Dreiser in the objects that fill what were the free spaces of America. Encoded for him in the artifacts we have produced is not the power of individual men—who, after all, *did* build or even dream the skyline of New York?—but of what Dreiser calls "mass ideals." "I wish to make it perfectly clear," he writes in "The Essential Tragedy of Life," "that I am by no means confusing the race with the individual, or vice versa. What a race may do, and what man may, are two very different things. The race, representing the totality of active creations and pushed on by dynamic forces from below, may be, and in so far as one can guess is, a huge success." Dreiser's cataloguing of the visible evidences of this "dynamic force" is in a voice that continually loses its individual authority, and I in no way intend this as a criticism. Like other admirers of Dreiser, I am compelled by the very fluctuations and unsteadiness of his voice, revealing as it does the extraordinary degree to which he can be intimidated by the Things he describes, even by the banalities of conversation he reports: "There is a world of accumulated feeling back of the trite dramatic expression," he assures us. Anything for Dreiser, a skyscraper or a shop window, is part of the hieroglyph of "the race." It is nagging to ask that in the face of this there should be in his style anything like a firmly consistent individual presence.

Concluding this book with Dreiser, there is of course a temptation to find in him some culmination of the issues I have raised about self and environment or to treat him as a historical-literary link between the nineteenth and twentieth centuries. But in its emphasis on the dialectical struggle over these issues in the style of individual works and on the similarities proposed between writers separated by more than a century, as are Emerson and Fitzgerald, this book has denied itself the benefits of culmination or prediction. We can look forward from the Dreiser who in *Sister Carrie* hears "The voice of the so-called inanimate!" to the comic-apocalyptic writers of the present decade, where, as in the works of Thomas Pynchon, human beings drift into the category of the inanimate. But having done so, we are cheated of progression by reminders from R. W. B. Lewis that we can look back from them to Melville. Melville's Ishmael also finds the essence of man buried under accumulations of history, and he takes a quite darker view than does Dreiser of what this accumulation tells us about the race:

> Winding far down from within the very heart of this spiked Hotel de Cluny where we here stand—however grand and wonderful, now quit it;—and take your way, ye nobler, sadder souls, to those vast Roman halls of Thermes; where far beneath the fantastic towers of man's upper earth, his root of grandeur, his whole awful essence sits in bearded state; an antique buried beneath antiquities, and throned on torsoes! So with a broken throne, the great gods mock that captive king; so like a Caryatid, he patient sits, upholding on his frozen brow the piled entabulatures of ages. Wind ye down there, ye prouder, sadder souls!

As Charles Feidelson points out, the passage suggests that the lost potentialities of man are smothered under accretions of the ages, under what Melville calls, in an image Dreiser himself might have used, "the fantastic towers of man's upper earth." Radically unlike one another as they are, *Moby-Dick* and the works of Dreiser are in some sense about their own voracious accumulations of material, about, in Melville's case, a vast allusiveness to the literary, technological, philosphical authorities that cripple the free articulation of individual consciousness. Of *Moby-Dick* the book as of Moby-Dick the whale, Ahab might cry that it "heaps me."

It may be that as a historical and scientific development the power evoked by Dreiser and described by Henry Adams now feeds at an accelerated rate on its own creations. It may be, too, that human consciousness, failing to develop at a pace with the technology it has created, is to be reduced to the muteness of Dreiser's characters or to the monomania of Melville's. But American literature chose to confront this horror, in Cooper's *The Crater* as well as in *Moby-Dick*, before history verified it. And it continues to confront it after the verifications. These more recent confrontations are if anything less grim than the earlier ones. In Faulkner and Fitzgerald, in Nabokov and Mailer is a resurgence of the Emersonian dream of possibly "building" a world out of the self in a style that is that self. The effort in *Lolita* to preserve an "intangible island of entranced time" succeeds no more than did the efforts in *The Crater*, over a hundred years before, to preserve an island paradise from the contaminations of modern democratic America. But such efforts are celebrated by these and by the other American writers perhaps because success *is* forbidden them by realities other than style, by exigencies of time and space. The effort is celebrated because even out of the perverse design of Nabokov's hero there emerges those marvels of human ingenuity, those exuberances of imagination, those extravagances of yearning that create the objects they yearn for—these are the evidences still in American literature of the continuing struggle of consciousness toward some further created being and some other world.

ANN DOUGLAS

# Studs Lonigan and the Failure of History in Mass Society: A Study in Claustrophobia

James Farrell's novel *Studs Lonigan* (1932–1935), the story of the short, doomed life of an Irish Catholic boy in Chicago's South Side, is usually hailed as a masterpiece. Less fairly, it is often regarded as Farrell's only major work. It is striking that Farrell's critical popularity, confined to the 1930s, did not match, nor begin to cover, his achievement. The conventional argument goes that Farrell has written voluminously and in vain since *Studs* was completed in 1935.[1] It seems hard to deny that Farrell has used overproduction as a substitute for adequate support, that writing itself became almost the sole means of fueling his motivation to write, and that this situation, for a writer as politically oriented as Farrell, was not entirely healthy. But, contrary to received opinion, Farrell has written many important and compelling works since *Studs Lonigan*: innumerable short stories, the Danny O'Neill pentalogy, the *Bernard Clare* trilogy, shorter novels like *This Man and This Woman*, and a handful of critical essays striking in their demand for and recognition of honesty in art.[2]

Perhaps the central reason for Farrell's neglect is that he has confronted a problem modern America has determined to evade: our sense of history predicates a vision of Anglo-Saxon progress and expansion which our intellect no longer supports. Unlike most of his contemporaries, Farrell does not veil this dilemma. His lack of "ambiguity," in the sense that Henry James demonstrated and Lionel Trilling explicated the term ("ambiguity" is

From *American Quarterly* 29, no. 5 (Winter 1977). © 1977 by the Trustees of the University of Pennsylvania.

125

quite different from the sense of "mystery" Farrell rightly claims as characteristic of *Studs* and his other books),[3] is essential here. "Ambiguity" is more closely related to our experience of ourselves in history than might at first be apparent. Criticism itself, with its leisured origins, is a form of intellectual activism implicated in an a historical consumer culture. A central concept of the last decades of criticism, "ambiguity" provides both an acknowledgement of the difficulties of interpretation and a complex obfuscation of the possibility of conflict and the need of change. "Ambiguity" marks the vestiges of the process of struggle best defined by the dialectical consciousness; "ambiguity" depends, among other things, on nostalgia for this consciousness.

Farrell's work begins with his admission that our sense of historical mission, our destiny of significant resolvable struggle, is failing, but this admission does not then transmute itself into a richly textured literary sensibility: admission instead becomes a dramatized insistence. In several senses, Farrell does not know how to change the subject. His unpopularity is in part due to his belief that "ambiguity" cannot long be the mainstay of a major literature. Literary critics, like other people, prefer to ignore work that eludes their means of analysis rather than develop new methodologies. Farrell needs less to be interpreted than experienced and confronted. Unlike most major authors since Henry James, although Farrell deserves critical attention, his work is not by definition involved with it; his fiction does not exhibit what I would call criticism-dependency.[4]

Farrell's prestige, then, coincided less with his merits than with a special set of circumstances operative in the 1930s. The Depression gave Americans their first intimation of the complexity and possible termination of their historical purpose, a suspicion that they inhabited a world unyielding to their intentions and conceptions. No twentieth-century author has understood and articulated this American fear better than Farrell. He once astutely described *Studs Lonigan* as "the aftermath in a dream of the frontier days";[5] Studs is a terrifying accretion of contracting possibilities. The titles, as well as the subject, of Farrell's more recent works—"The Vast Present," *The Silence of History* (1963), *What Time Collects* (1964), *Lonely For the Future* (1974), all part of a cycle called "A Universe of Time"—suggest his ongoing concern with the breakdown of our historical conceptions. History itself has always been the chief character of the American novel. Even in Faulkner's doomed world, the most tragic and vicious personages are partially redeemed by the simple fact that an historical process, the decay of the South, is working itself out through them. History does not cohere sufficiently in Farrell's fiction to provide myths available to his readers or his characters.

Bernard Clare, the writer-hero of a trilogy Farrell wrote in the 1940s and 1950s, leaves the working class district of Chicago in which he grew up to look for a "biography" in New York City. Clare knows he is "trying to make history of myself"; "Bernard Biography" he jestingly labels himself.[6] His effort is not successful. The intermittent need to experience our lives as though they were coincidental with history is never satisfied in Farrell's fictive world.

From the late 1920s, Farrell was aware that a kind of narcissistically self-involved image, fostered and shaped by the mass media, was doing the work of more objective criteria in determining the sense of status and self in lower- and middle-class Americans. Farrell dramatized in *Studs* that mass culture was the indispensable agent and analogue of our vanishing historical consciousness and that, in protecting people from the pain of historical awareness, it also deprived them of experience and of history itself.

In two essays on Hollywood published in 1944, Farrell made explicit his quarrels with American mass culture as manifested in popular movies of the day. Farrell begins by running through what by 1944 had become among intellectuals the standard objections to the film. Hollywood, he argued, with its packaged star system and formula pictures, is the archetype of capitalist production. Mass art, unlike genuine art which is often "painful, disturbing, difficult," can be quickly and heedlessly consumed by its devotees.[7] The movies, with their thematic fixation on the leisured class and the products of leisure, are a form of consumer-oriented self-advancement. Farrell grows more provocative as he deals with the movies' distortion of history. His particular target is a movie about Woodrow Wilson entitled *Wilson* which he wittily insists might better be called "History is Just an Old Time Song."[8] Farrell claims that history is presented in such so-called historical films not as a series of problems and actions, but rather as a gallery of dated artifacts to be nostalgically repossessed by the viewers: "Old time songs, styles in clothing, the design of vehicles are the most familiar means of registering the passing of time.... Time thus passes in most films as if it were without depth."[9] Mass culture makes time an object of consumption; history becomes as stagnant as an amusement park. Mass culture creates a totally self-referential world to replace the increasingly complicated historical one. In this world, while outmoded objects are incessantly being replaced by "updated" models, nothing is ever finally disposed of: everything is collected rather than comprehended. And, if nothing is disposed of, time clogs, "history" does not happen.

The 1930s represent the only decade in our history dedicated to some conscientious if minimal exploration of the meaning of the possible failure of our historical identity. Radicals and conservatives (or "humanists" as they called themselves),[10] surveying the debacle of the late 1920s and early 1930s in America, shared two convictions despite their fundamental differences. Both believed, as Farrell noted,[11] that any remedy for the crisis of American capitalism must be self-consciously "collective." They came to this belief not only through their disillusion with the individualism of the 1920s, but also through their less conscious intuition that "collective" society was the antidote to even the healthy version of the "mass" society which they denounced. Michael Gold, the Jewish editor of the left-wing New York-based magazine *The New Masses*, might attack the followers of that "literary snob," T.S. Eliot,[12] expatriate Anglican editor of the *Criterion*, but Gold's Utopia involved the cure of mass addiction to low-grade radio and movie fare as surely as Eliot's did. Both groups also agreed that a sense of historical motion could paradoxically be preserved only by a process of dislocation which had to be accepted by faith rather than by reason.

Eliot felt that the only viable future for America lay in the past, and in the English rather than in the American past.[13] The collective entity which fired his imagination was that represented by the Anglo-Catholic church; its rituals, Eliot believed, had once done for the people adequately the work mass culture with its fascist potential was now insanely mismanaging. Religion and its notions of cyclical reoccurrence had provided in the past, and still might provide, a refuge from history more substantial than escapism. Gold, and those who agreed with him, believed that America's future lay in Stalinist Russia; the U.S.S.R. should serve as a model for those Americans eager to regenerate their country. Class-consciousness alone, not obsolete ceremonies, could replace mass culture. If England was Eliot's ideal, the Soviet Union was Gold's. Gold disdained Eliot who called for a great leap backwards, but he himself was not asking for a great leap forward so much as an enormous step sideways; both Eliot and Gold implicitly demanded of America a willed self-repositioning in the historical sequence.

Farrell eventually found both platforms, humanist and communist, untenable, but he started, and continued, with his sympathies on the left.[14] It was the left he fought with, not the right; if he quarrelled incessantly with the radicals, he barely spoke with the conservatives: His fiction everywhere testifies to his perception that the traditionalism urged by the humanists was bankrupt; people milk their personal past for nostalgic purposes; they don't return to their collective history for political solutions. Patrick Lonigan, Studs' middle-aged Irish Catholic father, fantasizes often about the proverbial "good old days" when he was young; he muses over his parents' lives; he gives no thought, however, to the institutions which governed his progenitors' existence. He perceives the Catholic church simply as it expands or diminishes his personal sphere of opportunity. If blacks join his church, that's bad; if Father Moylan, a noted Catholic priest (modelled by Farrell on Father Coughlin) attacks Jews on his radio program, that's good. There is no evidence that Farrell intended his portrait of the Catholic church in *Studs Lonigan* (or in the Danny O'Neill and Bernard Clare books) to serve as a rebuttal to humanist aspirations for the church, but nothing in fact serves better. The Catholic church as Farrell presents it is already dominant in many Americans' lives; but with its waxen, mass-produced madonnas and its priests dedicated to the extremes of boosterism, it has become an ally, not an opponent, of mass culture. At best, Studs' parents and their friends go to church in much the same spirit Studs and his gang go to the movies, to have their prejudices reinforced and their discontent siphoned off in fantasy.

The logic of *Studs* is almost as destructive, however, to radical programs as to humanist ones. Every page of *Studs* demonstrates the impossibility that any significant number of Americans will look to foreign models for their future. Hatred of foreigners (not, of course, simply the foreign-born, but all those who aren't "us") characterizes everyone but Danny O'Neill and a few emigré radicals in *Studs*; and Danny and the emigrés are all expelled by one means or another from the Irish-Catholic Chicago community Farrell describes. In the first two parts of *Studs*, Farrell lets us into the consciousness of foreign or foreign-sympathizing characters. Such excursions are absent from *Judgment Day*, the last volume of the trilogy. It is the self-willed destiny of Studs' society that it will end by talking only to itself, whatever the cost. Studs is at his most pathetic at the start of *Judgment Day*; in bad health and low spirits, he is returning to Chicago by train from the country and a friend's funeral, and he thinks "how glad he was that he lived in a big city like Chicago" (466).[15] Farrell's city, unlike Dreiser's, never functions as a metropolis; it is a collection of warring provinces, a conglomerate of uncongenial, if similar, suburbs. There is no hope for internationalism or political sophistication in Studs' South Side. Ethnic prejudice comprises the very identity of Studs and his neighbors; because they don't know who they are, they cling to their pride in what they are not. The logic by which one arrives at a scapegoat is the only logic they are acquainted with; "niggers" are ruining their community, "Jews" and "reds" their prosperity. Ethnic insularity does not so much check class-consciousness as replace it.[16]

Farrell's book destroyed current radical programs; yet, through its peculiar kind of literary achievement as well as its chosen subject, *Studs* is sympathetic to a radical social critique. Farrell never condescends to his characters. His style, while more powerful and various than many critics have realized, is based on a principle of non-interference with his subject matter; *Studs* is superior to the world it describes precisely because it refuses at any given moment to be demonstrably better than that world. The novel's structure depends on Farrell's determination to reorder but not to omit any aspect of his material. We see Studs' world finally from Farrell's perspective, but we see all of it. Farrell's art is his commitment to integrity. At his worst Farrell is verbose but never distracted. It is shameful, terrifying, and finally intolerable to Farrell that large masses of Americans are living and dying as he shows us: ignorant, afraid, useless, incapable of thought.[17] These people's lives don't matter in any traditional sense available to the author or reader. If history is more than the passing of time and the recycling of matter, if its recognition involves an achieved personal sense of connection with forces larger than oneself, then these people have no history. Yet the extraordinary quality of *Studs*, as of much of Farrell's work, derives from his implicit insistence that these people's lives should matter; his characters should have a sense of "history."

A great deal has been made of Farrell's involvement with sociological theory and its visible effect on *Studs Lonigan*.[18] No one could deny that sociology—which one might define loosely as the examination of the status, interaction, and environment of social groups partially detached from the full context of circumstance—helped to form Farrell's literary technique. Yet it is less true to say that Farrell wrote sociological fiction than to say that he wrote about people so enmeshed and entrapped in the static stereotypes of their culture that their lives *are* sociology; they are not historical creatures. Sociology, in other words, is less Farrell's technique in *Studs Lonigan* than a kind of operative metaphor for the impoverished quality of middle- and lower-middle class existence in urban America. As I shall try to show, Studs himself has no language and no experience, whether societal, personal, or physical, which he can genuinely call his own.

*Studs*, despite its third person voice, is largely a stream-of-consciousness narrative with obvious and acknowledged affinities to James Joyce's work. The book opens with a description of Studs Lonigan's thoughts as he stands before the mirror in the bathroom on the night of his graduation from St. Patrick's grammar school:

> Studs Lonigan, on the verge of fifteen, and wearing his first suit
> of long trousers, stood in the bathroom with a Sweet Caporal
> pasted in his mug. His hands were jammed in his trouser pockets,

and he sneered. He puffed, drew the fag out of his mouth, inhaled, and said to himself:

Well, I'm kissing the old dump good-bye tonight.... He took another drag and repeated to himself:

Well, I'm kissing the old dump good-bye.(11)

There are a number of points to notice about Farrell's stream-of-consciousness technique as he uses it here and elsewhere. There is a confusion in Studs' mind (and presumably in his culture) between public and private exposure, a confusion so radical as to alter the very nature of the technique. "Said to himself" are the crucial words in the monologue just quoted. Studs is alone, but his solitude means simply that he is in rehearsal for a fantasied on-stage performance. His inner life is not a refuge from his outer life, nor even a complex counterpoint to it. In *Studs Lonigan*, consciousness itself has been demythologized, demystified, as it was not in Joyce's work. Stephen Daedalus' consciousness, like Leopold Bloom's, or Molly Bloom's for that matter, however complex, tortured, and confused it may occasionally be, operates like an internalized free university; any perception is theoretically allowed and possible. In contrast, Studs' mind has no free play at all; it is a collage of accepted clichés which Studs tries to correlate to his stunted psychic needs. Studs' consciousness is the reader's subject, never his or her guide. Studs never forms the material around him into perceptions, much less ideas. In a very real way, Studs has no inner life. His thought patterns could be said to constitute an external stream-of-consciousness.

A comparison between Farrell's technique in *Studs Lonigan* and Hemingway's in *The Sun Also Rises* (1926) may further elucidate my point. Hemingway, like Farrell and unlike Joyce, uses a narrative posture which apparently denies the full resources of consciousness. Yet Hemingway's assumptions, whatever their manifestations, are closer to Joyce's than to Farrell's. Hemingway's novel begins:

Robert Cohn was once middleweight boxing champion of Princeton. Do not think that I am very much impressed by that as a boxing title, but it meant a lot to Cohn. He cared nothing for boxing, in fact he disliked it, but he learned it painfully and thoroughly to counteract the feeling of inferiority and shyness he had felt in being treated as a Jew at Princeton.[19]

In *The Sun Also Rises*, the first person narrator frequently sounds like a third person. The "I" in the opening passage could be an authorial "I": the reader does not feel a pressing need for this voice to distinguish, explain, and personalize itself. As the story progresses, however, we realize that this impersonality is the mark of the narrator, the journalist Jake Barnes. The important point here is that the suppression of the ego felt in the opening sentences is a deliberate act for Jake as it is for Lady Brett or Bill. The main characters with the exception of Cohn, have chosen to repress themselves, and it is this choice which makes them Hemingway "heroes" and "heroines." Their choice is of course neither arbitrary nor totally voluntary. It is the brutal tragic history of war and the waste attendant on it which has made screening imperative; the past is dictating the terms of perception and articulation to the present. Yet the choice, no matter how limited, perhaps *because* it is so limited, is real. The power to select is a form of grace in Hemingway's world—Jake has it, Cohn does not; it is not a power formed by the scene from which the character selects, but one which precedes it. In other words, the Hemingway hero's sensibility is still elite.

Studs' monologues throughout *Studs Lonigan* reflect the loss of such epistemological mastery. Studs is an individual, and a real one; he is "there" as few characters in literature are "there," as we know our own selves to be "there." Farrell never lets us lose touch with the longing for self-fulfillment which animates Studs and which is our test of a unique human being. Studs' tragedy, hardly an unshared one Farrell implies, is that he is an individual who needs to be and feel himself, yet who has nothing but a cross-section of the mass mind to achieve that goal. Even when he is dying, his mind is filled with disjointed authoritarian images borrowed from his culture. He imagines that George Washington appears and shouts, "Your country right or wrong, but your country, my boy, jazz her." The Pope demands, "Do you receive the sacraments regularly?" (764). Living or dying, Studs' thoughts are prejudices, his feelings are escapist fantasies. Studs, not Jake Barnes, is the mutilated character.

The special quality of Studs' consciousness can be defined by a second comparison which Farrell calls to our attention. At one point in the final volume of the trilogy, Studs, pushing thirty, sees a gangster movie called *Doomed Victory*. He has gone to movies often in the preceding years; as his life gets less satisfying and comprehensive to him, he seems to go to movies with greater frequency, just as he listens to the radio more and is more nagged by what he hears there. What power of resistance his mind has to mass culture decreases as time goes on. Watching *Doomed Victory* Studs is absorbed; he identifies with the "tough" hero, Joey Gallagher, as he has never identified with a movie hero before: "he knew he was going to like this picture. It was going to be more like his own life than almost any picture he'd ever seen" (507). When Gallagher is shot at the end, Studs is disturbed: "Dead. Like a part of himself dying" (514).

We are told the plot of the film in detail. Whether intentionally or otherwise, Farrell made *Doomed Victory* an amalgam of the three most popular gangster films of the early thirties: Mervyn LeRoy's *Little Caesar* (1930), William Wellman's *Public Enemy* (1931), and Howard Hawks' *Scarface* (1932). The hero's character, however, seems modelled on that of Tommy Powers, the immigrant-gunboy James Cagney portrays in *Public Enemy*. Gallagher, like Powers, hangs around saloons in his youth; he too has a brother who is trying to make his way by honest work and whom he, like Tommy, considers a "sap" (508). Both characters have mothers whom they love and who love them but who will not accept their ill-gotten money. Both treat women brutally; Joey kicks one of his girls while Tommy grinds a grapefruit in the face of a young woman who has become a pest. The comparison can be summed up by saying that Gallagher is a Cagney hero, and Cagney was the archetypal gangster actor of the early 1930s.

This identification between Cagney and Studs is only partial—Studs is no hoodlum. Yet he dreams he would like to be one. Other observers have felt the vital link between the two. The choreographer Lincoln Kirstein, intent on creating American dance forms in the 1930s, was impressed with Cagney, originally trained in the song and dance routines of vaudeville. Kirstein believed Cagney's motions were the starting place for indigenous American dance, and he considered doing a Cagney-like interpretation of *Studs Lonigan*.[20] What is the ideal represented by the Cagney-gangster figure which so drew Kirstein, and Studs? The gangster is of course "tough," the word which Studs uses in the first part of his story to describe his self-image. The gangster's toughness, however, unlike that of the Hemingway hero also renowned for the same quality, is less a matter of suppression than of condensation. The Cagney hero always has a series of repetitive gestures or phrases (the faked little punch in *Public Enemy*, the phrase "Whadda ya hear? Whadda you say?"[21] in Michael Curtiz's *Angels With Dirty Faces* [1938]) on which he has taken out a patent. He cannot think or act in ways that are alternative to his environment, but he can adapt certain common mannerisms into a trademark. As Farrell's hypothetical title *Doomed Victory* suggests, the Cagney gangster achieves a temporary mastery over what has the final mastery over him: this is what constitutes his undeniable "class." His quick motions and fast remarks are a way of choreographing environment; he is still a puppet, but a dancing one. He is the glamorized apotheosis of what I have called external stream-of-consciousness.

Unlike the Hemingway hero, who would dominate American films in the next decade through the presence of Humphrey Bogart, the Cagney-gangster moves only in response to what is outside him. He mimics and mocks the world, and the world must have the last word in his life. The Hemingway-Bogart hero can be left alive, whatever his crimes; his inner life, which is not only real but ultimately inescapable, will punish him. The world is the Cagney gangster's inner life, and hence it must destroy him. After seeing *Doomed Victory*, Studs leaves the theatre depressed and disturbed by Gallagher's death: "Why couldn't it have ended differently? They didn't have to kill off Joey Gallagher. He was gloomy" (514). Gallagher's death, as Studs senses, foreshadows his own, not because he will be shot down in the streets, but because he too has no private resources. What is at work here in Cagney's style and in Studs' is not tragedy in any classic sense. There is no development; there is a system of check-counter-check. Studs and Cagney have no resources to comprehend and conquer their environment that it did not provide. Events and emotions are recyclings, not real happenings; in a world where protest is created out of the same stuff as what is protested, conformity is inevitable.

The language, verbal and physical, which the characters of *Studs Lonigan* use reinforces this picture of a closed, self-cancelling world. The book is in part a contest between two languages, neither of which expresses its users. As the story opens, the Lonigan family is eating supper before going to Studs' graduation. In a display of sibling sniping characteristic of American middle-class family life in Farrell's fiction, Studs tells his sister Frances to "go to hell." She responds indignantly: "'Why William Lonigan! Father, did you hear him insult me, swear at me, like I was one of those roughnecks from Fifty-eighth street I sometimes see him with.'" His father tells him to use "gentlemanly language." Studs replies, "'Aw heck, she's always blowing off her bazoo.'" Now Mrs. Lonigan chimes in: "'William, I wish that you wouldn't use such language. After receiving such a fine education ... I'm shocked'" (26–27). Studs' slang is a form of urban shorthand; his family tries to use a system of genteel ciphers. His mother and sisters, all three upwardly mobile in unattractive ways, call him "William"; the name "Studs" itself is a tacit declaration of war. Yet Farrell expects the reader to observe, not to arbitrate this linguistic contest: there is nothing to choose between the two modes of speech because they both exist only in response to one another. Mrs. Lonigan's and Frances' language isn't language; it's censorship. Studs' words are nothing but defiance of censorship, a defiance which in its repetitiveness acknowledges the supremacy of its opponent.

The barrenness of Studs' language is revealed by the fact that when he talks with those who talk as he does, the other members of his "gang," he has nothing to say. Much of what matters to him most, the beauty of the park, the tenderness he sometimes feels for girls and his own softer feelings, he labels "goofy" and refuses to talk about. His tough idiom seals him off. It is striking that Farrell puts a good deal of the conversation among the gang members into indirect discourse. Here is an example from the first book:

> Vinc said he had made a mistake. He didn't have any money. They ragged him. Weary sneered, grabbed Vinc's arm and told the group to frisk him. Studs grabbed Phil, and the gang got six bits out of the two of them.... Weary told some new dirty jokes. Paulie Haggerty then asked Weary about school, but Weary said the hell with it.... He said the family had taken him back home, and wouldn't make him do what he didn't want to (136).

This form of reporting flattens communication; the speakers are isolated, their words uncollated with motive or response. Like Studs with his family, they are trafficking in borrowed self-images, not talking.

The problem, constantly reiterated in *Studs Lonigan*, of how to talk to women and how to interpret in turn what they say is another instance of the inevitable failure of communication in the lower-middle-class world Farrell depicts. From adolescence on, Studs is confused about sex. At fourteen, Studs has a girlfriend, Lucy Scanlon. Lucy talks and thinks like Studs' sisters, whom he supposedly despises. One magical afternoon Studs and Lucy are sitting together in the park. Their happy mood is almost dispersed, however. Studs distances and antagonizes Lucy because he tells her his "goofy" thoughts about the breeze feeling like a pretty girl stroking silk (whenever Studs is happy, he instinctively uses metaphors); and, more important, because he takes her coyness at face value. Lucy wants him to be sexually demanding although she can't say so.

Weary Reilly, Studs' rival for preeminence in the gang, in contrast, attacks his girl, Helen Borax, during a game of post office despite all Helen's disavowals of sexual interest:

> He forced her to the bed.
> 'Stop touching me there, Stop!' she whispered.
> When he paused, breathless, she demanded an apology.
> 'Shut up!' he muttered.
> He bent down and kissed her.

'Unhand me, you cur. Take your hands off!' she whispered.
'Take your hands off or I'll scream!'
He pulled her to him and kissed her. She became limp in his
   arms....
She flung herself around him. Then he walked out (52).

There is humor of a bitter variety here. Helen "whispers" that she'll "scream." The best bred of the girls in Studs' neighborhood, she uses the language of an upper-class screen heroine while she behaves as she probably believes only a tramp would act. Weary has assumed here as he does elsewhere that the "niceness" middle-class girls in his world are socialized into peddling—their continuous protestations of purity, their delighted horror at masculine aggressiveness in any of its forms—is a pretense. With Helen Borax, he is vindicated.

Fifteen years after his encounter with Helen, however, Weary takes a young girl to a New Year's Party. In assuming that her fear of sex is a facade, he makes a terrible mistake. Despite the fact that she automatically dances in a provocative way with Weary, "Blondie" is a virgin, afraid of sex, and terrified of violation. In trying to defend the calling-the-bluff routine which constitutes his only act of perception, Weary must rape, beat, and nearly kill her. Weary is right that girls mouth platitudes even if they don't mean them; what he doesn't understand is that, by the paradox inherent in routinized culture, even if they *do* mean those platitudes, they still have to use them. They possess no language by which they can convey sincerity. At one point Studs and a friend called Paullie discuss the reasons that all girls, well-bred or otherwise, "wriggle when they walk"; they "had to," the two young commentators conclude (129). In other words, no matter how they feel, girls should move dirty and talk clean. They, like Studs, must project and meet stereotypic conceptions even if those conceptions don't express their feelings or are in themselves conflicting. Their "thoughts" are other peoples' thoughts; they too represent the external stream-of-consciousness.

It is symptomatic of Studs' nature and plight that he would take women, at least those in his social group, at their word. Studs, for all his vaunted toughness, is what we call a "nice guy." Late in the book, when he first sleeps with Catharine, the girl he is engaged to at his death, he imagines himself boasting to the group about "copping her cherry." It is typical of Studs that when he is next with his pals, some other guy is vaunting his sexual prowess (666); Studs is silent. In Studs' world such decency can only trap him further in the institutions and cliches which purport to convey decency. The fact that he possesses it only makes his entrapment meaningful, wrenching, and inevitable.

Not everyone in Studs' world is as trapped as he is, or in the same way. Farrell gives Studs two alter egos: the hoodlum Weary Reilly and the hard-working, intelligent Danny O'Neill. Both push, although in very different ways, outside the conventions which bind Studs. Weary from the start defies his parents; he has no interest in imagination or intellect; as we have seen, he specializes in treating women with sadistic violence. Weary is the least likeable character in the book; by being all the things Studs thinks he wants to be, Weary makes us aware of how much better Studs is than his self-designated ideal.[22] Studs reaches his nadir at the New Year's Eve party where Weary rapes "Blondie"; he also beats Studs up, thus reversing Studs' great victory over him some fifteen years earlier. It is important to remember, however, that Weary is then arrested (for the rape) and disappears from the book.

Danny O'Neill wins genuine freedom. As a boy, Studs wonders at Danny's ability to play "happy and contented by himself" (87). This autonomy helps Danny to use parochial school to fuel his incentive to reach for the ideas parochial school forbids; it enables him to get to the University of Chicago, to see the world he came from as "lies, lies, lies" (429), and to achieve a better life. Unlike Weary, he understands that the language of the Irish South Side is not so much inverted as meaningless. Danny would become the central figure in Farrell's great pentology, but it is significant that he, like Weary, vanishes from the closing portions of *Studs Lonigan*. Studs' career is not the only possibility for a young man on the South Side in the early decades of the twentieth century, but it is, and this is Farrell's point, typical.

Studs has enough ambition to avoid Weary's course and not enough to glimpse Danny's goals. Like many people, he has that modicum of drive which dictates that he will actually aspire to cultural stereotypes, and achieve nothing of value. Studs' first exchange with Weary in the men's room after the graduation ceremonies at St. Patrick's outlines his tormented middle-of-the-road position. The two boys are discussing a smart but sickly schoolmate:

> 'He's damned smart. Jesus! You know, if he'd a wanted tuh [*sic*] work, he could have had the scholarship to ... any of those schools that hold scholarship exams and give scholarships,' Studs said. 'But what the hell does that mean?' said Weary. 'Nothin,' said Studs (39).

Studs admires brains, but for the wrong reasons; he backs down before Weary without adopting Weary's attitude.

Both Weary and Danny are rebels, though Danny's rebellion is successful and Weary's is not. Studs is a conformist who becomes a stooge. At the start of the book, Studs and his father only imagine that they are in opposition. Despite Mr. Lonigan's disapproval of Studs' wild ways, he remembers, even with pride, similar escapades he pulled off as a young man. Unconsciously, he understands that running around is more likely to be a prelude to bourgeois endeavor than a denial of it. During the Depression, Studs sympathizes with his father's struggle for status. More importantly, both father and son believe the same phenomena are "real" even if they occasionally assign different values to them. Studs instinctively skips over a picture in the paper showing a cop beating a demonstrator; he would rather look at a shot of an attractive blonde. Patrick Lonigan, at the story's close, broken by the Depression, shattered by the imminent death of his favorite son, watches an enthusiastic band of Communist demonstrators; he has only the most fleeting moment of awareness that these people actually believe in what they are doing. Patrick then goes to a bar and gets drunk. It is not surprising that, although the young Studs quits school against his parents' wishes, he soon goes to work for his father, who runs a painting business. His father, in "helping" Studs, predictably co-opts him. At 29, Studs is still living at home. His last words before going to bed with what will prove a fatal case of pneumonia are "Mom, I'm sick. Put me to bed." He has just returned from an unsuccessful day of job-hunting; he has pulled himself up the stairs, and, with these words, he throws "himself weakly into the house" (761). He is back to stay from the tight-leashed excursion which was his life.

Studs has slipped gradually into total conformity, not because society has given him so much, but because it has given him so little so continuously that he can conceive of no alternative to acquiescence. Throughout the novel, Studs is subjected to a series of rituals which cannot accomplish their ostensible purpose. He does not grow up; he is processed. He puts on long trousers for the first time; he graduates from school; he goes to work; he gets engaged; and yet nothing has happened. The climax of these non-events is Studs' indoctrination not long before his death into the Order of Christy, a Catholic society to which his father also belongs. The initiation consists of confusing the new members by a melodrama in which a priest is apparently assaulted and a sick man brutalized by officers of the society. The show concludes with an invitation to the initiates to donate blood to the (supposedly) sick man, an invitation Studs, in a troubled bid for attention and significance, accepts. At this point, the presiding officer explains that the whole disturbance has been fabricated to test the "patience," "courage," "honor," and "charity" of the novices (580). There is no correlation between the scene the Order has created and the moral it tries to extract from it; but this discrepancy doesn't bother Studs or any of the other initiates, all of whom have a marvelous time. The tip-off to the cause of the ceremony's success is provided by Studs' reflection that "it was as exciting as a mystery movie. He'd never been present before when so many exciting things had happened" (375). Yet exactly what has happened? Studs' identity as a member of the audience and as a potential performer before it has been artificially charged and decharged.

There is no content in the forms of life that Studs has been socialized to define as "society"; the church, the family, the gang, none of them has substance. It is not surprising, then, that Studs knows nothing about the rituals which constitute experience. He misses out on the war; he dislikes his work; he never knows love or sexual pleasure. Studs, as a participant in and victim of mass culture, inevitably sees the world in terms not of institutions or even people, but of audiences. Like anyone without a coherent objective or subjective life, he is a creature of moods; indeed, moods might be defined here as the process by which anxiety does the work that ought to be carried out by a more elaborate range of feelings. Studs' moods are based on competitiveness. He incessantly imagines what others are thinking of him: are they admiring, preferably envying him—or scorning him? The principle of comparison is the closest approach he has to an idea. Studs talks to himself, and his dialogue consists of talking himself up or down. He can boost or deflate himself, but he can never evaluate himself. Increasingly, Studs knows that he hasn't gotten what he wanted, that "something [is] missing," that he is a "clown clear through" (649), but he never understands why. There is no rest for him, only failure.

Studs had only one thing going for him: his youth, his health, his body. These had inadvertently given him clues to a sense of freedom, buoyancy and pride altogether alien to his world. Farrell is aware that society can take over the mind more swiftly than the body. Studs could be said to have inherited mental conformity; we have seen that he is unable to express himself. Yet, until he is an adult, his physical life functions in part as an interpreter of lost languages. He loses the knowledge his body gives him; his terror at this loss is less the obsession with youth it seems to us, and to Studs, than the traumatized preoccupation with the period when all the odds were not against him. His physical self had provided his only metaphor for hope.

Each book of the trilogy includes a scene in which Studs goes swimming, and each time Studs is able to find less pleasure in the act. The first time Studs is fourteen and he goes with his friend, Ken, to the lake in the park. Studs is happy; he is in touch with himself, and, by a logical corollary, in touch with a world outside himself:

> They went out further. Only the lake was ahead of them, vast and blue-grey and nice with the sun on it, and it gave them feelings they couldn't describe. Studs floated, and looked up at the round sky…. It was too nice for anything. He just floated and didn't have anything to think about. He looked up at the drifting clouds. He felt just like a cloud (115).

He is at ease; he is moving outward and looking upward; his mind is less blank than blissfully fallow, receptive.

The second swimming episode takes place a decade later. Significantly, it is an indoor scene. Studs and another companion go to the Y pool. At first Studs feels out of breath and strained; he is out of shape from his years of smoking and drinking; but he gradually begins to exult "in a feeling of complete bodily freedom. It was swell" (330). The last episode occurs shortly before his death. He has taken his girl Catharine, who is now pregnant, to the shore. This time he barely notices the sun or the water; he obsessively compares Catharine and himself, usually unfavorably, to other couples on the beach. He is ashamed of her body, dumpy and pasty in her cheap bathing suit; he is ashamed of his own body, pale, small, wasted by his recent bout with pneumonia. When he tries to swim, he has a heart attack. He is pulled to shore; a doctor resuscitates him, and warns him that he must never swim again. The end is near. Out of a job, burdened with responsibilities for which he has no training other than a conventionally programmed expectation that they will one day be his, Studs physically and mentally has become a paradigm of tension.

It is no accident that the disease which kills Studs is a heart ailment. His consciousness narrows to a concentration on his heart: he has become a time-bomb. Time is terrifying because it is potentially divorced from experience; the hours and days notch Studs without enriching or even using him. At one point during the early days of the Depression, Studs and Catharine go to watch a dance marathon. Couples with swollen ankles and faces dark with fatigue cling to each other to stay upright, to respond to the prodding of the master of ceremonies. " 'I wonder when something is going to happen,' " Studs remarks to Catharine. " 'I guess this is what happens,' " she replies (681, 682). The dance marathon becomes a metaphor for Studs' existence; the m.c.

keeps alive that facsimile of hope expressed by stupefied endurance. Studs and Catharine stay for hours, waiting to "see if anything will happen" (693). Time functions as a vigilante on guard against the possibility of significance.

Studs' death, which occurs not long after the evening of the marathon, closes the book. Farrell describes it in brief but painful detail:

> He gasped. There was a rattle in his throat. He turned livid, his eyes dilated widely, became blank, and he went limp. And in the mind of Studs Lonigan, through an all-increasing blackness, streaks of white light filtered weakly and recessively like an electric light slowly going out. And there was nothing in the mind of Studs Lonigan but this feeble streaking of light in an all-encompassing blackness, and then, nothing.... The nurse covered the face of Studs Lonigan with a white sheet (819).

It is rare in the annals of the novel that a controlling consciousness be allowed to die, and to die on stage. Somewhat like Studs and Catharine at the marathon, the reader must confront how much harder it is to face the end of a hopeless enterprise than to witness the demise of a flourishing one. By writing his novel, Farrell has in part redeemed Studs' life, but chiefly as a warning, and one that has no easy juncture with whatever conscious wisdom we use to conduct our lives.

Studs' death testifies to the unwanted, unbearable perception that time passes as surely when experience is repeatedly postponed as when it is possessed. The shock value of the last scene is its cruel but necessary reminder that we can die without having lived, and that, in painful fact, our society has become committed to developing the mechanisms that will insure that we do so. Studs' life was borrowed and it never fit him; his culture maintained rather than sustained him. There are no answers here. That the Communist demonstration which Patrick Lonigan watched took place and gave joy to those who participated in it is important; but it is also important that the parade had no effect on Lonigan. If the marchers constitute history in America, history is a lonely affair. *Studs Lonigan* tells its readers what they must not forget, not what they must do; Farrell's objective is to force and discipline perception. He offers nothing to palliate our terror of space and time, of the failure of history, of the potential collapse of significance itself; he simply brings us face to face with our fear. Farrell warns that, while genuine resources may exist, we will not find them until we explore our induced commitment to the cheapest of palliatives.

## Notes

1. This argument is too conventional to need documentation. For an important recent collection of essays that evaluates this argument, see the James T. Farrell issue of *Twentieth Century Literature*, 22 (Feb. 1976), guest edited by Jack Salzman. This issue will hereafter be referred to as *TCL*.

2. See *The Short Stories of James T. Farrell* (New York: Grosset and Dunlap, 1937); *Judith and Other Stories* (New York: Doubleday, 1973); *A World I Never Made* (New York: Vanguard Press, 1936); *No Star Is Lost* (New York: Vanguard Press, 1938); *Father and Son* (New York: Vanguard Press, 1940); *My Days of Anger* (New York: Vanguard Press, 1943); *The Face of Time* (New York: Vanguard Press, 1953); *Bernard Clare* (New York: Vanguard Press, 1946); *The Road Between* (New York: Vanguard Press, 1949); *Yet Other Waters* (New York: Vanguard Press, 1952); *Gas House McGinty* (New York: World Publishing, 1933); *This Man and This Woman* (New York: Vanguard Press, 1952); *The League of Frightened Philistines and Other Papers* (New York; Vanguard Press, 1945); and *Literature and Morality* (New York: Vanguard Press, 1947).

3. See Dennis Flynn and Jack Salzman, "An Interview with James T. Farrell," *TCL*, 4.

4. I do not make this distinction to slight the works of Henry James, James Joyce, or Thomas Pynchon whose level of difficulty have helped to create modern criticism. I am pointing out that our tradition is one-sided, and that, while it is equipped to elucidate many works, it is less trustworthy in dealing with others that may be equally valuable. Lionel Trilling's praise of James and flat dismissal of Dreiser is an obvious case in point. See "Reality in America," in *The Liberal Imagination* (London: Martin Secburg and Warburg, 1951), 3–21.

5. Farrell to Sherwood Kohn, Dec. 10, 1960, quoted by Edgar M. Branch, "James T. Farrell: Four Decades After *Studs Lonigan*," *TCL*, 34.

6. *Bernard Clare*, 160.

7. *The League of Frightened Philistines*, 175.

8. Ibid., 195.

9. Ibid., 200–07.

10. I am not implying that all conservatives were "humanists," but simply that the humanists held a "conservative" view in comparison with the Marxists.

11. See James T. Farrell, "A Note on Contemporary Letters," *Earth*, 1 (Feb. 1, 1931), 2–5.

12. See Michael Gold, "Wilder: Prophet of the Genteel Christ" in Jack Salzman and Barry Wallenstein, eds., *Years of Protest: A Collection of American Writing in the 1930's* (New York: Pegasus, 1967), 236. For summaries of Gold's position, see Daniel Aaron, *Writers on the Left* (New York: Avon, 1961), passim. See also Joseph North, ed., *New Masses: An Anthology of the Rebel Thirties* (New York: International, 1969); Daniel Aaron and Robert Bendiner, *The Strenuous Decade: A Social and Intellectual Record of the 1930's* (New York: Doubleday, 1970), and Harvey Swados, ed., *The American Writer and the Great Depression* (Indianapolis: Bobbs-Merrill, 1966).

13. See T. S. Eliot, *The Idea of a Christian Society* (New York: Harcourt, Brace, 1940), and Malcolm Cowley's review in *The New Republic*, "Mr. Eliot's Tract for the Times," collected later in Henry Dan Piper, ed., *Think Back on Us: A Contemporary Chronicle of the 1930's* (Carbondale and Edwardsville, Ill.: Southern Illinois Univ. Press, 1967), 174–77.

14 For an account of Farrell's political position during the 1930s, see Alan Maynard Wald, "James T. Farrell: The Revolutionary Socialist Years," Diss. Univ. of California at Berkeley 1974.

15. References to *Studs Lonigan* are to the Signet edition (New York, 1965).

16. On this aspect of Farrell's work, see Barry O'Connell, "The Lost World of James T. Farrell's Short Stories," *TCL*, 36–51.

17. I am paraphrasing here the sentence Gorky used to describe the message of Chekhov's work, a sentence Farrell apparently finds important for his own work: "You live badly, my friends. It is shameful to live like this." See Farrell, "On the Letters of Anton Chekhov" in *The League of Frightened Philistines*, 71.

18. For a summary of the sociological influences and intention in *Studs* see the "Afterword" by Philip Allan Friedman in the Signet edition, 822–30. See also Blanche H. Gelfant, "James T. Farrell: The Ecological Novel" in *The American City Novel* (Norman, Okla.: Univ. of Oklahoma Press, 1954); and Richard Mitchell, "*Studs Lonigan:* A Scientific Novel," *Thoth*, 1 (1959), 35–43.

19. *The Sun Also Rises* (New York: Charles Scribner's Sons, 1926), p. 3.

20. See Lincoln Kirstein, *The New York City Ballet* (New York: Knopf, 1973), 41, and "James Cagney and the American Hero" in Stanley Kauffmann, ed., *American Film Criticism From the Beginnings to Citizen Kane* (New York: Liveright, 1972), 262–64. Please note: I am stressing only one role in Cagney's brilliant repertoire, but one dominant in his early gangster films, and crucial to Studs Lonigan.

21. Cagney took this phrase from a gangster he had known as a boy. See James Cagney, *Cagney by Cagney* (New York: Doubleday, 1976), 73.

22. I disagree with Alfred Kazin's interpretation of Studs Lonigan as an unsympathetic "petty bourgeois skunk" (*Starting Out in the Thirties* [Boston: Little, Brown, 1962], 33); Kazin's belief that Farrell "charged his work with [an] unflagging ... hatred of the characters in them" (*On Native Grounds: An Interpretation of Modern American Prose Literature* [New York: Harcourt, Brace, 1942], 380) is wrong. Farrell has said himself that "Studs is not presented unsympathetically" (Flynn and Salzman, op. cit., 2).

HAROLD KAPLAN

# Naturalist Fiction and Political Allegory

## ABSTRACTIONS OF FORCE—TROPISMS OF NEED

No one discriminates a choice or a motive very clearly in Dreiser's *Sister Carrie*. The characters exhibit, rather, a kind of tropism of need in the midst of a stream of force. Because of this, the novel has a consistency that makes it a classic of American naturalist fiction, a tribute to Dreiser's single-mindedness in reducing human action to simple responses of attraction and repulsion. In the early chapters the theme of force attracting need stands out: Carrie and Drouet meet in the city, and the sex of one and the money of the other are the media of their exchange of power.

The city is itself an overwhelming quantification of power, "a roar of life" that dominates its human agents and objects. Actually, it is the city, with its promise of satisfied desire, that seduces Carrie, and Dreiser describes her responsive wish to "make it prey and subject—the proper penitent, grovelling at a woman's slipper."[1] It is characteristic that desire should be expressed in the language of conquest, yet this is no mere metaphor; for desire in *Sister Carrie* is conceived of as a force among forces that, as such, inevitably tend to pose the issue of surrender or conquest. But this abstraction of force, whether sexual or otherwise, is inseparable from real things, the things that Carrie sees and wants and that the city provides: lights, food, handsome clothes, fine houses. Things are in the foreground of her attention, not people and

From *Power and Order: Henry Adams and the Naturalist Tradition in American Fiction.* © 1981 by The University of Chicago Press.

certainly not her own passions. Her seduction is preceded by a good dinner at a good restaurant, and Drouet's presence is epitomized in the flashing of his gold cuff-links. The scene is intended to support the author's declaration that "man is the victim of forces over which he has no control." Though Carrie is herself a force, certainly as Drouet and Hurstwood know her, and perhaps a central force in the city, she is still a victim:

> She could not realize that she was drifting, until he secured her address. Now she felt that she had yielded something—he, that he had gained a victory.... Already he took control. [*SC* 10]

But no one really has control, as we shall soon see, although the issue of victory and defeat remains alive. This is naturalism in its simplest expression: there is a contest; success and failure are real; but the conscious will, or conscience, is most obvious in its subordination. Carrie's conscience

> was no just and sapient counsellor.... It was only an average little conscience, a thing which represented the world, her past environment, habit, convention, in a confused way. With it, the voice of the people was truly the voice of God. [*SC* 82]

In some instances that voice might be strong, but there is always a stronger:

> She was alone; she was desireful; she was fearful of the whistling wind. The voice of want made answer for her. [*SC* 83]

Want is a strong power; it is located in the human person, but reduction makes it abstract. What is purely human may be "the voice of the people," here rendered as the voice of God, himself a habit and a convention. The interesting result is to assign human force to mental fictions and to move toward nonhuman terms for describing forces with greater potency and a greater claim on reality. The lights of the city have as strong an influence as the light in Drouet's eyes, Dreiser writes. But since we are directly told that Carrie felt only a minimal sexual attraction to Drouet, though "she felt that she liked him," it is plausible to judge that he is only the point of focus for the series of radiating "forces" that meet her in the city. On the very first pages Dreiser sets the terms for Carrie's "fall":

> Half the undoing of the unsophisticated and natural mind is accomplished by forces wholly superhuman. [*SC* 6]

In that sense, the sex drive impelling Drouet must be considered to be as "superhuman" as the power inherent in the crinkly ten-dollar bills he presses on Carrie at a strategic moment.

In this world, things that money can buy speak more eloquently than people, who hardly speak at all. Thus Drouet communicates to Carrie:

> As he cut the meat, his rings almost spoke. His new suit creaked.
> He was a splendid fellow. [*SC* 54]

And yet, with all the respect that goes to suits and rings, and for all the directness of their impact on Carrie, who is indeed attracted to them as by a magnet (the chapter title is "The Magnet Attracting: A Waif amid Forces"), the reader is simultaneously made aware that such things are symbols. Clothes are the signs of sexual value. They are indeed indispensable to it and to status as well, and Dreiser sums up Drouet by saying that good clothes are so essential to his composition that without them he is nothing. For the rest, he owned a strong physical nature—meaning a sexual drive—a love for various pleasures, and "the company of successful men."

Dreiser suggests that the other men in Carrie's life are more complex (the novel plots a curve from simplicity to complexity), but Hurstwood and Ames are hardly better able to transcend Dreiser's abstractions of force and desire. Ames represents Carrie's vague aspirations for something better; he comes from the sphere of education and culture, another frontier for Carrie to cross. Hurstwood, for all the simple power with which he is drawn and the overwhelming sense of social gravity in his fall, is the symbol of worldly poise and the prestige of the businessman's role and relationships. In fact, he is the symbol of nothing more than the idea of success, as he later becomes the symbol of worldly failure.

This rapid movement from the realism of facts, objects, and simple responses to symbolic abstraction is a significant characteristic of traditional naturalist fiction. There is no mystery in this; it is the direct consequence of a theoretical hunger that grows as fast as the mountain of detail heaped up by realist reporting. Things like Carrie's skirt or Drouet's rings are attractive in themselves as objects of desire or need, but they almost immediately become symbols of the power they generate, and *that* is their value.

This naturalist tradition obviously reflects the social symbol-making of a society of producers and consumers. Subordinating other values, things become the signs of the power asserted in gaining them. And so a simple desire or need is translated into a sign of the power needed to satisfy it. This tautological circle may be characteristic of a society given up to "conspicuous consumption," but here the chief point is to note the emphasis it receives in naturalist fiction and the way it is used to elaborate a structure of power values in that fiction.

Such values are allowed to overwhelm or even exclude distinguishing features of character. The discriminated qualities of Carrie as a person are subordinated to the sexual power she generates, first over Drouet, "the creature of an inborn desire" that urged him toward women "as a chief delight." Hurstwood is another helpless "moth of the lamp," who, unable to give up Carrie, sacrifices his established "success" for her. This is a bad tradeoff for him, since he loses what it was that gave him sexual power over Carrie in the first place. One might say that Hurstwood is the victim not so much of poor judgment as of his own insufficient power resources. It is clear that he cannot have Carrie without losing all his property to his wife and probably his job as well. The result is the abortive theft and flight, ending in the loss of his money, his job, his status, and, eventually, Carrie and his life. The drama could be called a specific example of naturalist tragedy, where, instead of an even exchange, one power cancels another, and a sexual force generated by Carrie engulfs and lays waste all the power that Hurstwood could claim as his own.

That power was money, and in simple seriousness Carrie understands that at the start. She holds what Drouet gave her in her hands, "two soft, green, handsome ten-dollar bills.... It was something that was power in itself" (*SC* 57). It was, indeed, "stored energy," a truth that reaches its dismal climax in the scenes describing Hurstwood's decline and fall, where Dreiser seems to count the gradual, almost dollar-by-dollar disappearance of Hurstwood's money. As Hurstwood declines to a physical shadow, losing all interest in Carrie, the accompanying refrain is the absence of money to buy meat or pay the rent. Although Carrie deserts his bed at that point, her action is not given any more emphasis, by either of them, than his failure to pay the rent.

However, once the issue is clearly power—and both sex and money become symbols of power conflict—the naturalist writer has access to dramatic significance and can escape the threat of triviality. The limitations on his resources for depicting character and action remain severe, but human experience can now be made meaningful by the use of at least one, and sometimes all, of three characteristic patterns: the pathos of victimization; abstraction of the characters as agents of a social or a biological force; and melodramatic violence. Violence is of course inevitable in fictional representations of power conflicts, but one of its advantages is the way it can link simplifications of motive to exaggerations of action, exaggerations that are quantitative, not qualitative, in their measure of power. Thus Hurstwood, almost stupid in the commonplace quality of his infatuation, commits a crime, breaking with all his previous life, in order to win Carrie. His eventual decline and suicide are the end products of the slow progression of that violence in his life, a violence buried beneath the problems of paying the rent and buying steak for dinner. Carrie herself is first a victim, then a survivor, and, finally, a winner, but Minna Hooven, in Norris's *The Octopus*, illustrates the latent melodrama in Carrie's sexual career. Minna has the choice of starving on the street or succumbing to prostitution. Her mother, separated from her on the streets of San Francisco, literally does starve to death. The diminished scale of characterization here is counterbalanced by accentuated pathos, by the vivid outline of social forces in action, and, above all, by the sharp impact of violence.

On the other hand, even the most extreme violence arouses a relatively minor response in naturalist characters. Emotions must not be complex or profound, though needs or wants may be drastic compulsions to act. Subjective experience is thus submerged by the imperatives of action, and neoscientific abstractions, whether of poverty or sex, dominate personal response. People are the creatures of natural and social forces. They must be kept from breaking though the thesis that controls them. It is stressed at the beginning that Carrie has a "rudimentary mind," and Norris's McTeague is almost an ape in his exaggerated animal sensibility; the instinctive and conditioned behavior of both is thus made more visible. The work of Dos Passos is characteristically naturalist, for, large and comprehensive as the world he describes may be, it is a world in which human sensibility is absent or is very early aborted.

It should be noted, however, that the emotional and intellectual retardation that characterizes the people of orthodox naturalist fiction serves an ideological point. The stunting of life becomes the ground for moral accusation: the poor can *afford* emotions no more than pleasure. We remember Minnie, Carrie's sister, and her husband Hanson in their dour puritan life of work, forbidding Carrie the chance to go to the theater. And Carrie herself really enjoys nothing so much as her moments as an actress, when she seems to come to life; it is as if both emotional and imaginative experience were restricted to fantasy, to life on the stage. The major effect of this on the reader is to make him sense a generalized repression, a universal poverty, in which all imaginative needs become one. Whether it is nature or society that has dictated this restraint, the weight is sensed as unbearable. One of the most relevant and expressive revolutionary slogans of our time was voiced in May 1968, when the French students wrote on their walls, "All power to the imagination."

To sum up, one can say that a study of literary naturalism leads to a series of paradoxes. A literature devoted ostensibly to the reporting of reality is found to be based on abstraction, allegory, and melodrama. The theme of power is in itself a simplistic abstraction of values. Dreiser accurately makes money its chief symbol. Money is undefined latent power; what you do with it is another matter. At the same time, money is the sign of success, the specialized status of power; and what money will buy provides further, secondary, signs: fine clothes, houses and carriages, the company of successful men and women, all of which, as Dreiser points out, both Hurstwood and Drouet need as much as they need sexual gratification or any other simple want.

More direct and tangible signs of power are communicated in the melodrama of the contest itself, no matter what is won or lost. Every desire or motive, and particularly sex, is faced by a contest, as when Carrie, at her first meeting with Drouet, feels that "she had yielded something, he had gained a victory." This may be petty realism, but the theme of life as a contest leads to greater exaggerations, as in *The Octopus*, in the brutal confrontations between the wheat ranchers and the railroad. Frank Norris was in fact the most melodramatic of naturalists, and he expressed his convictions as follows:

> Terrible things must happen.... They [the characters] must be twisted from the ordinary, wrenched out from the quiet, uneventful round of every-day life, and flung into the throes of a vast and terrible drama that works itself out in unleashed passions, in blood, and in sudden death.[2]

The statement is revealing, since one might suppose that the extraordinary and the grotesque do not embody the truth that naturalism seeks. It tells us, in part, that sensationalism compensates for the dullness of ordinary lives and of weak or incapacitated people. This is a literary need, and melodrama hovers over the pages of every naturalist novel; but this need is reinforced by naturalist thought. Exaggerated violence and victimization can prove a thesis of social conflict or demonstrate a historic truth that might be apocalyptic or redemptive. Marx himself was a "scientist" of the apocalypse, and his habit of combining realistic documentation with melodramatic finalities provides a close analogy with naturalist fiction.

Such marks of the apocalypse are clear traits of naturalist writing, as I shall observe later. The more subtle and paradoxical result of dealing obsessively with ordinary experience is the tendency to allegorize human types behind the mask of realism. Frank Norris again exhibits this trait more visibly than other naturalist writers. His pages are dominated by stereotypes, themselves melodramatic, of the poet, the banker, the western rancher, the man of the soil, the woman of the sexual soil, the miser of money, the miser of power. An example of the stereotype that becomes a caricature is Zerkow, the Jewish miser in Norris's *McTeague*, who achieves a degree of grotesqueness the author could not have intended:

> He was a dry, shrivelled old man of sixty odd. He had the thin, eager, cat-like lips of the covetous; eyes that had grown keen as those of a lynx from long searching amidst muck and debris; and clawlike, prehensile fingers—the fingers of a man who accumulates, but never disburses. It was impossible to look at Zerkow and not know instantly that greed—inordinate, insatiable greed—was the dominant passion of the man.[3]

The obsessively animal metaphor here seems clearly prompted by the need to abstract a force, to locate it in nature, and, at the same time, to pronounce a moral judgment on it. The passage illustrates, in Norris's vein of caricature, an ideological compulsion to focus on the simplest, clearest forces in any zone of conflict.

## Winners and Losers

Hurstwood attracts Carrie because he demonstrates all the signs of a successful man, "reflecting in his personality the ambitions of those who greeted him" (*SC* 150). Even his grace and suavity (which are his best qualities, Carrie notes) emanate from his success. The most impressive thing about him is his vocation as a professional master of ceremonies and greeter of the prosperous patrons of his elegant saloon. He "knew by name ... hundreds of actors, merchants, politicians, and the general run of successful characters about town" (*SC* 41). And, when he falls, in the second half of the novel, it is, in the largest sense, because he has lost his vocation: the function of greeting success and sharing in it.

The strong effect of Dreiser's novel results from his dynamic sense of the curve of fortune, a simple graph of the rise and fall of power. Thus the structure of *Sister Carrie* is based on the closest possible contrast between Carrie's rise and Hurstwood's fall, and human relations are dictated by the accompanying view of life as a contest for success and a struggle for survival. To a large extent, as I have said, the judgment of success is tautological:

success is what succeeds, as when Hurstwood's friends see in him only the reflection of their own ambitions. Dreiser was no doubt viewing the American city realistically when he saw that success there was its own excuse for being, no matter how achieved. But imaginatively, and for his own purposes, Dreiser adopted the success cult of American life by emphasizing its intrinsic force, as if the capacity to succeed were a quality inherent in some people and not in others. In Dreiser, success is not based on a gradual consensus among people. It is not a valuation at all but a force that seizes the judgment of others and compels their submission. When Carrie has her first success on the stage, for instance, the effect on her is described this way:

> She was now experiencing ... that subtle change which removes one out of the ranks of the suppliants into the lines of the dispensers of charity. She was, all in all, exceedingly happy. [SC 165]

With "the independence of success ... with the tables turned, she was looking down, rather than up, to her lover" (SC 161).

This turning of the tables is a motif that unifies Dreiser's story. The men in Carrie's life succeed each other in cycles: as one goes up, the other goes down. Hurstwood supplants Drouet, Ames replaces Hurstwood, each on the basis of some vaguely cited superiority in a competitive struggle. These comparisons of strength apply also to Carrie herself, who eventually is destined to look down from a pinnacle. The men, as they appear in the story, are stronger than she is; she then grows as if by absorbing their strength. This cycle is incomplete at the end, for Ames, the third man in Carrie's life, is defined only by comparisons, such as, "He seemed wiser than Hurstwood, saner and brighter than Drouet" (SC 271). (Comparisons had begun earlier, with simpler values, as when Carrie notes her preference for Hurstwood's soft leather shoes over Drouet's patent leather.) The reader never quite sees *what* is strong or wise or sane in Ames and may conclude that all values are comparative and stand for quantity, not substance, in the strangely abstract world of this naturalist novel.

The success of an actress is of course plausibly based on her ability to magnetize an audience, but it is suggestive that Dreiser limits his description of Carrie's gift to its effect on others. Her talent *is* the power she has over an audience, and it may consist more of chemistry than of art. Dreiser makes an explicitly parallel point about failure in his theory of "katastates," the chemical poisons generated by failure, which create depression and mental and physical deterioration (SC 274). Failure, like success, is a part of animal fate, and the least superstitious view of it is to refer it to biological old age, which Dreiser does to reinforce the more imaginative hypothesis of the chemistry of failure, which he had borrowed from a contemporary experimenter in physiological psychology.[4]

Thus Hurstwood's case illustrates the aging cycle: there is youthful flourishing and old decay, and the balance at middle age—where we find Hurstwood at the beginning of the story—can only tilt downward toward the grave. The cycle, and the sexual rivalry that it includes, is mirrored in the relation between Hurstwood and his wife; his taking of Carrie represents a biological defeat for her, and her bitterness is largely a response to that: "She was fading while he was still preening himself in his elegance and youth" (*SC* 177).

Her straightforward self-defense is to use her power over their money, and the chapter heading for Hurstwood's struggle with his wife, "Flesh Wars with Flesh," is not an exact description; for the mortified flesh of Mrs. Hurstwood takes comfort and revenge from the equally strong power of money, a kind of a variation on the theme of sex negotiating with money in the affair of Carrie and Drouet. This parallel between the sexual contest and the struggle for money must have a deeper source for Dreiser than the commercial culture's equation of everything with money; for when Hurstwood later tries for business success and fails, and fails to find or hold any sort of a job, Dreiser makes it clear that the major reason for this failure is not bad luck or social injustice but an inner failure of power, a deterioration that feeds on itself. It is true that Dreiser adds scenes that report on the marginal life of flophouses and soup kitchens and on a strike and its violence, but these provide only minor accents; they are part of the struggle for existence, though the roots are there for the politics that Dreiser later cultivated.

These reductive images of success and failure, of power as the abstraction behind the abstraction of success, all focus on the basic theme that life is a struggle. When Drouet is about to lose Carrie, he is described as like the emperor of China, unaware that his fairest provinces are being wrested from him. When Carrie begins to feel some alienation from him, the first effect is to make us see him as weak. This is a brief forecast of the more important later process of her being weaned from Hurstwood, where everything that happens accents his deterioration, and his weakness increases to the point where it would seem to the reader a totally ungrounded sacrifice for Carrie to stay with him. Dreiser manages this effect (and avoids any possible moral reproach for Carrie) by citing the decay of every faculty in Hurstwood, including even the capacity to feel hurt by her departure. His state is one of almost catatonic apathy, anticipating his eventual numb suicide.

The suicide scene illustrates the characteristic emotional flatness of naturalist fiction, the result of subordinating response to the movement of forces. For "the forces" do not simply overwhelm the capacity of a human character to define himself against them; rather, they *seem* to oppose themselves to a human interest but are then discovered to be the same as the natural process that determined the character's motive in the first place and then obstructed it. In other words, nature has its fifth column within every human organism. There is no contest in the last resort, as when, in Hurstwood's case, the blows of fate not only crush his strength but undermine his capacity to feel anything at all. The scenes describing his decline are perhaps the strongest in the novel; these are moments when naturalism seems to suggest its tragic possibilities and its authentic relation to biological fate. Perhaps *Sister Carrie* would have achieved tragic significance if Hurstwood had been given a more than rudimentary capacity for either thought or emotion. But how could he be given that when he has been described as a dying limb of life's organism, suffering a sort of self-amputation?

All the forces in Hurstwood's life are thus drawn into a single symbolic force. Dreiser has no interest in separate and opposite traits, as when a character might illustrate failure in one respect and continuing potency in another. Carrie, for instance, stops sleeping with Hurstwood when he manifests his decay of will and strength in his business ventures, but it appears that he himself loses interest in sex at the same time. The principle is illustrated with singular clarity in later fiction in the naturalist, tradition, in the work of Hemingway, for instance, and, with even more emphasis, in that of Henry Miller and Norman Mailer, where competence in sex or in fighting is linked to a generalized potency to be found also in art, sport, politics, and other areas in which power may be sublimated.

This monistic theme of power suggests that a man is on the mark, to be tested by nature, and that he can be utterly condemned or glorified. It is a question of salvation, really, or sometimes resurrection, as in the case of Francis Macomber in Hemingway's most complete parable of normative naturalism. When Hurstwood fails, his failure covers him like an infection, and he begins to look repulsive to Carrie. What she is brought to feel is plausible, and there is no need to question the tough psychological realism of Dreiser's treatment. But its wholesale effect—its lack of modification or struggle, certainly the lack of guilt on one side or even hurt on the other—declares a complete subordination of the human sensibility to the power process. Is this stoic acknowledgment or superstitious respect for natural potency? It is hard to tell, both here and in other naturalist writing; but the latter effect is the stronger one at the end of Dreiser's novel.

An English critic, John Fraser, quotes and endorses a general comment on American movies: "There is no ruling class here, only a Darwinian struggle that divvies up Americans into winners and losers."[5] But the movies here referred to simply reflect something that is widespread in popular writing and conversation, where people are defined as "winners" or "losers," as if branded by a mark on their foreheads. Dreiser's novel shares in this superstition, if only because it is in essence a part of the naturalist myth, with its extraordinary focus on the totalist concept of force. Character does not have several departments of need and gratification, such as family happiness, status, wealth, love, and comfort. All interpenetrate and affect one another, and pleasure cannot exist apart from their possession. Money and sex, particularly, are never separated; the possession of one makes possible the other, and both are linked with status and success.

The point of focus for Dreiser was, obviously, the competition for wealth in a capitalist culture and the assumption that you can buy anything with money and can have nothing without it. However, by the strength of his art, he creates a larger myth of power in which wealth is only the instrument of the struggle for survival and the means for making the most of biological destiny. Its possession is the sign that one has gained and maintained the maximum potency of natural being. Its loss, as well as the loss of sexual power, can mean something metaphysical in the end, as drastic as a doom from heaven.

## PASSIVITY AND VIOLENCE

Carrie, in her first relations with Drouet and Hurstwood, does not choose: she surrenders, they conquer. The passage between Drouet and Carrie implies a sexual contest, but the intention is actually to stress victimization and entrapment, both of which feature the weight of external or environmental "forces." Carrie has a minimal passionate involvement with both men, though Hurstwood has a stronger effect on her imagination. The theme for her action is "she could not resist," and, even when she has feeling, it seems only to mirror the stronger feelings of the men. In retrospect, the reader asks, why should she resist, and, if she does, with what force should she do so? It is made clear that Carrie is affected hardly at all by conventional prohibitions. As for a sense of danger to herself or to her real interests, it is quickly made evident that her life after her seduction is quite comfortable and even enjoyable, a great step beyond factory work and the grim life with her sister.

Resistance seems to be set up as an essential part of the sexual struggle: the woman resists as a matter of nature—almost, it seems, as if to invite male aggression. If she did not resist, she could not subsequently submit, and the male would be deprived of part of his sexual pleasure, which is conquest. This theme is clearest in the writing of Frank Norris, since his view of sexuality is closer to vitalism than Dreiser's, which remains sociologically oriented. In *McTeague* the courtship of Trina is marked by McTeague's animal awkwardness until he blunders into an embrace:

> He had only to take her in his arms, to crush down her struggle
> with his enormous strength, to subdue her, conquer her by sheer
> brute force, and she gave up in an instant. [*Mc* 65]

Nothing quite like this happens in *Sister Carrie*, though as an expression of what might be called the folkways of seduction Carrie offers Hurstwood the passivity the male desires and imposes on women: she is "the victim of his keen eyes, his suave manners, his fine clothes ... answering vaguely, languishing affectionately, and altogether drifting" (*SC* 171). There is pleasure in "drifting," but that sort of submission is not all the emphasis that Dreiser wants. Carrie is finally trapped by the deception with which Hurstwood gets her onto the train to Detroit. And when Hurstwood discloses his lie, as he must when the train gathers distance from Chicago, the possibility of getting off the train is put out of Carrie's mind by the late hour, the rain outside, and by her rather infantile desire to see Montreal and other distant places while she has the chance. Infantile is the right word for this sort of passivity, for submission to external force and deception emphasizes helplessness, fear, and reflexive or dependent emotions. Thus Carrie, at the point of surrender, though impressed by the supposed power of Hurstwood's emotion ("her resistance half dissolved in the flood of his strong feeling") must ask herself, "Where else might she go? ... He loved her, and she was alone" (*SC* 235). It is relevant to make the point that vulnerability, passivity, and dependent infantilism are all traits brought into the foreground by the deterministic sociology of force and frequently exploited in the naturalist politics of the "masses." The historical and cultural significance of naturalist fiction is suggested by the firm outline Dreiser gives to Carrie's need, her drifting or unfocused capacity to choose, and the web of circumstance that encloses Hurstwood as well as herself.

To stress the comprehensiveness of his view of motivation, Dreiser does not restrict passivity and infantilism to a dependent female, for Hurstwood makes the fundamental decision of his life in an essentially similar fashion. By the time he confronts the safe in his office containing the money he needs for escaping with Carrie, his external situation has reached a climax of frustration. Frustration is the keynote; and just as submission to external force characterizes Carrie, Hurstwood's attention is focused on the circumstances that block his way. It is almost as if Dreiser had forgotten to give play to the passion Hurstwood feels for Carrie, the inner drive that brings him to his predicament; we seem to know of his desire chiefly from the obstacles that stand in its way: his wife's control over his money, his employers' objection to divorce or scandal, Carrie's discovery of his marriage, and his absolute need for cash to finance his escape. These dominate his mind not only in this crucial scene but in the preparation for it. But to make sure that the reader does not look too closely for ordinary moral responsibility, Dreiser gives the final momentum to simple accident. Hurstwood has taken the money out of the safe, as if only to look at it desirefully, but the door clicks shut. Not knowing the combination, he is now condemned to making an embarrassing explanation the next morning, since his job, though he is the manager, has nothing to do with handling cash. The fatalism of chance is necessary to the stress on drift and dependency; no free agent can rival process here.[6] Indecision here does not indicate a struggle between the power of moral resistance and the force of temptation but rather a kind of personal stalemate, as Hurstwood, like Carrie, is manipulated almost helplessly in a field of forces both major and minor. Did the rainy weather that night in Detroit determine Carrie's future? It is impossible to give a simple yes to that, but both the rain and the force of gravity that swung the safe door shut are meant to weigh more than clear value choices, and of course the author excludes conscience entirely: "The true ethics of the situation never once occurred to him, and never would have, under any circumstances" (*SC* 221). Why this should be so is not really clear, and the dismissal of "ethics" seems quite as theoretical and arbitrary as a conventional moralism would be. Conscience disappears into a primitive and simple fear of the police when Hurstwood recognizes, after he is on the train, that "They would be after him" (*SC* 221).

However, this view of character as dominated almost exclusively by external forces and lacking an inner life makes possible the impressive exhibition of Hurstwood's decline as status and wealth desert him. Dreiser has drawn him from the beginning as a man of externals, taking his character from his job, where he functions as a hand-shaker with the mission of pleasing others, particularly the rich and successful. That this is all he is, or was, is conclusively demonstrated by the fact that hardly a trace of feeling in Carrie survives Hurstwood's progressive loss of job, money, and public status. It is a mistake, however, to regard this as reductively cold and unfeeling, for what the author is emphasizing is the public or social nature of suffering. That shadow of a man, Hurstwood, appeals to an essentially political concern. Externalized in his wealth and prosperity, empty entirely in his misfortunes, he may be intended for the care of social doctors who might replace one lost exoskeleton of identity with another.

Taking this view of character as controlled and automatistic, it would be easy for a behaviorist engineer to manipulate circumstances in Hurstwood's life to gain a different result, since Hurstwood himself is so amenable to arrangement. Offering his own naturalist premise in the text, Dreiser remarks that man was once naturally and successfully an animal and that now his whole purpose must be to function as smoothly again, by "learning" what nature once gave without instruction:

> As a beast, the forces of life aligned him with them; as a man, he has not yet wholly learned to align himself with the forces. [SC 67]

This absurd "evolutionary" development gives the intelligence, together with all of its civilized instruments, the paradoxical task of returning its owner to a happier original alignment with nature. A vitalist naturalism would more plausibly conceive that a harmony of this kind is better achieved through the instincts; the function of the authorial intelligence would then be not to map alignments with nature but to force them through deep penetrations of passion and instinct. However, since Dreiser gave the greater role to outward conditioning, there is in his work the accent on passivity that usually goes with a strong mechanistic emphasis. What should interest a student of naturalist fiction in general is the marked alternations between mechanistic and vitalist effects that occur, sometimes in the same work, with a large web of circumstances controlling action in one scene and explosive passion erupting in another.

Norris's writing makes this dualism of effect more directly evident. In *The Octopus*, Shelgrim, the corporate leader of the railroad, sums up the impersonality of power thus: "*Railroads build themselves....* Men have only little to do in the whole business.... Blame conditions, not men."[7] The temptation to passivity is evident, but the deeper temptation may be to identify with some "force," otherwise uncontrollable—to let it act *through* oneself and to profit by it, as Shelgrim surely does, though he says, "I can *not* control it. It is a force [and] I—no man—can stop it or control it" (*O* 396). Beyond surrender or manipulation there is the alternative of blind resistance, like that of the violent Dyke, who in Norris's novel is maddened to the point of participating in the destruction of his farm, his family, and himself.

What is important to note is the context of violence. When power is the measure and the multitude of men and women are found to be relatively impotent in the face of events and circumstances, it is almost inevitable that reactive violence *should* be the one alternative to the usual passivity. A desperate impulse to resist, like Dyke's, must lead to failure, but it points to the more promising possibility of collective resistance. Collective violence in many naturalist novels, like the streetcar strike in *Sister Carrie* or the ranchers' demonstrations in *The Octopus*, must be seen in the context of the dominant role assigned to social forces, like the Railroad or the impersonal City, and the helplessness assigned to individual protagonists. Given the drifting submission of most of the characters and the isolated self-destructive outbreaks of a few, the conditions are set up for socially meaningful and possibly effective violence through collective action. This requires no political ideology for its discovery. The conclusion seems inevitable from the premise that men are ruled by forces in conflict; for if this is true, the best way to avoid being the victim of a social force is to identify with it, and the only way to oppose one social force is to take sides with another.

### Victimization and Resentment

Stephen Crane's writing lacks the impressive documentation whose enormous weight finally gives Dreiser's work an effect appropriately related to the awe Henry Adams felt before the Dynamo. But Crane comes closer to revealing the impact of violence, for he presents the naturalist laws of conflict and victimization with such clarity that the reader knows, with some relief, that he is in the presence of a literary myth and not the hybrid product of literature, social science, and political ideology that is so often found in conventional naturalist fiction.

In Crane's *Maggie*, for instance, the boys fighting in the streets assume the bearing of "one who aimed to be some vague soldier, or a man of blood."[8] Pete is the "supreme warrior," and Maggie is helplessly attracted to him by the prowess of his fists, his fine clothing, and his contempt for the rest of the world. The city street is the scene of life's struggle, and Maggie's brother, Jimmie, forms himself in its image. "In revenge, he resolved never to move out of the way of anything, until formidable circumstances, or a much larger man than himself forced him to it" (*Ma* 15). Once Jimmie has learned to

respect only the fire engine, the symbol of superior force ("an appalling thing
that he loved with ... dog-like devotion" [*Ma* 16]) his relations with the rest
of the world must become conflict-oriented, and he typically adapts to the
world with the manifestations of a paranoid personality. This response is
grounded as firmly in his origins as though he had grown up with dangerous
wildlife in the woods. His mother, a monstrous creature of malice, could look
at Jimmie with an expression that "had the power to change his blood to salt"
(*Ma* 12). But the street was Jimmie's primary teacher, "a world full of fists,"
dominated only by the fire engine and, at times, the police.[9]

> To him the police were always actuated by malignant impulses
> and the rest of the world was composed, for the most part, of
> despicable creatures who were all trying to take advantage of him
> and with whom, in defence, he was obliged to quarrel on all
> possible occasions. [*Ma* 14]

Crane's constant stress on defensive belligerence in Pete and Jimmie,
the street warriors, is paralleled by the pathos of Maggie's complete
victimization. A superior force can arouse fear in victims but also, in the right
context, the "dog-like devotion" that Maggie feels for Pete: "To her the earth
was composed of hardship and insults. She felt instant admiration for a man
who openly defied it" (*Ma* 20). She herself has no capacity for resistance or
defiance, and Crane uses the pathos of her situation to add emotional appeal
to naturalist conflict. As the victim she makes a poignant contrast with
strength and in doing so provides the sentiment that is usually a part of the
cult of power. She is described, for instance, as a girl blossoming in a mud
puddle: "None of the dirt of Rum Alley seemed to be in her veins" (*Ma* 16).
Her chief role is to suffer and to dream, with dim thoughts of "dream
gardens" and a lover and faraway lands where "the little hills sing together in
the morning" (*Ma* 19). The aim of the plot is to sacrifice this innate
refinement to the coarse violence of the streets. As a woman, Maggie is the
virginal sacrifice to Pete's warrior pride and lust. But to compound the
victimization, she is also the child, remaining as she was, early in the story,
where she and Jimmie are described as two children huddling together in a
world full of savage animals. She is also as deluded as a child because she is
capable of imagining Pete as a man of the world, a cultured gentleman. This
is excessive irony on Crane's part, but it is symptomatic of the patronizing
sentiment that was strongly characteristic of early naturalist fiction, where
the people for whom the reader can be asked to feel sympathy are so often as
dependent and vulnerable as children. The pathos of weakness is linked to a

bias on behalf of the "oppressed," and this becomes visibly related to the fuller development of naturalist politics.

Characters so helplessly abused as Maggie are meant to arouse a sympathy based on the fact of their being doubly victimized by society. Maggie is first of all the victim of the street anarchy and the specifically sexual competition of street warriors like Pete, who considers her his natural victim, as Jimmie would, too, if she weren't his sister. This point is sharply made because Jimmie and their savage mother are the agents of the punishment that Maggie suffers for her sexual fall. When they throw her out to her final destruction as "a girl of the streets," they are asserting a moral standard in grotesque disharmony with their own behavior. Crane is not so concerned with the specific plausibility of this as he is in stressing that his victim is doubly oppressed: by the violence of the slum, where people are brought to the edge of savagery, and also, if contradictorily, by the repressive social forces that define wrong behavior and punish it.

The link in naturalist thought to large issues is suggested by one critic, Donald Pizer. Justly pointing out that Crane's characters exhibit "a core of animality and a shell of moral poses," Pizer, like many readers of naturalist fiction, devotes most of his attention to the "shell," that is, to the hypocrisy inherent in the system of middle-class morality. It is true that one is faced with an interesting complexity in trying to decide which is Maggie's greater enemy, the jungle life of sexual exploitation or the social persecution that comes later. As Pizer reads him, Crane is working with the double theme that men cannot control their destinies, which are determined by environmental and instinctual forces, but that they can, at least, destroy those systems of value that uncritically pretend to control naturalist fate. "If we do this [i.e., destroy these systems of value], a Maggie (or a Jennie Gerhardt) will at least be saved from condemnation and destruction by an unjust code."[10]

Here I think Pizer is reflecting accurately an ambivalence at the heart of naturalist writing, in which those who are powerless—the victims of either natural or social forces—are revenged when the writer attacks moral conventions as illusions or hypocrisy. The resentment of the victims, aroused by amoral biological or social fate, can be converted into a war against bourgeois morality. In *Maggie*, a youthful work, written in an age of muckraking and social reform, Crane was undoubtedly responding to deep currents of popular thought, in which society's laws are seen to oppress people, particularly the poor, and the police are dramatized as the enemy of those who are in fact society's victims. More oppressive than the police are the conventional moral stereotypes, which are embodied even in such wretched degenerates as Maggie's mother and the tough saloonkeeper who abuses Maggie and ejects her from his place. By a curious but typical maneuver, the sexual anarchy that abuses Maggie is made to seem the ally of the moral system that punishes illicit behavior.

Intensely conceived naturalist fiction like Crane's enables us to see the almost simultaneous action of two kinds of moral criticism: people are viewed as victims of repressive social standards, and they are seen as the victims of nature's violence. A moralizing naturalist writer tends often to link these two forms of oppression.[11] The more ideological fiction of Dos Passos illustrates the point by its repeated use of the effect of cumulative victimization and injury from both nature and society.

Many of the characters in Dos Passos's *USA*, for instance, begin their adult lives by experiencing sex traumas, which form their characters and seem to form even their political attitudes. There is the case of Janey, who in an early sexual experience weeps but thereafter reacts with "cold, hard feeling" when things upset her. Her defensive shallowness seems to be the basis of her later loyalty to her boss, Ward Moorehouse, and her coldness toward her unionizing brother, Joe. Moorehouse is a caricature of the businessman-opportunist, incapable of honest feeling, for he, too, like Janey, has been the victim of early disillusionment: he was trapped by his promiscuous first wife, Annabelle, into marriage after a sexual encounter. He and his later mistress, Eleanor Stoddard, a snobbish social climber, are partners in a worldly alliance, lacking passion of any kind. The sexuality of Barrow, the union leader who sells out labor, has become lecherous and dirty—"his eyes got a watery look."[12] In contrast, respectable "puritan" restraints are despised, even while sexual selfishness, cruelty, infidelity, and abuse are made the basis of lifelong trauma. Ward Moorehouse was sexually sentimental before being seduced by Annabelle, who is pregnant with another man's child. He "was twenty and didn't drink or smoke and was keeping himself clean for the lovely girl he was going to marry, a girl in pink organdy with golden curls and a sunshade" (*USA* 117).

Such illusions are meretricious; they represent a false social system and its standards. But truth is a rough taskmaster, and the truth of nature can be as ruthless to emancipated sensibilities as to those protected by conventional pieties. Dos Passos was obsessed by the rapacity of sexual appetites and the cold law of sexual competition, but it is not the violence of nature alone that touches his characteristic sensitivity. The naturalist portrayal of human life as subject to the casual drift of animal appetite and instinct could lead finally to the wholesale trivialization of existence. In this respect, as well as in his attention to the naturalist shock of violence, Dos Passos belongs to his own generation, that of Hemingway and Nathanael West. In all of these writers moral indignation is undermined and seemingly canceled by a philosophic defeatism, or, conversely, metaphysical outrage is added to legitimate social and cultural criticism.

The important hypothesis here is that a revulsion against biological fate, though rarely overt, is often covert in naturalist fiction and that a resentment bred by it can find its target in society, the established culture, and, of course, in politics. A clear illustration of this, I have suggested, can be found in the naturalist writers' treatment of sexual conflict in the context of a commercial society. Writers who show Marxist inclinations, like Dos Passos (in *USA*) and Dreiser, can treat sex as part of a system of exploitation: women trap men, men buy women. Sexual conflict is thus linked with competition for money; sex and money are both free-market exchanges of strength, and there is no mercy for the weak or the sentimentally deluded. But sex is at the same time presented as a deeper threat, as a form of primitive biological exploitation; it thus serves to join the injustice of society to the deeper injustice of nature.

Another example of a covert metaphysical despair that turns on society in revenge can be found in the naturalists' treatment of war, a theme that occupied so prominent a place in the works of Dos Passos and Hemingway and their contemporaries. War could be viewed (and was so viewed by Crane in *The Red Badge of Courage*) as the human form of Darwinian conflict, the competition between species becoming conflict between human groups. But in Dos Passos and others war is seen less as the outcome of primordial natural competition and more as a vice of civilization. It is not instinctive violence that dominates in this view of war but a kind of corrupt ethics called patriotism.[13] This violence, then, is inspired by a false value, a mendacious faith. Self-interest is, of course, the strong motive behind the patriotic bloodlust of cold, aggrandizing characters like Moorehouse and Eleanor, but it is a form of self-interest that no longer appears natural, i.e., Darwinian, but one bred and sanctioned by a social system. The war profiteers and careerists, the manipulators and opportunists, are all so deeply embedded in a system of illusory values and lies that the violence of the Darwinian principle of competition, or even the simple inevitabilities of physical suffering and death, have all been absorbed by a resentment directed against national and cultural ideologies.

Thus the war conflict, like the sex conflict, in Dos Passos's work (and in Hemingway's *A Farewell to Arms*) adds naturalist shock to revolutionary protest. The sum is a powerful double indictment, giving a political meaning to what might otherwise be considered universal, natural, and inevitable human suffering. The point is not that political meanings are invalid, particularly in the social conflict of wars; it is rather that these writers have piled the sum of human rage and frustration on the back of the political beast the way Ahab piled his on the White Whale. This may help to explain the historical success achieved by naturalist politics, in which a possibly nihilistic but essentially subversive hostility is transferred from nature, as the ultimate oppressor, to society or culture. Culture suffers the revenge of the deprived; failing to maintain faith in itself, accused of lying from the start in its assertion of ethical authority, as well as in its original claim to be linked with nature through an ominipotent God, it becomes the easiest target of contempt and rage. Its authority must be unmasked, not just because it is based on falsehood but because it can give no real protection from the greater enemy, nature itself. The intransigence of revolutionary doctrine in our era may be understood in the context of this great unsatisfied demand on society to protect human life from natural process or to rediscover an old harmony that promised safety and fulfillment.

The revolutionary implications of naturalist literature were clearly voiced from the start, mixed, as always, with impulses of revenge and hope. Zola declared the political force of his literary doctrine and foresaw the literary triumph of naturalism as coinciding with the victory of "the Republic, which is now in process of being established by science and reason."[14] In this he was the prophet of hope. But he understood, he said, why his enemies dragged him in the mud: "I quite see the reason. It is because we deny their *bon Dieu*, we empty their heaven, we take no account of the ideal, we do not refer everything to that abstraction."[15] And although Zola seriously claimed to emulate science in his pursuit of the truth, other reflections of his indicate that, when it came to "reality," the naturalist could be very selective and that his overriding interest was to destroy false idealizations. Guy de Maupassant was blunt in saying that, "When you look at it closely, the persistent representation of 'lower elements' is, in fact, only a protest against adherence to a poetical view of things."[16] In this he spoke for a revenging truth of fiction and science whose plain mission was to sweep the world of lies.

Revenge is really the only adequate word for describing the reflexive hatred of idealizations one finds in the naturalist literary tradition and in that branch of "modernism" most affected by it. In Europe, writers like Strindberg and Artaud come to mind. Malcolm Cowley noted early the penchant for self-injury in the writing of the American naturalists. He concluded that in this respect American naturalists were neither cynics nor realists but men who had been morally wounded and were flaunting their wounds in their writing. Intrinsically, Cowley says, the sense of moral fitness is strong in them; they believe in their hearts that nature *should* be kind, that virtue *should* be rewarded on earth, that men *should* control their own destinies ... ; they often give the impression of seeking out ugliness and injustice in order to be wounded again and again.... They seem to be flogging themselves and their audience like a band of penitentes.[17]

This insight lays bare the profound emotional dialectic that inhabits the spirit of both naturalist fiction and naturalist politics, a dialectic in which injury from nature becomes injury from society. In its own revolutionary commitment, Marxism illustrates the double alienation expressed in naturalist fiction. Capitalist society and all human history exhibit the law of naturalist conflict, the struggle between classes developing from the basic competition for survival. The real intention of naturalist politics is not to justify the law of dialectical conflict (though in theory a Marxist would deny any intention to arrest the essential law of history) but to lead conflict toward its only possible resolution, one that grows out of natural and historical process. Acceptance of nature's law is transferred from stoic endurance to hope, and that political hope is paradoxically based on moral revulsion from the economic law of the survival of the fittest and, one might say, from the general view of nature as a gigantic and universal system of exploitation. Thus the fervor of naturalist politics is inspired by its implied mastery over both social laws and natural forces (since its doctrine springs from the understanding of both social and natural forces) and by its ability to pose as the champion of man against both antagonists, sometimes alternately and sometimes both at once. The comprehensive effect of revolutionary naturalist politics is to make a brilliant resolution of the conflict between nature and society, lifting the oppressive weight of both from man. It can seem to satisfy two rival needs, emphasizing liberation in the first phase of the revolutionary cycle, as if to set nature free from the burden of culture; but then, with the second phase, it promises a new social order, one that will subdue the least threat of natural anarchy. The miracle is the frequent ability of a revolutionary program to promise both liberation and a new discipline at the same time.

## NATURALIST FICTION AND POLITICAL ALLEGORY

In *Sister Carrie*, Hurstwood's decline is played out against a background of social struggle; during a motorman's strike he works as a scab and is almost killed in street violence. Later he sinks into marginal survival in flophouses and soup kitchens. The fading of Hurstwood's personal power, the deterioration of all his faculties, supports the transfer of attention to the social issue. As the possibility of self-redemption or even personal enlightenment is canceled out, a moral responsibility is being offered to society. Nothing can be done for Hurstwood as an individual, and he can do nothing for himself; but that perception is a way of enforcing the shift of moral responsibility from particulars to universals, from individuals to groups. Biological fate dictates the short cycles of individual life and death, strength and the fading of strength, but for the species there is a recourse from this fate. Thus, all that is lost in the life of individuals—the possibility of purpose, the possibility of redemption—can be subsumed into history and into the effort to direct history through political action.

This is a way of defining the important role of politics in naturalist fiction. One imagines that the first requirement of a determinist politics is to propose the existence of victims whose helplessness simulates the conditions of the experimental laboratory Zola help up as the model for fiction. There is a great deal of melodramatic sentiment in an episode of Norris's *The Octopus* that describes the total victimization of the Hooven family through a series of misfortunes, beginning with the dazed confusion of an immigrant German farmer and ending with his violent death, the prostitution of his daughter, and the death through starvation of Mrs. Hooven on the streets of San Francisco. But no specific moral monster—no person—can be held responsible for these outrages. The sequence is set off by the selfish imperial power of the Railroad, but, once it starts, fortuitous accidents appear to play a strong role, as when Mrs. Hooven's note, directing Minna where to find her, is lost. It becomes evident, however, that these "accidents" are due to the inscrutable operation of "Forces" massed against human beings and their powerless hopes and needs. Since these Forces partake of the metaphysical, resistance to them, if any is possible, must operate on the same level. Thus moral or political programs assume the same feature—equally abstract and impersonal and with equal authority—as historic fate.

In Norris's work this idea is used almost as a formula for the presentation of ethical sentiments and judgments. A shocking extremity of suffering is visited on an extremely vulnerable person, and both the suffering and the vulnerability are the products of the impersonal movement of "forces." Ethical outrage is thus pitted against a nonethical power, and the resulting dramatic effects are the most significant ones in the story.[18] For instance, Magnus Derrick and his rancher friends go to great lengths to put his son Lyman into a position of political power in the contest between the wheat-growers and the railroad corporation. They realize that they must do as the Railroad does, and so Lyman's election is won through political bribery. The aristocratic Magnus Derrick feels trapped and humiliated by this imitation of the vulgar power plays of his enemies, but the helplessness of this sentiment is illustrated when his son, himself bribed with the promise of great wealth and power, turns against his father and sells him out. Our horror at this betrayal is not undermined by the author's neutral view of overwhelming forces pitted against the feeble, subjective ethics of men. Neutrality and cynicism are possible reactions, but the response dictated by the author, even if it is masked by objective detachment, remains one of moral outrage. Thus the naturalist view retains its moral bias even as it presents an impersonal estimate of the enemy's power and a cold determination to wield an equal power.

Therefore, when Norris has Shelgrim, the Railroad leader, say "Blame conditions, not men," and "I can *not* control it. It is a Force," the effect is not necessarily one of submission to fate. What must be sought is a counterforce, equally inscrutable, equally the product of "conditions, not men." Norris finds this in the vitalist force of the Wheat, stronger than machines and money and, in effect, the guardian of the real interest of men, which is their share in the vitalist process. Meanwhile, if an interest is at stake or an outrage is to be revenged, the needed superior force can be brought into play if men are transformed, allegorized, into "conditions." Behrman, the active Railroad manager on the scene, is allegorized in this way. He is finally extinguished by suffocation in an ocean of wheat, poured into the hold of the ship, where he has been trapped. And, most welcome of all, no human agent has exacted this punishment. It is an accident, or rather a "condition," as if the Wheat itself had decided finally to punish Behrman, the agent of the Railroad.

Behrman's role is representative of the process of political abstraction—a process that Norris, in the eagerness of his convictions, was one of the first to emphasize in American naturalist fiction. Dos Passos, in a documentary vein that contrasts with Norris's melodrama, indicates again how naturalist fiction adapts to political allegory. The programmatic effect of Dos Passos's *USA* trilogy is the complete subordination of individual lives to the historic social process. Public life so overwhelms private life that the fragments of lives we are presented with in Janey and Joe, Moore-house and Eleanor, seem only illustrative footnotes to large events. The "Headlines" supply a drama that is almost entirely missing in the narrative. In effect the reader is told to go to the "Newsreel" sections of the text for the real story; it is the public themes, essentially political, that determine what is significant. The result, of course, is to lean on political ideology, to let general patterns of judgment interpret these lives for us. And in an even more suggestive link with naturalist politics, the passivity of most people—the ordinary, everyday people—in *USA* opens up the distinctive role given to the leaders and inventors, the manipulators of things and persons, who are featured in the "Biographies" that regularly interrupt the narrative text. The general run of characters are pressed into the roles of average victim or average opportunist and profit-maker. Their lives are tedious and routine; there are no large moments, no charged excitements, even on a personal level. In contrast, the "Biography" sections feature heroes or villains like Eugene Debs, Big Bill Haywood, Henry Ford, J. Pierpont Morgan—each a public monument who casts a giant shadow. These strong characters may be as much identified with social "forces" as the little people, but they are separated from the mass because of their strength, their vividness, their real effect on the social process. These people manipulate and handle power, but their motives are inaccessible, their humanity minimal, perhaps because images of power tend to leave such terms behind. In combination with the army of small characters, they feed the paranoid tendencies of the political imagination, the world divided between men of great power and the people of the mass, who are singled out, if at all, for their representative qualities or else, as the occasion demands, for the pathos of their suffering.[19]

The author's distinctions between good and bad people are obvious in the contrast he draws between public characters like Bill Haywood and Henry Ford, but the miniature characters are also categorized. Thus Janey, though not as sympathetic as her working-stiff brother Joe, is a loyal and forlorn stenographer, the conventionally burdened female, with definite limits placed on her life. Above her on the social scale, Eleanor Stoddard is an egotistical snob, striving to move to higher class and cultural levels and rendered emotionally frigid by her ambition and struggle for money. Though she becomes a manipulator of esthetic values, these have been made shallow and pretentious not by her character but by her context: the way of life and social psychology she is supposed to illustrate. It is a blameworthy way of life—or so we can judge when Eleanor accepts money from her working-class father while hating him and promising herself never to see him again. There is not much reason for her hostility except for the aura of low beginnings that clings to him. When she finally allies herself with Moorehouse, we can expect any sort of rottenness from both of them. But their evil is quite impersonal and dehumanized. The prejudice against them, communicated to the reader, is abstract and as class-oriented as Eleanor's own revulsion from her father.

This moral thinness of character is a weak dramatic basis for presenting human relationships; the social pattern is obviously strong and determining, and yet there is watery response and very limited allegiance in the actual relationships we observe. In *USA* people move in and out of each other's lives without producing much effect; even those who are closest to each other, like Janey and her brother Joe, seem absentminded when they meet again. Joe and Mac leave home as young men almost as a matter of course, feeling not the vaguest homesickness or yearning for something lost. Transient lovers like Annabelle and Moorehouse or Janey and Burnham illustrate a general principle: people come close, engage, and then drift apart.

All this might be described as the accurate report of a decadent, disheartened society, and so I believe it was taken by most readers in their first response to it. But considered judgment suggests that these effects are the product of an abstract political vision, one that tells us that generalized social forces and simple natural instincts dominate people's lives. In that view, survival is the most important of motives, and, following from that, the range of motivations is severely limited. There is the need for money; there is social ambition—that is, the struggle for power and status; and there is sex. Beyond that, or, rather, draped over them for concealment, there remains the pseudo-ethic of conventional respectability. The formula is a familiar one and central to the myth of naturalism. Values are fictions, instincts are real, behavior is selfish. A typical tradeoff is the one that takes place between Moorehouse and Annabelle, his first wife, after the early wounding of his young and conventional sexual idealism (one siege of weeping and he becomes an opportunist again). Basically, they exchange for what they each need: Ward wants money and sex, Annabelle wants respectability—and sex. This barrenness of motive should dull the reader, and, if it doesn't, it is perhaps because the reductive simplicity is on a universal scale. There is, of course, the possibility of violent response in any sequence dealing with sex, and Dos Passos does not forget violence in the highly visible pattern of a naturalist myth of sex. The rule in such fiction is somewhat as follows: violence or erotic demonstrations will increase in proportion to the lack of psychological nuance and complexity of character. The simplest example is the violence that breaks from Norris's McTeague, as if in revolt from his own numb intelligence and inarticulateness. And, in Dos Passos, it is striking to see how often an erotic crisis or some personally experienced physical abuse is made to interrupt and season the massive sociological documentation. The effect in general terms is one of alternation between triviality and sensationalism. If the social documentation is boring, the naturalist novelist has a remedy available in the devices of melodramatic political allegory or in the "realism" of sexual shock and violence.

Both dramatic violence and the panorama of sociological abstraction are by-products of the naturalist's reductive view of character, but a more significant result is the spirit of condescension implicit in it. In naturalist fiction the poverty of the characters' responses is often conveyed by infantile simplicities of style, and, with sometimes powerful dramatic irony, this style is used to describe even the most serious and painful experiences. The dominant stylistic influences on Dos Passos were surely Hemingway, Stein, and Sherwood Anderson, although he lacks the intense stoic drama or poetic primitivism that enlivens their works. And, what is also more evident in Dos Passos's writing, the infantilism of style has the effect of emphasizing the infantile vulnerability of characters. The reader's moral sympathy must focus first on a generality of suffering, a social condition, and second on a mass dependency that begs for protection and direction.

The question arises, why did two or more generations of writers feel it necessary to diminish the moral size and personal strength and intelligence of their characters? Was it because they turned to ordinary people for their subjects? Was it because an oppressive and corrupt social system had reduced most people to these dimensions? Or was it the response to tendentious thinking about human nature based on social and biological naturalism? It is a bothersome question, seemingly reversible in terms of cause and effect, because it is affected by various uncontrolled factors. It may be that the bottom half of human society could never exhibit more than this narrow range of sensibility, having neither the opportunity nor the capacity for making meaningful choices. Therefore, a literature of the "people" must do what it can with such limitations and risk being reductive and patronizing, as a politics of the "people" will also risk forms of paternalist and authoritarian intervention. On the other hand, the limitation may be in the point of view, in which a simplified, empirical, reductive understanding of the typical case, the average human being, always produces distortions.

These allegorical effects of naturalism are pushed to an ideological extreme in Frank Norris's work, perhaps because, ambitious to write an American epic, he rightly understood that he was dealing with mythic substance. In *McTeague*, for instance, the struggle for money plays the central dramatic role, and it is doubtful that this is a response to the social reality that Norris knew best. Rather, it is a great and inclusive ordering principle, a surreal obsession that drives all the characters almost as blindly as it sweeps Zerkow, the miser, toward murder and self-destruction. Rival instincts and motives converge on this one point, greed, as when Marcus Schouler, after first accepting generously the loss of his girl, Trina, to McTeague, finds his friendship turning to jealous hatred when Trina wins a five-thousand-dollar lottery prize just before her marriage. Money is what cements and then divides her marriage, for Trina's new fortune, infecting her with greed, finally drives her husband to kill her. And when Schouler hunts McTeague to his death, his own greed for gold dominates his need for revenge, his hunter's sadism, and even his own instinct for survival.[20] This convergence of motives reaches an inventive climax when Norris shows Trina directly substituting money for sex: in a climax of miserly pleasures, she pours her gold onto her bed, undresses, and sleeps naked with it.

What Norris has done is to fuse biological and social abstractions of force, pour them into the same mold, and, in doing so, reach the point where social conflicts take on the metaphysical character of biological process and naturalist fate. To think of social and economic relations in such terms is to mythologize them and make them absolute. We see McTeague and Schouler magnified in that kind of metaphysical drama as they wrestle to their deaths even when they know they are already doomed by the desert and the loss of their supply of water. It is as if life cannot be allowed to end on any accent but violence. In this novel's context (which is intellectually based on the abstraction of economic conflict), Zerkow's murderous greed, Trina's miserliness, and Schouler's revenge are not strange pathologies; they are simple representations of the strongest force ruling behavior, the demon that drives history. If interpreted in a political spirit, what counterforce would not be justified in the effort to master it?

The allegory of "forces" in literary naturalism leads plausibly to the allegory of groups. There was sanction for this, it seemed, from Darwin; and if McTeague is large and violent on the scene, fighting for his survival, how much larger and more violent would the struggle be if it were not just for himself but for his species? Norris is a man of his intellectual period in the way he thrusts racial concepts and group stereotypes into the foreground of attention. In *The Octopus* the degenerate mixed-breed Spanish of California love the cruelty of the great rabbit slaughter, a kind of epitome of the novel's extended violence. The supreme villain, Behrman, is "Hebraic," cautious and scheming, as much without mercy as the Jew Zerkow in *McTeague*. Lyman Derrick, the renegade son, is described as having a dark face and popeyes, and it is repeatedly emphasized that he is foreign-looking. For contrast, we have sturdy Americans endowed with fair Anglo-Saxon strength and beauty.

If the hints of racism are strong in *The Octopus*, it is because Norris is dealing ultimately with "forces, not men," and so, appropriately, he will see groups when he treats of individuals. The crude stereotypes of race do not generally lend themselves to fiction, but the roots of racist judgment and feeling are present in the initial stereotypes of the forces that motivate men and rule life. Thus Behrman illustrates a mean lust for power, but Magnus Derrick represents the power drive absorbed in a generous and aristocratic, though fallible, principle of leadership. Such human divisions are easy to make and tempting. Vanamee represents the spiritual man, Presley, the man of conscience and poetry, and Annixter, to complete the triad of young protagonists, the virile man, dominated by physical action and the love of work. The women are even more distinctively classified. Hilda, representing vital sex, is linked with the earth and the wheat, while Angéle, also a spirit in nature, meets Vanamee's more intense and transcendental aspirations. Adams's Venus-Virgin figure is here divided into its components, but both are representations of energy, attracting and endowing the men. And the men, even the sympathetic figures, are accordingly dedicated to controlling some form of power. Vanamee, the mystic, wishes to control ultimate, supernatural forces; Presley, the poet, wishes to master experience and all its meanings; while Annixter, the man of action, wants to control the land and the wheat. The rest of the characters are driven in the same direction, though on more prosaic levels, preoccupied as they are with the direct objectives of economic and political power.

Such one-dimensional characters take their interest from the naturalist value conflicts they exhibit. In other words, they function as allegorical figures in a myth. Some exhibit positive vitalism, like Hilma and Annixter, while others represent the "soulless force," the ironhearted power of the Machine. The Machine, and the abstract power of money behind it, almost visibly compel Norris to elaborate the rival vitalist powers found in the Woman, the Wheat, and the People. (All such "forces" need capitalization, in Norris's view.) We sense the presence of another vitalist god in Race, though it does not receive the same explicit treatment. But a symbol that does link group forces comes forward in the idea of Empire. The work of Henry Adams suggests that the nineteenth-century cults of race and empire were vitalist, intended to rival the supremacy of science, technology, and finance, purging them of their dehumanizing implications. Norris exhibits the same response, paralleling Adams more clearly than any other naturalist fiction writer. In writing of the "great West," he calls up epic effects. It is the promise of empire, "vast ... vaster ... immensities multiplying," that inspires Presley with "stupendous ideas for which there were no names," and the "vast terrible song" he hears he calls the "Song of the People," though it is at the same time the song of Empire (O 33, 29). For Presley, the poet, these are gods: "The voice of God is the voice of the People," he says in his enthusiasm, and Norris writes, "He *believed* and so to him all things were possible at once" (O 377, 255).

The main point is that these abstractions *are* "believed"; they are the basis of political religions, though the political implications may seem contradictory. The energy of empire is equated with the energy of race, of the species, and that, of course, is reactionary in trend. At the same time, the energy of life in the species is also translatable into the political energy of the people, a revolutionary concept.[21] The final enemy of the Railroad Trust, the only power capable of breaking its grip, had to be the People. Here was a power that transcended individuals and came from nature; it had the strength of the species, a conquering strength condensed in the theme "the individual suffers, but the race goes on" (*O* 448). The People aroused are an "awakened brute," an "enraged beast"; but when the People are also a "god," as in Presley's vision, it is clear that the animal metaphors are there to endorse the life-force in collective humanity.[22]

To imagine the power of the Railroad and its money is to understand the stimulus for inventing the symbol of the People. On one side was corporate power—not human, but a machine alternately showing its face of steel or its face of paper, made of legal writ and money. On the other side, there is a gathering of victims but a possible reversal of their weakness to strength—to power with a human face. Again the political implications are strong. How do two collective abstractions negotiate with each other? They can't without contradicting their nature, their defined essence. Therefore, they fight in order that one, not the other, may survive. Violence is the necessary outcome of political allegory, one might say, since any other resolution—except, of course, the total enervation or decadence of one side—is inconsistent with the abstraction of historic conflict and rival powers.

In the background of this violence, this war of symbolic concepts, one sees an inherent moral irresponsibility in the "forces." But, as Shelgrim, the great corporate leader, suggests, the shift of responsibility to a "force" grants all the more license for violence in individuals. And we see in *The Octopus* that the very stress on group force tends to throw up a leader figure of giant proportions, for he is the symbol of that force. Shelgrim remains a threatening and omnipotent shadow, but Magnus Derrick, the leader of the ranchers, lives up to the proportions of his name until his final collapse. He has great personal magnetism—the force of his cause, his group identity, flows into him—and the ranchers can plausibly surrender to his power because, in terms of the novel, that power becomes their own.

Actually, as soon as Shelgrim identifies himself as an "ungovernable force," he suggests the existence of a force opposing him. The People, in battle with the "iron-hearted master of steel and steam," are equally ungovernable when enraged. Norris makes this explicit in the mob scene where the ranchers confront the railroad men at the Hooven ranch. As the alternative to passive drift and hopelessness, the "enraged beast" authorizes an explosive resistance, in any form it may take. Norris writes of a "war to the death" almost as a reflexive comment. This is more than rhetoric, for naturalist conflict tends to reach this extremity. The law of survival directs that two naturalist forces in conflict cannot remain in stalemate, nor, as I have said, can they negotiate without compromising their identity as a "force."

Ungovernable or enraged, a terrible power "not to be resisted," the People are nevertheless a welcome force because they represent the transference of power to a vitalist principle that attracts belief. On the model of Henry Adams, one might rather pray to it than to the Dynamo. The important need—and Norris's response to it is almost formulaic in the naturalist tradition of writing—is to make power humanly accessible and still do it justice, still mark out a stoic respect for nature's truth.

## NOTES

1. Theodore Dreiser, *Sister Carrie* (Boston: Houghton Mifflin, 1959), p. 6. (First published in 1900.) (Subsequently referred to as *SC*.)

2. Henry David Thoreau, *Walden*, ed. Sherman Paul (Boston: Houghton Mifflin, 1057), p. 15. (First published 1854.)

3. Frank Norris, *McTeague* (San Francisco: Rinehart, 1950), p. 31. (First published in 1900.) (Subsequently referred to as *Mc*.)

4. Ellen Moers gives a full account of Dreiser's friendship with Elmer Gates, during the time he was writing *Sister Carrie*, in *Two Dreisers* (New York: Viking, 1969), pp. 158–69. As an amateur physiological psychologist, Gates seems to have supplied strong evidence for the mechanistic and "chemistic" themes of Dreiser's intellectual life; these were later to be more impressively supported by the work of Jacques Loeb.

5. John Fraser, *Violence in the Arts* (London: Cambridge University Press, 1974), p. 167 n.

6. The more famous instance of Dreiser's need to blur choice is the ambiguous murder in *An American Tragedy*, where Clyde Griffiths literally stumbles into his crime.

7. Frank Norris, *The Octopus* (Boston: Houghton Mifflin, 1958), p. 395. (First published in 1901.) (Subsequently referred to as *O*.)

8. Stephen Crane, *Maggie* (New York: Norton, 1979), p. 6. (First published in 1893.) (Subsequently referred to as *Ma*.)

9. Tony Tanner, in his book on contemporary American fiction, *City of Words* (London: Jonathan Cape, 1971), is one of the first critics I know of to give appropriate stress to themes and effects he calls "the American paranoia": "The possible nightmare of being totally controlled by unseen agencies and powers is never far away in contemporary American fiction" (p. 16). See, particularly, his discussions of Thomas Pynchon and Norman Mailer (ibid., chaps. 7 and 15).

10. Donald Pizer, *Realism and Naturalism in Nineteenth-Century American Literature* (Carbondale, Ill.: Southern Illinois University Press, 1966), pp. 127–31.

11. The modern theme of linking violence with repression came to its most direct expression in the politics of Wilhelm Reich and his literary followers. One of the latter, Norman Mailer, illustrates how compatible this theme is with literary naturalism. The hero of Mailer's famous essay "The White Negro" is the psychopathic victim of society who cures himself by violence. He replaces "a negative and empty fear with an outward action ... even if the fear is of himself, and the action is to murder. The psychopath murders—if he has the courage—out of the necessity to purge his violence, for if he cannot empty his hatred then he cannot love, his being is frozen with implacable self-hatred for his cowardice" (*Advertisements for Myself*, p. 347).

12. John Dos Passos, *USA* (New York: Random House, 1937), p. 312.

13. Norman Mailer brought these aspects of war-making together in *The Naked and the Dead*, using General Cummings as his archetype. Mailer recognized the latter's fascism as a form of naturalist politics and played vigorously on the themes of power, conflict, and order in the experience of other characters. In this, as in other respects, one can read Mailer's work as the most revealing contemporary expression of traditional naturalist themes.

14. Emile Zola, "Naturalism in the Theatre," in *Documents of Modern Realism*, ed. George J. Becker (Princeton, N.J.: Princeton University Press, 1963), p. 202.

15. Zola, quoted by W. S. Lilly, "The New Naturalism," ibid., p. 280.

16. Guy de Maupassant, "The Lower Elements," ibid., p. 250.

17. Malcolm Cowley, "A Natural History of American Naturalism," ibid., pp. 444–45.

18. See Tony Tanner's excellent discussion of Manichean naturalism in his *City of Words*, pp. 141–52.

19. Norris, as might be expected, provides an illustration of this authoritarian principle: in *The Octopus* the leader of the ranchers, Magnus Derrick, is a magnified man, six feet tall, a cavalry officer with a hawklike nose. The others instinctively look up to him; there was "a certain pride of race in him" (*O* 44). He has the instinct to be master, as others are born to be followers.

20. If greed is fate in Norris's novel, so is instinct. The instinct of the hunted compels McTeague to run for his life, beyond his own choice or sense of direction. He is matched against a fatal process, and finally all that can move him to act on his own behalf is a sixth sense, "an obscure brute instinct," which tells him when he is being pursued and makes him run again (*Mc* 300). It is plausible to invoke a sixth sense against something so mysterious as naturalist fate, the point being that naturalism treats events on a metaphysical scale and can appeal to superstition, despite the initial commitment to empirical science.

21. In Norris's novels these convergences of the dominant political currents of his time are clearly revealed, and they illustrate a relationship difficult to see elsewhere between neo-Darwinian racism, imperialism, and American populist thought.

22. Following is a passage from a classic sociological text, originally published early in this century, in which the imagery of the "People" is also eloquently naturalistic. The authors are writing about the silence of farm workers in England during the nineteenth century, who allowed their experiences to be interpreted solely by upper-class ideologies and spokesmen:

> religion, philosophy, and political economy were ready with alleviations and explanations which seemed singularly helpful and convincing to the rich. The voice of the poor themselves does not come to our ears. This great

population seems to resemble nature, and to bear all the storms that beat upon it with a strange silence and resignation. But just as nature has her power of protest in some sudden upheaval, so this world of men and women—an underground world as we trace the distance that its voices have to travel to reach us—has a volcanic character of its own, and it is only by some volcanic surprise that it can speak the language of remonstrance or menace or prayer, or place on record its consciousness of wrong. [John L. Hammond and Barbara Hammond, *The Village Labourer* (London: Longmans, 1911), pp. 242–43]

R I C H A R D   L E H A N

# American Literary Naturalism:
## The French Connection

Most studies of literary naturalism begin with Zola's *Le Roman expérimental* (1880) and explain this movement in scientific/literary terms. The argument centers upon Zola's use of Prosper Lucas's *Traité ... de l'hérédité naturelle* (1850) and especially Claude Bernard's *An Introduction to the Study of Experimental Medicine* (1865), which supplied the basis for Zola's definition of the experimental novel. Zola wanted the novelist to function like a scientist—to observe nature and social data, to reject supernatural explanations of the physical world, to reject absolute standards of morality and free will, and to reveal nature and human experience as a deterministic and mechanistic process—by which he meant controlled by scientific explanations of matter. For Zola, all physical reality was made of matter, and all matter was subject to natural laws, explainable in scientific terms. Both the idea of miracles and of the imagination were suspect: there were no miracles in nature, and the best novelist was an empirical observer rather than an imaginative creator. Influenced by both Lucas's and Bernard's theories, Zola believed that man was finally a product of his heredity and environment, that life was simply the play of temperaments in a social context, subject to human observation and description: "I wanted to study temperaments and not characters ...," Zola wrote; "I chose beings powerfully dominated by their nerves and their blood, devoid of free will, carried away by the fatalities of their flesh."[1]

From *Nineteenth-Century Fiction* 38, no. 4 (March 1984). © 1984 by the Regents of the University of California.

This explanation of literary naturalism is obviously true to a point. No one can deny the influence of the new scientific and medical theories on Zola and some of his contemporaries, especially the Goncourt brothers, Edmond and Jules, in novels like *Germinie Lacerteux* (1864) and *Madame Gervaisais* (1869). But what this kind of discussion omits is the true social and historical basis of literary naturalism—the willing ability of these writers to examine the cultural matrix in a way it had not been examined by previous novelists. We are all familiar with the *Rougon-Macquart* novels and the assumption about temperament and heredity that Zola brought to this famous twenty-volume study of two families. But Zola subtitled this work *A Natural and Social History of a Family under the Second Empire*, and we tend to minimize what he meant by "social history" as revealed in the eighteen-year span (1852–1870) that makes up the novels.

It is this social/historical/cultural dimension of naturalism which I should like to address in this essay. My argument is that literary form—here literary naturalism—cannot be divorced from a historical process that saw the movement from a landed to an urban economy, saw the rise of the bourgeoisie and at least the appearance of republican government, and that was ultimately founded upon empirical/scientific assumptions about reality which, coupled with the new technology and power of money (new banks and credit theories), led to the impulse of nationalism and the rise of empire. In this context, the English/Puritan Revolution, the French Revolution, and the American Revolution/Civil War are historically not only similar but, when examined along a spectrum of time (from 1660 to 1865), reveal the same kind of "turnings" away (which is what the word "revolution" means in its generic sense) from a feudal/aristocratic world toward a modern urban/commercial/industrial world. Defoe and Dickens were among the first to observe this phenomenon, which occurred in England from the seventeenth to the nineteenth centuries; Balzac and Zola were among the first to observe it in France; and Norris and Dreiser in America. That the British experience precedes both the French and American experience by one hundred to two hundred years is explained by the fact that the commercial/industrial revolution began in England in the seventeenth century, in France in the eighteenth, but not in America until the nineteenth century. The novels of Defoe and Dickens are very different from those of Zola and Dreiser because the urban experience in Paris and New York/Chicago was very different from the London of either Dickens's or Defoe's time.

But with Defoe there is a radical change in the nature of the novel. We move from the placeless world of Sidney and Lodge, held together by typological patterns, to the concrete world of modern London and the New World. Dickens depicted the grotesque details of this world a century later, and Zola picked up where Dickens left off—moving us away from sentiment (the power of the human heart to address social evil) to a commercial/industrial world driven by the power of its own mechanisms, creating both the splendor of Haussmann's Paris and the degradation of the industrial slums. Later Norris, who was influenced by Zola, and Dreiser, who was not, would show the same historical process at work in New York, Chicago, and San Francisco. In this context, naturalism is more than a literary movement, more than just the workings of shared assumptions about heredity and environment, and it becomes inseparable from the historical processes of modernism, which moves us away from the land to the city, away from the world of craft to the world of factories, away from the manor house/cottage to the townhouse/tenement, away from the lord of the manor to the city speculator, away from the domination by the aristocracy to the domination by the high bourgeoisie who had begun to control political and financial institutions (parliament and national banks of credit) in the name of national policy and imperial longings. One can obviously chart this transition in the novels of Balzac and Zola, just as one can less obviously chart it in the novels of Hawthorne and Faulkner. In this context, what was happening in the nineteenth-century novel, especially in America and France, becomes part of a shared cultural and historical experience.

II

A study of Zola's world must begin in 1830, ten years before his birth, when Louis Philippe took over the political reins of France in the name of the Second Republic. One historian tells us: "It was not long before liberals came to see that their idealism was misplaced; the system of divine right and ultra-royalism had been driven out, only to be replaced by a regime of landlords and capitalists with a bourgeois monarch. There was not much to choose between the two." Under Louis Philippe, France became a commercial, urban, industrial country. Industries like textile manufacturing were taken over by machines. The invention of the steam engine freed such industries from water power supplied by rural rivers and brought them to the city, creating a major shift in population. In 1820, France had sixty-five steam engines of low horsepower; in 1830, six hundred of ten thousand horsepower; and in 1850, five thousand of over sixty-six thousand horsepower. By 1840, over 672,000 men, 254,000 women, and 130,000 children were working in French factories, far outnumbering the older and more traditional urban trade workers (tanners, dyers, hatters, masons, and smiths). Much of this new industry was being financed by English investors—Rothschilds, Barrings, and Hopes—who had amassed fortunes supplying the money base for the English industrial revolution.[2]

The transition in December of 1848 from Louis Philippe to Louis Napoleon Bonaparte was not as abrupt a change as it first appeared. Three years after Louis Napoleon became president, on 2 December 1851, Paris was occupied by troops loyal to the new president. One year later, Louis Napoleon became Napoleon III, the Emperor of the Second Empire, with a new constitution of 14 January 1853 codifying his powers. Once again a liberal revolution had given way to a conservative political reaction, the new power consolidated by the new emperor.

Zola later saw these events as the betrayal of the liberal cause. But many historians have stressed the enlightened aspect of Napoleon III's regime. Canals and rivers were dug or widened, keeping open one of the best transportation systems in Europe. And Baron Georges Haussmann (1809–1891) was hired to remove medieval and build modern Paris. Haussmann demolished almost 20,000 slum dwellings and built 43,777 new homes; he lengthened the Rue de Rivoli from the Bastille to the Concorde, built the Boulevards Saint-Michel, Sébastapol, Strasbourg, and Magenta. The Saint-Martin canal was covered and transferred into a boulevard. The Bois de Boulogne and Vincennes were made into public parks, and in a new spacious context such urban buildings as the Louvre, Hôtel de Ville, the Palais Royal, the National Library, Notre Dame, and the Opéra became monuments. Paris became the center of Europe with six great railroad lines converging on the capitol. In 1855 and in 1867, Paris hosted the World's Fair, and in 1856 the Congress of Paris. Under Napoleon III new credit lines were established by two lending institutions—the Crédit Mobilier, which handled primarily industrial loans, and the Crédit Financier, which handled primarily agrarian loans. When Napoleon came into power, 74.4 percent of France was rural; when he lost power in 1870, 68.9 percent of France was rural. In that time Paris almost doubled in population, and a number of urban centers came into being: Lyon, Marseille, Bordeaux, and Lille.[3]

Zola captures the sweep of these events in his *Rougon-Macquart* novels, written between 1871 and 1893, a period covering slightly more than twenty years after the Second Empire but including the years from the eve of the Second Empire (1851) to the French defeat at the Sedan during the Franco-Prussian War (1870), or as Zola puts it in his introduction "from the perfidy of the coup d'état to the treason of the Sedan."[4] Zola describes these years from the point of view of the countryside, where a greedy peasant class begins to consolidate power, and from the point of view of the city, where a new middle class rises to power under the auspices of Napoleon III.

Zola's sequence begins with *La Fortune des Rougan*, which describes the origins of the two families, the Rougons and the Macquarts, both springing from the defective blood of Adélaïde Fouque (Aunt Dide), who marries the respectable Rougon, by whom she has a son, Pierre. After her husband's death she takes the drunkard Macquart as her lover, by whom she has a son and a daughter, Antoine and Ursule. Until 1830 the inhabitants of Plassans (based on Zola's own Aix-en-Provence) were fervent Catholics and Royalists. But when it became evident that Louis Philippe would triumph, they "deserted the cause of legitimacy, and gradually espoused the great democratic movement of our time. With the revolution of 1848, the nobility and the clergy were left alone to labor for the triumph of Henri V" (pp. 77–78). When, in turn, the Republic fell, the Rougons prey off the ruins and become rich: "Mixed up with the various phases of the crisis, they rose on the ruins of liberty. These bandits had been lying in wait to rob the Republic; as soon as it had been strangled, they assisted in plundering it" (p. 80).[5]

Zola describes the political shifts of the peasants in the countryside as they jockey for power in the Second Empire. Such novels as *La Fortune des Rougon* (1871), *La Conquête de Plassans* (1874), *La Faute de l'abbé Mouret* (1876), and *La Terre* (1887) treat this world—and an unpleasant world it is as Zola pricks the bubble of pastoral illusion. But the center of the *Rougon-Macquart* novels is the center of France—Paris—to which many of the townspeople come in search of a heightened sense of self, in search of power at its functioning center. The Paris novels are *La Curée* (1872), *Le Ventre de Paris* (1873), *Son Excellence Eugène Rougon* (1876), *L'Assommoir* (1877), *Nana* (1878), *Pot-Bouille* (1882), *Au Bonheur des Dames* (1883), *La Joie de vivre* (1884), *L'Œuvre* (1886), *La Bête humaine* (1890), and *L'Argent* (1891). Whereas *Germinal* (1885) and *La Débâcle* (1892) are not city novels, they depict action that has its origins in the economic and political meaning of the city. Thus over half the novels in the series deal with the world of Paris, and the rest cannot be separated from its influence.

*La Curée* (1872) is the first novel to establish the meaning of Paris as both the center of France and the center of Zola's narrative world. Aristide Rougon comes to Paris from the provincial town of Plassans to hunt *la curée* (the quarry). In Paris he joins his brother Eugène, a minister in the Emperor's government, and his sister, Madame Sidonie, a courtesan. Early in the novel Aristide looks down over the entire city from a restaurant window on the Buttes Montmartre and sees Paris much as Eugène de Rastignac sees it at the end of *Le Père Goriot*, as a world to be plundered and conquered.

Aristide's wife, Angèle, dies, leaving him with a son and a daughter, and he marries Renée Béraud Du Châtel, the daughter of a retired magistrate who is pregnant with another man's child. At the suggestion of his brother, Eugène, he changes his name to Saccard—which suggests both money (sac d'écus) and ruin (saccage)—and goes about his way making a fortune out of Haussmann's rebuilding (that is, out of the ruins) of Paris. Saccard has a vision of Paris before it is rebuilt, and by speculating on what real estate to buy or sell he amasses a fortune in a short period of time: "Paris was then disappearing in a cloud of plaster dust. The times that Saccard had predicted on the heights of Montmartre had come. The city was being slashed to pieces with sabre strokes and he had a finger in every slash, in every wound."[6] Like Balzac, Zola depicts a city that creates its own reality, motivating the ambitious to a greed that separates them from family and establishes commodity rather than human relationships. As Saccard becomes more involved in his financial speculations, Renée spends more time with her stepson, Maxime Saccard, eventually falling in love and seducing him. Zola finds a metaphorical equivalent for narrative action, and in *La Curée* it is incest. When Saccard eventually surprises Renée and Maxime at their lovemaking, he uses this moment to force his wife to sign over her property to him, more interested in his bourgeois respectability and his power to make money than he is in his own relationship with wife and son. The most pathetic character in this novel is Renée, whose love is betrayed twice—by father and by son—in a world where money is the final power.

Zola continues the story of Saccard in *L'Argent* (1891), another novel about the power of money, as the title indicates. *L'Argent* is a more ambitious novel than *La Curée*. Zola based his plot upon a financial scandal in the Third Republic involving an engineer named Eugène Bontoux, who engaged in foreign speculation financed by L'Union Générale, a bank (with close ties to the Pope) which was attacked and defeated by the financial forces of James de Rothschild. Zola saw in this incident a modern paradigm: the bank as the center of the city, financing investments all over the world, caught up in the forces of political and religious strife, its workings effecting directly or indirectly the lives of people all over the world. Saccard goes to the center of this world when he meets a young engineer, Hamelin, who needs help financing a silver mine in Palestine. Connected with this scheme are spin-off investments in railroads, steamship lines, and foreign banks. Zola is here describing the beginnings of the world city—the visible tower of the financier with its invisible power, the beginning of the cartel-like financial deals, the movement of capital and the control of the underdeveloped lands of the world.

Money is a force greater than military or political power. Even when Saccard's plan is defeated and his scheme collapses, the money he has engineered has built new cities and brought remote lands into the grip of the modern world: "The village of five hundred inhabitants, born at first around the mine in process of exploitation, was now a city, several thousand souls, a complete civilization, roads, factories, schools, fertilizing this dead and savage corner."[7] Caroline, Hamelin's sister and Saccard's mistress, comes to see money as simply an amoral force, supplying the means by which the daring speculators like Saccard control and are controlled, the means by which we transform the landscape, build cities, and subsume other nations and lands. Money may corrupt but out of such corruption comes new life, or so Zola says at the conclusion of the novel: "Money ... [is the] muck-heap in which the humanity of tomorrow grows ... the ferment of all social vegetation.... Why, then, blame money for the nastiness and crime of which it is the cause? Is love less polluted, love that creates life?" (p. 435). What Zola shows so clearly in *L'Argent* is how power is transformed through the workings of the city—in this instance through its financial institutions. The biological process of life and death have been transformed in the modern world, moved from the realm of nature to the realm of the city. In *Le Ventre de Paris* (1873) and *Au Bonheur des Dames* (1883), he analyzes this idea in some detail, describing two kinds of market place—the Halles Centrales, supplying food, and the modern department store, supplying material goods. Thus the city organizes the means to satisfy biological needs as long as one has money. It is in the getting of money that modern man reveals his basic nature, which includes a combativeness that he did not leave in the jungle. In the *Rougon-Macquart* novels, Zola shows how modern urban institutions are really systems of control—control over the landscape, over natural and industrial resources, and finally over the people themselves. Zola's is a world of physical force operating within terms of physical limits, and if one person gets more than his share, another must get less. He sees this system as ultimately both exploitive and destructive, and he depicts the evil of the system in the very best of the novels which make up the *Rougon-Macquart* series: *L'Assommoir, Nana, Germinal, La Bête humaine, La Terre,* and *La Débâcle.*

*L'Assommoir* (1877) is one of the first French novels to depict the life of true working-class people—a subject the novel did not seriously entertain before Zola—which perhaps explains why the novel received so much critical attention when it was first published. "I wanted," says Zola in his preface, "to depict the inevitable downfall of a working-class family in the polluted atmosphere of our urban areas."[8] The context for this novel is the same as in

*La Curée* and *L'Argent* because in *L'Assommoir* money also sets limits in the lives of the characters, although the effect is more brutal when applied to the working class. Gervaise very carefully figures how much money she needs to free her and Coupeau from their squalid room and to establish her own laundry. As she approaches that sum, her plans are seemingly dashed when Coupeau falls from the roof and fractures his leg. Saved by a loan from the fauning Goujet, the boltmaker whose own world is being threatened by the new machinery, Gervaise once again struggles to put her own life in order. And indeed, *L'Assommoir* is a novel about the failure of this class to take control of their lives, to establish a necessary order. Zola praises Coupeau's and Gervaise's initial energy and delight in their work. He symbolically has Gervaise keep her bankbook in the back of a grandfather clock, and money and time wisely spent thus become equated in this novel. But such energy seemingly cannot be sustained, especially in the face of continued disappointments; and first Coupeau and then Gervaise herself become more passive, give way to drink and then finally to self-abandonment. Once again Zola has quantified an experience: he does not morally condemn Gervaise—only shows life weighing more heavily upon her day by day until the weight trips the balance and the scale falls. It is the accumulative effect of their lives that finally destroys these characters, who live from beginning to end on a very primitive level of being—food, sex, and drink constituting the ends of life for the working class. The scene where Gervaise, Coupeau, and their wedding party go to the museum is a brilliant stroke because they are totally out of place in this bourgeois setting, in awe of the polished expanse of floor, puzzled by the paintings on the wall that have no connection whatever to their daily lives.

And it is in the squalor of this world that Nana, the daughter of Gervaise and Coupeau, is born. Later Nana will realize that only money can save her and that the easiest way to such power is through selling her one possession—her body. Zola depicts in *Nana* a public world—the theater, the restaurant, and the hotel—a world in which Nana can come from nowhere and become the center of attention once she displays her body and sensual charms. Zola also depicts the upper realm of the bourgeoisie and the aristocracy, and we quickly move from city streets to luxurious salons: at the peak of her success Nana's rooms are as luxurious as any. In this way, Zola exposes the shallowness of upper-class life, the emptiness of such people whose money and power come from the work of others, whose lives lack substance and direction, and who seek pleasure as an end in itself. Such pleasure is in itself transient: the more they have, the more they want. Nana becomes the fatal attraction for all of the major characters in the novel—

Count Muffat, Steiner, Georges and Philippe Hugon, Marquis de Chouard, Count Xavier de Vandeuvres—and each, in one way or another, is destroyed by such contact. The critic Fauchery, no better himself then the world he condemns, points the moral of Zola's narrative in his article, "The Golden Fly," in which he describes Nana as a product of the "dunghill" world, carrying her "rottenness" upwards to contaminate the aristocracy. "She becomes a blind power of nature, a leaven of destruction, and unwittingly she corrupts and disorganizes all Paris."[9] This conceit, however, is not totally true because the aristocracy itself has already become corrupted—weakened by its own superfluous connection to the new sources of money and power, dissipating its energies on sensuous pleasures that lead to a fateful decadence. Count Muffat is the character who best embodies this process, and his gradual decline from a respected aristocrat to a masochistic plaything of Nana's enlists as much sympathy from the reader as disgust. But disgust is the end product of this world, the reader's final response to it—disgust at Muffat and the empty world of the aristocracy; at Fontan, the actor whose violence seems as necessary a consequence of this world as Muffat's decadence and whose anger leads to sadistic beatings of Nana; disgust at Satin, a gutter-rat with whom Nana has a lesbian affair; and, finally, disgust at Nana herself, who is carried away by her own excesses. Almost all of the action that involves Nana takes place in a world of great luxury—of gold-plated and silver-adorned salons and boudoirs—the money for which comes from the dying world of the aristocracy, of a landed, property class embodied by a Muffat whose financial and moral defeat become one. Nana and her followers mutually infect each other in a world where death is the only end product. Nana dies of smallpox at the end of the novel, her suppurating, purulent body inseparable from the corruption of the aristocracy, whose death is harbingered by the call of the mob—"A Berlin! A Berlin! A Berlin!"—which signals the Franco-Prussian War and the end of the Second Empire. Zola saw the health of a society as inextricably connected with the way it works and the way it controls the wealth and power that come from work. Once the aristocracy was displaced from the true economic processes of a commercial/industrial world, the seed of death was within it. Nana simply exploits the destructive process that is already at work, and since she is an inextricable part of that process, her own destruction is also guaranteed. Zola's understanding in *Nana* goes beyond that of portraying a courtesan in a corrupted world to enabling the reader to understand the very reasons for such corruption.

Zola depicts the opposite world of *Nana* in *Germinal*, in which he takes us into the northern coal fields where the miners are on strike. Such strikes had occurred at La Ricamarie, Rive-de-Gier, Aubin, and Anzin; Zola actually visited the coalfields of Anzin and used his observations there as the basis for his novel. *Germinal* is a richly detailed, highly charged novel that graphically depicts the woeful life of coal mining. A mining family like the Maheus finds itself caught between two kinds of economic power. On the one hand, we have the owners and the investors and managers, embodied by Grégoire, and Hennebeau. Grégoire has inherited shares in the colliery bought by his grandfather for 10,000 francs, which now provide an annual income of 50,000 francs. And Hennebeau was a former worker who rose through the ranks to a position as manager and now believes in and protects the system. Both are well-meaning, decent men, but unsympathetic to the worker's plight because any change in the system would be to their disadvantage. On the other hand, we have those who represent the workers. Étienne Lantier, the central character, is the self-educated, idealistic socialist who has read Marx and who believes that the value of a product is created by the work that it brings into being. Rasseneur is the trade unionist who believes a settlement must be worked out within the system by the principals involved. And Souvarine is the revolutionary anarchist who believes the system must first be destroyed and rebuilt outside the restrictions of capitalism. If Zola repudiates the paternalism of a Grégoire, he also repudiates the radical solution of a Souvarine: the workers end up as victims of both extremes; Grégoire feeds off their helplessness, whereas Souvarine destroys those who oppose him and hence their means to work. It is not clear whether Zola finally gives consent to the positions of Rasseneur or Étienne. He appears to repudiate both of them as leaders, since the mob of workers turn on them individually on two separate occasions and since the workers themselves seem to embody a force—like the force of nature—that will overpower the idle and the destructive and, in some vague Darwinian way, create a higher purpose that will redeem the system from within. Étienne comes to realize that

> it was clear that everything must go wrong as soon as any one man sought power for himself. Hence the fiasco of this much-trumpeted International which, instead of creating a new world, had merely witnessed the piecemeal break-up of its mighty army through internal strife. Was Darwin right, then, was this world nothing but a struggle in which the strong devoured the weak so that the species might advance in strength and beauty? ... For if one class had to be devoured, surely the people, vigorous and young, must devour the effete and luxury-loving bourgeoisie? A

new society needed new blood. In this expectation of a new invasion of barbarians regenerating the decayed nations of the old world, he rediscovered his absolute faith in a coming revolution, and this time it would be the real one, whose fires would cast their red glare over the end of this epoch even as the rising sun was now drenching the sky in blood.[10]

Zola thus makes clear that the worlds of *Nana* and *Germinal* are really one—that the workers who produce the wealth that allows the luxury of Nana are also the means of transforming the system. Almost everything in Zola's world comes back to the nobility of work, and he becomes absorbed in this part of the solution to the extent that he never really addresses the equally serious questions of who will lead the new workers, and who will control the master who controls the masses. Zola takes us in *Germinal* to the doorstep of a totalitarian world without realizing that that is what he has done. It is not that he was unaware that he was dealing with the forces of power—*La Bête humaine* reveals his fascination with that subject—it was just that he never really knew who was to be trusted with the new power that would come from the fall of a decadent ruling class.

In the *Rougon-Macquart* novels, Zola shows how the effects of a commercial/industrial process are transforming the city, the provinces, and the relationship between man and his work. In *La Terre*, he shows how this process reached a peasant world and transformed the land. Zola once said, "I should like to do for the peasant in *La Terre* what I did for the working man in *Germinal*."[11] The main character, Jean Macquart, is the brother of Gervaise of *L'Assommoir* and an uncle of Nana, Ètienne, and Claude. His travels have taken him to Beauce, a small market town in the grain-growing plains, the center of which is Chartres. What Zola reveals through the telling of Jean's story is that the feudal system has passed forever; the land has been bought up by the new bourgeoisie like Hourdequin or absorbed by greedy peasants like Fouan and his brutal son, Buteau. Zola depicts a brutal world in which the possibility of a pastoral past is pure literary invention. Greed and suffering seem to be the by-products of this life, and always have been. But now the small farmer is being bought out by the larger property owners who "use machinery" and, in some instances, participate in "large capital turnover."[12] The peasants who remain on the land feel betrayed: "We've got to get back to the Revolution! We were diddled. The middle class took the lot and, by God, we'll make them hand it back" (p. 234). Zola depicts the land as a counter-force with its life-giving rhythms. But he also shows that the land will never be "handed back"—that the farmer, large or small, is part of a process controlled by the new mechanics of the city. As Hourdequin explains, the land is "being crushed out of existence by taxes, foreign competition, the continual increase in labor costs, the flight of capital into industry and the Stock Exchange" (p. 157). The city has reached out and absorbed the land, but the peasants do not realize this. They become brutal in their desire to keep the land, and participate in a destructive process, as the murders of Fouan and Françoise reveal. Thus Zola ends the novel with a reference to the inseparability of life and death—a new season upon the land that seems to take its being from death: "Here were the Dead, there was the Seed; and bread would be springing from the Good Earth" (p. 500).

This bread will be taken to the markets of Paris to feed the city, and the world of *La Terre* is only a small part of a larger commercial/industrial process which reveals new sources of power. Zola's *La Bête humaine* extends the theme of the new power, although here Zola's interest is drawn toward technology as a source of power. In the center of this novel we have the murder of Judge Grandmorin, a Royalist and the president of the Western Company railway system; the judge is murdered by Roubaud and his wife, Séverine, after Roubaud has learned that Grandmorin seduced Séverine when she was an orphan child. Once again Zola depicts the ruling class as morally corrupt, provoking a destructive violence in others. Such a violence seems also directly a part of Jacques Lantier's inheritance, and he moves in a seemingly conditioned way from lust to an eagerness to murder. Zola superimposes upon this pathological condition Jacques' obsession with the locomotive on which he is the engineer: "He had loved this engine for all the four years he had been driving it.... He loved this one because it had the rare qualities that go to make a worthy woman."[13] Lust, murder, and the machine thus become connected in a strange and unexplained way, and the train seems to control and hold sexually the violence that Jacques turns back upon women. And yet that violence seems inseparable from the train itself. Four deaths occur either on a train or as a train passes, and when Pecqueux, the fireman, and Jacques fight and then fall in Dickensian fashion beneath the wheels of the train, their violence seems to be absorbed by the force of the train itself. The mechanical power of the train seems larger than the world it occupies, as Zola describes it crashing through huge snowbanks and crossing the land in a blur of speed. As Jacques Ellul has pointed out, there can be a direct connection between a technological and a totalitarian society, since efficiency—order and control—is the common denominator between them.[14] In *La Bête humaine* Zola once again ends a novel on the note of blind, undirected power working in an uncontrolled way as the train—"its engine without engineer or fireman, its cattle-cars filled with troops howling patriotic airs"—hurtles through the night "going to war" (p. 384), a symbol of the new commercial, industrial, technological society without true leader or direction: "Without a master, through the blackness, a blind, deaf beast, unleashed with death, it sped on, and on, loaded with cannon-fodder, with soldiers stupid with exhaustion, drunk, singing" (p. 384).

*La Débâcle* picks up exactly where *La Bête humaine* ends with soldiers going off to fight in what will prove to be the disastrous Franco-Prussian War. Once again, Jean Macquart of *La Terre* is the central character of this novel, which opens with him on the front. *La Débâcle* serves as a historical conclusion to the *Rougon-Macquart* novels (as *Le Docteur Pascal* will serve as a conclusion to the genetic and familial aspect of the story). Zola realized that an act of historical violence was necessary if France was to break from Napoleon III, and he anticipated the Franco-Prussian War before it happened. The corruption of the empire, radiating from Paris outwards, had been the theme of the major novels, and Zola had shown how such corruption had infected every limb of the society from the aristocracy, separated for generations from the land, to the high bourgeoisie in their banks and offices of exchange, to the peasants and mine workers whose greed and strife have interrupted the sacred office of work. The loss of 17,000 French soldiers in the Sedan becomes a great sacrificial act to bureaucratic and military incompetence—and even more so to a society that has produced wealth and luxury by exploiting the land and the people. Even in war the emperor travels in luxury, with carriages and vans so full of "silver plate and bottles of wine, hampers of provisions, [and] fine linen" that it takes two hours to unload them.[15] Such extravagance demands a price, draws life out of the empire, and leaves it vulnerable to attack from outside. Jean and Maurice, two men of opposite class and temperaments, come together as friends to embody the solidity that could be France's. But this solidity is betrayed from within, and France is divided, as Jean's unwitting killing of the Communard Maurice graphically symbolizes.

The geographic center of the *Rougon-Macquart* novels is Paris, but Zola depicts it as a diseased center, a diseased heart that could no longer energize its extremities. The center must be purged, and the final scene in *La Débâcle* is that of Paris burning—"burning like some huge sacrificial fire" (p. 508). The novel closes with the hope of a new Paris that will somehow draw its strength from the land—from the good, simple people, like Jean, with their love of the earth and their capacity for work. Maurice's dyings words to Jean reflect this belief: "Go and take up your pick and trowel, turn over the soil and rebuild the house!" (p. 504). And Zola's final words underscore this hope: "The ravaged field was lying fallow, the burnt house was down to the ground, and Jean, the most humble and grief-stricken of men, went away, walking into the future to set about the great, hard job of building a new France" (p. 509). The naturalistic vision seems to return to "renewal" through "eternal nature, eternal humanity" and the promise of toil. In the *Rougon-Macquart* novels Zola shows how deeply political is the nature of this vision and what can happen when an old feudal and new commercial society are cut away from the land and the people and the vitality of redeeming work.

III

There was no American novelist who covered the panorama of economic and historical activity of a Zola. But collectively there were hundreds of novels which did for America after the Civil War what Zola did for the Second Empire. Indeed, the aftermath of the Civil War in America parallels the kind of historical changes taking place in France between 1848 and 1870 as both economies moved from a landed to a commercial/industrial world. In America this period witnessed the rapid growth of cities, the rise of corporate businesses, the influx of immigrant labor, and the practice of wretched working conditions. One commentator has put it: "The result was an all but incredible skyrocketing of industrial production. From the Civil War to 1900, capital invested in manufacturers increased ... five or six times over; the money value of factory products mounted with similar speed; and in certain basic industries, such as steel, the growth in productive output was immensely larger even than this. Correspondingly, the number of cities of 8,000 or more inhabitants at least trebled."[16] Many of the American writers depict this economic transition from the point of view of the upper classes, and thus their position differs markedly from Zola's sympathy toward a proletariat and an emerging working class; but even among the more conservative writers in America, we find an increasing sympathy for the hardships of the new poor and a growing distrust with a system that can be corrupted by the new forces of big business. Elizabeth Stuart Phelps, for example, sympathetically depicts the plight of mill workers in *The Silent Partner* (1871), and other novels which treat workers or the poor are Thomas Bailey Aldrich's *The Stillwater Tragedy* (1880), Amanda Douglas's *Hope Mills* (1880), Mary Hallock Foote's *Cœur d'Alene* (1894), and Francis Hopkinson Smith's *Tom Grogan* (1896). Novels which depict the rise of speculative finance and industrial wealth are Henry Francis Keenan's *The Money-Makers* (1885), Charles Dudley Warner's *That Fortune* (1899), Garrett P. Serviss's *The Moon Metal* (1900), David Graham Phillips's *The Great God Success* (1901), Robert Barr's *The Victors* (1901), Will Payne's *The Money Captain*

(1898) and *On Fortunes Road* (1902), H. K. Webster's *The Banker and the Bear* (1900), Samuel Merwin's *The Honey Bee* (1901), and Merwin and Webster's *Calumet "K"* (1901) and *The Short Line War* (1899), and Harold Frederic's *The Lawton Girl* (1890) and *The Market-Place* (1899). And novels which depict the corruptive effect of the new economy, either on the system or on the individual, are Rebecca Harding Davis's *John Andross* (1874), J. W. De Forest's *Honest John Vane* (1875), J. G. Holland's *Sevenoaks* (1875), Edgar Fawcett's *An Ambitious Woman* (1883), F. Marion Crawford's *An American Politician* (1885), Thomas Stewart Denison's *An Iron Crown* (1885), Paul Leicester Ford's *The Honorable Peter Stirling* (1894), Hamlin Garland's *A Spoil of Office* (1892), Henry Blake Fuller's *The Cliff-Dwellers* (1893) and *With the Procession* (1895), and almost all the novels of Robert Herrick, but especially *The Gospel of Freedom* (1898), *The Web of Life* (1900), *The Real World* (1901), *The Common Lot* (1904), *The Memoirs of an American Citizen* (1905), *Together* (1908), and *One Woman's Life* (1913).

The cumulative effect of these novels is more impressive than the individual achievements of most of these authors, almost all of whom have fallen out of the canon. We thus have a literary substratum which belies the supposed indifference of the gilded age to the actual workings of their economic system and the subsequent abuses it produced. As in Zola, we can move in these novels from the boardrooms of power and wealth to the salons where the wealth is displayed, to the legislating halls which the wealth controls, to the mills, factories, and mines that produce the wealth at great human sacrifice and suffering. Although the voice depicting the latter experience is certainly muted, we are still far removed from what Walter Rideout calls the "radical novel."[17] American fiction had to go through its own version of literary naturalism before that kind of experience could take place, and the two most influential practitioners of American literary naturalism were Frank Norris and Theodore Dreiser.

The connection between Norris and Zola is a direct one. Norris probably did not know Zola's work when he lived in France as a student from 1887 to 1889, but he had certainly discovered Zola by 1890 or shortly afterward when he was an undergraduate at the University of California at Berkeley. Norris's treatment of physical degeneration is the basis for *Vandover and the Brute* (1914), which he worked on early in his career but which was published posthumously. In *McTeague* (1899) Norris treats the same theme but counterpoints it against a social backdrop, which includes a consideration of the mine fields of California, the social mix of San Francisco, especially the Polk Street area, and the compulsion for money. The stories of Trina and McTeague, and Maria and Zerkow are studies of greed, of people driven to pathological behavior by the desire for gold and money. Zerkow, compulsively driven by his delusion that Maria possesses a set of golden dishes, will murder her. McTeague will murder Trina for the five thousand dollars in gold pieces that she counts every day and takes to bed with her. And Marcus Schouler will turn on McTeague when he loses Trina—and the five thousand dollars. The desire for money turns love and friendship to murder and hate. Poverty has the same degenerative effect on Trina and McTeague that it has on Gervaise and Coupeau in Zola's *L'Assommoir*; and it creates in *McTeague* the same homicidal tendencies that sexual love and passion inculcated in Jacques Lantier in *La Bête humaine*. The influence of Zola on the early Norris is evident on almost every page.

But Norris was not content simply to depict the pathology of naturalism. By March 1899, in a letter to William Dean Howells, Norris indicates that he had the idea for an "epic trilogy" dealing with wheat—its production (*The Octopus*), distribution (*The Pit*), and its consumption (the never-completed *The Wolf*). Like Zola, Norris wanted to write a series of novels describing the economic forces that were changing modern society from an agrarian to an urban base. He also wanted to work out his idea of the West—his belief that the direction of modern civilization, with some starts and stops, had been moving along a western frontier, jumping the Atlantic after the Crusades, progressing across the American continent, and then jumping the Pacific when the American West was settled. Dewey's exploits at Manila and the landing of United States marines in China during the Boxer Rebellion in 1900 were significant events in the documentation of this thesis.[18] His trilogy would begin at the present cutting edge of the frontier (California), move eastward to the commodity markets where wheat was bought and sold speculatively (Chicago), and end where the movement began, where the life-giving wheat was now consumed (Europe). What Norris wanted to show was how modern capitalism had created a world city where economic events thousands of miles removed had life-threatening consequences for markets all over the world. In *The Octopus*, for example, he describes the telegraph lines that connect the ranchers

> by wire with San Francisco, and through that city with Minneapolis, Duluth, Chicago, New York, and at last the most important of all, with Liverpool. Fluctuations in the price of the world's crop during and after harvest thrilled straight through to the office of Los Muertos, to that of the Quien Sabe, to Osterman's and to Broderson's. During a flurry in the Chicago wheat pits in the August of that year ... Harran and Magnus had

sat up nearly half of one night watching the strip of white tape jerking unsteadily from the reel. At such moments they no longer felt their individuality. The ranch became merely the part of an enormous whole, a unit in the vast agglomeration of wheat land the whole world round, feeling the effects of causes thousands of miles distant—a drought on the prairies of Dakota, a rain on the plains of India, a frost on the Russian steppes, a hot wind on the llanos of the Argentine. (p.44; see also pp. 216–17)

The plot for *The Octopus* (1901) came mainly from a shoot-out in May of 1880 between agents of the Southern Pacific Railroad and wheat farmers of Tulare County in the southern part of the San Joaquin Valley. The railroad had originally encouraged ranchers to settle the land given to it by the government, promising the settlers that the land would be sold to them at a minimal price. Once the land was improved, the railroad raised the price. When the ranchers protested, the railroad sent in deputies to dispossess them. In the fight that followed, seven men—five of them ranchers—were killed. While Norris's sympathy in *The Octopus* was clearly with the ranchers, he showed how they also had been corrupted by money, how they were exploiting the land for immediate gain, and how they were also leaving a legacy of greed, of bribery and of deceitful influence:

> They had no love for their land. They were not attached to the soil. They worked their ranches as a quarter of a century before they had worked their mines.... To get all there was out of the land, to squeeze it dry, to exhaust it, seemed their policy. When at last the land, worn out, would refuse to yield, they would invest their money in something else; by then they would all have made fortunes. They did not care. "After us the deluge." (p.212)

There were no innocents in this economic process—only the working of the wheat, a force which somehow, and this is the vaguest part of Norris's thinking, is working for the Good, an idea the opposite of which the novel better documents (cf. pp. 405, 446, 457–58).

While most of the action in *The Octopus* takes place in the San Joaquin Valley, San Francisco is an all-pervading presence. There the railroad, the Octopus, has its headquarters, and there Shelgrim (modeled on Collis P. Huntington) lectures Presley on the philosophy of force—a philosophy which absolves the railroad from moral responsibility. The liaison between the ranchers and the city is S. Behrman, the banker and local agent for the railroad, who is most instrumental in dispossessing the ranchers. What used to be a symbiotic relationship between city and countryside has broken down in *The Octopus;* the city seems to feed off the land—as the sumptuous dinner at the end metaphorically suggests—and deplinishes without ever restoring. Like Zola, Norris depicted in *The Octopus* a shift in cultural values—a movement away from the land to the city as the source of the new power, the wheat as a force in itself being funneled through the city to markets all over the world.

In his next novel, *The Pit* (1903), Norris further develops this theme. The central character in *The Pit* is Curtis Jadwin, who tries to corner the wheat market, and the central situation involves the Chicago Board of Trade, which buys and sells wheat options, thus helping to set the price of wheat worldwide. Norris convincingly shows Chicago as a center into and out of which energy flows—not only the energy embodied in the trains and barges that come into Chicago everyday but the energy behind speculation which binds Chicago to the West and the prairie states where wheat is produced, and to Europe where the surplus will eventually be sold. Chicago was a "force" that "turned the wheels of a harvester and seeder a thousand miles distant in Iowa and Kansas," the "heart of America," a force of empire that determined "how much the peasant [in Europe] shall pay for his loaf of bread."[19] But as central as Jadwin and Chicago are to Norris's story, the wheat is even a greater force, larger than both. Norris effectively depicts in *The Pit* a world of limits—the naturalistic belief in a physical, quantitative world—and when Jadwin tries to raise the price of wheat beyond the "limit" that wheat will go (p. 346), the market breaks and he is a ruined man. Every man and every social institution has its limit, and even abstract matters like wheat speculation are governed by laws that ultimately come back to nature—back to the land, back to the wheat, and to the forces out of which life germinates, a theme Norris energetically shared with Zola.

This becomes the infrastructure of Norris's world. The social structure follows as does the superstructure of art and intellectual pursuits. But everything eventually comes back to the wheat and the land, just as all life ends in the grave. Curtis Jadwin's wife, Laura, helps carry this theme. We first see her at the opera, where talk of wheat speculation can be heard competing with the singing. Laura—arrogant, self-concerned, cloying when she is not childishly independent—is torn between two men, Curtis, the man of practical energy, and Sheldon Corthell, the artist, a woman's man, sensitive to life's beauty but passive and effete. Laura's instinct drives her toward Curtis, and although she wavers when Jadwin gives all of his time to his business affairs, she remains faithful to him at the end; Norris hereby gives priority to the world of business over the world of the salon, the man of action over the man of art, of bold venture over esthetic pursuits, perhaps because Jadwin is closer to the workings of wheat as it moves, perpetuates, and transforms life. Norris never finished the third volume of his story about wheat, never got to Europe, where the consumption of wheat would be the final step in this cycle of life. But thematically a third volume was not necessary. Norris had already shown how the growing and selling of wheat touches the lives of everyone, worldwide; and he clearly documented the economic assumption behind literary naturalism.

Norris died in 1902 at the age of thirty-two, too young to leave a literary legacy of his own except for the influence that he had on Theodore Dreiser. Norris was the reader for Doubleday, Page and Company when Dreiser submitted his manuscript of *Sister Carrie* to this firm, and Norris supported the publication of the novel, even after Doubleday had had a change of mind and wanted to break his contract with Dreiser. Dreiser never forgot Norris's help and friendship; he was equally moved by Norris's literary achievement, especially *The Pit*, his favorite among Norris's novels. There is no question that *The Pit* had an influence on two of Dreiser's own novels— *The Financier* (1912) and *The Titan* (1914).

But despite the influence, *The Financier* is a very different novel from Norris's *The Octopus* or *The Pit*. In Norris's novels, as in Zola's, the emphasis is upon the workings of an economic system and the way individual characters fit into that system. In Dreiser's *The Financier*, the emphasis is upon the rise and fall and rise again of a young financier genius, Frank Cowperwood (modeled on Charles Yerkes), who makes a fortune in the Philadelphia brokerage business before he is indicted and found guilty of using public funds for speculative purposes. By the end of the novel, Cowperwood is out of prison and making another fortune when the house of Jay Cooke fails. In *The Financier*, Dreiser puts the emphasis upon the obsessive nature of Cowperwood, who early in life decides to be a money-man, and how the genius for this work is part of his temperament and nature. He also puts the emphasis upon Cowperwood's desire for the good things in life, especially his love for the beautiful, including the beautiful Aileen Butler, whom he pursues with the same intensity that he pursues money. Despite the differences in their lives, Dreiser superimposed upon Cowperwood many of his own personal traits and qualities. Dreiser also conveys in *The Financier* a sense of a city, Philadelphia, and of America itself coming of age. The story is told against the backdrop of life just after the Civil War when cities were beginning to overarch the land and speculative money was being directed to new enterprises in the West, especially to those involving the railroad. Men of immense wealth like Jay Cooke took advantage of this situation:

After the Civil War this man, who had built up a tremendous banking business in Philadelphia, with great branches in New York and Washington, was at a loss for some time for some significant thing to do, some constructive work that would be worthy of his genius.... The project which fascinated him most was the one that related to the development of the territory then lying almost unexplored between the extreme western shore of Lake Superior, where Duluth now stands, and that portion of the Pacific Ocean into which the Columbia River empties—the extreme northern one-third of the United States. Here, if a railroad were built, would spring up great cities and prosperous towns.... It was a vision of empire, not unlike the Panama Canal project of the same period.... His genius had worked out the sale of great government loans during the Civil War to the people direct.... Why not Northern Pacific certificates? For several years he ... [organized] great railway-construction corps, building hundreds of miles of track under the most trying conditions, and selling great blocks of his stock, on which interest of a certain percentage was guaranteed.... However, hard times, the war between France and Germany, which tied up European capital ..., all conspired to wreck it. On September 18, 1873, at twelve-fifteen noon, Jay Cooke & Co. failed for approximately eight million dollars and the Northern Pacific for all that had been invested in it—some fifty million dollars more.[20]

Like Norris, Dreiser knew that the system was larger than the individuals who made it up and that it depended upon the subtle workings of events worldwide. When the Franco-Prussian War tied up European capital, Cooke's house failed—just as the Chicago fire of 1871 brought ruin to Cowperwood/Yerkes. In all of these novels, the realm of force operates in terms of laws of its own.

This is specifically the thesis of Dreiser's next novel, *The Titan*. Here Cowperwood has moved to Chicago where he is successful in establishing a gas trust before he puts into operation a plan to monopolize the streetcar system. Chicago itself embodies an energy that parallels Cowperwood's drive, and the destiny of the city and the man seem inseparable. Cowperwood's desire to have, to possess, is extended to women, and the subplot of this novel involves his affairs with a host of women—Stephanie Platow, Cecily Haguenin, Florence Cochrane, Caroline Hand, and Berenice Fleming. His acquisitiveness in business and in love engenders a swarm of powerful and committed enemies. As he multiplies enemies and angers the citizens of Chicago with his financial schemes, Cowperwood brings into operation a counterforce that finally defeats him. As in Zola's novels, Dreiser's fiction takes place in a world of limits, controlled by what Dreiser called the "equation inevitable." This is the term Dreiser used to convey his belief in the circularity and repetitiveness of life which stemmed from antagonistic forces canceling each other out. Life ultimately becomes its own justification in this kind of world—all human activity ultimately transient, all men part of an agency that works through them. Both Zola's and Dreiser's characters have moments—artistic moments like those of Claude Lantier and Eugene Witla and Cowperwood himself—when they intuit such secrets, intuit also the beauty of life. For in Zola and Dreiser, beneath the ugliness of an industrial/urban process is a redeeming color and vitality. Unfortunately, those who intuit the beautiful most often fall victim to ideals or illusions, miscalculate the meaning of a mechanistic reality, and perish in disillusionment. Such was the fate of Claude Lantier in *L'OEuvre;* such is the fate that Cowperwood foresees for Governor Swanson in *The Titan;* and paradoxically such in some ways was Cowperwood's fate. It is often fatal in naturalistic fiction to dream oneself out of tune with the kingdom of force.

It was such obsession with the theme of force that led other naturalistic writers to move beyond the conventional novel to the subgenres of utopia and dystopia—novels of ideas which depict the kingdom of force, sometimes out of control, a theme that obviously connects these novels with Zola, Norris, and Dreiser. Zola had seen—although not always clearly as we saw in our discussion of *Germinal*—that the technological/industrial society depended upon efficiency, that efficiency demanded control, and that the instruments of control were one step away from totalitarianism. Zola's mob, like Nathanael West's in *The Day of the Locust* (1939), reveals the potentiality for anarchy when it is undirected and the potentiality for fascism once it is controlled. The existence of a mass always implies the dangers of a master. Edward Bellamy seemed unaware of such political consequences in *Looking Backward* (1888), a fantasy vision of the year 2000 in which America has given way to a kind of technocracy—a technological society made up of an industrial army in which all the goods that are produced are shared equally among the populace on a kind of pro rata basis. Giving control of this system to an engineer-dictator does not seem to bother Bellamy, who believes that satisfying basic human needs takes priority over other activities and justifies the dangers of a technocracy. Mark Twain was not so sanguine, and he answered Bellamy in *A Connecticut Yankee in King Arthur's Court* (1889)—as did Ignatius Donnelly in *Caesar's Column* (1890), both of which try to come to terms with the misdirected consequences of industrial power.

Set in the technological wonders of New York in 1988, *Caesar's Column* describes another futuristic city. But here the city is torn by political strife stemming from two factions: a wealthy oligarchy that controls the army, and an abused proletariat which gets control of the mob. Once the oligarchy is overthrown, the leaders of the mob consolidate their own power, and the whole process starts over again. As in naturalistic fiction, power and its ability to corrupt remain constant. By the end of the novel, the principal characters have escaped to Uganda in Africa, where they attempt to break the circuitry of power by establishing a kind of socialistic state in which the major sources of wealth are owned in common, the land is shared, gold and silver no longer remain the basis for the value of the dollar, and all forms of interest are outlawed.

Jack London in *The Iron Heel* (1908) picks up where both Bellamy and Donnelly leave off. He also begins with a capitalistic oligarchy in control of a profits system, protecting their wealth with a police force and army, which are not needed so long as the people give consent to a superstructure of religious and literary ideas that reinforce the status quo. But a discontented labor force brings the crisis to a head, and through a series of revolts (for London, unlike Bellamy, the transformation of wealth from one class to another must involve a violent process) the oligarchy is finally overthrown, but not before the execution of London's revolutionary spokesman, Ernest Everhard. London was not a hundred percent right in his predictions of the future. He was wrong in his Marxist belief that the middle class would be absorbed into the proletariat and that there would be an effective international labor movement. But basing many of his assumptions upon Marx's theory of surplus value, London does predict the fight over world markets, the coming of World Wars I and II, the rise of Japan as an eastern empire, the need for stockpiles and subsidies and the destruction of surplus goods, the buildup of the military, and the rise of trusts and multinational corporations. And behind it all, he insists, is the working of power as a mechanical force in a world of limits—an idea voiced by the capitalist Wickson when he says that the oligarchy will triumph over the revolution: "We will ground your revolutionists down under our heel, and we shall walk upon your faces"—because the oligarchy controls the "Power. Not God, not Mammon, but Power."[21] The novels of Bellamy, Donnelly, and London thus begin where Zola's and Norris's novels end—with the power of a commercial/industrial class out of control and about to be transformed. The utopian writers hence fantasize what is implicit in the naturalistic novel and take it beyond itself to the doorstep of science fiction.[22]

At this point, naturalism plays itself out and gives way to forms of a totalitarian vision or a world-city fantasy; and indeed, its tendentious aspects were carried over and applied to different political, economic, and cultural matters as we moved away from the commercial/industrial city of the nineteenth century to the totalitarian/world city of the twentieth century. Perhaps the last of the pure naturalists in this context was Upton Sinclair, who comes the closest to being an American Zola. Sinclair took on the whole economic process in naturalistic terms and, similar to Zola, wrote novels dealing with speculative finance (*The Metropolis* and *The Moneychangers*), the meat, coal, and oil industries (*The Jungle, King Coal,* and *Oil!*), and journalism and education (*The Brass Check* and *The Goose-Step*). As Zola protested against the fate of Dreyfus, Sinclair protested against the execution of Sacco and Vanzetti (*Boston*). To be sure, Sinclair never had Zola's dramatic sense, and allowed his novels to become too talky and tendentious (George Orwell once referred to Sinclair as a "dull, empty windbag"); but, like Zola, Sinclair never separated the novel from the world in which he lived, nor from his sense of immediate experience; he also, like Zola, never forgot that such experience flowed from invisible channels of power and control.

Literary naturalism was an important movement in the development of the novel. As a movement it supplanted the sentimental novel and was in turn supplanted by modernism (the literary movement, not the period). Naturalism supplanted the sentimentalism of a Fielding's Squire Allworthy or a Dickens's Mr. Brownlow when it was no longer convincing to have the sentimental hero resolving the major conflicts of the novel through the power of the human heart to do good against the forces of a purely commercial/industrial world. And naturalism itself was supplanted by modernism when the generation of T. S. Eliot, Ezra Pound, James Joyce, and Virginia Woolf rejected the scientific basis of naturalism, turned away from the human detritus of the industrial process, escaped in turn to the world of the salon or into esthetic concerns, and replaced the mechanistic assumptions of naturalism with the more organic elements of symbolism and myth, relying on a human consciousness and a theory of time mainly derived from Henri Bergson. After World War II, literary naturalism was all but dead, perhaps because so many of its assumptions came too close to the racial and genetic theories associated with Hitler and Nazism. Also, after World War II, an industrial society, especially in America, gave way to a service society based upon the processing of information and the need for electronic communication. The nature of labor changed—work did not make money so much as money made money—and the multicorporation and the world city came into being; the world of Zola gave way to that of Thomas Pynchon. But this network of change should not diminish our interest in what naturalism did for the novel, supplying, as I have tried to suggest, the narrative context for studying the historical consequences of the movement from land to city, of the rise of the financial and speculative institutions, of the rise of a factory and industrial system controlled by a privileged few, and of the effects of such a system in human and environmental costs worldwide. In conceptualizing and codifying these ideas and putting them into literary practice, Zola did for the industrial society in literary terms what Marx did in economic and Lenin in political terms. Every naturalistic writer who followed Zola, particularly in America, which was coming into its own industrial era, remained directly or indirectly in his debt.

## NOTES

1. Bettina L. Knapp, *Émile Zola* (New York: Ungar, 1980), p. 21. For further critical information on Zola and literary naturalism see Matthew Josephson, *Zola and his Time* (New York: Garden City Publishing, 1928); Elliot M. Grant, *Émile Zola* (Boston: Twayne, 1966); Joanna Richardson, *Zola* (London: Weidenfeld and Nicolson, 1978); Graham King, *Garden of Zola* (New York: Barnes and Noble, 1978), Brian Nelson, *Zola and the Bourgeoisie* (London: Macmillan, 1983). Two important essays on Zola are by Georg Lukàcs in *Studies in European Realism* (New York: Grosset and Dunlap, 1964), pp. 85–96, and Harry Levin in *The Gates of Horn* (New York: Oxford Univ. Press, 1963), pp. 305–71.

2. John B. Wolf, *France, 1814–1919* (New York: Harper and Row, 1963), pp. 71, 281, 113, 131.

3. Wolf, *France, 1814–1919*, p. 278.

4. Émile Zola, *La Fortune des Rougan*, trans. E. Vizetelly (London: Vizetelly, 1886), p. vi. Further references to this novel will be shown parenthetically in the text. Since the Vizetelly editions are unreliable, all translated passages have been checked against the original French. There is a serious need for a better translation of the lesser-known Zola novels.

5. Those who are familiar with William Faulkner's novels cannot help but see a similarity here between Zola's Rougons and Faulkner's Snopeses.

6. Émile Zola, *La Curée*, trans. E. Vizetelly (London: Vizetelly, 1886), p. 107.

7. Émile Zola, *L'Argent*, trans. E. Vizetelly (London: Vizetelly, 1886), p. 434.

8. Émile Zola, *L'Assommoir*, trans. Leonard Tancock (New York: Penguin Books, 1970), p. 21.

9. Émile Zola, *Nana*, trans. E. Vizetelly (New York: Modern Library, 1927), p. 246.

10. Émile Zola, *Germinal*, trans. Leonard Tancock (Baltimore: Penguin Classics, 1954), p. 494.

11. "King, *Garden of Zola*, p. 219.

12. Émile Zola, *La Terre*, trans. Douglas Parmée (New York: Penguin Books, 1980), p. 156. Further references to this novel will be shown parenthetically in the text.

13. Émile Zola, *La Bête humaine*, trans. Louis Colman (New York: Julian Press, 1932), p. 159. Further references to this novel will be shown parenthetically in the text.

14. Jacques Ellul, *The Technological Society*, trans. John Wilkinson (New York: Knopf, 1964).

15. Émile Zola, *La Débâcle*, trans. Leonard Tancock (New York: Penguin Books, 1972), p. no.

16. Walter Fuller Taylor, *The Economic Novel in America* (Chapel Hill: Univ. of North Carolina Press, 1942), p. 25. Taylor bases his statement on statistics derived from Ernest Ludlow Bogart, *The Economic History of the United States* (New York: Longmans, 1907), pp. 381–82, 400–402.

17. Walter Rideout, *The Radical Novel in the United States, 1900–1945* (Cambridge, Mass.: Harvard Univ. Press, 1956). Rideout's study is a valuable introduction to the social novel at the turn of the century. A related study, also helpful in discussing late nineteenth- and early twentieth-century novels, is Joseph Blotner's *The Modern American Political Novel, 1900-1960* (Austin: Univ. of Texas Press, 1966). For a version of literary naturalism in America different from mine see Charles Child Walcutt, *American Literary Naturalism: A Divided Stream* (Minneapolis: Univ. of Minnesota Press, 1956), and Donald Pizer, *Realism and Naturalism in Nineteenth-Century American Literature* (Carbondale: Southern Illinois Univ. Press, 1966).

18. Frank Norris, "The Frontier Gone at Last," *The Responsibilities of the Novelist* (New York: Doubleday, Doran, 1901), pp. 71, 74, 77. Norris restates this thesis in *The Octopus* (New York: New American Library, 1964), pp. 227–28. Further references to this novel will be shown parenthetically in the text. There are two studies of Zola's influence on Norris: Marius Biencourt, *Une Influence du naturalisme français en Amérique* (Paris: Marcel Giard, 1933) and Lars Ahnebrink, "The Influence of Émile Zola on Frank Norris," *Essays and Studies on American Language and Literature* (Uppsala, Sweden: A. B. Lundequistska Bokhandeln, 1947).

19. Frank Norris, *The Pit* (New York: Grove Press, n.d.), pp. 62, 120; cf. also p. 189; further citations to this novel appear in my text.

20. Theodore Dreiser, *The Financier* (New York: Dell, 1961), pp. 526–28.

21. Jack London, *The Iron Heel* (Westport, Conn.: Lawrence Hill, 1980), p. 63.

22. For the reader who would like to follow the idea of technological power in science fiction, the following novels are illustrative: Mark Adlard's *Interface*, *Volteface*, and *Multiface*; Isaac Asimov's *Foundation*, *Foundation and Empire*, and *Second Foundation*; Arthur C. Clarke's *Childhood's End* and *The City and the Stars*; Samuel R. Delany's *The Fall of the Towers* and *Dhalgren*; Jonathan Fast's *The Secrets of Synchronicity*; Jane Gaskell's *A Sweet, Sweet Summer*; Mark S. Geston's *The Siege of Wonder*; Robert A. Heinlein's *Stranger in a Strange Land* and *The Moon is a Harsh Mistress*; Ursula Le Guin's *The Word for World is Forest* and *The Dispossessed*; Stanislaw Lem's *The Cyberiad* and *Solaris* (on knowledge and information as power); Walter M. Miller's *A Canticle for Leibowitz*; Frederik Pohl and C. M. Kornbluth's *The Space Merchants* and *Gladiator-at-Law*; Mack Reynolds's *Black Man's Burden, Boarder, Breed, Nor Birth, The Best Ye Breed*, and *Mercenary from Tomorrow*; Robert Silverberg's *A Time of Changes*; Clifford D. Simak's *City*; and Norman Spinard's *The Men in the Jungle* and *The Iron Dream*.

MICHEL FABRE

# Beyond Naturalism?

That Richard Wright is a naturalist writer has generally been taken for granted by American critics. In his review of *Lawd Today*, entitled "From Dreiser to Farrell to Wright," Granville Hicks proceeded, not incorrectly, to show that

> ... he could scarcely have failed to be influenced by James T. Farrell who was just beginning to have a strong effect on American fiction. As Farrell had learned something about documentation from Dreiser, so Wright had learned from Farrell.[1]

When he reviewed *The Outsider* for the *New York Times*, the same critic noted:

> ... if the ideas are sometimes incoherent, that does not detract from the substance and the power of the book. Wright has always been a demonic writer, and in the earliest of his stories one felt that he was saying more than he knew, that he was, in a remarkable degree, an unconscious artist.[2]

Other reviewers even seemed to regret that Wright attempted to deal with ideas. In his review Orville Prescott stated that "instead of a realistic sociological document he had[d] written a philosophical novel, its ideas

From *The World of Richard Wright*. © 1985 by the University of Mississippi Press.

dramatized by improbable coincidences and symbolical characters."[3] And Luther P. Jackson outspokenly lamented that the

> words of Wright's angry men leap from the page and hit you between the eyes. But Wright can no more resist an argument on the Left Bank than he could a soapbox in Washington Park. The lickety-split action of his novel bogs down in a slough of dialectics.[4]

It is clear, then, that Wright is regarded not as a novelist of ideas or as a symbolist, but as an emotionally powerful creator who writes from his guts and churns up reality in a melodramatic but effective way because he is authentic, close to nature, true to life. Conversely, the critics's displeasure at his incursions into other realms than that of social realism proves only that there are elements in his writing which cannot be reduced to their favorite image of him as a hard-boiled naturalist. The question then becomes: to what extent is he part of the naturalistic stream in American literature? Is he, in fact, sufficiently a part of it for his works to be judged, and found satisfactory or wanting, only according to that perspective? Or is his originality so strong that it cannot be adequately accounted for in terms of the Dreiser/Farrell line of succession, and does this therefore necessitate a reassessment of what is commonly held for American literary naturalism?

It is not my purpose here to reopen the long-debated question of what exactly naturalism is. In his preface to *American Literary Naturalism, A Divided Stream*, Charles C. Walcutt described it as "a beast of protean slipperiness" which, soon after it had sprung from the fountain of Transcendentalism, divided into rebellious, idealistic social radicalism on one side and pessimistic determinism on the other; consequently, the assertion of the unity of nature and spirit, the equality of intuition and reason was somewhat diminished.

If we consider naturalism as a philosophy, it is clear from the start that Wright's perspective is only very partly akin to it. He had read Darwin's *Origin of Species* but he probably did not even know of Herbert Spencer, the true philosophical cornerstone of American naturalism. If he did, his Communistic leanings set him early on the side of Marx against the Spencerian view of the "survival of the fittest." To him, the fittest were the productive workers, not the parasitic upper classes. Insofar as he was a Marxist, "the organized exercise of the social will" meant the liquidation of the bourgeoisie.

Estranged as he was from God by the oppressive religious practice of his Seventh-Day Adventist grandmother, Wright was also prone to eschew Transcendentalism as well as the very American belief that physical progress reflects spiritual progress. His childhood taught him that knowledge could indeed bring freedom, and self-education became his only means of escape from the cultural ghetto. But if knowledge can make man similar to God, he later discovered that too much knowledge can bring man beyond good and evil so that he ends, isolated from his fellowmen, in the position of a "little God" who has no right to act as one. This is the lesson in existential absurdity to be derived from *The Outsider*. Thus, at times Wright comes close to the naturalistic vision of determinism, which conceives of man as an accident, or an epiphenomenon caught in a general movement toward universal rest. This is apparent in a long (still unpublished) piece of poetry he wrote in the mid-fifties to celebrate the manifold incarnations of life. In it he deals with a force that works through man, and that inhabits him for a time, making him the vessel of a principle he cannot control. This force, though, does not tend toward static, cosmic rest; rather, it aims at self-fulfillment and unlimited expansion, it gropes toward a kind of pantheistic harmony in which matter and spirit are one. If this is Transcendentalism of a kind, it represents only a transitory stage in Wright's thinking. On the whole, he is a humanist who retains the Marxist perspective as an ideological tool, and who believes in ethical responsibility, and a certain degree of free will in a world whose values are not created by a transcendental entity, but by the common workings of mankind.

Insofar as naturalism is opposed to romanticism as a philosophy, it attacks the unscientific values of tradition and evinces a distrust of those natural forces that man cannot control; it thus corresponds to one facet of Wright's personality. If we look at an early short story, "Superstition," and at a later one, "Man, God Ain't Like That," we find that both denounce the obscene power that such beliefs—and Wright deliberately makes no difference between religion and superstition—can wield over the spirit of man. There, Wright is largely a rationalist. Similarly, when he advocates the cultural liberation of African nations, he still upholds the idea that what was good for Europe, insofar as rationalism and technology are concerned, should be good for the Third World: colonialism has unwittingly given Africa the tools for her own liberation from her religion-ridden ancestral past, and the new African leaders should seize that opportunity to step boldly into the twentieth century. Such is Wright's contention—an opinion which encountered strong opposition on the part of many African intellectuals at the 1956 Congress of Black Artists and Writers in Paris.

Where America was concerned, however, Wright held somewhat different views; he often regretted that his country had no past and no traditions (however unscientific or irrational they might be).

Like many naturalists before him, Wright feared the forces that reason cannot control, forces that lie within the darkest recesses of man's soul, and his descriptions of Africa evoke at times Conrad's sense of horror in *Heart of Darkness*. Mostly he fears the forces man has unleashed and can no longer subdue, like the overpowering social systems that stifle the development of individuality.

A brief survey of Wright's many-faceted *weltanschauung* shows him to be inconclusively close to or remote from what passes for the common denominators of the various American naturalists. His position oscillates between Marxism and humanistic Existentialism.

We ought to remember that he is not primarily a thinker but a novelist, and therefore, that whatever may be characteristically naturalistic in his fiction is more likely to have resulted from his personal experience as a poor black American or from his early readings and stands as an embattled writer. Although naturalism is as protean as a set of literary forms and techniques as it is as a philosophical view, it is, nevertheless, on these forms that the brunt of our analysis must rest.

In the often-quoted episode from *Black Boy* in which he relates how he was spiritually saved by reading a few American novelists to whom he had been introduced by Mencken's *Book of Prefaces*, Wright mentions Sinclair Lewis's *Main Street*, Dreiser's *Jennie Gerhardt*, and *Sister Carrie*, as well as Stephen Crane:

> I was overwhelmed. I grew silent, wondering about the life around me. It would have been impossible for me to have told anyone what I derived from these novels for it was nothing less than a sense of life itself. All my life had shaped me for the realism, the naturalism of the modern novel, and I could not read enough of them.[5]

Two things are important in this statement. First, the experiential basis of Wright's literary outlook ("all my life had shaped me for the realism, the naturalism of the modern novel"); second, the apparent lack of distinction between realism and naturalism; he seems to consider the two terms practically interchangeable. In this piece, written in 1943 after he had established his reputation as a novelist, Wright considers naturalism loosely, as simply another version of American realism; he is mostly interested in it because it provides an authentic sense of life and an understanding of the American scene:

> *Main Street* ... made me see my boss, Mr. Gerald, and identify him as an American type ... I felt closer to him though still distant. I felt that now I knew him, that I could feel the very limits of his narrow life.[6]

Such naturalistic novels convinced Wright that his life, hemmed in by poverty and racism, was not the only life to be circumscribed. Even the lives of the powerful whites that he had pictured as glamorous were restricted by uncontrollable circumstances. All men were encompassed by the same definition of the human condition. In a sense, Wright is relieved to see that white people don't escape man's common destiny; the racial gap artificially established by them tends to disappear, yielding at the same time to a more social perspective of rich versus poor, and to a universal humanistic view. Realistic/naturalistic fiction is thus defined, through Wright's own experience, as an eye-opener, in opposition to the romantic tales, the dime novels, the detective stories, the blood and thunder episodes he relished primarily because they provided him with an escape from everyday life. Romantic fiction became for him a synonym of evasion and vicarious revenge, wholly artificial because it precluded meaningful action. Naturalistic fiction provided him with a means of liberation through understanding. Although he sometimes read it, he contritely admits, as he would take a drug or dope, he generally derived from it a new social perspective.

> The plots and stories in the novel did not interest me so much as the point of view revealed.... I could not conquer my sense of guilt, the feeling that the white men around me knew that I was changing, that I had begun to regard them differently.[7]

That early impact upon his sensibilities was to last. Throughout his life, he considered Dreiser, his favorite American master, a literary giant nearly on par with Dostoevsky. Nothing indicates that he had read such early naturalists as Harold Frederic, Hamlin Garland, or even Frank Norris. Yet, he knew the works of Gorki, Hauptmann, George Moore, London, Stephen Crane, and Sherwood Anderson. Anderson appealed to him because of his revolt against small-town life in *Winesburg, Ohio*, and because of the essentially instinctive realism of his portrayals of domestic revolt. Anderson, like Wright, neither apologized for himself nor submitted to naturalistic despair; rather he tended to make of personal freedom a sort of mystic quest and to consider fiction as a substitute for religion—a thing in which Wright also characteristically indulged.

Later, the discovery of James T. Farrell's works and his personal acquaintance with him in the mid-thirties had some impact on his own writing, as is apparent in *Lawd Today*. True, Wright certainly derived more from Conrad or Poe with regard to the expression of moods; from Henry James and Hemingway with regard to the use of symbols; from Gertrude Stein with regard to speech rhythms; and he learned from Joyce, T. S. Eliot, and above all, Dostoevsky. Yet, the impact of the American realists was important because it came first and because it closely corresponded to Wright's own experience. There is a kinship between the lives of Dreiser and Wright that goes beyond literary theories. From the first, Dreiser was hard pressed by suffering, and the destitution of the existence to which he was born suggested to him a vision of men struggling aimlessly in a society which excluded them. American life he could thus identify as a figure of distant, capricious destiny.[8] He grew up hating the narrow-mindedness and helplessness of his family and was so overpowered by suffering that he came to see it as a universal principle to the point that he considered only the hand of fate where others saw the political and economic evils of capitalism.

Isn't that largely what happened to Wright? The sufferings due to poverty and family disruption, the narrow-minded religion practiced at home, the subservient attitudes of the family figures of authority caused him to question and to rebel against the order of things. He too hated the threadbare woof of his spiritually deprived childhood so strongly that he tended to generalize it in his oft-criticized declaration about black life.

> I used to mull over the strange absence of real kindness in Negroes, how unstable was our tenderness, how lacking in genuine passion, we were, how void of great hope, how timid our joy, how bare our traditions, how hollow our memories, how lacking we were in those intangible sentiments that bind man to man, and how shallow even was our despair ... what had been taken for our emotional strength was our negative confusion, our flights, our fears, our frenzy under pressure.[9]

He too disliked his father who had relinquished his responsibilities; he too deplored his mother's inefficacy; he too had a brooding boyhood and the lonely joys of wallowing in books. He too came to experience destiny as an unexpected dispensation of fate, particularly brutal in the case of his mother's stroke, and he started to build up the precariousness of his own life into a philosophy. At twelve, he held "... a notion as to what life meant that no education could ever alter, a conviction that the meaning of living came only when [he] was struggling to wring a meaning out of meaningless suffering." He concluded:

> It made me want to drive coldly to the heart of every question and lay it open ... love burrowing into psychology, into realistic and naturalistic fiction and art, into those whirlpools of politics that had the power to claim the whole of men's souls. It directed my loyalties to the side of men in rebellion; it made me love talk that sought answers to questions that could help nobody, that could only keep alive in me that enthralling sense of wonder and awe in the face of the drama of human feelings which is hidden by the external drama of life.[10]

If Wright followed Dreiser along the road of pessimistic determinism and stressed the helplessness of man, it also appears that the racial oppression he suffered enabled him to find the cause for his own, and his people's, sufferings in the hatred of the surrounding white world. Severed from knowledge and from the mainstream of American culture, he tried to join it. A victim of oppression, he directed his efforts toward rebellion. Thus, he partly escaped Dreiser's deep pessimism while his reverence for the invisible helped him maintain a sense of wonder and awe in front of his existential dilemma.

The fact that Wright came of age, in a literary sense, under the aegis of the Communist Party and during the Depression largely accounts for the special tenor of his naturalism. The revival of naturalism in the thirties corresponded to Wright's efforts to adapt his writing to a style he could achieve relatively easily. Among the John Reeders he found for the first time a milieu akin to, and favorable to, his preoccupations. That was the time when America was being educated by shock, and the impact of the crisis on the values of American culture was probably stronger than the repercussions of the economic crash upon the capitalist system. The rational character of the social structure seemed to disintegrate, and its existential components were revealed through the alienation of the individual from a society which did not care for him. Wright had experienced this since his childhood in Mississippi and could thus translate his own experience into general terms. His desire to use words as weapons, after the fashion of Mencken, in order to achieve some kind of liberation, had also become a nearly general tenet. The novelists of the thirties seemed heir to new obligations and were called upon to leave their ivory towers and become politically relevant. Authenticity, which had always been Wright's criterion, was rehabilitated to stand against artiness. A comparable movement had already taken place at the turn of the century, when Frank Norris supposedly declared, as he embraced naturalism out of hatred for so-called pure literature, "Who cares for fine style, we don't want literature, give us life." And in Europe, the social studies of Émile Zola had developed in opposition to the stylistic achievements of Flaubert's realism. Yet, in the thirties, a new sense of urgency was added, and Wright felt strongly confirmed in what he believed his mission as a writer to be.

> In their efforts to recruit masses [the Communists] had missed the meaning of the lives of the masses, had conceived of people in too abstract a manner. I would try to put some of that meaning back. I would tell Communists how common people felt, and I would tell common people of the self-sacrifice of communists who strove for unity among them.[11]

There was indeed a deep convergence between Wright's idiosyncratic attraction to violence (or compulsive counter-violence) and protest, and, on the other hand, the social attitude of the committed writers of the times as Alfred Kazin has analyzed it with perspicacity.[12] Of course, there did not remain much of the original philosophy of naturalism in that attitude. It was taken for granted that the writer should be a tough guy. In fact, most of the so-called proletarian writers were the sons of the bourgeoisie, but they considered themselves as starting from scratch and rejected literary traditions. On the contrary, Wright came from the lower classes, was largely self-educated, and had been kept from a literary tradition; he tried to invent one for himself, and this explains why he could endorse writers in the thirties who, like T. S. Eliot, were often attacked by the left as "decadents."

Also, the hardness of naturalism was more or less instinctive to those writers who tended to see life as oppression. Wright had really suffered oppression, so he could be vehement about what he repudiated. They all shared a common belief in social determinism, not the biological determinism of Spencer or even Dreiser, but the conviction that man is made and crushed by his social background and environment.

As Kazin further emphasizes, proletarian naturalism generally had narrow categories and ready-made prescriptions. It was assumed that the embattled novel ought to be relatively fast-paced so that the reader could be stimulated into active sympathy with the right cause; accordingly, thought was often subordinate to action, and the characters developed in a predetermined way toward class-consciousness. The novelists did not pose psychological problems whose refined variations constituted the novel proper. The strategy, Kazin argues, consisted in beginning with a state of fear or doubt which action dissipated. One always found a great deal of facts and documentation which answered for documentary realism.

This enumeration of the characteristics of the proletarian novel nearly amounts to a description of Wright's outstanding success of the period, i.e. *Native Son*.

Above all, Wright is conspicuous by his use and abuse of violence. This theme of violence was revived in fiction where it tended to become a demonstration of economic and social dislocation and a reflection of the state of the American system. Wright's own inclination to violence in fiction (in life he abhorred physical violence) could mirror the violence inflicted by American society, pass for the counter-violence of the oppressed Negro, and prefigurate revolutionary violence. This was also the case for Erskine Caldwell and, to a degree, for James T. Farrell, both of whom displayed real excitement in reporting capitalistic decay. One may wonder, indeed, whether those novelists—in spite of their different political affiliations, temperaments, and styles—were not united by this coming of age in a time of catastrophe, a time which corresponded to their deep need for terror. Such terror in Wright hardly finds release except in a kind of obsession with details of utter brutality; the endings of his novels are not cathartic. Although Bigger discovers that he is what he killed for, this does not really free him from his alienation. On the contrary it fills Max with horror at the thought of his own (and the Communists') failure. *Native Son* differs noticeably from the standard proletarian novel in that the protagonist does not achieve real social and political consciousness; as a piece of propaganda, it is much weaker than "Fire and Cloud" and "Bright and Morning Star," in spite of the opinions of the reviewers and critics of the time. The writing of violent novels thus appears, above all, to be a search for emotional catharsis, maybe for vicarious fulfillment; this is what Wright meant when he said that writing "drain[ed] all the poison out of [him]."

Brutality is also, at times, deliberate and calculated to shock the reader. Because bankers's daughters had wept when reading *Uncle Tom's Children* and thereby found relief, Wright says in "How Bigger Was Born" that he wanted *Native Son* to be so taut, so hard that they would have to face it without the relief of tears.[13] This cultivation of violence often brings him closer to

Dostoevsky who excels in depicting characters under extreme stress—think of Raskolnikov or Karamazov before and after the murder—than to the American naturalists. The naturalists's supposed contempt for style and their refusal of sensationalism do not apply to Wright and is certainly better exemplified by James T. Farrell's deliberate literalness of description. Farrell renounces effects to such a degree that this becomes an attribute of his writing (his writing is far more barren and clinical than Dreiser's, whose epic imagination took him, like Zola, into wild and beautiful flights). By accumulating details with detachment and also with some cruelty to his characters, Farrell achieves a sort of stone-like solidity, which is a monument in itself. Not so with Wright. There is in him a great attention to detail, but he depends much more for his effects upon the sweep and the suspense of narrative rather than upon the accumulation of revealing evidence—with the exception of *Lawd Today*.

At times, Wright's realism is quite naturalistic. He does not attempt to create simply the illusion of reality; after a careful study of life, he sometimes resorts with evident relish to nearly photographic verisimilitude. This, of course, is true mainly for descriptions and details, and is best documented by *Lawd Today*. This is also true for reactions and attitudes. For instance, while Wright was writing *Native Son*—in which he depicts in deterministic terms, "the story of a boy born amid poverty and conditions of fear which eventually stopped his will and control and made him a reluctant killer"[14]—the Robert Nixon case broke out in Chicago, and the novelist was quite happy to copy verbatim some of the *Chicago Tribune's* descriptions of the murderer and to use the brief prepared by attorney Ulysses Keys. Wright also resorted to authentic sources in order to present a view of the racist reactions of the white reporters—perhaps he did so to forestall any possible challenge by his critics. Why did he desire such literalness? One may surmise that he wanted to emulate Dreiser, who had based *An American Tragedy* on the Grace Brown/Chester Gillette case. In several other instances, however, Wright goes beyond that need for undebatable proof and documentation. As I have tried to show elsewhere, even in a novella as surrealistic and existentialistic as "The Man Who Lived Underground," Wright did not use Dostoevsky's *Notes from Underground* as a source, but used instead a glaring account of the subterranean adventures of a Hollywood delinquent he had lifted from *True Detective Magazine*. Likewise, we have to go back to actual events in order to find the origin of his humorous and imaginative "Man of All Works." "The Man Who Killed a Shadow" actually comes from the Julius Fischer case, which attorney Charles E. Houston had related to Wright shortly before his departure for France. Wright secured a transcript and nearly contented himself with narrating it: describing, for instance, the way the defendant had strangled and clubbed with a stick a librarian, Catherine Cooper Reardon, because she had complained about his work, Wright went as far as lifting whole sentences from the court record; even details which one could think came from his imagination and zest for horror, such as the use of the victim's pink panties to wipe her blood from the floor, are borrowed from the official transcript. Again and again, whether for details or plot episodes, Wright goes back to actual occurrences. Of course there is in this something of the painstaking search for documentary proof that he greatly admired in Émile Zola. An interview he gave to a Swedish newspaper in the late fifties shows how much he wanted to imitate the French naturalist master. Just as Zola, notebook in hand, jotted down information about prostitutes when he wanted to write *Nana*, we discover that Wright, not satisfied with copying real letters from American sailors to Spanish prostitutes in *Pagan Spain*, also tried to buy similar letters from French prostitutes when gathering documentation on GI's in France for the last volume of his Fishbelly trilogy.

To Wright, the document, designed as proof, is nearly sacred. His industrious research into the facts can sometimes be ascribed to the necessity to check actual details because of a lack of personal experience: for instance, apropos of the arraignment of Tyree in *The Long Dream*, he had to learn the details of Mississippi court procedure. In other instances his journalistic zeal seems to be a carry-over from his beginnings as a correspondent for the Harlem Bureau of the *Daily Worker*. As was the case with Crane, Norris, London, Dreiser, and many muckrakers, Wright's schooling in the writing profession began partly in a newspaper office, hence his reverence for the document as objective record. Yet, contrary to Sinclair Lewis, he never turns the novel into a sort of higher journalism, and it might be truer to say that his best journalism—articles like "Two Million Black Voices" or "Joe Louis Discovers Dynamite"—derives its power from a nonjournalistic interest in time, locale, and dramatic sequence.

Among the many reasons for the importance of the authentic record in Wright's fiction, two seem to prevail: first, the obligation of a black writer to substantiate his most trifling indictments of the white system; second, but not least, Wright's naive pleasure in discovering that reality is often more fiction-like than fiction itself and in persuading the reader of this.

As far as form is concerned, a commonly held opinion is that the naturalists did not really care for the niceties of style. This may be true of a few proletarian novelists who disguised their ignorance in literary matters as a deliberate contempt for refined "bourgeois" aestheticism. This may be true of Farrell; and it may even be partly true of Dreiser, though his clumsier attempts at elegance are the result of a failure rather than a lack of care. This is never true of Wright, who always evinced a deep interest in style. His best-known pronouncement about writing, "Blueprint for Negro Writing," stresses the balance between content and expression. Indeed he takes writing seriously, sometimes awfully so; for him it is no gratuitous game, but a weapon, a vital, self-justifying activity, a means to change the world.

In his eyes, to write well was not sufficient. He did, for instance, censure Zora Neale Hurston because the "sensory sweep of her novel [*Their Eyes Were Watching God*] carries no theme, no message, no thought."[15] And he praised Carl Von Unruh because his comprehension of the problems of Fascism in *The End Is Not Yet* "lifts him, at one stroke, out of the class of fictionneers and onto the plane of writers who through the prophetic power of their vision, legislate new values for mankind."[16] For Wright, the ideal for people "writing from the Left," as he does, should be to "create in the minds of other people a picture that would impell them to meaningful activity."[17] This quest for the meaningful even leads Wright to assert that Stephen Crane's *Maggie: A Girl of the Streets* is simply a coldly materialistic picture of poverty (while Jack Conroy's *The Disinherited* is the picture of men and women groping their way to a new concept of human dignity[18]) and to find Arna Bontemps's or Langston Hughes's novels more relevant, though not better, than *Sister Carrie* because their characters are "haunted with the desire to make their lives meaningful."

The strength of true fiction comes above all from the nature of writing itself, which must achieve a nice balance between form and content; "the limitations of the craft constitute its greatest virtues. If the sensory vehicle of imaginative writing is required to carry too great a load of didactic material, the artistic sense is submerged," Wright states in "Blueprint for Negro Writing."[19] This explains why he did not hesitate to fight the attempts of CP leaders who wanted him to propagandize. He did so in the name of personal freedom and also for the validity of an art defined by intrinsic criteria; in a reply to the Jewish liberal critic David Cohn, he says:

> Mr. Cohn implies that as a writer I should look at the state of the Negro through the lens of relativity and not judge his plight in an absolute sense. This is precisely what, as an artist, I try NOT to do. My character, Bigger Thomas, lives and suffers in the real world. Feeling and perception are absolute, and if I dodged my responsibility as an artist and depicted them otherwise, I'd be a traitor not to my race alone but to humanity.[20]

Art certainly requires a "point of objectivity in the handling of the subject matter," yet, Wright will never define it through extrinsic criteria: "In the last analysis," he answers engraver Antonio Frasconi in a beautiful letter dated November 1944, "the artist must bow to the monitor of his own imagination; must be led by the sovereignty of his own impressions and perceptions; must be guided by the tyranny of what troubles and concerns him personally. There is no other true path."[21]

Wright himself spent hour upon hour trying to master the craft of fiction, experimenting with words, with sentences, with scenes; and with the help of other novels or prefaces after he had found grammar books and style manuals quite useless, he tried patiently to make his writing jell, harden, and coalesce into a meaningful whole. When he was successful, stories such as "Big Boy Leaves Home" or "Down by the Riverside" are proof that he was able to blend and to fuse elements and techniques borrowed from Joyce, Hemingway, Gertrude Stein, Conrad, and even James. His single-mindedness can, at times, be reminiscent of the efforts of Flaubert, whom he greatly admired. Proust's *Remembrance of Things Past* also filled him with boundless admiration and equal despair because he felt unable to do as well. In one of the most revealing chapters of his autobiography, Wright confesses:

> My purpose was to capture a physical state or movement that carried strong subjective impressions, an accomplishment which seemed supremely worth struggling for. If I could fasten the mind of the reader upon words so firmly that he would forget words and be conscious only of his response, I felt that I would be in sight of knowing how to write narrative. I strove to master words, to make them disappear, to make them important by making them new, to make them melt into a rising spiral of emotional climax that would drench the reader with a sense of a new world. This was the single end of my living.[22]

Here we are far indeed from the supposed naturalistic/proletarian distrust for fine writing!

The major difference between Wright's view of how fiction should depict the lives of the common people and what the believers in scientific determinism tried to achieve in fiction can be found in Wright's opinion of Nelson Algren's *Never Come Morning*. The preface he wrote for that novel considers a few of the literary strategies which could have been used for the treatment of Bruno Bicek and his friends: some writers would have resorted to satire or humor, others would have "assumed an aloof 'social worker' attitude toward it, prescribing 'pink pills' for social ills, piling up a mountain of naturalistic detail."[23] Wright, by the way, did *not* go in for such techniques and he believed that Algren's perspective excelled all of those because he "depicts the intensity of feeling, the tawdry but potent dreams, the crude but forceful poetry and the frustrating longing for humanity residing in the lives of the Poles of Chicago's North West Side."[24]

Here, the importance attributed to intensity of feeling over naturalistic detail, the insistence on the forceful poetry of commonplace lives is somewhat unexpected; yet, is this not what Wright attempted when he depicted Bigger Thomas' or Jake Jackson's frustrated longings for a movie-like world? And, at the same time, is not such a statement in the very vein of a Frank Norris who considers naturalism, as incarnated by Zola, as another kind of romanticism?

In "Blueprint for Negro Writing," Wright seems to be responding to Norris' desire that ordinary characters "must be twisted from the ordinary" when he prescribes:

> The presentation of their lives should be simple, yes; but all the complexity, the strangeness, the magic, the wonder of life that lays like a bright sheen over the most sordid existence should be there. To borrow a phrase from the Russians, it should have a *complex simplicity*.[25]

This is a way of claiming equal treatment for all in the field of literature, hence a political statement. At the same time, Wright is convinced that no literature exists without romance, without "the bright sheen" of illusion—he dedicated *Native Son* to his mother, who taught him as "a child at her knee, to revere the fanciful and the imaginative." He was convinced that art had little to do with scientific objectivity (not to be mistaken for authenticity and honesty) and that:

> An artist deals with aspects of reality different from those which a scientist uses. My task is not to abstract reality but to enhance its value. In the process of identifying emotional experience in words, paint, stone, or tone, an artist uses his feelings in an immediate and absolute sense.[26]

Literature is thus less the depiction of the actual world than the representation of emotional experience through words. The world interests Wright only insofar as it affects the individual, as it is perceived, experienced, acted upon, or reacted against. He places the emphasis on emotion, the emotional potential of the material, the emotion to be aroused in the reader, the emotion of the creator at work. It may be in that last domain that his intimate convictions about literary creation bring him the farthest from the theoreticians of the experimental novel and "laboratory creation." He does not view writing as a conscious production in which intellect and critical sense are unceasingly called upon to regulate fancy. His conception is rather dangerously close to the Romanticists' definition of inspiration. Being a rationalist and an agnostic, if not an atheist, he confesses there is something paradoxical in such a view, and he honestly admits this contradiction:

> I abhor the very notion of mysticism; yet, in trying to grasp this [creative] process in me, I encounter a reality that recedes and hides itself in another reality, and, when hunted too openly, it alters its own aspect, chameleon-like, thereby escaping introspectional observation. I sigh, shrug, leave it alone, but still trust it, welcoming it when it comes again.[27]

Doesn't this half-reluctant admission amount to a recognition of the contingency of visitations of quasi-divine inspiration? Further on, Wright recalls that, preceding the writing of all his books, not only fiction but even travel narratives, he had been invaded by a feeling of estrangement from his surroundings, a sense of "being possessed by a slow stirring of the emotions, a sort of haunting incitation as though ... vainly seeking to recall something long forgotten."[28] He owns that he had no power over these creative moods, that they came when they wanted, and that no distraction could dislodge them until the writing of the piece had actually drained them off. Such a perspective defines the writer as the instrument of a power which inhabits him temporarily, coerces him to express it, and then leaves him after these strange visitations. This is strongly reminiscent of Wright's description of the working of the life force in a poem of his that was mentioned previously. It corresponds to a fatalistic creation, because it becomes, in this view, a process which takes place without much actual effort on the part of the writer:

> I was aware of subjective movements ... finally being strung out in time, of events spelling a sequence, that of interlocking images shedding that kind of meaning we associate with a 'story'.... Such moods ... suck themselves into events, long past and forgotten, declaring them their personal property; then to my amazed

delight they telescope alien and disparate images into organic wholes.... A crime story in a newspaper evokes a sense of excitement far beyond the meaning of the banal crime described, a meaning which, in turn, conjures up for some inexplicable reasons its emotional equivalent in a totally different setting and possessing a completely different meaning.[29]

Even more significant than his conception of inspiration is the definition Wright provides of a "story": it is not so much an organized plot carried out through narrative, as it is a "sequence of interlocking images shedding [a] kind of meaning." "Meaning" here is emotional rather than intellectual, and the image-pattern stands for the essential element. A close reading of Wright's symbolic, often dream-like fiction reveals that the crudely apparent three-to-five-act dramatic structure is only an external framework which supports a finely woven symbolic texture. The dramatic framework is mainly a means of prodding the narrative onwards at the hectic pace required by the narrow time limits of the classical tragedy (these time limits are actually narrow in *Lawd Today*, *Savage Holiday*, and even *Native Son*; they are made to seem narrow in *The Outsider* and *The Long Dream* by the selection of important scenes and by glossing over several months in a few sentences). As a result, Wright's narrative derives its emotional unity not so much from the plot or even the breathless rhythm with which he carries the reader forward, as from the "complex simplicity" of its associational imagery. Again, this brings Wright closer to the expressionists (or the impressionists, for that purpose) than to the naturalists. But does not the power and beauty of *Sister Carrie* derive less from Dreiser's objective presentation or see-saw-like structure than from its weird and emotionally laden images? Isn't this true also of the glittering world of *Nana* or Flaubert's *Madame Bovary*?

In the last resort, can't the best naturalists be declared great *because of*, not in spite of, their diffuse romanticism or epic vision? It may well be that the tendency to weave emotion and passion into documentation and reportorial accuracy is the secret of successful naturalistic writing and that naturalism should be reassessed in that light. Rather than sheer reaction against romantic exaggeration, it would appear to be a semi-conscious attempt to rationalize the sense of doom which was so keenly felt by the romantics. Scientific theories were introduced into the naturalists' critical and conceptual views of literary creation, but did they ever turn the novel into a scientific process? On the contrary, they tended to subordinate and assimilate science to the imagination. What they considered slice-of-life authenticity, what Wright believed to be real and authentic in his novels because it rested upon documentary proof, was often only a starting point, as he admitted toward the end of his career.

> A crime story in a newspaper evokes a sense of excitement far beyond the meaning of the banal crime described, a meaning which, in turn, conjures up, for inexplicable reasons, its emotion equivalent in a totally different setting and possessing a completely contrary meaning.[30]

If the setting and meaning are thus totally "contrary," can the original reports still be considered as relevant proof of authenticity?

Wright's conception of the artistic aim is, in the final analysis, that of a technique directed at bringing the reader, through poetic ecstasy or shock treatment, to acceptance of a new consciousness. A sort of alchemistic strategy (he actually uses and abuses the terms "to blend" and "to fuse") must be devised in order to drench the reader with the sense of something unheard, a result which could not be achieved by demonstrative logic or philosophizing. It is not surprising, then, that Wright should compliment Fritz Von Unruh because his novel is:

> ... a marvellous nightmare which has the power to shed light upon your waking hours. It depends for its continuity not upon the logic of two plus two equals four but upon the blooming of opposite images, upon the linking of widely disparate symbols and events, upon the associational magic of passion.[31]

"The linking of widely disparate symbols" was the touchstone of "good" surrealistic imagery in the eyes of the French surrealists; they considered the image more successful as the symbols were more distant and unrelated. At the root of Wright's fondness for what he calls surrealism one finds not a reading of the French surrealists (although Wright liked Dali's paintings and wrote a poem in homage to Aragon) but rather the influence of his grandmother whose Seventh-Day Adventism connected in his eyes ordinary reality with remote beliefs and, even more, the influence of the blues with their typical ability to bring together seemingly unrelated elements of the American Negro's existence and blend them into a new, meaningful whole.

Another, more obvious, trend of Wright's fiction, which, at times, differentiates him from the naturalists, is his sensationalism. True, such sensationalism could pass for an answer to Norris's demand that a naturalistic tale must possess "a violent and energetic greatness," that the characters must be "wrenched from the quiet, uneventful round of ordinary life and flung into the throes of a vast and terrible drama that works itself out in unleashed passions, in blood and sudden death." Certainly, if the naturalists thrive on the appearance of power and gross effects (which might be defined as expressionistic), then Wright is very much of a naturalist because he retains a great deal of the awareness of American naturalism. Viceral writing is his forte; critics generally agree that he is "a born storyteller" with all the implications of such a definition. Yet, if he willingly resorts to suspense, melodrama, coincidence, and subjection of character analysis to plot and storytelling, does not Wright do so mostly because of his early schooling in the stock techniques of popular fiction? In his mind, rawness and brutality are associated with fantasy and the gothic, i.e., another kind of romanticism. Here, the influence of Edgar Allan Poe is prevalent; in the most gruesome epidsodes of *Native Son*, for example, Wright blends two such apparently irreconcilable trends as gothic horror and sadism and, on the other hand, matter-of-fact, slice-of-life reporting. Perhaps he was able to do so because of his early ability to live simultaneously on the level of everyday destitution and that of evasion through popular fiction. The tenets of naturalism would impose upon Bigger a passive character, one subject to the workings of determinism and fate; we are made to share in his subordinate behavior through a quasi-reportorial rendition of his physical and psychosomatic reactions, sensations, and half-formulated thoughts. At the same time he evolves, by implication, in a world which is more that of Dostoevsky's *Crime and Punishment* than that of Dreiser's *An American Tragedy*, and by indirection he is enlarged into a King-Kong stereotype (quite consistent with the Rue Morgue murderer)—all without losing any of his humanity, because the reader is compelled to see the whole scene from his eyes.

Wright's conception of fiction as a magic telescoping of disparate elements if certainly linked to his childhood discovery of the power of the written word. He read with the feeling that he was performing a forbidden act, and, indeed he was, given the reactions of his grandmother, who saw fiction as a creation of the devil, and the attitude of the Deep South, which banned Negroes from public libraries. As much as the educational power of fiction, its capacity to arouse wonder was always important to him. As a Communist, he emphasized the former without renouncing the latter. He made ready use of the naturalistic and proletarian perspective, but only among other possible ones. Only in the late twenties did the philosophy of social determinism answer his questions concerning the restrictions which had been imposed upon him: universal determinism posited the equality of the oppressed Negro and his white oppressor under the common sway of human destiny. Wright could then consider the absurdity of the world through the eyes of Dreiser, who, he wrote, "tried to rationalize and justify the defeat of the individual in biological terms; with him it was a law of the universe."[32] Yet he could no more accept subjection and powerlessness as a universal law, since subjection amounted to his own slow death in a racist setting, than he could his grandmother's attempt to explain his mother's illness in terms of his own impiety and God's ensuing wrath. Determinism provided him, at best, with only a transitional belief, soon superseded by the optimistic social revoluionism of the Marxist faith. When he could no longer believe in the irreversible progress of History in Communism, Wright had to face again the absurdity and precariousness of the human predicament but he did so in terms that were closer to Russian, German, or even French existentialism. Existentialism left a way open for the creation of values by man, for individualism, and for solidarity, in a fashion that even the optimistic Spencerian brand of determinism could not. At the same time, existentialism satisfied Wright's tragic sense of life. The novel which best illustrates this shift in his philosophy (or rather the different emphasis he placed on different philosophies at different times) is undoubtedly *The Outsider*. Its first section, derived as it is from the then-unpublished *Lawd Today*, is strongly naturalistic, not only in the piling up of documentary detail but in the fashion in which economic, family, and sexual ties determine both Cross Damon's and Jake Jackson's life. That Wright has to resort to violent circumstances and largely coincidental plot in order to break off with this materialistic setting and deterministic definition of Damon's life is irrelevant here. The break is significant because it represents a jump into existential freedom and into an absurd world beyond the laws of "normal" causation. Cross will lie, kill, burn a church, drive to suicide the woman who loves him, act like one of those "little Gods" he so vehemently condemned for their ruthless use of power, only to finally discover the necessity of human solidarity and some kind of moral law. The break in the style is itself a significant transition from naturalistic reportage in didactic, philosophical prose, somewhat in the fashion of Sartre's *Les Chemins de la Liberté*. Although Wright's contribution to that type of fiction is of historical importance, we must confess that he is not at his best as a stylist when he resorts to such long-winded arguments and that the jump from naturalism to the philosophical novel does not always suit his talents.

He, on the contrary, effected the change from naturalism into what he would call surrealism quite successfully in "The Man Who Lived Underground." It is revealing that the piece was begun as a novel, in whose naturalistic first part the protagonist was a victim of circumstances: the police arrested him and beat him up on suspicion of a crime he had not committed. This part (which was suppressed from the published novella) ended with Fred Daniels's literal jump outside reality into the underground world of the sewer. Chance allowed him to escape in the way Cross Damon later did, but necessity and a search for an emotional relationship also drove him back above ground and into the hands of his torturers. In the same way, Damon owns on his deathbed that man cannot bear absolute solitude, that he must establish a bridge with other men, that the necessity of man's determinism must, in some way, be acknowledge. As a change from naturalism into another kind of literary strategy, "The Man Who Lived Underground" is a success because surrealism, as we tried to show, better suits Wright's passion for gothic detail and violence than philosophical didacticism. It appears that Wright functions best as an artist whenever, in his own words, he is able to "fuse and articulate the experiences of man, because his writing possesses the potential cunning to steal into the inmost recesses of human hearts, because he can create the myths and symbols that inspire a faith in life."[33]

To that end, American naturalism, both as a philosophy and as a literary technique in the line of Dreiser and James Farrell, provided him only with a starting point; then either, as we suggested, a larger definition of naturalism must be given—if it is to encompass the many facets of Wright's writing—or it must be recognized that he often overstepped its boundaries. Wright's attraction to the fanciful, the mysterious, the irrational always proved too strong for him to remain attached to his self-declared rationalism and deliberate objectivity. His heavy reliance upon visceral and violent emotions may account for this inability. Far from being a limitation, it turns out to be one of the major resources of his narrative power, in the same way that his obstinate refusal to submit to authority and his insatiable curiosity concerning everything human certainly led him to ask some of the most relevant questions of our time.

## NOTES

1. Granville Hicks, "From Dreiser to Farrell to Wright," *Saturday Review*, March 30, 1963, pp. 37–38.

2. Granville Hicks, "Portrait of a Man Searching," *New York Times Book Review*, March 22, 1953, Sec. 7.

3. Orville Prescott, review of *The Outsider*, *New York Times*, March 18, 1953, p. 29.

4. Luther P. Jackson, "Writer's Outsider," *Newark News*, April 5, 1953.

5. *Black Boy*, (New York: Harper and Row, 1945), p. 219,

6. Ibid., pp. 218–219.

7. Ibid.,

8. See Charles C. Walcutt, "Theodore Dreiser: The Wonder and Terror of Life," in his *American Literary Naturalism* (Minneapolis: University of Minnesota Press, 1956), pp. 180–87.

9. *Black Boy*, p. 33.

10. Ibid., p. 88.

11. Richard Wright, "I Tried To Be a Communist," in *The God That Failed*, ed. Richard Crossman (New York: Harper & Bros., 1949), pp. 107–08.

12. See Alfred Kazin, *On Native Grounds* (New York: Harcourt, Brace and Co., 1942), especially "The Revival of Naturalism."

13. Richard Wright, "How 'Bigger' Was Born," in *Native Son* (New York: Harper & Bros., 1940), pp. 29–30. Wright's phrase certainly was an allusion to Eleanor Roosevelt's reactions; she had found the book beautifully moving and had said so in her *New York Post* column.

14. "Interview," *Bulletin Board*, June, 1950.

15. Richard Wright, "Between Laughter and Tears," *New Masses* 25 (October 5, 1937): 25.

16. Richard Wright, "A Junker's Epic Novel about Militarism," *PM Magazine*, May 4, 1947, p. m3.

17. Richard Wright, "Writing from the left," (Unpublished typescript, p. 3, Wright Archive, Yale University Library).

18. Ibid., p. 1.

19. Richard Wright, "Blueprint for Negro Writing," *New Challenge*, Fall 1937, p. 63.

20. Richard Wright, "I Bite the Hand That Feeds Me," *Atlantic Monthly*, June 1940, p. 826.

21. "An Exchange of Letters: Wright to Frasconi," *Twice a Year*, Winter 1944–45, p. 258.

22. Richard Wright, *American Hunger* (New York: Harper and Row, 1977), p. 22.

23. Richard Wright, "Introduction" to Nelson Algren's *Never Come Morning* (New York: Harper, 1942). p. ix.

24. Ibid.

25. Richard Wright, "Blueprint for Negro Writing," p. 60. Here Wright comes quite close to Ellison's opinion that the heritage of the American Negro is made of many influences. He adds that "Eliot, Stein, Joyce, Proust, Hemingway and Anderson, Gorki, Barbusse, Nexo and Jack London no less than the folklore of the Negro himself should form the heritage of the Negro writer. Every iota of gain in human thought and sensibility should be ready grist for his mill no matter how far-fetched that may seem in its immediate application."

26. Wright, "I Bite the Hand That Feeds Me," p. 826.

27. Richard Wright, "Roots and Branches," (Unpublished typescript, p. 5, Wright Archive, Yale University Library).

28. Ibid.

29. Ibid.

30. Ibid.

31. Richard Wright, "A Junker's Epic Novel about Militarism," p. m3.

32. Richard Wright, "Personalism," (Unpublished typescript, p. 1. Wright Archive, Yale University Library).

33. Wright, "Blueprint for Negro Writing," p. 59.

PHILIP FISHER

# The Naturalist Novel and the City: Temporary Worlds

The opening scene of *An American Tragedy* leaps into new territory of the self in as striking and profound a way as the scene of the *petite madeleine* in Proust. A seedy little band is walking the streets, perhaps a family, but not enacting themselves as family. They are "the man-in-the-street," omitted in the attention of others who, likewise walking, scan or muse in the way one does as a "passerby" in the absence of events that solicit attention. Suddenly the band stops, two adults, four children. This is nowhere, no place. Suddenly it is a place they make up as they begin to sing. Now it is an improvised church, on the spot, and in singing they become ministers and choir, the passerby, their attention now solicited, must choose to become or refuse to be the congregation, audience, members of this half-hour church. In the middle of nowhere they have improvised a world, temporary, voluntary (only they accredit themselves "ministers," each person in the congregation is a self-appointed instant member of this church). On the spot a social structure exists with roles and tactics forced into existence under what seems emergency conditions: as someone might decree, "For tonight this square of sidewalk is my bed," or as someone can find himself in a storm and transform what was a moment before "newspaper" into "umbrella."

This fragile, ad-hoc world transforms itself again, now into a business. The congregation is asked for money, is sold tracts. This is, after all, how these people get their living. Now each one in the congregation must

From *Hard Facts: Setting and Form in the American Novel.* © 1985 by Oxford University Press.

225

contribute or refuse to "support" these people. The half-hour service ends, the congregation transforms itself into walkers by drifting away, becoming "the man-in-the-street." The ministers and choir move on, becoming walkers. The place becomes nowhere, no place again. No trace, no "evidence" as the book will later name all traces of the past, remains. The experience, the roles, the physical reality of the church within which each lived for half an hour, dissolve.

No role exists unless it is honored like paper money in the eyes of others who must, in order to validate my role, not simply approve or permit, but enact a complementary role. They must become co-performers. If all passersby lower their eyes and walk on when a man begins to preach in the streets, they rule by their co-performance that he is performing the role of madman, not that of minister. Without the co-performers no one is anything at all. They are passersby.

The tactics for being someone under emergency conditions, conditions that are permanently temporary, fragile, improvised (without any prestructuring past), and absolutely dependent on the cooperative enactment of others, these are the essential tactics of identity in the city world of *An American Tragedy* or *Sister Carrie* where the profession of actress names this general condition precisely.

In choosing to begin with Clyde "in place," performing, but resentful of a squalid, theatrical self-enactment, Dreiser abandons the comforting sentimentality of the innocent central character. Typically, the novel of adolescence depends on an outsider who sees such structures first as an observer, then makes up himself by choosing among them. Such outsiders have a self that they invest with social position, career, and wife, usually in ways that express or publicize the nature of that self. In Dreiser no outsider exists, no innocent. Clyde begins in state, experiencing what was for Nietzsche the characteristic feeling of western civilization—resentment. Every motion of his life compounds flight and desire, neither feeling exists even for a moment except in the presence of the other. As the motion of desire is given in the metaphor of shopping, so its opposite is generated literally with more and more overt force in the book; Clyde flees his family (metaphorically); he runs from the auto accident (literally); after the murder he becomes a fugitive (totally absorbed in flight).

Bluntly put, within Dreiser's novel the question of authenticity never exists. Clyde has no self to which he might be "true." Literally, he is not yet anyone at all. For the calm or even frantic possession of himself Clyde substitutes an alertness to the moods of others, to their "take" of him. By the end of the book the lawyer's projection of the jurors' take, designs every gesture Clyde will make. Ultimately, Clyde lives in their moods, borrows their being, as he had earlier borrowed Gilbert's appearance, until we have to say he is more often them than himself. So attentive is he to his observer that he springs to life as a reflection of what the observer appears to have seen. He gets his "self" moment by moment as a gift from the outside. He murders by imitation (after reading of a drowning in the newspaper) as he loves by imitation (his being mistaken for Gilbert).

Throughout the novel Clyde is in motion towards or away from worlds he does not merge with. Fleeing or yearning, running or shopping, seducing or aborting, saving money to buy, planning to do, hoping for—"if" and "if only," could he only ...": Dreiser begins hundreds of sentences with these words. The two motions to embrace and to murder, possess and amputate are sharpened and magnified by the staircase plot. With each turn the circumstance is wider, the matter more ultimate, but the same matters are, with each new circle, once again in view. Finally, at the same lake he seems ready at once to snatch at the social world he most desires and annihilate the clinging world from which he cannot be free.

Nowhere in Dreiser's novel is there the slightest trace of society, as that word is understood in nineteenth-century novels. Instead there are worlds, like the world of the Green-Davidson Hotel, the social world of the Giffiths, the world of condemned prisoners at the penitentiary, the shabby rural world Roberta comes from, the sexually languid world of the girls who work for Clyde. These worlds are islands of varieties of aura, some glamorous, some contaminating. Everyone in Mrs. Braley's rooming house appears to Clyde to be from "the basement world." He speaks of the "better atmosphere" of the Union Club in Chicago. No distinction expresses the fact that whereas he *lives* in the rooming house, he was a servant in the Union Club. The atmosphere soaks in equally. In the city all aura is translated into places, and the moments of entering a new atmosphere, whether of the restaurant the bellboys visit on their night off, the living room of the Griffiths mansion, the death row, or the dyeing room of the factory—these are among the most perfectly crafted moments of Dreiser's novel. Places supplant manners. In communities, in societies, manners were the codes of behavior, often most precise in speech and language, encoding deference or intimacy, reserve, assumption or condescension—codes of behavior that enact the rules of presence, the way in which we enter or situate ourselves in each other's experience. Places in Dreiser give out this social grammar once located in behavior, in manners, in the implications of conduct.

Zola was the first to abandon society as the object of public representation for the new post-social topic of "worlds." However, in Zola these islands have economic and systematic integrity based on work: the entire world of the coal mines in *Germinal,* the world of land and farming in *La Terre,* the military world of *Le Débâcle.* Each is a rational sector of experience, known by the array of types, the kinds of language or experience, the appropriate modes of sexuality, humor, pride, and violence. Public, permanent compartments of society, they imply the larger, total society even while the magnification Zola applies, the isolation of spheres, makes them seem absolute. The food world, the art world, the sex world of *Nana* are all paradoxically still within a world, although courtesan, artist, grocer are monomaniacally absorbed in their sectors of work.

For Dreiser the worlds are neither economic, nor public, nor are they permanent centers of activity. Worlds are not generated by the webs of work, because in Dreiser work itself is only one kind of atmosphere, enthralling to the bellboy of the Green-Davidson Hotel, contaminating to the worker in the "basement world" of the collar factory. Work is just another place where one is seen by others and fixed by their looks that melt self and atmosphere together. Dreiser's worlds are temporary, magical improvisations like the little religious world on the street, or the perfectly named "Now and Then Club" through which Sondra engineers her flirtation with Clyde and his entry into the social set. Every boarding house is a world, the hotel bellboys have their own world of nights out at restaurants and brothels or outings in the country. Even the condemned man, Clyde, and his two guards on the trip to Auburn prison make up a world performing itself for the crowds who gather to see the now-romantic murderer. The guards feel honored and proud (as Clyde once felt walking with Hortense) to be seen with the murderer. His aura gives them identity: they are "the murderer's guards" with a genitive construction as potent as the erotic genitive Clyde feels for "his beloved's breasts." Murderer and guards form one aural body as Clyde working at the Green-Davidson is a limb of one aural body that includes guests, employees, furniture, renown, position in St. Louis, and lights.

So many fragile, transient worlds exist in Dreiser's novel because the root meaning of world here is anything outside the body that, if seen by another, contaminates or glamorizes the self. When Clyde walks with Hortense she decorates him, testifies to him. Two lines of energy contribute to the power of worlds to share being, to lend identity: the first is the force of collective identity, the second, the magic of places.

Collective identity in the novel is more substantial than individual identity. Being "one of" the Griffiths or "one of" the Green-Davidson bellboys or "one of" the prisoners condemned to death, is a more precise matter than being Asa Griffiths or Ratterer or even Clyde Griffiths. The novel describes "sets" or bands, clubs or cliques. Many of the sharpest representations in the book are of days Clyde spends within a precise identity set. Dreiser brilliantly records the life of groups, factory workers moving through the streets to work or the camping trip of the social set. He is remarkably indifferent to kinds of life that cannot be described as ongoing— activities or groups that one "joins."

Experiencing oneself as "one of" this or "one of" that is the primary way of constituting a self in the novel. The material is outside the body in sets. "He felt he would like to caress her arm.... Yet here he was a Griffiths— a Lycurgus Griffiths—and that was what now made a difference—that made all those girls at this church social seem so much more interested in him and friendly" (I, 210). Or again: "He danced with her and fondled her in a daring and aggressive fashion, yet thinking as he did so, 'But this is not what I should be doing either, is it? This is Lycurgus. I am a Griffiths here. I know how these people feel toward me'" (I, 213). The perfect concision of identity: I am a Griffiths, *Here*. I am a bellboy, here. I am a condemned prisoner, here. These are the absolute figures of identity: collective and limited by that terrible word *Here*. Both set and setting are around the self. Dreiser notes that the old death row was literally a row with all the cells side by side so that the prisoners never saw one another, never saw the "Them" that each was "one of." In the new death row—to Clyde's fastidious distaste—the cells face and the men become a hysterical, visible set acting out in front of each other variations of their common fate and identity. Architecturally, the state of New York has taken account of the new conditions of self by making the setting enforce a set.

The first act of looking at someone in the book is to look *around* him. Clyde feels humiliated to know that as the eyes of others come to focus on him in the street the "around" that they notice first is the shabby religious family that he must wear like an irritating garment. Because the savor of worlds replaces the savor of individual character within the body, Dreiser designs a web of metaphors to represent this new condition. Clyde often wears a uniform, the first metaphor of "set" identity. First as a bellboy, later as a servant at the Union Club, then as a businessman, finally as a prison inmate. Uniforms designate both sets and one specific place within a setting, as in a resort hotel the casual clothes of the guests define their places, the formal uniforms of the elevator operators, theirs.

More profound than uniforms is the territory Dreiser calls "manner," a stylized, collective tone of behavior. After a time in the Union Club, Clyde, though a servant, takes on the aloof, sexless manner of the successful businessmen there. Manner is absorbed, not learned. The power of adopting a manner depends on an interior blankness over which many colorations can pass. In court Clyde's attorneys coach him in a manner, and when shaken he must look to the eyes of his lawyer whose return look will recall him to what he is supposed to be.

A more brilliant device of collective identity than either uniforms or manner is the resemblance between Clyde and his cousin Gilbert. The blur between the two identities creates the entire plot of the novel. Because Clyde has the manner of the Union Club and is first seen by his uncle Samuel within its civilized aura, and because he resembles in a striking way the manufacturer's son Gilbert—a double "rented" being—he is invited to Lycurgus and given a job. Again, Sondra Finchley offers a ride to Clyde, having mistaken him for Gilbert; then begins her flirtation with him and opens society to him. She continues, at first, only to irk Gilbert, to strike at Gilbert by taking up his neglected cousin. It is only because he can so easily be "taken for" someone else that Clyde can exist in Lycurgus as "himself."

Identity, blurred or collective, externalizes the question of who I am, converts it into the question, Who do they take me for? Who does it look like I am to them? A stunning scene enacted again and again in the book could be called "looking around to see who I am." At the collar factory Clyde approaches the secretary guarding the door.

> "Well?" she called as Clyde appeared.
> "I want to see Mr. Gilbert Griffiths," Clyde began a little nervously.
> "What about?"
> "Well, you see, I'm his cousin. Clyde Griffiths is my name. I have a letter here from my uncle, Mr. Samuel Griffiths. He'll see me, I think."
> As he laid the letter before her, he noticed that her quite severe and decidedly indifferent expression changed and became not so much friendly as awed. (I, 184)

After his capture people come to see him and he sees himself in their eyes:

> Their eyes showed the astonishment, disgust, suspicion or horror with which his assumed crime had filled them. Yet even in the face of that, having one type of interest and even sycophantic pride in his presence here. For was he not a Griffiths—a member of the well-known social group of the big central cities to the south of here. (II, 162)

Dressed as a prisoner, his hair cut, he sees himself as others might:

> There was no mirror here—or anywhere—but no matter—he
> could feel how he looked. This baggy coat and trousers and this
> striped cap. He threw it hopelessly to the floor. For but an hour
> before he had been clothed in a decent suit and shirt and tie and
> shoes, and his appearance neat and pleasing, as he himself had
> thought as he left Bridgeburg. But now—how must he look? And
> tomorrow his mother would be coming—and later Jephson, or
> Belnap, maybe. God!
>
> But worse—there, in that cell directly opposite him, a sallow
> and emaciated and sinister-looking Chinaman in a suit exactly
> like his own, who had come to the bars of his door and was
> looking out of inscrutable slant eyes, but as immediately turning
> and scratching himself—vermin, maybe, as Clyde immediately
> feared. There had been bedbugs at Bridgeburg.
>
> A Chinese murderer. For was not this the death house? But as
> good as himself here. And with a garb like his own. Thank God
> visitors were probably not many. (II, 348)

A magnificent scene. Dreiser at a moment like this has no equal. Clyde
imagines the "other" and then finds him out there as another version of
himself. The Chinaman is the first installment of his "set" which he accepts
by reminding himself: that's what I am *here*, in this setting. He ends grateful
to be invisible. In miniature this scene recapitulates the curve of the book,
and its sinister constituting glance that destroys, the glance of the Chinaman,
is the world glance returned when Clyde looks around to see who "I" am.

On the street singing hymns he is wounded by "who" the bystanders
take him to be. In court the eyes of the jury take him to be a murderer. The
sexually vital girls he meets at the church social take him to be a Griffiths,
and Clyde knows well the difference between being taken to be one of the
Kansas City Griffiths and one of the Lycurgus Griffiths. Contaminated or
magically ennobled, in either direction he is a blank center engulfed by
worlds.

Often the aura of a world is precisely located in a building, a space that
becomes a metonymy for that world. The Green-Davidson Hotel in Kansas
City where Clyde works as a bellboy is evoked with rapture and desire. The
hotel has more being, more reality than anyone within it. To each it rents out
a part of its self so that the pale creatures become "someone who works at
the Green-Davidson" or "someone staying at the Green-Davidson." Clyde

looks at the Alden farm or the Griffiths mansion and sees them as "selves," as what could be taken for his self by others were he within. He shudders or feels exhilarated, threatened, or tempted by them in that intimate way most people feel only about *actions*. We feel honored or shamed by what we have done because, in our sense of self, what we *do* expresses and announces what we are. It is the one transmission from the portable, interior self. In Dreiser, this decisive burden of *actions* is taken over by settings. The two fundamental settings are clothes and the slightly larger garments that we wear called houses or rooms. Both are the first elements of the self around the body. The Griffiths' factory makes collars, an article of clothing. All of Clyde's money goes into clothes, a more widely visible self than one's room or house which one must leave behind much of the day. Decisive clues against him at his trial are his two straw hats, his clothes and suitcase. Hortense offers to exchange sex for a coat, and in one of the greatest of Dreiser's scenes, Clyde goes in desperation to a clothing store to learn from a clerk selling him ties where he can locate an abortionist.

Clyde is never intimately sculptured by his actions. He does not seem to do them. Every decisive event in his life is an accident, a mistake, or a confusion. In the existential sense, he does not "do" his life. For that reason his acts are not essential to who he is. He seems peculiarly absent at the most decisive moments, such as when an auto accident kills a child. To Clyde, Roberta dies by accident, really, and what was he in the boat but "someone" holding the camera she bumped her head against? He does not participate in what he does, but he does participate in where he is. These places index who we must take him to be, and they can be found outside him, while the accidental moral life of his acts goes its irrelevant way within. Being here and not there has replaced doing this and not that.

As a pun the word "place" suggests physical space, social station, and occupation at the same time. But for all the desperate importance of worlds and places within worlds, Clyde is never seen at home. He seeks admission or flees confinement, he desires and flees; worldless. The two haunted spaces of the novel where Clyde enacts his life are hotels and water. He begins work in a hotel, lives in the small-scale hotels that are rooming houses, finishes his life in the state-run hotel known as a prison. His outing with the bellboys and Hortense takes them to a hotel in the country, and before Roberta's death they go from hotel to hotel in the resort area. A hotel is an ideal home, like the street church with which the book begins, for improvised, overnight worlds.

Yet hotels *are* worlds. The Green-Davidson in Kansas City has a dense, alluring presence in spite of its changing cast. Dreiser can sketch in precisely the "world" of each of the rooming houses Clyde lives in—their manner, their tone, their place in the scale of society. Because they are worlds there exists a kind of visual rule to judge who does or does not belong there: who is, as we say, "out of place" there. The acute vision of the book does not rest with situating Clyde in transient, improvised worlds, temporary worlds, but in representing him as fundamentally worldless, unable to "belong there" even in temporary worlds. At the end he is dead, not of justice, nor of social revenge, but of a new disease: worldlessness.

Within every world there are defective positions, reserved for those who are deeply "out of place" there, who don't belong, but are permitted to be on the spot if they agree to admit in some clearly announced way that their case is an exemption. The servants at the Union Club are poor boys permitted to bask in the aura of the club, sharing its dignified manner, treated with the civility of all relations there, even to be seen as part of this world—as Clyde is first seen by his uncle Samuel—but at the cost of signifying by their uniforms that they are there by permission and don't in fact belong. They participate in aura without membership in the world. This is Clyde's social place at every moment in the book. When invited to the Griffiths' mansion he can come only at the cost of their constant reminders that he is a poor cousin, there on tolerance as an act of kindness. In the social set that he cannot afford Sondra slips him seventy-five dollars so he can pretend to pay their way, and the money itself is his stigma. Even when he descends to a world, in the menial work of the factory, he is seen there as exempt since, as the nephew of the owner, he may suddenly no longer be a fellow worker but a boss. With the Griffiths set he is an outsider, but in every other set he is equally an outsider because the others see him as a Griffiths. Every world is doubled by his presence inside it.

On his first day at the Green-Davidson Hotel Clyde is called to Room 529.

> [He was then...] sent to the bar for drinks ... and this by a group of smartly dressed young men and girls who were laughing and chatting in the room, one of whom opened the door just wide enough to instruct him as to what was wanted. But because of a mirror over the mantel, he could see the party and one pretty girl in a white suit and cap, sitting on the edge of a chair in which reclined a young man who had his arm around her.
>
> Clyde stared, even while pretending not to. And in his state of mind, this sight was like looking through the gates of paradise. Here were young fellows and girls in this room, not so much

older than himself, laughing and talking and drinking even.... (I, 44–45)

Clyde sees the scene of youths like himself but mysteriously different, privileged, worlded, but he sees it in a mirror glimpsed through a crack in a door someone holds almost closed against him. His uniform and purpose there are the distance for which the slightly open door is a metonymy. He sees only an image, a fiction in the mirror. Later in the novel, the newspaper is this mirror. Clyde, with touching innocence, tells Sondra he has been following the social life of her set "in the newspaper." He reads in the newspaper of a drowning at a lake that gives him, in his empty resentment of Roberta, a crime that he can imitate. And in a stroke of grotesque brilliance, Dreiser has Clyde's mother support her trip east by acting as a reporter for a newspaper, writing up the sentencing to death of her own son!

The newspaper or mirror is a periscope in the novel, feeding images from worlds to other worlds. The newspaper is a metonymy for the world hunger Dreiser associates with the city, the torment of proximate worlds that one can never enter, turned into a self-torment by reading about even more fantastic, unavailable worlds.

Clyde enters always with a talisman or trick that simultaneously admits him and curses him: his uniform gives him the glimpse of the hotel paradise, his resemblance to Gilbert tickets his entry to Sondra and her set, the slipped seventy-five dollars pays his way into the camping vacation.

The most perfectly orchestrated scene of defective membership that marks Clyde throughout is his joining the campers after the murder of Roberta.

> For although met by Sondra, as well as Bertine, at the door of the Cranston lodge, and shown by them to the room he was to occupy, he could not help but contrast every present delight here with the danger of his immediate and complete destruction....
>
> If only all went well, now,—nothing were traced to him! A clear path! A marvelous future! Her beauty! Her love! Her wealth. And yet, after being ushered to his room, his bag having been carried in before him, at once becoming nervous as to the suit. It was damp and wrinkled. (II, 123)

These "althoughs," "ifs," "if onlys," "and yets" are the permanent structure of his doubled world, every world becomes conditional, concessive, possible, yet in becoming possible, impossible. For the very same reason the door is opened, a foot is held against it to open it only a crack.

That Clyde is askew within every world is demonstrated in his helplessness when he tries to connect within a world. He does not know how to find an abortionist because he belongs neither to the middle-class world whose doctors accommodate when a "problem exists" (as we learn from the attorney's story) nor to the working-class world where lore and gossip would supply him with the name of a back-alley abortionist. His life being arranged with mirrors, he has no connections anywhere and ends up in a clothing store desperately trying the clerk's knowledge of "solutions." Later Dreiser carefully shows that were Clyde of the Griffiths world the entire crime would have been hushed up. On the other side, were he an ordinary factory worker no one would have cared. Because the jury can resent him as a well-connected seducer of a poor girl while the Griffiths deny him as "not really one of us," he is important enough to exterminate but not important enough to rescue. Justice, through the choice of lawyers and legal maneuvers that Samuel Griffiths can buy for Clyde, is a matter of sets and worlds, too.

What is his name? Clyde Griffiths (of the Kansas City Griffiths)? Harry Tenet (his name during his flight after the car accident)? Clyde Griffiths (of the Lycurgus Griffiths)? Clifford Golden or Carl Graham (the names he uses to register at hotels with Roberta)? At his trial the evidence against him consists of matters of identity. How can he explain his two straw hats, the wet suit? His is the first murder in literature in which the weapon is a camera. Dredged up from the lake it contains identifying pictures that along with Roberta's letters that he forgot to burn turn the jury against him decisively.

In *An American Tragedy*, defective membership means not only having no world but also having no self. Deprived of set and setting, having no group which we can say he is "one of," Clyde drifts into the inevitable worldless acts: murder and then execution. Unable to erase the signs of his set through abortion or murder he is caught halfway through the door and imprisoned on the threshold. Literally, death row is such a threshold since the men there are no longer legally alive but not yet dispatched. Like the sidewalk church with which Dreiser began, it is a temporary, self-contained world of fixed roles under emergency conditions. The ever stronger meaning of the adjective "emergency" as we move from the improvised church, to the emergency of abortion, to the flight after murder, to death row suggests the inner nature of what Dreiser means by tragedy. For him tragedy has a circular or spiral quality where each return to what seems to be the same predicament is in fact located farther from the center. The tragic account that he created in the 1920s is less complex and less profound than the neutralized, half-tragic, half comic account present two decades earlier in

*Sister Carrie*. In fact, it is the earlier novel that is structured around the city itself in its entire range of possibilities, and in that novel Dreiser invented his most striking vocabulary for the urban privileged setting.

MICHAEL DAVITT BELL

# The Revolt Against Style:
# Frank Norris

"Had you given the Prize to Mr. Dreiser, you would have heard groans
from America; you would have heard that his style—I am not exactly
sure what this mystic quality 'style' may be, but I find the word so often
in the writings of minor critics that I suppose it must exist—you would
have heard that his style is cumbersome, that his choice of words is
insensitive, that his books are interminable."
                —Sinclair Lewis, "Nobel Prize Acceptance Speech" (1930)

"I detest 'fine writing,' 'rhetoric,' 'elegant English'—tommyrot. Who
cares for fine style! Tell your yarn and let your style go to the devil. We
don't want literature, we want life."
                —Frank Norris to Isaac F. Marcosson (1899)

Frank Norris has become for many literary historians perhaps *the*
representative American naturalist—particularly, in the 1980s, in the work of
the so-called new historicists—and for clear and good reasons. For instance,
when Mark Seltzer proposes in "The Naturalist Machine" (1986) that
"production, both mechanical and biological, ... troubles the naturalist novel
at every point" and that the naturalist novel devises "a counter-model of
generation," he insists that such a model "operates in a wide range of
naturalist texts." But he has chosen to focus on Frank Norris, he explains,
because Norris is "the American novelist who most conspicuously and

From *The Problem of American Realism*. © 1993 by the University of Chicago.

compulsively displays both these anxieties about generation and the aesthetic machine designed to manage them."[1] Norris, for the new historicists, is a kind of cultural seismograph, his compulsions and anxieties nicely registering the wide variety of ideological formations and cultural practices that he shared with his era, and it is also important that he was the most conspicuous and overt proponent, among his American contemporaries, of literary naturalism. Yet for all his historical centrality, Norris is one of the most incompetent practitioners of his craft across the whole range of the American canon. I am referring here simply to his *writing*, his labored and lugubrious *style*. I will be fleshing out this observation shortly, and the point is hardly controversial; all I would add to it for the moment is that Norris's style in fact gets worse over the course of his brief career, more prone to clichéd purple prose, to unintentionally hilarious bathos, to strangely inappropriate (yet often hideously extended) metaphor.

In arguing for Norris's centrality, it should be recognized, new historicists are by no means arguing for the literary *value* of his work; nor, of course, is there any necessary contradiction between Norris's growing incompetence as a writer of English and his current status as representative American naturalist. Restraint is probably not the first quality one looks for in a seismograph, and it well may be Norris's ineptitude that allows his compulsions and anxieties to play so freely and conspicuously across the surface of his prose. But I want to argue for a more direct connection: I want to argue that the obvious defects of Norris's style were, in effect, *learned* and that this deliberate learning was a product of growing commitment to what he took literary "naturalism" to be. Norris, it is important to recognize, was a representative naturalist even to himself; he strove to *become* a representative naturalist; and what commitment to naturalism entailed for him was above all a kind of deliberate literary self-impairment, a revolt against "style."

## THE ROAD TO NATURALISM

Benjamin Franklin Norris, Jr., was born in 1870.[2] His mother was "artistic"; she had been an actress before her marriage, and while matrimony ended her career it did not abate her devotion to literature and culture. Norris's father, by contrast, was a man of practical affairs, a self-made business success who had little use for art or literature and who wanted his eldest son and namesake to follow in his footsteps. This contrast between a "feminine" world of culture and a "masculine" world of "real" business dominated Norris's childhood and adolescence and left its mark on nearly everything he wrote before his untimely death in 1902—not only on his fiction but also on his essays about the nature and function of literature, about the need for naturalism in fiction. Norris spent the 1894–95 academic year at Harvard, studying writing with Lewis E. Gates. Here he worked on a novel begun earlier, finally published in 1899 as *McTeague;* he also wrote a draft of *Vandover and the Brute,* which was not published until the manuscript was discovered in 1914. He produced five more novels before his death. *Moran of the Lady Letty*—his first novel to be published, although it was third in order of composition—appeared in 1898. *Blix* was published in 1899, soon after *McTeague,* and was followed by *A Man's Woman* in 1900. Norris then embarked on what he called his "Wheat series," a projected trilogy with one volume to be devoted to production (and set in California), a second devoted to distribution (and set in Chicago), and a third devoted to consumption (and set in Europe). The first of these volumes, *The Octopus,* appeared in 1901, bringing its author his first real taste of fame. Norris died shortly after finishing the second volume, *The Pit,* which was published posthumously in 1903. The third volume was never begun.

In the course of a very brief career, then, Norris wrote seven novels, producing at the same time numerous stories and essays. This is an impressive performance, and it would seem to indicate the triumph of his mother's influence over his father's, of the "artistic" woman over the "practical" man of business. Yet even while he fulfilled his mother's ambitions, Norris fully shared his father's (and his father's culture's) devaluation of the "literary" as feeble and effeminate. "Life," he declared again and again, "is more important than literature.... Life is better than literature" (7:179).[3] Artists, in his fiction, are almost always treated with contempt and ridicule, and he delighted in the idea that his own novels were anything but "literary." His characteristic stance is clear in a letter he wrote in 1899, thanking Isaac F. Marcosson for his favorable review of *McTeague:* "What pleased me most was the 'disdaining of all pretentions to style.' It is precisely what I try most to avoid. I detest 'fine writing,' 'rhetoric,' 'elegant English'—tommyrot. Who cares for fine style! Tell your yarn and let your style go to the devil. We don't want literature, we want life."[4] This stance, moreover, constitutes the central plank in Norris's campaign for literary naturalism. "I've lived by doing things," announces one of his characters, "not by thinking things, or reading about what other people have done or thought; and I guess it's what you do that counts, rather than what you think or read about" (3:234). To put it crudely but accurately, a naturalist for Norris is a writer who "counts."

"Zola," Norris writes in "A Plea for Romantic Fiction" (1901), "has been dubbed a Realist, but he is, on the contrary, the very head of the Romanticists." Whereas "Realism ... notes only the surfaces of things," and confines itself to "the drama of a broken teacup, the tragedy of a walk down the block, the excitement of an afternoon call, the adventure of an invitation to dinner," Zolaesque "romance" breaks through this surface to explore "the unplumbed depths of the human heart, and the mystery of sex, and the problems of life, and the black, unsearched penetralia of the soul of man" (7:164–65, 167–68). Five years earlier, in 1896, Norris set forth much the same argument in an essay in the San Francisco *Wave*, "Zola as a Romantic Writer." "Naturalism," Norris here insists, "is a form of romanticism, not an inner circle of realism." Because Zola deals with "the lower—almost the lowest—classes," his work is not "purely romantic"; but neither is it "realism." "It is a school by itself," Norris concludes, "unique, powerful beyond words. It is naturalism."[5]

Norris's principal contribution to the definition of naturalism is his notion that it is a synthesis of "romance" and "realism," but if we wish to understand what this synthesis meant to him we must recognize that the key terms, as he used them, had far less to do with literary theory, with a discrimination of fictional modes, than with a personal effort to transform the meaning of his identity as a writer. For instance toward the end of *Moran of the Lady Letty* the terms "real" and "romance" are used in a quite suggestive way as virtual synonyms. After discovering his manhood at sea and in the thrill of killing a man in hand-to-hand combat, the hero, Ross Wilbur, returns to San Francisco, to discover that he no longer fits into its feminized social world. "He had known romance," we are told, "and the spell of the great, simple, primitive emotions." A few pages earlier Wilbur himself expresses the same idea in somewhat different terms. "We've come back to the world of little things," he announces. "But we'll pull out of here in the morning and get to the places where things are real" (3:314, 309). The meaning of "real" here has little to do with any philosophical definition of reality; rather the ocean is more "real" than the city because it is bigger, because life on it is more exciting. This is why Norris can equate the "real" with "romance," and to say in this sense that something is "real" is merely to say that it is an exotic antithesis of the ordinary routines of middle-class life—which is precisely the sense in which Norris advocated the rejection of Howellsian realism in favor of romantic naturalism.

The trouble with Howells, Norris writes in the 1896 essay on Zola, is that his characters "live across the street from us, they are 'on our block.'" "One can go even farther," he adds. "We ourselves are Mr. Howells's characters, so long as we are well behaved and ordinary and bourgeois, so long as we are not adventurous or not rich or not unconventional." What, by contrast, is the appeal of Zola? Norris says nothing about such things as "experimental" method or determinist philosophy, qualities normally associated with naturalism; what matters instead is that Zola's characters "are not of our lives ... because we are *ordinary.*" The expansion of this point tells us a good deal about just what naturalism meant to Norris, and why it appealed to him:

> To be noted of M. Zola we must leave the rank and the file, either run to the forefront of the marching world, or fall by the roadway; we must become individual, unique.... Terrible things must happen to the characters of the naturalistic tale. They must be twisted from the ordinary, wrenched out from the quiet, uneventful round of every-day life, or flung into the throes of a vast and terrible drama that works itself out in unleashed passion, in blood, and in sudden death. The world of M. Zola is a world of big things; the enormous, the formidable, the terrible, is what counts; to teacup tragedies here.[6]

Here as always Norris understands naturalism entirely in terms of the writer's material, but this is the least of the passage's interest. Ross Wilbur, we recall, turns to "romance" from "the world of little things" and in so doing becomes a "real" man. Norris turns to naturalism for precisely the same reason: it offers him, he seems to believe, a connection to "a world of big things," and the concern with size is suggestive. Norris's version of naturalism sounds like nothing so much as a prospectus for a body-building course, promising to turn the ninety-eight-pound literary weakling into a dynamic he-man, one who "counts" in the domain of masculine "reality." Thus did naturalism offer Norris what he apparently needed and wanted: a way of following his mother's footsteps, as it were, in his father's boots.[7]

Donald Pizer writes that "although ... Norris's critical essays are poorly written, repetitious, and occasionally plain silly, they nevertheless contain a coherent critical attitude of some importance."[8] No one can doubt the importance of Norris's ideas—they are typical of a good deal of the thinking that characterized American literary modernism in the 1890s and early twentieth century—but the truth is that nothing in Norris's essays is sillier than the critical attitude that underlies them, and even to describe Norris's call for naturalism *as* a critical attitude may be to invite misunderstanding. For the terms in which he espouses the new fiction are not finally terms of criticism; they are rather the terms of crude fantasy, the fantasy of a writer haunted by the specter of "effeminate" irrelevance, dreaming of a virile fiction that "counts" because it dismisses the "literary" in order to keep step with "the marching world." There is of course nothing wrong with a writer wishing to rescue literature from the excessively "literary"—wishing to return it to "reality," to the life and language of actual people. This has been the project of many writers, of Wordsworth, for instance, or Whitman. Yet what distinguishes Norris's ambition from theirs, even more than an obvious difference in achievement, is the crudeness of his idea of reality. It is almost always tinged, or more than tinged, with sexism and racism; white, Anglo-Saxon males always seem to have a corner on the "real." The art of the novelist, according to Norris, is "of all the arts ... the most virile.... It is not an affair of women and aesthetes" (7:158–59).[9]

An even more basic problem is that Norris cannot invoke his idea of "reality," in his essays or in his fiction, without resorting to a language of sodden and inflated cliché. One thinks of such things as "flung into the throes of a vast and terrible drama that works itself out in unleashed passions, in blood, and in sudden death"—or "the unplumbed depths of the human heart, and the mystery of sex, and the problems of life, and the black, unsearched penetralia of the soul of man." Such language hardly convinces one that its author has a very precise sense of the reality to which he thinks literature should turn; instead, it indicates clearly what should be clear by now in any case, that Norris's conception of literary naturalism was based on the crudest sort of *fantasy* of the "real." Behind such rhetoric there lurked a serious dilemma, a dilemma inevitable once Norris had accepted the assumptions on which his idea of naturalism was based. To insist on the distinction between "literature" and "life," and to choose "life" over "literature," was not to solve the problem of his vocational identity but to compound it—by cutting off the very bough on which he himself had chosen to perch. In another literary essay, "The Novel with a 'Purpose,'" Norris briefly glimpses his predicament: "The artist," he writes, "has a double personality: himself as a man and himself as an artist." As a "man" he may care about his materials, but to the "artist" in him they "must be ... a matter of the mildest interest" (7:23–24). Thus even the naturalistic novelist, the novelist with a "purpose," is finally beset by a fundamental schizophrenia, torn between the antithetical identities of "man" (identifying with his "big" characters and materials) and "artist" (regarding both with aloof detachment); moreover in order to function as an "artist" he must at least temporarily *cease* to function as a "man." Norris soon retreats from this insight, ending his essay with the passage quoted in the prologue to Part Two of this study, the passage in which fiction is allied with "the Great March" and the novelist is grouped with "leaders," "teachers," "great divines," and "great philosophers"—all united in their muscular pursuit of "a well-defined, well-seen, courageously sought for purpose" (7:26). This retreat is hardly surprising, since to have followed his insight to its logical conclusion would have been to undermine the whole rationale for a fiction that "counts" in the world on the world's own terms.

The confusions and fallacies rampant in Norris's writings about naturalism are obvious, and it may seem mean-spirited to pick on him. Nevertheless, it is of the utmost importance that we understand the nature and basis of his thinking about literature. We must recognize that the ultimate significance of naturalism for Norris, like the ultimate significance of realism for Howells, was far more centrally personal than literary. We should recognize, too, that Norris's assumptions have been shared, in one form or another, by a great many so-called American naturalists—who have sought, like Norris, to neutralize suspicions of the irrelevance of literature by suppressing the "literary" and insisting on the primacy of a fantasy of masculine "reality." In any case, understanding the nature and basis of Norris's thinking about literature allows us to ask what may be the most important question about his example: How, exactly, did his confused idea of naturalism, and the personal and vocational conflicts that lay behind this idea, affect the fiction he wrote during his brief literary career?

## NATURALISM AND STYLE

Toward the end of 1898 Norris wrote to Howells, who had seen promise in Norris's first published novel, that its successor, *McTeague*, would be quite different: "It is," he explained, "as naturalistic as Moran was romantic." A year later he wrote to Isaac Marcosson that the novels published immediately following *McTeague*—*Blix* and *A Man's Woman*—had been diversions, but that he now vowed to change: "I am going back *definitely*," he wrote, "to the style of MacT. and stay with it right along.... The Wheat series will be straight naturalism with all the guts I can get into it."[10] Literary historians and critics have come to regard *McTeague* and at least the first volume of the "Wheat series," *The Octopus*, as Norris's most important novels, and they have agreed, by and large, that part of what distinguishes them is their cultivation of naturalism. It is far from clear, however, just what qualities in the novels this classification refers to. For instance, if we understand naturalism mainly as indicating a certain kind of subject matter—the underclass rather than the middle class, the brutal and sordid rather than the genteel—the label certainly would seem to suit *McTeague*, Norris's tale of an uneducated San Francisco dentist whose increasingly sadistic relationship with his wife culminates in her murder, but it hardly seems to suit *The Octopus*, whose rancher heroes, locked in struggle with the railroad, are wealthy capitalists, middle-class entrepreneurs. To Norris's contemporary readers the world of *The Octopus* might have seemed exotic, but it would not have seemed sordid.

If we follow Zola's lead, and see naturalism as "scientific" or "experimental" fiction, the term seems even less appropriate as a description of Norris's practice. There are in his novels scattered gestures toward the idea of determinism, but they remain gestures: Norris's "science," in this sense, is at bottom melodramatic and moralistic. He frequently indulges in meditations on the supremacy of amoral "forces"—most notably toward the end of *The Octopus* when the poet Presley, shocked by the railroad's victory over his friends the ranchers, comes to an "explanation of existence" couched in what popular thinking in the 1890s might have taken to be "scientific" terms:

> Men were naught, death was naught, life was naught; FORCE only existed—FORCE that brought men into the world, FORCE that crowded them out of it to make way for the succeeding generations, FORCE that made the wheat grow, FORCE that garnered it from the soil to give place to the succeeding crop. (2:343)

But such meditations are seldom pertinent to what actually happens in Norris's fiction; throughout *The Octopus*, for instance, the railroad has been driven to combat the ranchers not by any demonstrated laws of nature or of the marketplace but by the conventional and melodramatic villainy of characters like the jowly railroad agent, S. Behrman. In the last analysis, Norris has little interest in exploring the actual mechanism by which "forces" and "conditions" influence human behavior; on this score, too, the conventional notion that his fiction is naturalistic would appear to rest on rather shaky ground.

Yet all of this may be beside the point. Norris, like Zola, dismissed considerations of style from the discussion of naturalism, yet as Larzer Ziff has observed, "one cannot have *no* style," and Norris in fact cultivates a number of distinguishable styles. "Disregard for style," Ziff writes, "is, as Norris unconsciously shows, in constant danger of being bad style, bad art," and it is not difficult to find in Norris examples of perfectly dreadful writing; he had, as John Berryman put it, "a style like a great wet dog."[11] Still, it is not enough simply to say that Norris had a "bad" style; there are more important matters to be pursued. What, for instance, are the precise qualities of Norris's various styles? In what sense or senses might we describe these characteristic styles as being "naturalistic"? What, finally, is the relationship between Norris's stylistic practice and his own conception, however vague or confused, of literary naturalism?

Let us begin with the most obviously "naturalistic" prose in Norris. In *McTeague*, for example, dentistry is described in a technical language clearly acquired through research. McTeague makes "'mats' from his tape of non-cohesive gold"; he makes "'blocks' to be used in large proximal cavities," "'cylinders' for commencing fillings," and so on (8:15). Still, while dentistry provides a fund of convenient symbols in a novel whose main characters are obsessed with gold, the factual details of dentistry, the actual procedures and the specialized language used to describe them, remain at best tangential to Norris's concerns; and once the real business of the novel gets going the language quickly veers away from the obvious naturalism of technical terminology and detail. For instance, when McTeague is first attracted to Trina Sieppe we are told that "suddenly the animal in the man stirred and woke; the evil instincts that in him were so close to the surface leaped to life, shouting and clamouring"; a kiss leads to an authorial meditation on "the changeless order of things—the man desiring the woman only for what she withholds; the woman worshipping the man for that which she yields up to him"; of Trina's response to this kiss we are told that "the Woman within her suddenly awoke" (8:26, 73, 77). This is the sort of language to which Norris always resorts, in his fiction as in his critical essays, when he wants to describe the "reality" he conceived to be the true subject of naturalistic fiction. This language has little to do with factual detail, with observation, or with any scientific effort to understand and explain physical or emotional processes; instead, it relies relentlessly on melodramatic metaphor and abstract assertion. The activities of McTeague's "evil instincts" are purely (and more or less inconceivably) metaphorical—"leaping," "shouting," "clamouring"—and this reliance on metaphor, and the epithet "evil," tell us a good deal about the depth of Norris's commitment to scientific objectivity. Finally, important nouns here are characteristically preceded by the definite article—"the man," "the animal," "the woman"—and they are likely as well to come out capitalized—as in "the Woman." This is a language not of scientific description or explanation but of abstract, melodramatic cliché. In *The Octopus* and in its sequel, *The Pit*, Norris gave this language free rein.

For *The Octopus* Norris researched wheat ranching and California politics; for *The Pit* he went through a crash course in the intricacies of commodity speculation; but in both books the nominal subjects are repeatedly swamped in waves of abstraction and melodramatic metaphor. While a description of a wheat harvest near the end of *The Octopus* mentions such things as "header knives," "beltings," "the separator," "the agitator," along with "cylinders, augers, fans, seeders, and elevators, drapers and chaff-carriers" (2:325), the next to last paragraph of the book is far more typical of Norris's treatment of his subject:

> *But the* WHEAT *remained.* Untouched, unassailable, undefiled, that mighty world-force, that nourisher of nations, wrapped in Nirvanic calm, indifferent to the human swarm, gigantic, resistless, moved onward in its appointed grooves.... [T]he great harvest of Los Muertos rolled like a flood from the Sierras to the Himalayas to feed thousands of starving scarecrows on the barren plains of India. (2:360)

Norris's political research for *The Octopus*, unlike his research into wheat ranching, does play an important part in the book's action, providing the details for the story of the ranchers' unsuccessful effort to elect their own railroad commission and thus resist punitive increases in the rate charged for shipping their crop to market. Yet even here the details of political manipulation and countermanipulation keep dissolving into the abstract rhetoric of the "big" and "vital." For instance, when the ranchers unite to resist the railroad, the narrator enlarges considerably on the significance of their action:

> It was the uprising of The People; the thunder of the outbreak of revolt; the mob demanding to be led, aroused at last, imperious, resistless, overwhelming. It was the blind fury of insurrection, the brute, many-tongued, red-eyed, bellowing for guidance, baring its teeth, unsheathing its claws, imposing its will with the abrupt, resistless pressure of the relaxed piston, inexorable, knowing no pity. (1:271)

Except for the curious addition of a "relaxed piston" (which in spite of its relaxation still exerts "pressure") this eruption of "the brute" sounds a lot more like what happens to McTeague, and to so many of Norris's characters, than it sounds like any conceivable political meeting. Here "The People," capitals and all, are virtually interchangeable with such things as "the man," "the animal," or "the Woman," and the "resistless pressure" of this force (the word "resistless" occurs twice in this brief passage) makes it sound more than a little like the wheat itself, at the close, "gigantic, resistless, moved onward in its appointed grooves." The problem, of course, is that this rhapsodic description bears no relation whatever to its supposed subject, the formation of the Ranchers' League to combat the railroad. These capitalists are not in any sense "The People"—nor, for that matter, is any actual "mob" (let alone "*the* mob") involved in their coalition or in any of their subsequent actions.

The same sort of movement, from concrete detail to a quite irrelevant assertion of large "force," also characterizes Norris's last novel, *The Pit*. Much of the book's action turns on details of speculation in grain futures: Curtis Jadwin corners the market in May wheat only to destroy himself by trying to extend this corner to a July harvest made much larger by his own inflation of wheat prices, and in the story of his rise and fall we learn about such things as "bulls" and "bears," "selling long" and "selling short," or "covering" contracts to deliver grain on a specified date. These things matter in *The Pit* in ways that the details of dentistry, for instance, do not matter in *McTeague*. Still, these details, too, are finally tangential to the direction of Norris's deepest concern; what ultimately matters about Jadwin is that he is another "big" man who unleashes the "forces" in himself only to be beaten by even larger "forces." It is thus no surprise that the complex machinations of commodity trading are repeatedly buried beneath Norris's characteristic language of melodramatic metaphor. To cite only one example, here is some of the narrator's account of Jadwin's difficulty holding to a vow to stay out of speculation:

> Try as he would, the echoes of the rumbling of the Pit reached Jadwin at every hour of the day and night. The maelstrom there at the foot of La Salle Street was swirling now with a mightier rush than for years past. Thundering, its vortex smoking, it sent its whirling far out over the country, from ocean to ocean, sweeping the wheat into its currents, sucking it in, and spewing it out again in the gigantic pulses of its ebb and flow.
>
> ... The great Fact, the great Result which was at last to issue forth from all this turmoil was not yet achieved. Would it refuse to come until a master hand, all powerful, all daring, gripped the levers of the sluice gates that controlled the crashing waters of the Pit? He did not know. Was it the moment for a chief?
>
> Was this upheaval a revolution that called aloud for its Napoleon? (9:247–48)

To believe that this is in any sense naturalism is to believe that Napoleon rose to power as water commissioner of Paris, after a period of severe flooding.[12]

My point here is not simply that Norris's stylistic excesses are ridiculous, although the impulse to raucous laughter is often irresistible. The main importance of Norris's persistent cultivation of rhetorical melodrama, rather, is that it indicates quite clearly what is going on at the heart of his fiction. He cares very little if at all for factual or "scientific" detail—for specialized language or, what is far more important, for the specific biological, mechanical, economic, or political processes this language describes. He always shifts from the literal to the metaphorical, and he draws his metaphors—unlike Melville, say, or Thoreau, or Pynchon—not from the process he is supposedly describing but from a severely limited stock of conventional and interchangeable clichés about the emergence of vague, "resistless" forces: "the brute," "the mob," "the crushing waters," whatever. It would thus appear that Norris's conception of naturalism affected the style of his fiction in a rather direct way: one can easily understand the appeal of such metaphors to a writer who wanted something "big," who longed to escape "the quiet, uneventful round of everyday life" in order to join "the throes of a vast and terrible drama that works itself out in unleashed passions, in blood, and in sudden death." Even the abstract vagueness of this language would seem to be functional: Norris's was, after all, a *fantasy* of "reality," of "force," and detailed understanding does have a way of dampening ardors for the exotic. Still, to associate the style that emerges from Norris's needs and fantasies with what has normally been meant by "naturalism" is to throw critical seriousness to the winds—or, as Norris himself might have preferred it, into the smoking vortex.

The story of the effect of Norris's ideas on his style does not end here, however, for Norris has another arguably "realistic" or "naturalistic" style, at least in his earlier fiction. For instance, in *Vandover and the Brute*, written during Norris's year at Harvard in 1894–95, there is an interesting description of the home of Ida Wade, a "fast" young woman whom the hero, Vandover, eventually ruins:

> The front door stood at the right side of the parlour windows. Two Corinthian pillars on either side of the vestibule supported a balcony; these pillars had iron capitals which were painted to imitate the wood of the house, which in its turn was painted to imitate stone. The house was but two stories high, and the roof was topped with an iron cresting. There was a microscopical front yard in which one saw a tiny gravel walk, two steps long, that led to a door under the front steps, where the gas-meter was kept. A few dusty and straggling calla-lilies grew about. (5:59)

Here, suddenly, is a Norris halfway between Mark Twain and Nathanael West, relying not on melodramatic inflation but on ironic understatement. The progression from "Corinthian pillars" to the "gas-meter" is very nice, and those "iron capitals ... painted to imitate the wood of the house, which in its turn was painted to imitate stone," could be straight out of West's *The Day of the Locust*. For the reader accustomed to the inflated Norris, the deft and quiet irony of such passages is positively astonishing. It is not simply that they grow out of observation of the world Norris knew, rather than the out of the "big" world he fantasized, although this fact is important.[13] What is most surprising is that a writer in whose work irony (at least intended irony) is usually absent cultivates it here quite deliberately and skillfully. The Wades's world is seen on its own terms and yet is judged in quite other terms; narrator and reader stand aloof, seeing in the quietly reported details of this world what its inhabitants could never see themselves.

There is a fair amount of this sort of writing early in *Vandover*, although it soon retreats before the advance of the "serious" Norris, with his story of how Vandover "rushed into a career of dissipation, consumed with the desire of vice, the perverse, blind, and reckless desire of the male" (5:181). In *McTeague*—written for the most part, like *Vandover*, in the mid-18990s—the ironic style is sustained longer, which is surely one of the reasons the book now strikes many readers as Norris's most successful novel. For instance, we are told that on one wall of his Dental Parlors McTeague has hung "a steel engraving of the court of Lorenzo de' Medici, which he had bought because there were a great many figures in it for the money." We are later told about Trina Sieppe's taste in pictures, about her admiration for "the 'Ideal Heads,' lovely girls with flowing straw-coloured hair and immense, upturned eyes. These always had for title, 'Reverie,' or 'An Idyll,' or 'Dreams of Love.'" At a theater with Trina and her mother and brother McTeague is much impressed with the performance. "That's what you call musicians," he announces, "gravely." "'Home, Sweet Home,' played upon a trombone," adds the narrator, impersonating the admiration of the naive spectators. "Think of that! Art could go no farther" (8:3, 170, 87–88). The whole account of this visit to the theater, while the humor is sometimes a bit overdone, is a comic tour de force, as is the account of McTeague's and Trina's wedding, managed with military precision by Trina's blustering father. "Not Stanley penetrating for the first time into the Dark Continent," writes the narrator, "not Napoleon leading his army across the Alps, was more weighted with responsibility" (8:131). Significantly, the heroic analogies here used ironically are precisely the sort that Norris will later use

seriously and straightforwardly—for instance, in *The Pit*, when Curtis Jadwin
wonders whether the "maelstrom" is calling aloud for its "Napoleon."

In *McTeague*, moreover, this ironic aloofness is not confined to
moments of comedy or satire. After a visit to Trina's family McTeague stays
the night, sleeping in Trina's room (which she has vacated). He stands in
front of her open closet, staring in fascination at her clothes. "All at once,"
we are told, "seized with an unreasoned impulse, McTeague opened his huge
arms and gathered the little garments close to him, plunging his face deep
amongst them, savouring their delicious odour with long breaths of luxury
and supreme content" (8:69). Such things as "savouring," "delicious odour,"
"luxury," and "supreme content" sound, in their excessiveness, like Norris's
own purple rhetoric, but here they work because their excessiveness is the
point: these terms express McTeague's emotions, not the narrator's, and in
recognizing their ironic function we recognize our distance from McTeague,
from his moment of fetishistic indulgence, a distance we share with the
narrator. The same sort of narrative aloofness characterizes one of the best-
known passages in *McTeague*—the description of Trina's death, after she has
been beaten into insensibility by her husband:

> Trina lay unconscious, just as she had fallen under the last of
> McTeague's blows, her body twitching with an occasional
> hiccough that stirred the pool of blood in which she lay face
> downward. Toward morning she died with a rapid series of
> hiccoughs that sounded like a piece of clockwork running down.
> (8:320)

There is a good deal of Norris's customary rhetoric in *McTeague*—
abstract, melodramatic, overly insistent, and utterly without irony—but what
gives the book its power is Norris's ability for the most part to maintain the
distinction between himself and his characters, between the artist and his
materials, between, as we might put it, "literature" and "life." The most
curious fact about Norris's career, in this connection, is that what he
discovered in the mid-90s, in *Vandover* and *McTeague*, he rapidly unlearned;
in *The Octopus* and *The Pit* there is almost nothing like the aloof irony of
*McTeague* at its best. At the beginning of the second volume of *The Octopus*,
as the setting shifts briefly from the San Joaquin valley to the genteel world
of San Francisco, we have a momentary eruption of satire, directed mainly at
an "artistic" woman named Mrs. Cedarquist who surrounds herself with a
coterie of cultural charlatans, but it is hard to find much irony of this sort
elsewhere in the book. Descriptions of nature are "poetic" in the worst sense,

while descriptions of habitations and their decoration, in both *The Octopus* and *The Pit*, are almost uniformly without either irony or point. To understand Norris, then, we must try to understand what happened to him between the writing of *McTeague* in the mid-1890s and the writing of *The Octopus* and *The Pit* at the end of the decade.

In this light we should look at the initial description of Norris's most obvious surrogate in *The Octopus*, the poet Presley, who conforms with almost ludicrous precision to the conventional stereotype of the "artist." He has "the forehead of the intellectual," along with "a delicate and highly sensitive nature"; "one guessed," we are told, "that Presley's refinement had been gained only by a certain loss of strength" (1:6). An important part of the "artistic" baggage he must slough off in order to discover himself as a "man" is an effete lack of sympathy with "the people"—meaning, in this case, not the big ranchers but those far below them in the economic hierarchy. "These uncouth brutes of farm-hands and petty ranchers," the narrator tells us, "grimed with the soil they worked upon, were odious to [Presley] beyond words. Never could he feel in sympathy with them, nor with their lives, their ways, their marriages, deaths, bickerings, and all the monotonous round of their sordid existence" (1:3). This whole issue of sympathy with the "sordid" might remind us of Olive Chancellor's need to mortify her taste, in Henry James's *Bostonians*; but in terms of what happens in *The Octopus*, this issue is a red herring—since very few "farm-hands and petty ranchers" appear in the book and none of them is an important character, especially to Presley. Norris's raising of the issue of sympathy is important, however, because it reveals how closely, by the time he wrote *The Octopus*, he associated lack of sympathy with artistic alienation, with the irrelevance of literature to life. And what matters is that such lack of sympathy was precisely the hallmark of the irony in *McTeague*, signaling again and again the aloofness of the narrator, his distance from the "sordid existence" of his characters. Given Presley's need to identify with "the people," is it any wonder that such irony is almost totally missing from *The Octopus* and *The Pit?*

By the time he wrote *The Octopus*, Norris had apparently convinced himself that he could be a "man" only if he could identify with his materials, with "the world of big things," and while such a belief may have helped assuage his personal and vocational anxieties, it left little room for satire and irony—which could hardly be used, in any significant way, to describe the ranchers who were after all Norris's projections of his own fantasy of "reality." To put it bluntly, then, Norris's theory of naturalism would seem to have destroyed his power as a writer. It compelled him to turn away not only from the *idea* of style but from the actual style and stance of his best novel, a novel largely written before its author began to theorize about fiction. Norris's insistence on the absolute distinction of "life" and "literature" set forth the terms of a self-fulfilling prophecy. Proclaiming again and again that he was a "man," Norris ultimately ceased to be an "artist." Lionel Trilling complained, years ago, about "the chronic American belief that there exists an opposition between reality and mind and that one must enlist in the party of reality."[14] This belief lies at the heart of Norris's essays and novels: dismissing "style" and the "literatary," he ended up writing a style that is literary in the very worse sense of the term, and he turned from the irony of his best early fiction to a "reality" that is in fact a tissue of the very crudest fantasy. Norris's faults, this is to say, are not incidental; they are the products of what he conceived naturalism to be and to require. He wanted above all to enlist in the "party of reality," to join "the marching world," and in this respect his example is prophetic of a good deal of what has passed for naturalist thinking, in American fiction and criticism, in the years since his death.

## Notes

1. "The Naturalist Machine," in *Sex, Politics, and Science in the Nineteenth-Century Novel*, ed. Ruth Bernard Yeazell (Baltimore: Johns Hopkins University Press, 1986), 116. Norris also looms large, for example, in Walter Michaels's *The Gold Standard and the Logic of American Naturalism* (Berkeley: University of California Press, 1987), particularly in the title essay, and he is one of the three principal subjects (the other two being Jack London and Theodore Dreiser) of June Howard's *Form and History in American Literary Naturalism* (Chapel Hill: University of North Carolina Press, 1985). For a recent dissent from the connection of Norris with naturalism, see chap. 1, "Norris's Dubious Naturalism," in Barbara Hochman, *The Art of Frank Norris, Storyteller* (Columbia: University of Missouri Press, 1988), 1–19.

2. The principal source of biographical information remains Franklin Walker, *Frank Norris: A Biography* (Garden City, N.Y.: Doubleday, 1932). Valuable briefer accounts of Norris's career include Maxwell Geismar, *Rebels and Ancestors: The American Novel, 1890–1915* (Boston: Houghton Mifflin, 1953), 1–66; Kenneth Lynn, *The Dream of Success: A Study of the Modern American Imagination* (Boston: Little, Brown, 1955), 158–207; and Larzer Ziff, *The American 1890s: Life and Times of a Lost Generation* (New York: Viking, 1966), 250–74.

3. Parenthetical volume and page references to Norris are to *The Complete Works of Frank Norris*, 10 vols. (Garden City, N.Y.: Doubleday, 1928).

4. *The Letters of Frank Norris*, ed. Franklin Walker (San Francisco: Book Club of California, 1956), 30–31.

5. *The Literary Criticism of Frank Norris*, ed. Donald Pizer (Austin: University of Texas Press, 1964), 72.

6. Ibid., 71–72.

7. There would of course also appear to be a fair amount of sexual anxiety lurking in Norris's concern with "big things" and "little things." For instance, in *Moran of the Lady*

*Letty*, when Wilbur kills a Chinese beachcomber, we are told that "all that was strong and virile and brutal in him seemed to harden and stiffen in the moment after he had seen the beach comber collapse limply on the sand under that last strong knife-blow" (3:290). What matters most here, of course (as is also true of the comments on Zola), is that masculine force is equated with aggressive violence. Compare Mark Seltzer's observation that "a capitalizing on force as a counter to female generativity in particular and to anxieties about generation and production in general may help to explain, at least in part, the appeals to highly abstract conceptions of force in the emphatically 'male' genre of naturalism" ("The Naturalist Machine," 121).

8. *Realism and Naturalism in American Fiction*, 98.

9. On this aspect of Norris's thought, see especially Maxwell Geismar's *Rebels and Ancestors*, 1–66.

10. *The Letters of Frank Norris*, 23, 48.

11. Ziff, *The American 1890s*, 270; Berryman, *Stephen Crane* (New York: Meridian, 1962), 288.

12. Particularly intriguing in this passage is its jarring introduction of literal liquid ("from ocean to ocean") into the metaphorical cascade of "maelstrom," "vortex," and "ebb and flow." And the suggestion that "the great Result" would "refuse to come" without the intervening grip of "a master hand" might recall Mark Seltzer's observation that "creation, in Norris's final explanation, is the work of an inexhaustible masturbator, spilling his seed on the ground, the product of a mechanistic and miraculous onanism"—placing "power back into the hands of the immortal and autonomous male technology of generation" ("The Naturalist Machine," 124).

13. According to Maxwell Geismar, for instance, *Vandover* is a "key novel" because it deals with "that young western aristocracy—the sons of the rich—which was Norris's natural medium" (*Rebels and Ancestors*, 52–53).

14. "Reality in America," in *The Liberal Imagination* (New York: Scribner's. 1976), 10.

DONALD PIZER

# Contemporary American Literary Naturalism

Literary Naturalism has had an equivocal career and reputation in America. Though seemingly attuned to American life in its concreteness and circumstantiality, it also runs counter to the predominant strain of optimistic moralism in the American character. In addition, in a country still afflicted with a powerful residue of religious fundamentalism, the sexual sensationalism of naturalism—Trina McTeague, for example, lying naked on her gold coins—has never failed to attract condemnation.[1] Yet, as Willard Thorp noted in 1960, in a study of major tendencies in modern American literature, naturalism in America has "refused to die,"[2] with this refusal made even more singular in the light of its early demise in England and on the Continent.

In my recently published book, *Twentieth-Century American Literary Naturalism: An Interpretation*, I sought to account for the persistence of naturalism in America.[3] After examining the various manifestations of naturalism in American fiction from the 1890s to the early 1950s, I came to the conclusion that a major reason for the endurance of the movement has been its dynamic adaptability. While critics of American naturalism have since the beginning attempted to fix on it a static philosophical center derived from Emile Zola's ideas—materialistic determinism and the like—naturalist writers have refused to constitute themselves into a school. They have rather continued to do what they have always done—to write with

From *The Theory and Practice of American Literary Naturalism: Selected Essays and Reviews.* © 1993 by the Board of Trustees, Southern Illinois University.

distinctive personal individuality about "hard times" in America, hard times in the sense both of economic and social deprivation and of the malaise of spirit arising out of such deprivation. And they have continued as well to impose on this material of national failure conscious efforts to explain—to explain both specific ills and, by extension, the nature of all experience—efforts which move their fiction strikingly toward the symbolic and allegorical in expression. Naturalism has been in America a literature in which the writer depicts man under pressure to survive because of the baleful interaction between his own limitations and the crushing conditions of life and in which the writer also proffers, through his symbolism, an interpretive model of all life. It is a fiction, in brief, that is both powerfully concrete and provocatively expansive. What has varied in the history of naturalism in America is not the writer's commitment to the depiction of the inadequacies of American life. Rather, it is the nature of American life itself—its particular social reality and intellectual preoccupations—that has changed and that has thereby resulted in the varying themes and strategies of the American naturalistic novel—in its dynamic character, in short.

The three periods of hard times in American life since the late nineteenth century that have seen major outbursts of literary naturalism are the 1890s, the 1930s, and the late 1940s and early 1950s. In the 1890s, the shock of the realization that man now had to exist both in a mechanized urban present and in an animal past stimulated an often ideologically fuzzy but fictionally brilliant effort to constitute new myths and symbols of man's condition in the modern world. Whether depicting man as animalistic brute, as a confused soldier in a smoke-obscured battle, or as a searcher for a place of warmth in a cold, anonymous city, the naturalists of this decade were seeking ways to present man as more circumscribed by his nature and by the conditions of life than was usually supposed. During the 1930s, a new generation, responding to the breakdown of the American economic system, continued the search for adequate symbolic constructs to express their concern. But now, responsive as well to the full tide of literary modernism and to the striking example offered by Dreiser's *An American Tragedy* of 1925, they sought—at a moment when the American system and thus the American dream appeared to be at near collapse—to dramatize above all the blighting of the felt inner life by the cultural and economic poverty of America. James T. Farrell's Studs Lonigan, a potentially warm and even poetic young man misshapen by a street ethic, is the archetypal figure in the naturalism of the decade. The naturalism of the late 1940s and early 1950s was far more "cosmic" in tenor, as befits a phase of American history when the euphoria of the immediate postwar years was replaced by the fear and mistrust of the

Cold and Korean wars, the McCarthy era, and the birth of an international atomic age. The question raised by such naturalistic novels as Norman Mailer's *The Naked and the Dead* and William Styron's *Lie Down in Darkness* was whether the notion of human freedom had validity within the struggle for power that occurred in such symbolic centers of modern life as the army and the middle-class family.

The permanence, and vitality of naturalism in America is, I believe, also due to the presence in it of the modern residue of the tragic impulse. Naturalism, from Hurstwood's decline and death to Dos Passos's "We stand defeated America," has always been a literature of failure. Yet contrary to much received opinion, the naturalist depiction of human and social inadequacy is not equivalent to passive acceptance. The naturalist is not a neutral recorder of futility and fallibility in all their phases. Underlying his fiction is a powerful remnant of the sense that life has meaning and dignity— if not freedom—despite its frequent collapse into chaos and death. So the naturalist will dramatize the pathos of the waste of human potential in the lives of those feeling temperaments, a Clyde Griffiths or Studs Lonigan, who lack the cunning and strength to overcome the structured visions and expectations of their limited worlds. Or he will encourage our sympathy for the Joads of America, men of simple needs, who unsuccessfully attempt to maintain an even keel in an unstable universe. Or he will render the self-driven efforts by a Henry Fleming or a Sergeant Croft to obtain knowledge in a world clouded with ambiguity. These are of course neither conventional tragic sentiments nor conventional tragic heroes. No Hamlets or Lears here. Rather, there is a modern approximation of the essential tragic paradox— that the potentially wonderful creature which is man frequently goes crashing down to destruction and death.

I would like to devote the bulk of my paper to a preliminary and necessarily selective account of what I believe to be a contemporary resurgence of naturalism in American fiction. Since the late 1960s we have again had "hard times" in America. The two initial causes were of course the prolonged and costly and fruitless Vietnam War and the Watergate affair, both of which implied a major breakdown in America's global and national ethical character. These were followed in the mid and late 1970s by the crisis in the American city (the blight, violence, and bankruptcy of New York are indicative), by a severe recession deepening into near-depression, and by the fear that the world, with America's aid, was hastening into a nuclear holocaust.

I will discuss three recent works of fiction as examples of reactions to this new sense of hard times and of yet another phase of American literary naturalism. Each work derives from its writers's distinctive response to a specific inadequacy in contemporary American life, and each is also in a tradition of analogous responses by earlier naturalists to similar conditions. So Joyce Carol Oates's *them* of 1969 is a novel of the deprivation and violence of urban life. Like Crane's *Maggie* of 1893, it seeks to demonstrate, as Crane said of his novel, that "environment is a tremendous thing in the world and frequently shapes lives regardless."[4] So Norman Mailer's *The Executioner's Song* of 1979, like Dreiser's *An American Tragedy*, dramatizes, within a story of crime and punishment, the failure of our social and legal response to human need and desire. And so Robert Stone's *A Flag for Sunrise* of 1981, like Frank Norris's *The Octopus* of 1901 and John Steinbeck's *The Grapes of Wrath* of 1939, explores in the context of national social and political conditions the interplay between religious conviction and determining social reality in American life.

Of course, it is difficult to be more than suggestive in any selective study of a literary tendency or movement. One's specific choices and thus larger theses are always open to question and challenge. Nevertheless, these are three large-scale, important, and compelling works by three major contemporary novelists. Any perceived relationship among the works should therefore throw some light on one of the directions of contemporary American writing.

*them* is probably the best example in contemporary American fiction of the conscious effort by a major writer to recover and renew the themes and fictional conventions of American literary naturalism. The novel details the fortunes of a poor midwestern family, the Wendalls, from late in the Depression to the Detroit riot of the summer of 1967. Almost every characteristic of the naturalistic city novel, from *Maggie* and *McTeague* through *An American Tragedy* and *Studs Lonigan*, is present in *them*. When we first meet Loretta Wendall, the mother of the two principal figures in the novel, Maureen and Jules, she is a young girl whose own mother is dead and whose father is a drunkard. Through a series of brutish husbands, she raises her children without love or guidance in a slum setting of drink, unemployment, petty crime, ethnic prejudice, and violence. Except for the powerful sympathetic bond between Maureen and Jules, the emotions of the family are those of their world—envy, anger, fear, and hate. The novel opens with Loretta's jealous brother shooting her teenage lover while he sleeps in her arms, and it closes with Jules killing a policeman during the Detroit riot. Between these two deaths occur such staples of slum fiction as prostitution and rape, additional murders and attempted murders, alcoholism and drug addiction, and violence of every description. So full and rich is Oates' use of the "classic" matter of naturalistic fiction that one wonders if it is not with tongue in cheek that she claims, in her Author's Note to the novel, that she has not exaggerated the life depicted. "Indeed," she writes, "the various sordid and shocking events of slum life, detailed in other naturalistic works, have been understated here, mainly because of my fear that too much reality would become unbearable."[5]

Although Jules and Maureen Wendall are part of this world of spiritual and material deprivation, they both wish to be something else and something more. Oates appears to have chosen dual protagonists—a brother and sister—to stress that whatever their differences in sex, temperament, and specific experience, Jules and Maureen, because of the general similarity of their lives and fates, constitute one of the paradigms of slum experience. Both are dissatisfied with their lives and make early unsuccessful attempts to escape—Maureen to the library, where it is quiet and there is a chance to dream; and Jules to the streets, where there is at least an illusion of freedom. But for both figures these tentative early efforts reflect a far deeper need—to escape being a Wendall. So when Jules's father dies, Jules, as he recalls his father's life, realizes the danger of himself slipping into that life. The core of his father's life, Jules now knows, was anger. "Anger for what? For nothing, for himself, for life, for the assembly line, for the cockroaches and the dripping toilet. One thing was as good as another" (147). But Jules will not take this road. Instead, "Money was an adventure. It was open to him. Anything could happen. He felt that his father's essence, that muttering dark anger, had surrounded him and almost penetrated him, but had not quite penetrated him; he was free" (147).

Money, in fact, is not only an adventure, a means, but an end in itself. For money is one of the principal attributes of "them"—the middle-class world of wealth and possessions in which, Jules and Maureen vaguely and inarticulately feel, the self is somehow free from all that impinges on it in their present lives. And, they discover, the most available and seemingly effective way to acquire money and admission to the world of "them" is through sex and love. As Dreiser had demonstrated in *Sister Carrie* and *An American Tragedy*, upward mobility is often achieved through the bedroom and the altar. The first two parts of *them* (the novel is divided into three sections) are devoted to two such parallel efforts by Maureen and Jules. In the first section, Maureen, while still a schoolgirl, allows herself to be picked up by an older man. She asks for money for the sex she has with him, sex which she responds to unfeelingly and mechanically. But her step-father sees her with the man, finds the money she has hidden, and in a jealous rage beats her so severely that she remains psychically wounded for many years. In the second section of the novel, Jules becomes deeply obsessed with Nadine, an upper middle-class girl from Grosse Point. Oates tells us about Jules in this stage in a Dreiserian passage:

> He thought of himself as spirit struggling with the fleshly earth, the very force of gravity, death. All his life he thought of himself in this way....
> Of the effort the spirit makes, this is the subject of Jules's story; of its effort to achieve freedom, the breaking out into beauty, in patches perhaps but beauty anyway, and of Jules as an American youth.... (274)

Nadine is like Sondra Finchley, the rich girl of Lycurgus whom Clyde Griffiths views as a paradise to be gained. Nadine is what the spirit seeks as beauty because she is escape and freedom and hope, and she is to be won by a force in Jules that is both love and, as he tells her, "something deeper" than love because of its semireligious nature. But Nadine is "them"; she may be desired and indeed provoke desire, but her response to adoration is "cold," "steely," "limp," and "numb." When at last she permits Jules to make love to her, she fails to have a sexual climax. After spending a day and night with Jules, Nadine, feeling degraded and defiled, shoots him. Like the class that she symbolizes, she seems to beckon and offer herself, but in reality she holds herself back and then seeks to destroy Jules because of her fear that in being possessed she will become what he is.

The first two sections of *them* thus present us with analogous stories in which Maureen and Jules are almost destroyed by their effort to scale the walls into the bastion of "them." The last section of the novel dramatizes their equivocal success in achieving their goal. Maureen offers the clearest example. At twenty-six, she decides that she must at last "escape the doom of being *Maureen Wendall* all my life" (338). To marry—anyone, so long as he is not of her class and world—is to gain this new identity. So with an amoral cunning, rather than her earlier ingenuous selling of herself, she sets her sights on her night school teacher, a poor graduate student with a wife and children. He leaves his family for Maureen, they marry and move to the suburbs, and Maureen becomes pregnant. She tells Jules at the close of the novel, "I'm going to forget everything and everybody.... I'm a different person" (507).

Jules adopts less obvious but fundamentally similar means to at last reach "them." Down and out, he is picked up by some university radicals as an example of the suppressed working class. Through them, he meets a slumming upper-class girl—also from Grosse Point—whom he rapes and turns into a prostitute. During the Detroit riot, he kills a policeman, but after the riot he becomes a spokesman for the radical position. The end of the novel finds him going to California to work in a government antipoverty program. Both Maureen and Jules, it is clear, have adopted the weapons of their world—cunning, shrewdness, and ruthlessness—in order to escape it. They are now angry, but the directionless anger that imprisoned their father is now a means toward freedom because it is a directed anger toward the class they wish to join. Jules's prostitution of the young girl and Maureen's stealing of her husband away from his wife and children are conscious acts of anger and vengeance against the world of "them" that had earlier denied them access. The Detroit riot, with its destruction of property and attack on order, becomes to Jules a symbol of this new freedom of anger. As he wanders the burnt-out streets, "He was drifting with freedom, intoxicated with freedom. That was what he had tasted in the air ... freedom. The roofless buildings, already burnt-out, looked up into the sky in a brazen, hopeless paroxysm of freedom" (492).

Of course, though Jules and Maureen have "escaped," they have done so at such cost to themselves and to others that we are left with little sense of victory. The wasted streets of Detroit are apt testimony to the hate forced upon Jules as the price of freedom, he who had earlier tried love. But like Clyde Griffiths, who had also been forced into hate and anger by the inexorable pressure of his desires in the face of an immovable wall of class, Jules—and Maureen—also suggest in the strength of their need the permanence of the condition that is the human spirit seeking relief and fulfillment. Jules and Maureen as an American boy and girl desiring something better in life than to be a Wendall reveal both the terrible hazards accompanying an effort of this kind and its vitality. To reach "them" by the means Jules and Maureen use at the close of the novel is not estimable, Oates appears to be saying, but to be seeking still, after their earlier crushing defeats, is a revelation of the inexhaustible strength of man's quest for a better life.

Something of the same ambivalence characteristic of the naturalistic tragic ethos is present in Oates's own role in *them*. One of Maureen's teachers in night school is Oates. Maureen is deeply envious of Oates's career, marriage, and home, and when Oates gives her a failing grade in the course, Maureen is bitter and angry. "You failed me" (335), Maureen writes Oates, playing upon her grade and the deeper failure of Oates to respond adequately to Maureen's nature and needs. But though Oates did not reach out to Maureen—as few of us are capable of doing—she did shape an account of her that constitutes an attempt to understand and thus to make at least partial restitution. So, as in much tragic art, the writer, through his creation of an art object, testifies both to his helplessness in the face of the human dilemma and to his efforts to understand and to help others toward understanding.[6]

Norman Mailer's *Cannibals and Christians,* a collection of miscellaneous pieces published in 1966, contains a poem entitled "The Executioner's Song."[7] Throughout the poem Mailer plays on the various meanings of the verb "to execute." The song of the executioner who dispatches criminals is also that of the artist who executes in the sense of to perform. In particular, the artist, like the executioner, seeks to "kill well and bury well"—to bring a work of art from its sources in life to its paradoxical "dead" form as an art object. And like the executioner, the artist also sits in judgment on his subject. As the executioner claims in a central passage of the poem,

> If I could execute neatly
>     (with respect for whatever romantic imagination
>     gave passion to my subject's crime)
>     and if buried well,
>     (with tenderness, dispatch, gravity
>     and joy that the job was not jangled ... )
>     well, then perhaps,
>     then might I rise so high upon occasion
>     as to smite a fist of the Lord's creation
>     into the womb of that muse
>     which gives us poems....

The poem strikingly anticipates Mailer's effort, over ten years later, to tell the story of Gary Gilmore, a criminal executed for murder in 1977. Like Dreiser in *An American Tragedy,* which is also a massive account, based on documentary sources, of a sensational story of crime and punishment in America, Mailer in *The Executioner's Song* seeks to execute well—to recreate Gilmore's life with respect for the "passion" of the inner man, and to communicate through expressive form the complex and mixed emotions— the tenderness and gravity—of a tragic event.

Gary Gilmore would seem to be as unpromising a subject for a tragic work as was Chester Gillette, the prototype of Clyde Griffiths. The product of a broken and poor home, Gilmore had begun in adolescence his lifelong pattern of lengthy periods in prison followed by brief respites on the "outside." By April 1976, when he was released from a federal penitentiary in Illinois, he had spent eighteen of his thirty-five years behind bars. On parole in Provo, Utah, he has within a few months of his release again drifted into a life of drinking, drugs, theft, and flare ups of violence. He has also begun to live with Nicole Baker, a nineteen-year-old girl who has been married three times (the first at fourteen) and has two children. After an intense but brief period of love, Nicole leaves him because of his fecklessness and rages. Needing money to pay for a pickup truck he covets, and angry at Nicole, Gilmore commits robberies on consecutive nights, on both occasions killing an unarmed man needlessly and in cold blood. He is apprehended, tried for murder, and sentenced to be shot. At this point, Gilmore attracted national attention by refusing to appeal his conviction. Because of a Supreme Court ruling, no one had been executed in America for over ten years. Thus, the legal and moral issues raised by Gilmore's willingness to die, as well as the sensationalism inherent in a prospective execution after so many years, made him "news." Reporters and publicists rushed to Salt Lake City to compete for his story. Despite last minute appeals by the American Civil Liberties Union, Gilmore was executed by firing squad on January 17, 1977, a little over nine months after leaving the penitentiary.

Mailer explains in his Afterword to *The Executioner's Song* that the work "does its best to be a factual account of the activities of Gary Gilmore."[8] But he goes on to note that he has also tried to write "a true life story ... as if it were a novel"—to achieve accuracy but also "intimacy of ... experience" (1053). For the factual basis of Gilmore's life, Mailer relied on and often used verbatim a large body of documentary material—court records, Gilmore's letters, published interviews, and so on. He turned most of all to some fifteen thousand pages of transcribed interviews with Gilmore and with those who knew him or were associated with him during his Utah period, from Nicole Baker to friends, family, attorneys, and relatives of the murdered men. In this respect, *The Executioner's Song* resembles Truman Capote's *In Cold Blood* of 1965 and other exercises in the form that has come to be known as the New Journalism or Non-Fiction Novel. The writer seeking to recreate a sensational contemporary event—a crime or disaster—relies heavily on the reporting skills of himself and others but then molds this material into a fictional form that includes the representation of the interior life of the principal figures in the event. But though *The Executioner's Song* resembles *In Cold Blood* in this and other ways, it differs from Capote's and similar works in that Mailer—either as anonymous journalist or named author—is not present in the work. Capote in *In Cold Blood* and Mailer in several of his earlier efforts in the New Journalism help create meaning and form either through their presence in the narrative as participants in the event as it happens or as seekers of meaning in the event after it has occurred. But Mailer as personality or overt authorial presence is completely absent from *The Executioner's Song.* Instead of relying upon himself as focus of meaning and as shaping presence in the narrative. Mailer achieves theme and form in *The Executioner's Song* by his successful and powerful exploitation of two major fictional techniques—the dramatization of the inner life of the figures in the story through free indirect speech, and the division of the work into two strikingly juxtaposed halves.

*The Executioner's Song* ranks with Zola's *L'Assommoir,* Joyce's *Ulysses,* and the narrative portions of Dos Passos's *U.S.A.* as a work that relies almost completely for its principal fictional effect on the device known as *style indirect libre* or free indirect speech. Mailer shifts his point of view focus frequently in the work—from major figures such as Gilmore and Nicole to a host of minor ones, most of whom appear only briefly. But whoever is the center of interest at any one moment has his or her appearance, actions, thoughts, and feelings reported to us by the narrator in a prose style appropriate to that person. The omniscient narrative voice still performs the traditional function of selecting and ordering that which is presented to us, but the substance of what is presented is in the diction, syntax, and tone characteristic of a specific person or class of persons. Mailer makes this device known to us at the very opening of the work, when Gilmore arrives in Utah. The point of view focus at this moment is Brenda, Gilmore's breezy, good-natured, and forthright cousin, who recalls him as a child. Mailer's reporting of her unspoken recollection is in a slangy, colloquial style appropriate to Brenda's background and temperament: "Gary was kind of quiet. There was one reason they got along. Brenda was always gabbing and he was a good listener. They had a lot of fun. Even at that age he was real polite. If you got into trouble, he'd come back and help you out" (5).

This device pervades the work even, as often happens, when the point of view figure is being depicted externally—when his thoughts and emotions are not being engaged, as when Val Conlin, a used car dealer, is described by the narrative voice as "a tall slim guy with eyeglasses" (136). The "guy" in this passage is of course not Mailer's conventional usage, nor can it be attributed directly to Conlin, who is not the reflective center at this moment. Rather, it is what can be called generically true—that is, it is true to the general usage of Conlin's class and occupation and therefore tells us something both about Conlin's world and, indirectly, about Conlin himself.

This massive exercise in free indirect speech—almost eleven hundred pages which render the minds and feelings of Gilmore and those around him by engulfing us in their habitual language—leads us to believe, in the end, that we know these figures truly as they are because events and people appear before us seemingly directly—in the language of their lives—rather than as shaped through the interpretive medium of an author. Mailer has achieved, though by different means, Henry James's ideal of the representation of experience through the dramatic expression of consciousness.

Free indirect speech can play two not necessarily mutually exclusive roles in a work. Because it distances the narrator from his characters, it can serve a powerful ironic and satiric function, as it does fully in *Madame Bovary* and *U.S.A.* and occasionally in *The Executioner's Song* when Mailer is dealing with the conservative Mormon world of Utah. But its far more prevalent and significant use in Mailer's book is to create that sense of intimacy of knowing that he noted as a goal in his Afterword. Most of all, we come to know Gary Gilmore. At first, we know him as most others initially see him in Utah—a man too anxious to gain too quickly what he wants (money and a good job, a car, a girl) and therefore forcing and bullying and creating resistance and resentment in others that eventually pushes him into criminality. But as Gilmore's portrait deepens through our constant experience of him—both Gilmore himself and the effect he has had on others in the past and present— we come to understand the desperation that underlies his frustrated and failed life and the tormented self-destructiveness behind his actions. Like Perry Smith in Capote's *In Cold Blood*, Gilmore pulled a trigger out of the unrelieved pain, anger, and frustration of a lifetime, emotions which were now hotly renewed by the loss of Nicole.

As he gradually deepens our awareness of Gilmore's tortured life, acute intelligence, and frequently self-deceiving emotionalism, Mailer relies not only on free indirect speech but also on an even more immediate entry into Gilmore's psyche, his prison letters to Nicole. In a characteristic passage, Gilmore writes to Nicole about what his life in prison would be if he is not executed.

> What do I do, rot in prison? growing old and bitter
> and eventually work this around in my mind to where
> it reads that I'm the one who's getting fucked around,
> that I'm just an innocent victim of society's bullshit?
> What do I do? Spend my time in prison searching for
> the God I've wanted to know for such a long time?
> Resume my painting? Write poetry? Play handball?
> Eat my heart out for the wondrous love you gave me

that I threw away ... because I was so spoiled and
couldn't immediately have a white pickup truck I
wanted? What do I do? We always have a choice,
don't we? (306)

The choice he makes now, to die, is the consequence of the choice that he
knows he did not make earlier, to live with Nicole. Out of our understanding
of his realization of the complex depths of his nature, we are ready to accept,
by the close of the book, two disinterested judgments on Gilmore as a social
and human being. "The system has really failed with this man" (447),
comments the district attorney who prosecuted him, while a hard-boiled
publicist notes that "Even the people that didn't like him, liked him" (894).

Our deepening engagement in the life and nature of Gary Gilmore has
yet another characteristic. As we encounter the resentment of Gilmore's
friends and relatives, the love and despair of Nicole, the anger of his victims'
families, and the sense of duty fulfilled of attorneys and judges, we realize
that the work also seeks to render the full interwoven web of suffering, of
fear, of awe, and of self-righteousness that is the consequence of any violent
act. There are no anonymous, faceless perpetrators, victims, bystanders, or
judges in *The Executioner's Song*. All, from motel desk clerk to office typist,
are brought to life by the language that is the color of their natures. And all
are caught up in the tragedy of a broken and destroyed life. The work is
ultimately not so much about murderers and victims as about the essential
tragedy of life.

The tragic character of *The Executioner's Song* also benefits from
Mailer's second major technical device in the work, his division of it into two
balanced parts, "Western Voices" and "Eastern Voices." Each has its own
narrative center: in the first, the crime, concluding with Gilmore's
conviction; in the second, the imprisonment, ending with his execution.
Each is also an exploration of characteristic "voices"—of the modes of
expression that represent habits of thought. Gilmore of course predominates
as a "voice"—as a center of attention—in both parts. But in addition to him,
the first section dramatizes principally Gilmore's Utah world, the second the
largely Eastern (or West Coast Eastern) world of newspaper, magazine, and
TV journalists who flock to Utah to merchandise, as one of them puts it,
Gary Gilmore's dance of death. Chief among these and the major figure in
the second half of the book aside from Gilmore is Lawrence Schiller, a free-
lance publicist who, after much wheeling and dealing, succeeds in getting the
rights to Gilmore's story.

Schiller, we soon realize, is a complex and ambiguous figure. Shrewd and ruthless, he is also a man of considerable natural warmth. He therefore begins to respond to Gilmore with a deep and disturbing ambivalence. Gilmore on his way to the execution chamber is both a salable commodity and a human being about whom Schiller begins to feel strongly. So Schiller is racked with guilt, and like any man suffering the pangs of conscience he begins behaving erratically—salving his conscience by refusing one deal while in self-torment reaching out to complete another.

Gilmore and Schiller—Western and Eastern voices—represent the complementary halves of the American experience as rendered in *The Executioner's Song*. In social terms, Gilmore's story is an indictment of the American "system" that destroys its repressed classes, Schiller's is an almost mock-epic account of American media hype, of the American middle-class craving for human interest sensationalism. But far more movingly and profoundly, the two stories constitute one of the tragic centers of the American experience—that both the criminal punished by the system and the publicist profiting from the system suffer basically the same anguish and self-hate because of their desire to gain what life—the system—appears to offer them. In the face of the deep moral ambivalence that accompanies desire in America, Gary Gilmore and Lawrence Schiller are brothers in pain.

Robert Stone's *A Flag for Sunrise* is in the tradition of American naturalism represented by Frank Norris's *The Octopus* and John Steinbeck's *The Grapes of Wrath*. Like these large-scale novels of the turn-of-the-century and the 1930s, Stone's work is centered on a fundamental social and ideological crisis of his day—in this instance, the implications for American life of the use of our immense economic and political power to affect the lives of people elsewhere. And like these earlier works, the depiction in *A Flag for Sunrise* of the seemingly universal degradation of modern life is leavened by at least one portrait of a visionary voice and a heroic action.

The novel is set principally in the imagined Caribbean republic of Tecan. Tecan is a heightened model of the nature of American activities in the Third World; in particular, its character suggests that we are doomed to relive our experience in Vietnam again and again. Poor, diseased, and ruled by a corrupt and ruthless military dictatorship, Tecan is controlled by American economic interests and by the CIA, both of which justify their suppression of a native revolutionary movement on the grounds of possible Soviet involvement. Except for its revolutionaries and missionaries, animality is the dominant moral style of Tecan. The novel opens with a police lieutenant demanding absolution from a priest for the mindless murder of a young girl; it closes with the lieutenant again asking the priest for absolution, but now for the brutal murder of a different girl. The lieutenant says to the priest, "I am not an animal ... I believe there is a spiritual force,"[9] but his actions belie his belief. Tecan, we soon discover, epitomizes, in exaggerated form, the operative ethic of the world at large. So a CIA agent claims, in his attack on what he calls an indulgence in "moral posturing":

> We're at a very primitive stage of mankind [he says],
> that's what people don't understand. Just pick up the
> *Times* on any given day and you've got a catalogue of
> ape behavior. Strip away the slogans and excuses and
> verbiage, the so-called ideology, and you're reading
> about what one pack of chimpanzees did to another.
> (26)

In this world of Tecan, where "apes" mouth but do not believe in or act upon the old pieties, there come together three Americans whose joint attitudes and fates constitute the modern condition. Justin is already on the scene as a young nursing nun at a small, remote mission on the Atlantic coast of Tecan. She is a woman who has an intense need to believe in the possibility of order and justice, but her faith has been shaken by her years in Tecan, and she is about to laicize. Pablo is an American Coast Guard deserter. He is, as we come to know him as he works his way down the Caribbean, a vile human being—unscrupulous, vicious, and small. He is consumed and made dangerous by a paranoic belief that someone is "fucking with my head" (65). If Justin and Pablo are almost allegorical representations of a vague and formless good on the one hand and an animal malignancy on the other, Holliwell—the third major figure in the novel—constitutes the ambivalent center of man's modern ethical possibilities. An anthropologist who had worked for the CIA in Vietnam and who feels deeply guilty about it, he nevertheless permits himself to be recruited, without openly acquiescing, into investigating reports of revolutionary activity at the Tecan mission. "It would be strange," he thinks to himself, half-cynically, "to see people who believed in things, and acted in the world according to what they believed. It would be different. Like old times" (101). Holliwell is thus the American ethical psyche in its present mixed condition. As Justin notes, though he is tall and well-built, his face "bespoke softness and self-indulgence" (234)—the moral flabbiness of a man of "dry" spirit who believes justice is "only a word" and who "took things as they were" (245). Initially a man of good intentions, he has been dragged into moral compromises and self-evasions by the pressures, fears, and loyalties of life, and now scarcely knows where he stands—whether he has come to Tecan to spy on the revolution or to support it.

The three figures meet and interact at the mission in the days immediately before and during the outbreak of the revolution. Justin has been recruited into the cause and permits the mission to be used as a post, while Pablo is a seaman on a boat running guns for the revolution, guns that are to be landed at the mission. On the day before the fighting begins, Justin and Holliwell become lovers—he impelled to seek her "white goodness" to slake "the hangover thirst of his life" (299), she identifying the possibility of love with hope for the achievement of other ideal constructs. But their lovemaking is a failure. She "eludes" him, and afterwards they are "all separate again in their loneliness and fixedness, illusions of union fled" (379).

At sea, Pablo kills the rest of the gunrunning crew and completes the sale, but because he is wounded and cannot man the boat alone, he is forced to come ashore at the mission. Holliwell, realizing that he is now under suspicion by both sides, confesses his CIA connection to Justin and promises that he will not inform on her. When he is picked up by the police, however, he does indeed implicate her—ostensibly to save her, but also to save himself. When fighting breaks out, Justin, Holliwell, and Pablo are at the mission. Justin decides that the wounded Pablo and the endangered Holliwell must be put to sea in a small boat, where they will presumably drift into safety; she is to remain behind to aid the wounded revolutionaries.

The close of the novel is a reprise and summation of its central themes. Justin is captured and is beaten to death by the police. But in her death there is triumph of a kind. Earlier, after she and Holliwell had made love, she had bitterly repeated the first lines of an Emily Dickinson poem that begins, "A Wife—at Daybreak I shall be—/Sunrise—Hast thou a flag for me?" (380). There were no flags at sunrise for her in the consummation of her earthly love; only regret and anger at her betrayal by Holliwell. But now, in the transforming of belief into meaningful act, she does fulfill the promise of the poem. For as the rest of the poem reveals, the "Wife" of the opening line is the conventional image of the bride of Christ, the Christ who takes to his bosom at death all those who believe in Him. Justin, as a nun, had married Christ once before, but now—as a martyred fighter for justice—the marriage is truly consummated. As though in response to the concluding lines of the poem—"Eternity, I'm coming—Sir/Savior—I've seen the face—before!"—Justin cries at the moment of her death, "Behold the handmaid of the Lord" (416). Meanwhile, adrift at sea, Holliwell recognizes the pure animal evil of Pablo and therefore the danger he presents. He seizes a knife from the dozing Pablo, stabs him, and pushes him overboard. But as Pablo sinks,

Holliwell sees in his face not evil but "a brother's face, a son's, one's own. Anybody's face, just another victim of ignorance and fear. Just another one of us..." (431).

The naturalistic ethos of the novel is clear. Justin may have her flag at sunrise, but Holliwell—who is rescued—has his life. The lesson of Tecan is that good and evil are both vulnerable, good because of the risks it runs in a largely corrupt world, evil because it is essentially ignorance and fear. Survival is a trick of a shrewd and in the end ruthless moral ambivalence, a quality of mind that is an adaptation to the mix of surface moral coloration and amoral struggle characteristic of all life. Holliwell survives—he has his own flag at sunrise, as he himself ruefully notes—because of his potent moral flexibility. The man who tells Justin, after she has accused him of betraying her, that he is uncertain in his own mind if he did so but that "When I decide what happened, ... I'll decide to live with it" (408), outlives the open and decisive moral natures of both Justin and Pablo.

Like other epic naturalistic novels, *A Flag for Sunrise* joins an often sensationalistic plot and a complex of social, political, and religious ideas. And like such works, it dramatizes both the persistence of a visionary ethic and its tragic fate in a world of accommodation to what the apologist for "things as they are" in Frank Norris's *The Octopus* called "conditions"[10] and what Holliwell names "this whirling tidal pool of existence" (244).

The three novels that I have been discussing support the notion that, as in the past, naturalism owes its continued existence to its ability both to draw upon earlier naturalistic expression and to adapt its interests to those of the contemporary scene. Of past naturalists, it is undoubtedly Dreiser who casts the longest shadow over the present moment—in particular the Dreiser of *An American Tragedy*, the Dreiser whose concern was the destructive distinction in American life between a rich and self-satisfied nation, with a rhetoric of opportunity, and the social and moral realities of growing up poor. But also occupying an enduring place in the American literary consciousness are the epic naturalists of the 1930s—Farrell, Steinbeck, and Dos Passos—who sought to render the entire American scene as an admixture of broken promises and an occasional tragic visionary.

The traditional matter, themes, and forms of earlier American naturalistic fiction are thus still with us. Limited and deprived characters still struggle to stay afloat in a world of violent destructiveness, and the novels in which they appear still shape themselves into symbolic expressions of major flaws in the American experience. As in much naturalism of the past, the naturalistic occasion is still that of a closed social and moral world and of a figure seeking some way out. Usually not succeeding, but nevertheless seeking. On the evidence of the works that I have been discussing, however, it would seem that for contemporary naturalism "hard times" are now above all the continued failure, for much of our population, of American urban life, and the continued failure, for all of us, of our role abroad. Indeed, the single richest rein of naturalistic fiction during the 1970s—the Vietnam war novel, including Stone's earlier work, *Dog Soldiers*—derives directly from this second concern.

In form, contemporary naturalism continues—as in the 1930s and late 1940s and early 1950s—to absorb much current fictional experimentation. Mailer's combination of the New Journalism and an absolute reliance on free indirect speech, Oates' turn to the self-reflexive novel, in which she is a character in the novel we are reading, and Stone's poetic symbolism are further evidence of the unwillingness of American naturalists to accept the critical cliché that naturalism is merely a joining of massive documentation and sensationalistic event.

Naturalism thus continues to live in America—not only in the novel but less obviously though still powerfully in documentary narrative (as in Michael Herr's *Dispatches*) and in the film (as in *The Deer Hunter*). I bring the news of its continued existence not in celebration, since its presence is a sure sign that writers have again sensed that "hard times" are here. But like it or not, naturalism is again with us.

## NOTES

1. Fuller discussions of the conventional American hostility to naturalism can be found in Donald Pizer, "American Literary Naturalism: The Example of Dreiser," *Studies in American Fiction* 5 (May, 1977): 51–63, and Don Graham, "Naturalism in American Fiction: A Status Report," *Studies in American Fiction* 10 (Spring 1982): 1–16.

2. Thorp, *American Writing in the Twentieth Century* (Cambridge: Harvard Univ. Pr., 1960), p. 180.

3. (Carbondale: Southern Illinois Univ. Pr., 1982).

4. *Stephen Crane: Letters* ed. R. W. Stallman and Lillian Gilkes (New York: New York Univ. Pr., 1960), p. 14.

5. *them* (New York: Vanguard, 1969), p. 12. Citations from this edition will hereafter appear in the text.

6. In a 1976 interview, Oates noted that both the Author's Note to *them*, in which she described her relationship to the "real-life" prototype of Maureen, and Maureen's letters to her (pp. 329–40) were in fact fictitious. (See Joanna V. Creighton, *Joyce Carol Oates*, New York: Twayne, 1979, p. 65.) Oates' admission, however, does not affect the thematic function of the Oates-Maureen relationship within the novel itself.

7. (New York: Dial, 1966), pp. 131–32. The poem was initially published in 1964.

8. *The Executioner's Song* (Boston: Little, Brown, 1979), p. 1052. Citations from this edition will hereafter appear in the text.

9. Robert Stone, *A Flag for Sunrise* (New York: Knopf, 1981), p. 13. Citations from this edition will hereafter appear in the text.

10. Shelgrim to Presley, in *The Octopus* (Garden City, N. Y.: Doubleday, Doran, 1928), I, 285.

BARBARA HOCHMAN

# The Awakening and The House of Mirth: Plotting Experience and Experiencing Plot

... the trouble was with plot....
Kate Chopin, "Elizabeth Stark's One Story"

Many women novelists tell a story of female defeat. Nineteenth-century fiction is particularly full of women characters who cannot make peace with the options available to them in their society, characters who cannot fulfill their needs or resolve their conflicts. Rarely if ever do these protagonists find a form through which to tell others their story as (at least to some extent) their novel-writing creators did.

Like their protagonists, Kate Chopin and Edith Wharton are often said to have failed in creating a "new plot" for "women's lives."[1] Yet the identification of writer and character should be entertained with caution. For Chopin and Wharton themselves, professional authorship meant redefining their position as women within turn-of-century American society. The novelistic enterprise also meant reaching an audience with their version of a woman's life—only partially a version of their own. Many aspects of the fiction-writing experience itself, inscribed in The Awakening and The House of Mirth, suggest the complexity of the relationship between these authors and the characters they create. In both texts a tension emerges between the figure of a defeated female protagonist and, obliquely yet insistently, that of a writer forging grounds of articulation and thereby a place in the world.[2]

From The Cambridge Companion to American Realism and Naturalism: Howells to London, ed. Donald Pizer. © 1995 Cambridge University Press.

Certain parallels between these authors and their characters are inescapable, of course. Edna and Lily stem from the same class and background as their creators. For the young Chopin and Wharton themselves, as for many a "frail vessel" in nineteenth-century fiction, life options were severely limited by convention: marriage was the prime locus of adult female choice. The presumed "career" for a woman of Chopin and Wharton's class and background was social and domestic. Professional authorship was socially dubious—particularly "indelicate in a female," as Wharton put it.[3] Her autobiography repeatedly notes the disapproval that her literary ambitions encountered within her family and throughout her social world.

The notion of art as a socially precarious borderland is clearly expressed in both *The Awakening* and *The House of Mirth*. When Edna Pontellier sketches and thinks of becoming an artist, the misanthropic musician, Mlle Reisz, warns her that art is only for "the brave soul ... that dares and defies."[4] As for Lily, though aesthetic taste is one of her defining qualities, her own closest approach to *making* art is the notorious scene of *tableaux vivants*. There, in one of her finest (or most devastating) moments, Lily temporarily makes a work of art out of herself, appearing on stage as a figure in a painting.[5]

I suggest that despite certain self-evident grounds of analogy between Chopin or Wharton and their characters, the question of art becomes a watershed, a clear sign of the writer's separation from the protagonist who enacts her conflict rather than either resolving or articulating it. Unlike the writer who achieves pleasure, control, and distance in the act of writing, Lily and Edna are at best partial or failed artists. However, to reflect upon Lily and Edna as failing in the search for voice and form is not only to underscore their distance from women writers who have found both; it is also to clarify the two novels' recurrent focus on the nature and function of aesthetic experience, including the experience of narrative.

Up to a point, both *The Awakening* and *The House of Mirth* neatly exemplify the "naturalist" plot of individual decline, with its concern for the pressures of environment and circumstance, and its focus on forces (both inner and outer) beyond the control of the characters.[6] Like many "naturalist" writers, Chopin and Wharton reject a plot in which marriage becomes the ground of closure (as it does in the work of Dickens, George Eliot, William Dean Howells and sentimental/domestic American fiction). Instead, raising questions about marriage at the outset, both *The Awakening* and *The House of Mirth* follow their protagonists through progressive isolation to death (as in such naturalist works as *L'Assommoir*, the Hetty plot of *Adam Bede*, *Maggie: A Girl of the Streets*, *McTeague*, *Sister Carrie*).

Chopin and Wharton's use of the naturalist mode has several interesting implications. A woman's decision to write fiction for the late-nineteenth-century literary marketplace immediately signaled a bid for position in a male-dominated professional world. By employing a "naturalist" structure, Wharton and Chopin also sought authorial status beyond the confines of "women's" writing.[7] It would be difficult to find a late-nineteenth-century fictional model more clearly associated with male authorship and "virile" fiction[8] than the naturalist plot of decline. However, in adapting the naturalist plot to their purposes, Chopin and Wharton made some original changes. Through their handling of narrative time, in particular, they complicated the sense of downward slide typical of most naturalist texts—that relentless descent with its "few landings or level places."[9]

Throughout *The Awakening*, the forward movement of narration is modified by lyric passages and recurrent leitmotivs that foster a sense of stasis or free play without hampering the progress of the story.[10] As we shall see, *The House of Mirth*, too, intermittently undercuts the reader's sense of straightforward progression through narrative time—while maximizing other rewards of temporary immersion in a fictional world. Thus, for Chopin and Wharton, "naturalism" becomes both a vehicle for conceptualizing a woman's vulnerability and a way of redefining certain pleasures of the fiction-reading experience.

Compared to such naturalist heroines as Trina McTeague, Carrie Meeber, or Maggie Johnson, Edna and Lily are well educated and very sophisticated. Their greater access to "culture," however, does not give them either a sense of autonomy or a sense of community. *The Awakening* was originally entitled *A Solitary Soul*. Both that phrase and the following early description of Edna are equally applicable to Lily: "She had all her life long been accustomed to harbor thoughts and emotions which never voiced themselves.... They belonged to her and were her own, and she entertained the conviction that she had a right to them and that they concerned no one but herself" (48). When Edna tells Mme Ratignolle that she would give up "life," but not her "self," for her children, Edna's friend cannot grasp the distinction. The two women "did not appear to understand each other or to be talking the same language" (48). Despite increasing self-awareness as the novel unfolds, Edna's attempts at expression are never understood by others. Lily's efforts to articulate the life-issues that concern her are similarly fitful and unsatisfactory.

A failure of voice separates Edna and Lily from the writers who created them. Yet an illuminating analogue emerges between the challenge of the novelist *as* novelist and the protagonists' groping attempts at articulation. In a sense, Edna and Lily fail precisely where their authors succeed, defeated in "life" by their lack of several elements indispensable to fiction writing: not just a sense of plot, of how to structure and articulate one's story, but a sense of the relationship between fiction and reality, artists and audience, teller and tale. If we pursue the contrasts and parallels between the writers and protagonists with care, we shall clarify certain aspects of the characters' defeat while elucidating the meaning and function of fiction writing for Chopin and Wharton themselves.

At a critical juncture in the plot of *House of Mirth*, Gerty asks Lily to explain the events that result in Lily's disinheritance and ostracism from society. "[W]hat *is* your story," Gerty asks, "I don't believe anyone knows it yet."[11] "My story?" Lily replies: "I don't believe I know it myself. You see, I never thought of preparing a version in advance as Bertha did—and if I had, I don't think I should take the trouble to use it now" (236). Lily never takes that "trouble"; after her death, Selden struggles pointlessly to "unravel ... the story" from Lily's "mute lips" (347).

Unlike Selden, Gerty tries valiantly to elicit that story while Lily is alive. "I don't want a version prepared in advance," Gerty insists,

> "but I want you to tell me exactly what happened from the beginning."
>
> "From the beginning?" Miss Bart gently mimicked her. "Dear Gerty, how little imagination you good people have!" (236)

Lily claims that there is no way to establish the "beginning" of her story; it was in her cradle, she speculates—in her upbringing, or perhaps in her blood, via some "wicked pleasure-loving ancestress" (236). Moreover, Lily argues that the believability of a story is in any case relative, dependent on the power and influence of the teller. Thus, unlike Gerty, Lily sees no point in telling her friends "the whole truth" (235).

> "The whole truth?" Miss Bart laughed. "What is truth? Where a woman is concerned, it's the story that's easiest to believe. In this case it's a great deal easier to believe Bertha Dorset's story than mine, because she has a big house and an opera box, and it's convenient to be on good terms with her." (236)

As Lily sees it, stories need to be planned, preconceived, carefully plotted, in order to persuade. But this is precisely what Lily cannot or will not do—either after her retreat from Monte Carlo or later, when Rosedale proposes his own well-made, if melodramatic, "plot" to neutralize incriminating rumors about her. "I don't believe [those] stories," Rosedale says (268), offering to marry Lily if she will silence Bertha by threatening to reveal her old love-letters. "But [the stories] are there," Rosedale continues, "and my not believing them ain't going to alter the situation" (268). Now it is Lily's turn to be naïve:

> "If they are not true," she said, "doesn't *that* alter the situation?"
> He met this with a steady gaze.... "I believe it does in novels, but I'm certain it don't in real life." (268)

Although Lily sees Rosedale's point, she refuses his offer. Throughout the novel, Lily herself is repeatedly accused of "art," of achieving only "premeditated effects" in her social relations (3, 69, 70, 75); but she is singularly incapable of the kind of sustained and painstaking plotting that ensures Bertha's or Rosedale's success in society.

By refusing to tell anyone her story and rejecting all plots, Lily renounces the project of being believed or even heard, progressively isolating herself until, alone in her boardinghouse room, she seeks oblivion in drug-induced sleep. Cradling an imaginary baby in her arms, she finds the greater oblivion of death. Rosedale's distinction between "novels" and "real life" is cogent here, for whereas Lily renounces plot and is destroyed, it was precisely by articulating and controlling Lily's story that Wharton became a best-selling novelist.[12]

It is particularly illuminating to juxtapose Lily's storytelling failure with Edith Wharton's storytelling success. In Wharton's own account, "storytelling" was not merely her "job" or "vocation" (*BG* 119). In *A Backward Glance* storytelling is also given the credit for creating Wharton's "personality," being her "first-born," her own "real self," her very soul (112, 115, 119, 124). Such metaphors reflect a sense of deep identification, even merger, between Wharton and her stories. Yet, at another level, Wharton maintained a considerable distance from what she wrote for publication. For one thing, *House of Mirth* tells the story of a fictional character—not her own. For another, Wharton exerts impressive control over the very elements of Lily's story that Lily fails to conceptualize. Lily may not know what her story "is," or even where it began; but Wharton cannot possibly tell Lily's story (indeed no one can tell *any* story) without, at the very least, a firm idea of beginnings and endings. Moreover, as we shall see, Lily lacks not only the novelist's gift for narration, but also the writer's perspective on the difference between what Rosedale calls "novels" and "real life."

Like Lily, Edna Pontellier fails to tell her story. Unlike Lily, however, Edna repeatedly tries her hand at art. She not only sketches, she is (again, unlike Lily) both a reader and a responsive music-lover. Thus the figure of Edna, making "art" and responding to it, reflects many aspects of aesthetic experience. From this point of view, one of the most resonant scenes in *The Awakening* is the one where Edna does tell a story—a story that (perhaps like Chopin's own) both is and is not about herself.

The occasion for Edna's storytelling is the dinner to which her husband invites his friend and family physician Dr. Mandelet. Disturbed by the sense that his wife is "not herself" (57), Mr. Pontellier hopes that the doctor will observe Edna at dinner and perhaps offer some insight. With the help of warm claret and cold champagne, Mr. Pontellier is impelled to share his "amusing plantation experiences [and] recollections." Edna's father, in turn, tells a more "somber" story that seems to prompt an equally dubious tale on the doctor's part: "the old, ever new and curious story of the waning of a woman's love ... [and its return] to its legitimate source after days of fierce unrest" (70). Implicitly, this story gives rise to Edna's own:

> [The doctor's] story did not seem especially to impress Edna. She had one of her own to tell, of a woman who paddled away with her lover one night in a pirogue and never came back. They were lost amid the Baratarian Islands, and no one ever heard of them or found trace of them from that day to this. It was a pure invention. She said that Madame Antoine had related it to her. That, also, was an invention. Perhaps it was a dream she had had. But every glowing word seemed real to those who listened. They could feel the hot breath of the Southern night; they could hear the long sweep of the pirogue through the glistening moonlit water, ... they could see the faces of the lovers, ... drifting into the unknown. (70)

Edna's storytelling is a brief but crucial moment in *The Awakening*, one that dramatizes many issues in both Edna's life and Chopin's art. The passage, to begin with, repeatedly stresses the indistinct boundaries between reality and fiction. Despite Edna's attribution of a source for the tale, the narrative voice twice repeats that Edna's story is her own "invention,"—

"[p]erhaps ... a dream." Nonetheless, "every glowing word seemed real to those who listened" (70). Few readers fail to perceive the resemblance between Edna's situation and that of the "imaginary" woman she describes. Her own recent boat ride with Robert is the high point of her summer's experience, the touchstone to fairy-tale pleasures she can never recapture. Moreover, the image of the woman lost in the sea without a trace points forward to Edna's own end. The doctor, for his part, directly identifies Edna with the woman in her story:

> He was sorry he had accepted Pontellier's invitation.... He did not want the secrets of other lives thrust upon him.
> "I hope it isn't Arobin," he muttered to himself as he walked. "I hope to heaven it isn't ... Arobin." (71)

The doctor's response to Edna's story sharpens the focus on Edna's inner state and raises questions about her future. From the doctor's point of view, those "glowing word[s]" that seemed so "real to those who listened" simply reveal Edna's own wishes, thinly disguised. Yet by presenting Edna's story both as "invention" and as personal revelation, the passage invites speculation not only about the relationship between Edna's narrative and the feelings or events in her own life. It also raises questions about *Chopin's* "invention": what does Chopin herself mean by telling the story of an imaginary woman in *The Awakening?*

Some of the differences between Edna's act of narration and Chopin's become clearer when we juxtapose Edna's storytelling with other moments of representation dramatized in the novel. Edna repeatedly makes sketches in the course of *The Awakening*, gaining "satisfaction from the work in itself" (73) and even earning money in the process. Yet her sketching has neither the impact nor the intensity of her single storytelling moment. One reason for the difference, I suggest, is the clear separation between artist and object that informs Edna's every attempt to draw. She works, at her best, with "sureness and ease" (73)—never with passion or abandon. In this sense, Edna's relation to sketching is not unlike Mme Ratignolle's relation to music. Mme Ratignolle plays the piano partly for her children's benefit, partly to fulfill a social function. Her musical evenings occur regularly, "once a fortnight." They were "widely known, and it was considered a privilege to be invited to them" (55).

Mme Ratignolle's music (like Edna's sketching) provides pleasure and diversion for both artist and audience. It constitutes neither disruption nor danger to anyone. By contrast—and more like Edna's storytelling experience—the piano playing of Mlle Reisz has the power to disrupt Edna's equilibrium, eliciting passionate responses. Edna's relationship to Mlle Reisz's music thus raises questions about the nature of aesthetic response, the accompanying sensation of freedom, and even the dynamics of narrative. The questions raised by Edna's recurrent abandon and "exaltation" when listening to music are similar to those raised by her storytelling interlude: questions about loss of self and the threat of inner dissolution; questions about the boundary between the self and surrounding reality.

Hearing the strange, ugly Mlle Reisz play the piano, Edna feels as if her entire being is absorbed into the intensity of aesthetic response. Edna herself associates such experience with freedom: by way of "her divine art," Mlle Reisz "set [Edna's] spirit free" (78). Yet the "joy and exaltation" (80) that Edna experiences when listening to Mlle Reisz is full of contradictions. Edna's responses to this music are more problematic than her own view of them. Directly arousing Edna's "passions" (27) in one instance, Mlle Reisz's piano leaves her "sobbing" in another—"just as she had wept one midnight at Grand Isle when strange new voices awoke in her" (64). Despite the awakening of new voices in Edna, she only sobs. In fact, the scene at Grand Isle presents Edna's state as more conducive to incoherence and dissolution than to any articulation (such as "new voices" might imply). Far from moving toward articulation in the course of her experience, Edna progressively refuses the orderly sequences and constraining forms not only of social reality but of language itself.[13]

Thus, in the scene just alluded to, after a quarrel between Edna and her husband, Edna refuses to speak. She withdraws to the porch alone, rocking and crying: "There was no sound abroad except the hooting of an old owl ... and the everlasting voice of the sea that broke like a mournful lullaby upon the night" (8). Edna is figured here as both mother and child. Inarticulate and overwrought, she cries, simultaneously rocking and soothing herself. Like many other elements in *The Awakening*, this early image of Edna points to a state of emotional or developmental nondifferentiation—confusion, or fusion—for which the most resonant recurrent image is the sea.

The sea, repeatedly evoked in the course of *The Awakening*, is seductive to Edna throughout. The epitome of a fluid, unbounded, "everlasting" space and "unceasing" sound, the sea is figured here and elsewhere as a voice. Yet the sea-voice, singing its "mournful lullaby," also provides a sharp contrast both to the voice of any actual singing mother and to any human voice that uses language: "The voice of the sea is seductive, never ceasing, whispering, clamoring, murmuring, inviting the soul to wander for a spell in abysses of solitude, to lose itself in mazes of inward contemplation" (15). Maze and abyss, "clamoring, murmuring," "never ceasing," the undifferentiated voice of the sea, unlike a speaking voice—certainly unlike a narrative voice—is everything but linear and sequential. Inviting the soul to "lose itself," suggesting a physical enclosure in which to "wander for a spell," the sea-voice is neither articulate as language nor conducive to differentiation or autonomy. On the contrary, like Mlle Reisz's music, it invites loss of self, merger, immersion. It also refuses the traditional requisites of every story: not only no language, but ("never-ceasing") no beginning and no end.

All of Edna's most intense, responsive moments are explicitly marked by a blurred sense of beginnings and endings. Not only is the boundless, fluid, "unceasing" aspect of the sea often underscored; Edna herself repeatedly associates the sea with her one extended and recurrent childhood memory: "[walking through] a meadow that seemed as big as the ocean ... [the little girl] threw out her arms as if swimming when she walked, beating the tall grass as one strikes out in the water.... I felt as if I must walk on forever without coming to the end of it" (17–18). The experience of endless, nonpurposive movement through an unbounded area is directly linked for Edna not only with field and sea but, still more inclusively, with her emotional state during her experience at Grand Isle ("Sometimes I feel this summer as if I were walking through the green meadow again, idly, aimlessly..." Edna says [18]). In addition, the very qualities associated with the endless field walk, the "never ceasing" voice of the sea, and the summer that Edna hopes will never end, also characterize Edna's most intensely vital aesthetic experience: when Mlle Reisz plays Chopin in the city, Edna is so absorbed and exalted, that she "did not know when the Impromptu began or ended" (64).

I have said that Edna's obliviousness to beginnings and endings is an indispensible component of her "joy and exaltation" (80). She is repeatedly drawn to a space or a state characterized by its lack of apparent beginning or end. Still, *The Awakening* shows with brutal clarity that exaltation itself *always* comes to an end. And when it does, the result is neither freedom nor articulation—only increased vulnerability: "the exuberance which had sustained and exalted [Edna's] spirit left her helpless and yielding to the conditions which crowded her in" (32).

Thus, throughout *The Awakening* there is destructive as well as liberating potential in Edna's experience of the "sensuous," "seductive," "never ceasing" sea (as in the sense of "endlessness" associated with her field walk). The well-known passage about the "whispering, clamoring" sea—invoked again during Edna's final swim—is preceded by a less frequently noted comment: "... the beginning of things, of a world especially, is necessarily vague, tangled, chaotic and exceedingly disturbing. How few of us ever emerge from such beginning! How many souls perish in its tumult!" (15).

Although the language of Genesis here heightens the sense of potential creation implicit in Edna's "beginnings," this passage simultaneously underscores the danger Edna faces, the difficulty of emergence. From Edna's earliest childhood memories, through her rocking/crying/self-soothing experience and her engagement with the sea, her chances of "emerging" are in doubt. Thus the text is pervaded by a concern with the complex relation between beginnings and endings; yet Edna herself seems to live only in the present moment. Unlike the novelist (who uncharacteristically identifies herself with Edna's dilemma here: "How few of *us* ever emerge from such beginning"; my emphasis),[14] Edna never conceptualizes or articulates for herself the clash between her wish for merger and her need for emergence. Indeed, like Lily, who repeatedly "crave[s] ... the darkness [and silence] made by enfolding arms" (157), Edna seeks not to articulate her plight, but rather to escape from the inexorable forward march of chronological or historical time, from all plots and stories with beginnings and endings.[15] Even more than Lily, who cannot say where her own story begins and yearns to "drop out of the race" (40), Edna actively courts immersion in experiences that reproduce the "exaltation" of timelessness, the feeling of walking on forever with no sense of an ending.[16]

We have noted that Lily's experience, like Edna's, is characterized by the wish to disregard beginnings, refuse prearranged versions, renounce all plots. In addition, the figure of Lily, like the figure of Edna, raises questions about the status of exalted moments, whether triggered by life or by art. Lily's experience, like Edna's, repeatedly involves moments of intensity that seem to liberate the self, but that may instead merely hasten its destruction. Nowhere in *The House of Mirth* are the rewards and dangers of such moments more apparent than in Lily's stage appearance as Reynolds's Mrs. Lloyd. Moreover, this episode as a whole, and Lily's self-representation on stage in particular, are directly informed by the writer's concept of narration itself.

Among the "vision-making influences" (140) singled out for particular emphasis in Wharton's evocation of the tableaux is one element in the "the producing of ... illusions" (141) that draws attention to the very question raised by Edna's doctor/dinner story—the relation between the storyteller (or, in this case, actress) and the character represented:

> the participators [in the tableaux] had been cleverly fitted with characters suited to their types....
> Indeed so skillfully had the personality of the actors been

subdued to the scenes they figured in that even the least imaginative of the audience must have felt a thrill of contrast when the curtain suddenly parted on a picture which was simply and undisguisedly the portrait of Miss Bart. (141)

Until the moment Lily herself appears on stage, the "personalit[ies] of the actors" are "skillfully ... subdued to the scenes" represented. If we now substitute the idea of an *author's* personality for "the personality of the actors," we have here a formulation that might have been written by any of Wharton's novelist contemporaries, describing late-nineteenth-century American fiction. Indeed, the norm of representation as expressed with regard to the actresses at the Welly Brys's sounds very like the typical realist or naturalist aesthetic.

In critical essays and reviews, Frank Norris, Theodore Dreiser, Henry James, and Wharton herself repeatedly emphasized the importance of effacing authorial presence and letting "situations speak for themselves," in James's words.[17] Norris explicitly advocated "the suppression of the author's personality" in fiction.[18] Wharton herself rejected the notion of the author's "intrusion ... among his puppets."[19] But to underscore the connection between this cornerstone of realist narration and the artistic strategy in the Brys's tableaux is further to highlight the problematic exemplified by Lily: "when the curtain suddenly parted on a picture which was simply and undisguisedly the portrait of Miss Bart ... there could be no mistaking the predominance of personality.... Lily Bart ... had shown her artistic intelligence in selecting a type so like her own that she could embody the person represented without ceasing to be herself" (141–2).

In this passage Lily's aims are seen to be quite different from those of the other actresses. Far from subduing her personality to the represented scene, Lily's "artistic intelligence" is said to consist in her capacity to represent another woman—a figure not herself—while remaining, even representing, herself at the very same time. This description thus raises a number of questions. Like Edna's storytelling it points beyond the character's momentary performance to her daily life in society. At the same time, it points beyond Lily altogether to Wharton's position in relation to her own projected fictional "illusion."

The difficulty of representing one personality while remaining another can be easily applied to Lily's problem in "reality," her life-problem. When the novel begins, Lily thinks she can become Mrs. Percy Gryce without ceasing to be "herself." But in the course of her experience she encounters the difficulty (even impossibility) of this particular balancing act. Perhaps, the novel suggests, there *is* no way to represent otherness and yet remain oneself—except in art.

Even within the confines of stage illusion, however, Lily's approach creates difficulties. After the performance Lily delights in her sense of success. She "had not an instant's doubt as to the meaning of the murmur greeting her appearance…. it had obviously been called forth by herself and not by the picture she impersonated" (143). Yet Lily's certainty about the "meaning of the murmur greeting her appearance" is misplaced. As the text demonstrates in some detail, the "unanimous 'Oh!' of the audience" is comprised of multiple and contradictory responses to Lily's "flesh-and-blood loveliness" (141). Those responses range from Van Alstyne's lascivious sense of "what an outline Lily has" (146) or Stepney's disapproval of Lily "standing there as if she was up at auction (166) to Gerty and Selden's conviction that the stage has revealed nothing less than "the real Lily …, divested of the trivialities of her little world and catching for a moment a note of that eternal harmony of which her beauty was a part" (142).

Paradoxically, Selden's sense of contact with transcendent harmonies through Lily is quite as dependent upon the visible presence of Lily's body as the responses of Stepney or Van Alstyne. For Selden, Lily's "poetry" is inseparable from her physical being. Selden is entranced by "the suggestion of soaring grace … the touch of poetry in her beauty that Selden always felt in her presence yet lost the sense of when he was not with her" (142). If Lily's "poetry" is embodied in her body, however, the fact returns us once more to our point of departure: the difference between author and protagonist. Unlike a novelist, Lily uses her own body to project images. Moreover, for her—as for Edna telling her dinner story—total immersion in (and immediate feedback from) the act of representation is an indispensable element of aesthetic performance. For susceptible members of the audience, Lily's effectiveness on stage, like the impact of Edna's storytelling (or like Edna's response to Mlle Reisz's piano) depends upon the blurring of boundaries between art and life, fiction and reality, being oneself and being another. Lily's impact on her audience, the intensity of her delight in performance—like Edna's—joins teller/actress and listeners/spectators by temporarily transposing all concerned to an unaccustomed mode of being.

Such epiphanies—the sense of participation in a magic realm—may be seen as a major component of all aesthetic experience, including reading. (Indeed, nineteenth-century educators and librarians often argued against reading fiction on related grounds. Wharton herself was forbidden to read novels as a child.) As we have seen, neither Lily nor Edna accepts the limitations of aesthetic experience: they deny both their own separation from the objects represented and the short-lived nature of aesthetic response. On the contrary, they wish to prolong or reproduce such moments in "reality." That desire becomes a source of considerable danger to Edna and Lily alike.

Both *The Awakening* and *House of Mirth* invoke fairy-tale motifs to serve a double function: to underscore not only the delight of make-believe but also its time-bound tenuousness. Both books insistently thematize the question of time, setting Edna and Lily's escapist and transcendent impulses against multiple signs of time running out. Thematically, the protagonists' wish to escape or deny time is presented as a hopeless struggle. Yet, as we shall see, the desire for access to another world also provides an analogue to specific rewards of the reading experience.

The high point of Edna's dawning intimacy with Robert in the early chapters of *The Awakening* is their visit to the *Chenière Caminada*. This journey is punctuated by gamesome talk of the whispering "Gulf Spirit" and the pirogue they would sail in by moonlight someday. During the church service on the island, Edna is overcome by "a feeling of oppression and drowsiness" that causes her to flee—just as she fled in childhood from the Presbyterian service presided over by her father, finding refuge in the open field for her never-to-be-forgotten walk. When Edna leaves the island church, Robert takes her to a cottage "at the far end of the village":

> The whole place was immaculately clean, and the big, four-posted bed, snow-white, invited one to repose.... She took off her shoes and stockings and stretched herself in the very center of the high, white bed....
>
> Edna awoke ... with the conviction that she had slept long and soundly....
>
> "How many years have I slept?" she inquired. "The whole island seems changed. A new race of beings must have sprung up, leaving only you and me as past relics...."
>
> "You have slept precisely one hundred years. I was left here to guard your slumbers; and for one hundred years I have been out under the shed reading a book." (37–8)

Suggestions of Snow-White, Sleeping-Beauty, and Rip Van Winkle reinforce Edna and Robert's sense of shared magic. But after her return from the island, Edna is abruptly confronted by signs of passing time and change. The very next chapter opens with the news that Robert is going to Mexico. If he has realized that idylls do not last, Edna herself is startled: she does not understand how Robert can leave Grand Isle.

Several early encounters between Selden and Lily in *House of Mirth* reproduce the clash between transcendent impulses and time-bound realities. Lily and Selden's first meeting, setting the tone, is figured ironically as the "rescue" of a damsel in distress (4). Later, Lily and Selden's hilltop afternoon at Bellomont exhibits both the sense of delight and the sense of fleeting magic that characterize Edna's island experience.

> [Lily] had risen, and he stood facing her with his eyes on hers. The soft isolation of the falling day enveloped them; they seemed lifted into a finer air....
>
> They stood silent for a while after this, smiling at each other like adventurous children who have climbed to a forbidden height from which they discover a new world. The actual world at their feet was veiling itself in dimness, and across the valley a clear moon rose in the denser blue. (76)

Then, all at once, the mood is broken, with the abruptness of midnight striking:

> Suddenly they heard a remote sound, like the hum of a giant insect, and following the high-road, which wound whiter through the surrounding twilight, a black object rushed across their vision.
>
> Lily started from her attitude of absorption; her smile faded and she began to move toward the lane. (76)

Intruding upon the "finer air" of Lily's "new world," the motorcar puts an end to all magic. The sound of the motor returns Lily to social reality and passing time, to the story she had told the others (of having a headache that would keep her inside all afternoon), and to her own master plan of marrying the rich and stolid Percy Gryce—the very plot she has taken a break from by spending the afternoon with Selden.

Both Lily and Edna are approaching thirty when their stories begin. Both feel increasingly trapped by their sense of coercive "reality" shaping their lives. From the outset, both texts underscore the clash between the pleasures of impulse, idleness, and aimlessness on the one hand and the inexorable realities of social convention and time itself on the other. As we have seen, the experiences most relished by Edna and Lily are incompatible with their everyday lives, attainable only by denying social reality, or through dream, fantasy, "invention"—and art. Nonetheless, as we have also seen, both characters associate certain elements of art (particularly narrative art) with the very aspects of "reality" they most strongly resist. For them, magic moments are destroyed, not created, by those indispensible attributes of fiction which bring the imaginary worlds of *The Awakening* and *The House of Mirth* themselves into being: beginnings and endings, story or plot.

All fiction requires strategies for structuring plot and representing time. Naturalism, with its thematic emphasis on the conflict between the relentless movement of time and the characters' impotent resistance to that movement, generally presents its sequence of events in straightforward chronological order, with little of that flare for subverting the surface coherence of plot that we associate with the fiction of modernism or postmodernism. Both *The Awakening* and *The House of Mirth* have the extremely clean, streamlined, linear plots typical of naturalist texts. One extended flashback early in *House of Mirth* (chap. 3) and another in *The Awakening* (chap. 7) give a selection of details about Edna and Lily's childhoods, contextualizing their relation to their parents and providing perspective on the present situation of each heroine. Beyond that point, both stories seem to move ahead quite directly, with little perceptible circling. Yet despite the general sense of unimpeded progression characteristic of both plots, sophisticated maneuvers are at work in the manipulation of narrative time. Chopin, for example, would seem to conceive of *The Awakening* not primarily as a sequence of events, but rather as a seductive enclosure into which she would invite the reader. ("The voice of the sea is seductive, never ceasing, whispering, clamoring, murmuring...".) We have emphasized the contrast between the "unceasing," undifferentiated voice of the sea on the one hand and the articulation of a narrating voice on the other. Paradoxically, however, narration in *The Awakening* seems designed to evoke for the reader, through the reading process, an experience analogous to Edna's immersion in the boundless realm of field and sea.

The link between Chopin's sense of her own text and Edna's sense of the sea is not merely fanciful. After Robert's return from Mexico, when Edna runs into him in a garden restaurant, he notices that she is reading a book he himself has already read. He tells her how the book ends, "to save her the trouble of wading through it," as he says (105). Robert's image of "wading" for reading is worth some attention in a book so pervaded by the image of the sea. To "wad[e] ... through" a book merely to find out what happens at the end is a chore, something Robert would like to save Edna "the trouble of." I suggest that it is also antithetical to the reading experience that Chopin promotes in *The Awakening* itself. To wade in the sea is to keep one's feet on the bottom, to forestall the immersion that could make for a feeling of free forward movement (swimming) on the one hand, a danger of submergence (even the risk of drowning) on the other.[20]

All novel reading (at least until modernism) implicates a reader in a plot that creates suspense or curiosity, stimulating the reader to wonder "what will happen next," and especially "how will it end?" But a novel must keep the reader's wish to answer that question within bounds—must regulate the reader's involvement with the text, keeping him or her implicated in, and gratified by, the *process* of anticipation and delay itself. Otherwise, what is to prevent a reader from skipping ahead to the final scene?

Every writer must harness the forward movement that is indispensible to writing and reading fiction. Reading always involves such movement and encourages the projection of possible (anticipated) endings. In *The Awakening*, where the traditional momentum of the naturalist plot is modified by lyric passages and recurrent leitmotivs, Chopin generates a reading experience informed by a sense, not of rapid descent, but of timelessness or containment in a space that seems "free" even as it is always moving forward.

One measure of Chopin's control over narrative time is precisely her subversion of the forward thrust that characterizes most realist and naturalist plots.[21] The recurrent images and lyric passages in *The Awakening* complicate, even abrogate, a reader's concern with what will *happen* next. Unlike some of Chopin's own stories—and unlike *The House of Mirth*—*The Awakening* resists melodramatic encounters,[22] refusing climax altogether, creating instead a virtual sense of fusion between beginnings and endings.[23] That sense of fusion is reemphasized in the final passage by the repetition of previous motifs, the evocation of Edna's childhood memories, and the birth imagery that accompanies her disappearance in the sea.

Insofar as the act of reading fiction always separates one from habitual concerns and immerses one in a world of make-believe, the reading process may be seen as an undifferentiated state which one enters and from which one emerges.[24] As we have seen, the problem of emergence itself is underscored at an early point in *The Awakening*, with particular emphasis on the difficulty of emerging from the chaos that accompanies the beginning of "a world, especially." In the narrator's uncharacteristically explicit identification with Edna here ("how few of *us* ever emerge from such beginning ...") that "us" can of course be taken to include the reader as well as Edna and the narrator. However, while the aesthetic experience provided by *The Awakening* may approximate Edna's sense of immersion in a timeless realm (field, sea, or music), the act of reading allows fusion or merger only within safe boundaries. By engaging imaginatively with the fluid medium of narrative time, Chopin (like Wharton) makes the creation of an "in-between state" for readers a source of strength and satisfaction, even while demonstrating the inexorable power of time in "reality" and explicitly underscoring its role in destroying the protagonist.

Recent discussions of women's literature often concern themselves with the question of woman's "space." The issue is not merely one of physical space—a room of own's own—nor is it simply a question of woman's "place" in relation to either society or the literary canon. Many feminist critics speak of women's writing itself as "another 'medium'" (Jacobus), a "wild zone" (Showalter), a border or margin between established modes (Jehlen).[25] Far from constituting a purposive hurtle toward an end, the process of reading itself is a kind of "in-between state" that shares many qualities with the kinds of unbounded, or timeless, "magic-realms" repeatedly figured in both *The Awakening* and *The House of Mirth*. While all novels, in this sense, project "in-between" states for their readers, both Chopin and Wharton place particular emphasis on the temptation and danger of such states in "real life," even while taking pains to heighten the reader's own sense of immersion or suspension in an analogous condition.

Like Chopin, Wharton repeatedly subverts a reader's sense of straightforward progression through narrative time. In *The House of Mirth*, whenever Lily and/or Selden experience the impulse to stop time altogether, the strands of plot begin to split and the direct line of chronological sequence is obscured. Thus, in both novels, strategies of plotting reflect certain nonmimetic aims shared by Chopin and Wharton in projecting a narrated world for readers.

Early in the Bellomont section of *House of Mirth*, as Percy Gryce waits for Lily to accompany him to church, he temporarily loses himself in the pleasures of anticipation, reflecting "agreeably on the strength of character which kept [Lily] true to her early training in surroundings so subversive to religious principles." While nourishing "the hope that Miss Bart might be unaccompanied" (54), Gryce even enjoys the delay. But just when "the coachman seemed to be slowly petrifying on the box and the groom on the doorstep" (54)—that is, when time seems at a total standstill—the ladies' sudden entrance reveals that the clock has not stopped after all ("the precious minutes were flying"; 56) and in a flash "poor Mr Gryce found himself rolling off [to church] between four ladies for whose spiritual welfare he felt not the least concern" (55).

Gryce's delight in anticipation and delay is abruptly subverted. In the meantime—that is, at precisely the same early-morning time—Lily herself undergoes a related process. With the carriage come and gone, the scene shifts to a guest room where Lily still lies in bed. The *scene* shifts, but as far as *time* is concerned we are retracing the very moments during which Gryce waited expectantly for Lily.

Having "risen earlier than usual," fully intending to accompany Gryce to church (55), Lily lies in bed, luxuriating not only in her sense of physical well-being and her pleasurable memories of the night before, but in the certainty that her plot is working and that a secure haven (marriage to Gryce) is right within her grasp. Lying in bed, while the day seems stalled, Lily dwells delightedly in the assurance that she can easily elicit Gryce's marriage proposal—later. However, while Gryce waits for Lily, her own reflections on the events of the previous evening lead her to tremble between bleak visions of a future with Gryce and a still more chilling awareness of the bills on her night-table. With Lily's recollection of those bills, the narrative focus comes back—for the *third* time—to the moment when Sunday morning dawned at Bellomont: "Miss Bart, accordingly, rose the next morning with the most earnest conviction that it was her duty to go to church" (59).

Wharton's sleight of hand is impressive. While only a few moments pass in represented "reality" (Gryce waits, Lily reflects), considerable space in the text is devoted to providing multiple angles on the same brief span of time. Thus, through the circling away from and back over one particular moment, Wharton's handling of the sequence of incident and reverie reproduces quite closely, for the reader, a process repeatedly experienced by the characters: first the sense of time standing still, then the shattering of that illusion. The reader is held in slow motion, in suspension, in a sense of no time passing—not unlike Gryce and Lily themselves. However, once the spell is broken, for both reader and characters, it turns out that something decisive has occurred precisely because time has never really stopped. Lily has missed the coach; Gryce has gone to church without her, and Lily's marriage prospects are significantly reduced.

Wharton's structuring and pacing of narrative incident after the *tableaux vivants* scene reproduces in greater detail such circling away from and back over one limited stretch of time. Here, still more dramatically than on Sunday at Bellomont, a day that begins with the pleasurable denial of reality ends with the shattering of numerous illusions—a shattering at once more definitive and more destructive for Lily than the end of her plans for Percy Gryce.

The passage that renders Lily's awakening the morning after the *tableaux vivants* presents her once again in a state of delightful limbo. Selden has written, asking to see her, and Lily, who "could not bear to mar her mood of luxurious retrospection by an act of definite refusal" (147–8), has agreed to meet him the following day (while telling herself she can easily put him off when the time comes). Lily's state of delicious abstraction from habitual pressures is partly a result of her "luxurious retrospection" (147–8)—the memory of her "culminating moment of ... triumph" on stage (147). But it is also a result of what we might call "luxurious anticipation"—the pleasure of looking forward to her encounter with Selden (while reserving the right not to *have* it). Lily's taste for suspended moments of this kind is something she shares with Selden himself; it is perhaps the strongest tie that binds them. Immediately after the *tableaux vivants*, for example, although Selden's "first impulse was to seek Miss Bart," he is far from disappointed at failing to find her, because "it would have broken the spell to see her too soon": "... his procrastination was not due to any lingering resistance, but to the desire to luxuriate a moment in the sense of complete surrender" (143). Like Lily, Selden finds the sense of surrender particularly "luxurious" when kept short of realization. For him, as for her, delay is a special pleasure in itself. It is also (like anticipation) a pleasure particularly relevant to narrative.[26]

Thus two scenes juxtaposed in the middle of *House of Mirth* not only maximize the pleasures of anticipation and delay for characters and reader, but also underscore the various implications of illusion in life and art. The two scenes in question (Lily at Trenor's house, Selden at Gerty's) thematize the pressure of time running out for Lily while simultaneously deflecting the reader's attention from other aspects of passing time—including the simple fact that the novel's own midpoint has been passed and the end is fast approaching. In the dinner scene between Selden and Gerty, Selden luxuriates in his sense of both anticipation and delay, talking to Gerty of Lily, just to relish the moments until the "surrender" that he thinks is inevitable (162). By dwelling on Selden's idealized image of Lily, while averting the narrative focus from the *real* Lily and her doings at that moment, the text creates a sense of suspended time for both the reader and Selden himself.

No sooner does the text render Selden's misplaced sense of security, however, than it pointedly reemphasizes the relentless movement of time. While he talks expansively of Lily, confident in the future, events occur which transform Selden's sense of reality. When dining with Gerty, he is convinced that he can "separate the woman he knew from the vulgar estimate of her" (162). Even as he revels in this particular certainty, however, Lily is fending off Gus Trenor's aggressive sexuality; therefore, as Selden is walking home toward midnight, he sees Lily silhouetted against Trenor's door, about to get into a cab. It is only at this point that the reader, like Selden, is abruptly returned not only to the reality of Selden's moral cowardice (assuming the worst about Lily), but to the relation between causes and effects, made visible by the passing of time and the recombination of disparate narrative strands.

As in the scene where Gryce waits for Lily while Lily stays in bed, one effect of splitting the strands of a plot is a certain amount of inevitable distortion (or confusion) of linear time from the reader's point of view. While Selden idles at Gerty's, the reader, too, may experience a temporary sense of time standing still, a limbo or deadlock of anticipation matched against delay not unlike Selden's own. All time frames and lines of action recombine, however, when Selden sees Lily emerge from Trenor's door. At that point many illusions are dispelled, for characters and readers alike.

Through Wharton's careful handling of plot, then, both the feeling of time standing still, and the sudden realization of time having passed (two conditions so dangerous for the characters) are reproduced—in a harmless form—for the reader of the text.[27] *The Awakening* tells us at one point that "all sense of reality had gone out of [Edna's] life" (102). To a certain extent, a reader must willingly relinquish his or her hold on reality in order to read fiction at all. A "willing suspension of disbelief" is not the same thing, however, as an unwitting loss of all sense of reality. Thus, whereas Chopin and Wharton write fiction, Edna and Lily are destroyed.

Lily's lack of attention to the shape of her own story, and her unreflecting illusion of time-control, creates a sharp contrast with Wharton's extremely sophisticated understanding of narration and time. Similarly, we can point to the contrast between Edna's longing for a state with no beginning or end and Chopin's own control over beginnings and endings in narrative. As we have seen, however, Chopin (like Wharton) uses her text to implicate her reader in a recurrent sense not only of boundaries and limits but also of timelessness—an in-between state that shares certain qualities with Edna's experience listening to music (especially Chopin!), sailing to Chenière Caminada, or responding to the sea.

At the thematic level, *The Awakening*, like *The House of Mirth*, celebrates the joys of "exaltation" even as it exposes the futility of Edna's wish to sustain (or return to) her "culminating moments" of delight. Thus while Edna is "still under the spell of her infatuation" (54) with Robert several weeks after her own departure from Grand Isle, she repeatedly runs up against proof of time and change: Robert is gone, her sister marries, there are ten tiny new piglets at her mother-in-law's farm (102), and Mme Ratignolle, too, is about to give birth.

During Edna's last encounter with Mlle Reisz, she sits down to read Robert's most recent letter. Anticipating delight, Edna "hold[s the letter] ... in her hand, while the music penetrated her whole being like an effulgence, warming and brightening the dark places of her soul. It prepared her for joy and exaltation" (80). But when Edna reads of Robert's approaching return, she pulls Mlle Reisz's hands off the keys to get more information. The "joy and exaltation" of aesthetic experience is subverted by urgent expectations in material reality. Like Selden's sudden glimpse of Lily at Trenor's door, Edna's abrupt reentry into a time-bound realm short-circuits the sense of her "spirit set free," the feeling she generally achieves when Mlle Reisz plays the piano. Similarly, toward the end of *The Awakening*, the "intoxication of expectancy" (110) as Edna moves toward sexual union with Robert is interrupted by a knock on the door to request her presence while Mme Ratignolle gives birth. Pregnancy and birth constitute a kind of natural trope for the notion of time running out. Edna's suicide itself can be seen as a refusal to reenter the cycle of sexuality and birth that makes the presence of "a little new life" inescapable (109). Yet *The Awakening* also projects an entirely different, one could say more primal, image of mother and child. Despite the text's social critique of "mother-women" (10), the figure of mother and child—and of pregnancy itself—is, throughout *The Awakening*, one more vehicle for the idea of merger, the fluid symbiosis or fusion so "seductive" to Edna, and so threatening to the possibility of "emergence." Not surprisingly, Lily's final drift toward death in *House of Mirth* is also accompanied by the image of a mother and baby—rocking, intertwined, and interdependent. In the course of *House of Mirth*, Lily repeatedly longs for the shelter and darkness associated with a mother's arms (157).[28]

Both *The Awakening* and *The House of Mirth* are pervaded by a concern with modes of exaltation and fusion that ultimately make emergence impossible for the protagonists (though they are nonetheless, in themselves, a source of unique satisfactions). Unlike Edna and Lily, of course, both writers and readers can "emerge" from the chaos that constitutes the beginning "of a [fictional] world, especially." Different narrative structures, to be sure, implicate readers in different modes of immersion and emergence. But the start of every story involves a bid for connection between narrator and reader; and the end of every text involves loosening that bond, separation, and finally silence. Thus, in a sense, immersion and separation are always—inevitably—an issue for writers. Perhaps this is one reason why both male and female writers so commonly use birth motifs as a figure for the act of writing itself.

Many reading theorists stress the peculiar phenomenological status of the act of reading. Reading fiction in particular is an unusual condition that allows one, as reader, to be both oneself and someone else at the same time—

to experience (as Dorrit Cohn puts it) "what writers and readers know least in life: how another mind thinks, how another body feels...."[29] To read fiction is to experience (a bounded and temporary) sense of merger—such merger as, in Edna and Lily's experience, cannot be sustained in "reality."

The authors who created Edna and Lily as vehicles for exploring issues in their own experience of both life and art were effectively separated from their fictional heroines by the simple fact of having written these stories. It is not only that the authors master the time-bound medium of narrative, while the protagonists engage in a losing race with time and either refuse narrative altogether (Lily) or are threatened with dissolution by it (Edna); it is also that, for Chopin and Wharton, the control and order indispensible to aesthetic experience—what Wharton calls "precision in ecstacy" (*BG* 170)— becomes a source of satisfaction, not of fear.

A spirit "set free" through music or art cannot dwell in "exaltation" forever. If Chopin's or Wharton's narratives may be seen as ontological "borderlands," their own sense of absorption or merger in the writing of fiction is given free rein only within limits that enhance rather than undermine their capacity to project illusion by mastering plot, controlling narrative time, articulating a storytelling voice in language. It is precisely through their heightened consciousness of the limits inherent in magic realms that these writers are able to create such realms for both their characters and their readers.

Unlike Edna telling her story to the doctor, or Lily in the *tableaux vivants*, Chopin and Wharton sustain an awareness of the distinctions between fiction and reality, self and art and audience. At a certain point in *The Awakening*, Edna visits the Ratignolles and recoils from their relentless domesticity. "If ever the fusion of two human beings into one has been accomplished on this sphere it was surely in their union" (56). Such fusion ("on this sphere") is not to be envied, certainly not by Edna (or Chopin). But insofar as reading and writing enable one to fuse without fusing, to merge safely with another ("on this sphere"), Chopin and Wharton solve at least some of their protagonists' problems through authorship—representing otherness "without ceasing to be [themselves]."

### NOTES

1. Martin, p. 26. Cf. Showalter ("Tradition and the Female Talent"), p. 48; Gilmore, p. 80. On Lily's "inability to speak for herself," see Showalter ("Death of the Lady"), pp. 142, 145. Cf. Fetterley passim.

2. It is ironic in this context that whereas *The House of Mirth* became a best-seller and put Wharton on the literary map, *The Awakening* virtually put an end to Chopin's career.

(See Martin, pp. 8–10; Showalter ["Tradition and the Female Talent"], pp. 33–4; Kaplan, pp. 67–8.) But my main focus is the symbolic, not the social, effects of narration.

3. *A Backward Glance*, p. 223; cf. pp. 144, 217. Further references in the text are to this edition.

4. Chopin, *The Awakening*, p. 63. Further references in the text are to this edition.

5. On this much discussed scene, see Hochman, Steiner, Michaels, Seltzer.

6. The naturalist connection is rarely emphasized, perhaps partially obscured by the emphasis on Chopin and Wharton as trailbreakers in women's fiction. See Showalter ("Tradition and the Female Talent"), pp. 34–5. *The House of Mirth* is more often set in the "naturalist" context than *The Awakening* (see Kaplan, Michaels, Mitchell, Seltzer). Other generic models that could be noted are not directly relevant to the present argument. Wharton can, of course, be situated in the "novel of manners" tradition (see Lindberg); while *The Awakening* is often discussed in the romantic or transcendentalist context (see Balkman, Leary).

7. See Kaplan, pp. 69–74. Cf. Showalter ("Tradition and the Female Talent"), pp. 34–5, 44; Martin, p. 26; Gilbert, pp. 15, 29, 30–2.

8. See Norris, *Literary Criticism*, p. 13.

9. Dreiser, *Sister Carrie*, p. 244.

10. The pair of strolling lovers, the woman in black, the various birds, the sea itself— these attributes of *The Awakening* have received considerable attention. See Showalter ("Tradition and the Female Talent") on the text's "impressionistic rhythm of epiphany and mood" (43); Cf. Gilmore, pp. 80–1; Jones, p. 169; Horner and Zlosnik, p. 53.

11. Wharton, *The House of Mirth*, p. 236. Further references in the text are to this edition.

12. On Lily's rejection of plot see Bauer, pp. 124–5. Cf. Showalter ("Death of the Lady"), pp. 142–3, 154.

13. Controversy over Edna's experience has raged since the book first appeared (to hostile reviews). Subsequently neglected for decades, its rediscovery in the fifties has generated a wide array of readings. For a view of Edna's development that stresses Edna's "evolution from romantic fantasies of fusion with another person to self-definition and self-reliance," see Showalter ("Tradition and the Female Talent"), p. 33. Cf. Fryer, pp. 257–8.

14. On the narrator's tendency to "distance ... herself from Edna" see Jones, p. 165.

15. This concern of Edna's (and Chopin's) anticipates both Virginia Woolf's rendering of women's experience in *A Room of One's Own* and a central issue in much current feminist theory. For discussions of *The Awakening* in terms of "women's time," see Jones, pp. 157–8; Toth, pp. 275–6. Cf. Kristeva ("Women's Time"), pp. 187, 190–2, 207, and passim. In Kristeva's psychoanalytic theory, the unrecoverable unity of mother and child becomes the source of poetic language. On Kristeva's distinction between the "symbolic" mode and the "prelinguistic" ("semiotic") mode, see Kristeva *(Revolution)*.

16. Many critics engage Edna's and Lily's search for a form beyond time, space, and social reality. See Horner and Zlosnik, pp. 7, 24; Bauer, pp. 145, 148; White, p. 102; Fryer, pp. 257–8. On Lily's inability "to imagine existing in another element," see Horner and Zlosnik, p. 24; cf. Bauer, pp. 124–5. I am suggesting that, unlike Edna and Lily, Chopin and Wharton find "another element" for existence in and though writing.

17. James, "Ivan Turgenieff," pp. 174–5.

18. Norris, *Literary Criticism*, p. 55.

19. Edith Wharton, *The Writing of Fiction*, p. 91.

20. Chopin has harsh words for fiction that is not "seductive enough" to immerse a

reader totally. Of *Jude the Obscure*, Chopin writes: "you will just keep on munching a cream chocolate or wondering if the postman has gone by or if there is coal on the furnace" (*Complete Works*, p. 714).

21. For systematic examinations of narrative time, see Gennette, Rimmon-Kenan, Sternberg. In general, narratological approaches to temporal ordering have not engaged questions of gender.

22. That is, the scrubwoman selling letters to Lily, Rosedale meeting Lily leaving Selden's house in chapter I, Selden glimpsing Lily leaving Gus Trenor's house near midnight, Bertha banishing Lily from the yacht, and so on.

23. See Schweitzer, pp. 163–4, 185; Cf. Fryer, pp. 257–8.

24. On the reading experience as a ground of temporary merger between "self" and "other," see Bakhtin, p. 315; Poulet, p. 56; Iser, p. 293; Jacobus, p. 37.

25. In Jacobus's "other 'medium'" the self is temporarily "dissolved into writing" (37). Cf. Showalter (*New Feminist Criticism*), p. 262; Jehlen, p. 585.

26. On delay, anticipation, and narrative time, see Gennette, Rimmon-Kenan, Sternberg.

27. It may be relevant, in this context, that during the composition of *House of Mirth*, Wharton herself was (for the first time) subject to a writing deadline.

28. Cf. pp. 101, 176, 184, and note 15.

29. Cohn, pp. 5–6.


## WORKS CITED

Bakhtin, M. M. *The Dialogic Imagination*. Edited by Michael Holquist. Austin: University of Texas Press, 1981.

Balkman, Elizabeth. "*The Awakening*, Kate Chopin's 'Endlessly Rocking' Cycle." *Ball State University Forum* 20 (1979): 53–8.

Bauer, Dale M. *Feminist Dialogics: A Theory of Failed Community*. Albany: State University of New York Press, 1988.

Chopin, Kate. *The Awakening*. New York: W. W. Norton, 1976.

*The Complete Works*. Edited by Per Seyersted. Baton Rouge: Louisiana State University Press, 1969.

"Elizabeth Stark's One Story." In *The Awakening and Selected Stories*. New York: Penguin, 1986.

Cohn, Dorrit. *Transparent Minds*. Princeton, N.J.: Princeton University Press, 1978.

Dimock, Wai-Chee. "Debasing Exchange: Edith Wharton's *House of Mirth*." In *Edith Wharton: Modern Critical Views*, edited by Harold Bloom, pp. 123–37. New York: Chelsea, 1986.

Dreiser, Theodore. *Sister Carrie*. New York: W. W. Norton, 1970.

Fetterley, Judith. "The Temptation to Be a Beautiful Object: Double Standard and Double Bind in *The House of Mirth*." *Studies in American Fiction* 5 (1977): 199–211.

Fryer, Judith. *The Faces of Eve: Women in the Nineteenth-Century Novel*, New York: Oxford University Press, 1976.

Genette, Gerard. *Narrative Discourse*. Translated by Jane E. Lewin. Ithaca, N.Y.: Cornell University Press, 1980.

Gilbert, Sandra. "Introduction" to *The Awakening*. New York: Penguin, 1986.

Gilmore, Michael T. "Revolt Against Nature: The Problematic Modernism of *The Awakening*." In Martin, *New Essays*, pp. 59–88.

Hochman, Barbara. "The Rewards of Representation: Edith Wharton, Lily Bart, and the Writer/Reader Interchange." *Novel* 24 (1991): 147–61.

Horner, Avril, and Zlosnik, Sue. *Landscapes of Desire.* New York: Harvester, 1990.

Iser, Wolfgang. *The Implied Reader.* Baltimore and London: The Johns Hopkins University Press, 1974.

Jacobus, Mary. *Reading Woman.* New York: Columbia University Press, 1986.

James, Henry. "Ivan Turgenieff" (1874). Reprinted in *Theory of Fiction: Henry James,* edited by James E. Miller, Jr. Lincoln and London: University of Nebraska Press, 1972.

Jehlen, Myra. "Archimedes and the Paradox of Feminist Criticism." *Signs* 6 (1981): 575–601.

Jones, Ann Goodwyn. *Tomorrow Is Another Day: The Woman Writer in the South 1859–1936.* Baton Rouge: Louisiana State University Press, 1981.

Kaplan, Amy. *The Social Construction of American Realism.* Chicago: University of Chicago Press, 1988.

Kristeva, Julia. *Revolution in Poetic Language.* Translated by Margaret Waller. New York: Columbia University Press, 1984.

"Women's Time." In *The Kristeva Reader,* edited by Toni Moi. New York: Columbia University Press, 1986.

Leary, Lewis. *Southern Excursion: Essays on Mark Twain and Others.* Baton Rouge: Louisiana State University Press, 1971.

Lindberg, Gary. *Edith Wharton and the Novel of Manners.* Charlottesville: University Press of Virginia, 1975.

Martin, Wendy. "Introduction," *New Essays on The Awakening,* pp. 1–32. New York: Cambridge University Press, 1988.

Michaels, Walter Benn. *The Gold Standard and the Logic of Naturalism.* Berkeley and Los Angeles: University of California Press, 1987.

Mitchell, Lee Clark. *Determined Fictions.* New York: Columbia University Press, 1989.

Norris, Frank. *The Literary Criticism of Frank Norris.* Edited by Donald Pizer. New York: Russell and Russell, 1976.

Poulet, Georges. "Phenomenology of Reading." *New Literary History* 1 (1969): 53–68.

Rimmon-Kenan, Shlomith. *Narrative Fiction.* London and New York: Methuen, 1983.

Schweitzer, Ivy. "Maternal Discourse and the Romance of Self-Possession." *Boundary* 2 17 (1990): 161–86.

Seltzer, Mark. *Bodies and Machines.* New York: Routledge, 1992.

Showalter, Elaine. "The Death of Lady (Novelist): Wharton's *House of Mirth.*" In *Edith Wharton: Modern Critical Views,* edited by Harold Bloom, pp. 139–54. New York: Chelsea, 1986.

*The New Feminist Criticism: Essays on Women, Literature and Theory.* London and New York: Pantheon, 1985.

"Tradition and the Female Talent: *The Awakening* as a Solitary Book." In Martin, *New Essays,* pp. 33–57.

Steiner, Wendy. "The Causes of Effect: Edith Wharton and the Economics of Ekphrasis." *Poetics Today* 10 (1989): 279–97.

Sternberg, Meir. *Expositional Modes and Temporal Ordering in Fiction.* Baltimore and London: The Johns Hopkins University Press, 1978.

Toth, Emily. "Timely and Timeless: The Treatment of Time in *The Awakening,*" *Southern Studies* 16 (1977): 271–6.

Wharton Edith. *A Backward Glance.* New York: Scribner's, 1964.

*The House of Mirth.* In *Novels.* New York: Library of America, 1985.

*The Letters of Edith Wharton.* Edited by R. W. B. Lewis and Nancy Lewis. New York: Scribner's, 1988.

*The Writing of Fiction.* New York: Scribner's, 1925.

White, Robert. *"The Awakening." Mosaic* 17 (1984): 97–110.

DONNA M. CAMPBELL

# Dreiser, London, Crane, and the Iron Madonna

I

In "Women as Superfluous Characters in American Realism and Naturalism," Jan Cohn contends that naturalistic novels relegate women to a specific and very limited role. Women such as Laura Jadwin are not viable characters in their own right; rather, they exist as adjuncts to the real focus of naturalistic novels, the worlds of finance and business. Cohn is one in a long line of writers who have argued that characters, especially female characters, in naturalistic novels are not carefully delineated figures but crude sketches drawn to demonstrate some portion of naturalistic philosophy. Both the local color writers and the naturalists tended to create characters as types, but in their use of stereotypes, the naturalists showed that they held differing assumptions from those of their local color predecessors about the relative positions of character, reader, and narrator. Characters in local color works display the qualities of a particular region, whereas naturalistic characters show the effect of impersonal forces on a representative person; that is, the characters are signs of something larger than, and different from, either individuals or their regions. Implicit in this view of characters as types is the idea that somehow these characters are "other" than the author, and, by extension, the reader, who presumably shares the author's quick perceptions, level of education, and attitudes. The alterity of local color characters is a

From *Resisting Regionalism: Gender and Naturalism in American Fiction, 1885–1915.* © 1997 by Donna M. Campbell.

donnée of the movement, creating the outsider's view as an implicit norm against which the actions of the characters are judged.

The same vision of "otherness" or alterity is present in many naturalistic novels. In naturalistic novels, otherness is typically marked more by differences in class (delineated through dialect, level of education, economic circumstances, and ancestry of the characters) than by differences in time and locale.[1] Whereas some local color works, notably those of Sarah Orne Jewett, suggest exclusion from the community as a source of anxiety, naturalistic works threaten to include readers in the uncertain and frequently miserable world they depict, deliberately undercutting the safe position traditionally enjoyed by the reader. The fragility of a position based on something as rigidly enforced yet tenuously defined as class, particularly when, as in America, class itself is defined by the presence or absence of something as fluid as money, forces readers into an anxious identification with characters they might otherwise disregard.

Another sort of otherness or alterity exists in naturalistic novels: the idea of women as "other," as objects of study in themselves rather than as the representatives of human nature they had frequently been in local color fiction. Underlying this approach was a statement of alienation, not from women, but from a culture rigid in its insistence on stratified class and gender roles and its elevation of a feminine mode of literature. If establishing class as a basis for alterity was one naturalistic response to increasing industrialization, economic upheaval, and social and political uncertainty, then establishing gender as another basis surely reflects the need to express a similar anxiety, since gender roles as social constructs depend on something as strong or as fragile as the holding of mutual beliefs by members of a society. The threat is not that one can change from male to female, but that one can, as we have seen in chapter 4, become effeminate. By first divorcing female experience from the mainstream of human experience—treating women as "other"—and then by encapsulating certain female characters within the limits of stereotyping, naturalistic writers could achieve several aims at once, among them objectivity in representation, control over the parameters of feminine discourse, and the supersession of local color's perceived dominance of the literary magazines.

As men tacitly committed to social justice, Frank Norris, Jack London, Stephen Crane, and David Graham Phillips sympathized with the powerlessness of women in an inequitable social system, and they inverted and reinvented the stereotypes of fallen women to expose the economic basis of the double standard. Yet striving to create a new literature under a system they saw as dominated by feminine discourse, they exaggerated the power of "respectable" women and railed against the entrenched forces allied against young male writers. Their principal strategy for voicing this resentment was the inversion of existing attitudes on fallen women and the rearticulation of these women's stories. By examining these women's lives, and by surrounding with ambiguity the hitherto clear-cut moral judgments about them, the naturalists sought to "rescue" these women, not merely as stereotyped or sensationalized subjects for fiction, but as representative human beings worthy of study. The relegation of women to the status of "other" is preserved by emphasizing their role as objects of mystery or inspiration for male characters. Surrounding prostitutes with an air of indeterminacy provides the necessary distance.

A second means of expressing rage and regaining control of the prevailing feminine discourse was to discredit their attackers, the female figures whom the naturalists suspected were responsible for suppressing naturalism's depictions of "real life." The fallen woman's reliance on but a single defense—silence—contrasts markedly with the good woman's array of verbal and psychological weapons, as novels by London and Crane make clear. If the use of prostitutes as subjects suggests that "bad women" are or can be good, the opposing corollary is that "good women" can be bad—that is, life denying and repressive. In contrast to the prostitutes' silence, language proves to be the redemptive force for the male characters in Jack London's *Martin Eden* and Stephen Crane's *George's Mother*, as the use of what Norris called "the crude, the raw, the vulgar" emancipates male characters such as Martin Eden and George Kelcey from the dominance of feminine discourse. Both Kelcey's and Eden's respective liberations through language function as symbolic representations of the naturalists' own struggles.

The third response to local color and its ideals is a broader examination of the masculine and feminine social systems involved. If *George's Mother* shows the failure of local color virtues in a naturalistic world, *The Monster* shows that these virtues cannot flourish even in their natural habitat, the local color story. Evoking the local color conventions of order, praiseworthy virtues, a panoply of character types including strong spinsters, and storytelling, Crane uses the language and themes of naturalism to undercut the earlier tradition. *The Monster* stands as the consummate "outsider" story. It is a parable of alienation, not only that of Henry Johnson and Dr. Trescott, but of naturalism from the local color world that it had to destroy.

II

One of the naturalists' central premises was that the whole of life must be examined if one wished to present a truthful or, to use a favorite naturalistic term, "sincere" representation of reality. Frank Norris distinguished truth from accuracy by stating that the latter was merely a part of the truth, that in fact "it is not difficult to be accurate, but it is monstrously difficult to be True."[2] Representing the truth meant bridging the gap between two realities: to use Norris's metaphor, literature should not "stop in the front parlor and discuss medicated flannels and mineral waters with the ladies," but instead "be off upstairs with you, prying, peeping, peering into the closets of the bedroom, into the nursery, into the sitting room; yes, and into that little iron box screwed to the lower shelf of the closet in the library."[3] Sex and money, the two great unspoken forces of the Victorian age, were dragged out of the closet at last as legitimate, rather than covert, subjects for fiction.

The naturalists' fascination with fallen women, particularly prostitutes, has been well documented,[4] most recently in *Girls Who Went Wrong*, Laura Hapke's study of prostitution in turn-of-the-century literature. Hapke finds that, despite their commitment to truth, writers such as Crane, Frederic, and Phillips "revealed in their evasive attitude toward the prostitute both the genteel influence and their own ambivalence about the quintessential fallen woman."[5] The daring subject matter thereby masked the essentially conventional treatment of fallen women. Several of these tales end with retribution, the women either committing suicide, like Maggie Johnson, or being ravaged by disease, like Flossie in *Vandover and the Brute*. David Graham Phillips's Susan Lenox pays the price by being deprived both of all her illusions and of the man she loves. Even *Maggie: A Girl of the Streets* (1893, 1896), one of the earliest tales, can be seen as "essentially a tract, written by the son of a gentle Methodist."[6] Despite these limitations, for the naturalists the image of the prostitute forced to negotiate a hazardous existence with only her body and her wits as assets epitomized the struggle to survive in an indifferent universe. She therefore provided an appropriate proving ground for naturalism's deterministic theories. As a social outcast shunned by genteel society, she also gained a great deal of sympathy from the other (self-elected) outcasts, the naturalists.

The naturalists' investigations emphasized that the prostitutes' position as "merchandise" conflated commerce and sexuality, forcing the women, like their more fortunate peers, to objectify themselves as consumable commodities for the male gaze. For example, in *The House of Mirth*, Lily Bart views herself as "human merchandise," most obviously when, posing for the Wellington Brys' tableaux vivants, she markets not only her charm but her figure when she appears in the clinging robes of Joshua Reynolds's *Mrs. Lloyd*.[7] Within the rapt assembly of male admirers, each simultaneously admires publicly the ideal of womanhood that he projects onto Lily and assesses privately his ability to "buy" her. In the humbler world of *Sister Carrie, Maggie,* and *Susan Lenox,* the image of a woman posing for male purchasers pervades each work: Carrie Meeber trying on clothes for Drouet and appearing on stage in *Under the Gaslight;* Maggie Johnson parading the streets; Susan Lenox singing before rowdy riverboat crowds and trying on Paris fashions for her lover, Freddy Palmer. Possessing only themselves as a medium of exchange, they keep their market value inflated by infinitely deferring the process, implied by their promise of sexuality, of gratifying their purchasers' desires. The "successful" women, Susan Lenox and Carrie Meeber, accomplish this balancing act in two essential ways: by selling themselves sexually, they fulfill one half of the promise, but they deliberately maintain a distinction between the commercial self of sex-for-cash and the inchoate longings that comprise their personalities. Striving to maintain a cohesion between the commercial and the inner self, as Maggie and Lily do, drives down their value as commodities: Maggie, for example, gets few customers because when her identity becomes wholly bounded by her profession, she has nothing new to offer her customers; Lily, having gambled away her chances, cannot accept the distinction between commercial-sexual and inner self that her society demands, and her quest for maintaining herself as an integrated personality leads to her death. Obscured by the economic rather than sexual basis of human transactions, the whole issue of women's sexuality becomes distanced, as if of secondary importance.

Another form of distance arises from the novels' paradoxical figuration of exposure and concealment. The authors began, in fact, with the basic question posed by such autobiographical prostitute narratives as *Nell Kimball: Her Life as an American Madam* and *Madeleine: An Autobiography.* Indeed, it is the question that these and other "fallen women" declare is the one most frequently asked of them by their patrons: "What circumstances drove you to sell yourself?"[8] In asking this question, the naturalists skirt the edges of the white-slave narrative, the sensationalistic genre that reached its height of popularity in the Progressive Era with novels such as Harold Wright Kauffmann's *House of Bondage* (1910), a host of thinly disguised tracts like Clifford Roe's *Great War on White Slavery; or, Fighting for the Protection of Our Girls* (1911), and reports like George Kneeland's *Commercialized Prostitution in New York City* (1913) and the Chicago Vice Commission's *Social Evil in Chicago* (1911).[9] Kimball and "Madeleine" dismissed the "white slave" scare from their perspective as retired madams, yet these women felt, with some justice, that in asking this question men sought to buy some essential part of themselves, not merely their bodies, and they lied accordingly. "Madeleine" comments:

I had yet to learn that lying was a part of the profession.... and I had yet to learn that every man's vanity, regardless of how casual his intercourse with "one of the girls" may be, leads him to expect that she shall take *him* into her confidence, and tell *him* the truth about her family affairs ... and why she is adventuring in the primrose way, though he is quite ready to concede her right to "conceal hersel', as weel's she can, frae critical dissection" on the part of others.[10]

In seeking to perform this dissection, writers like Crane, Phillips, and Dreiser place themselves simultaneously in two positions. As sympathetic interpreters, they function as social intermediaries, reaching an audience, in effect a market, otherwise inaccessible to the prostitute. But as questioners, they resemble the prostitute's customers, a role that the reader doubly reenacts by asking the question (why did this woman sell herself?) and by paying (buying the book) to have the question answered. In uncovering what the prostitute seeks to conceal, the transaction of storytelling recapitulates her exploitation via the fictional invasion of her privacy, even as the exposure of social evils (like the clients' money) in the short term benefits her.

By their sympathies, however, and above all in their position as human beings attempting to sell a commodity that represents some portion of themselves, naturalistic writers acknowledge their kinship to the fallen women they describe. Living close to the edge of starvation, Crane, Dreiser, and London understood the factory worker's or shop girl's losing struggle to make ends meet on $5.00 a week. They generally viewed her fall into prostitution as a matter of economic necessity—and, in the case of kept women like Carrie Meeber, economic good sense. With almost obsessive repetition, they chronicle the minutiae of her existence: the sixty cents that Dulcie, of O. Henry's "Unfinished Story," must pay out for supper each week; the foolishness of Carrie Meeber for spending $1.25 on an umbrella; the eighty cents a day on which Susan Lenox calculates she must learn to live. The difference between these women and characters such as Martin Eden, Vandover, and Hurstwood, all of whom also agonize over pennies, is that the men's poverty results from an act of choice, either a refusal to take better-paying work, like Martin Eden, or a willingness to drift, like Vandover and Hurstwood. For women, the choice is really no choice. Prostitution places them at risk, but no more so, argue the naturalists, than the only other possibility open to them: monotonous jobs at inadequate wages. Turning out collars and cuffs like Maggie (and like Roberta Alden of *An American Tragedy*), punching out shoe uppers like Carrie, or pasting boxes and sewing hats like Susan Lenox (and Lily Bart) all offer physical and emotional debilitation similar to that of prostitution, but with less prospect of tangible reward.

Despite the naturalists' sympathy, presenting a portrait of fallen women that, in Norris's terms, could be both accurate and true proved to be difficult. Local color writers like Jewett, Freeman, and Cooke envision storytelling, especially women's storytelling, as a communal activity, one that by strengthening the community's bonds also helps to protect the community and its members from the incursions of a hostile world. The prostitute, however, lives a life of isolation, for, as becomes clear in *Susan Lenox*, the independence, better pay, and shorter hours she gains from her "immoral" life distinguish her from the virtuously downtrodden women who teach their daughters to shun her. She thus cannot participate in a community's storytelling rituals, and indeed her only defense is to "hoard" her story as a means of preserving a sense of self. Thus, like their real life counterparts, the fictional fallen women resist telling their own stories; for example, Susan Lenox, "[l]ike all the girls in that life with a real story to tell ... never told about her past self."[11] Deprived of the female communities that comprise a legitimate market for circulating stories and entrapped into a one-way economy of male purchasers that can only consume their tales (and lives), the fallen women operate within a preservationist ethos that, like Trina McTeague's, isolates even as it sustains them.

This resistance to language can be seen in the most saintly of their number, the heroine of Dreiser's *Jennie Gerhardt* (1911). Jennie fears the consequences of having her story told, although she gives herself to men with the noblest of motives: to save her family. Her story in fact resembles the "usual lies men like to hear" of an innocent, unsuspecting girl ruined by an older man of superior class.[12] At the age of eighteen, Jennie is seduced by Senator Brander and subsequently bears his child. Later, she attracts the attention of Lester Kane, the son of a wealthy manufacturer. After two chapters filled with his family's and his social circle's badinage about his unmarried state, Lester's "mind wandered back to Jennie and her peculiar 'Oh, no, no!' *There* was someone who appealed to him. That was a type of womanhood worth while."[13] Expressing her objections in a nearly inarticulate form, Jennie appeals to Lester precisely because of her difference; her resistance both to language and to his sexual demands contrasts with the linguistic and social voracity of those at the Knowltons' coming-out party. Indeed, the incidents of Jennie's life revolve around the stories she fails to tell and the silences she maintains; she keeps her involvement with Senator Brander from her family; her involvement with

Lester from her father; her supposed marriage from the neighbors; her child, Vesta, from Lester.

Jennie is nonetheless a "good girl" (344) and a "good woman" (410) as her father and Lester, the two most judgmental men in the book, tell her on their respective deathbeds. Part of her goodness is signaled by her lack of original language. As Carol Schwartz observes in "*Jennie Gerhardt*: Fairy Tale as Social Criticism," "Lester speaks the language of natural determinism, Jennie that of the nineteenth-century sentimental heroine."[14] Jennie "possesses a world of feeling and emotion" (338) and is "an ideal mother," although "[s]he isn't quick at repartee" and "can't join in any rapid-fire conversation" (339). Not being "quick at repartee" signals her essential difference from her rival, Letty Pace, for, having no social wiles, she achieves the greater naturalistic virtue of sincerity. Jennie is deficient in the kinds of speech commonly valued but eloquent in the language of feeling and gesture that allows Lester's imagination free play in envisioning her as his ideal woman. As a "good woman" who paradoxically chooses silence as her weapon, however, Jennie cannot capitalize on her strengths. Indeed, when Lester praises Jennie to Letty Pace as a "good woman" (339), Letty is quick to seize the linguistic advantage to reframe his definition: "Why, Lester, if I were in her position, ... I would let you go. I would, truly. I think you know that I would. Any good woman would" (341). At Gerhardt's funeral shortly thereafter, Lester watches Jennie: "The woman's emotion was so deep, so real. 'There's no explaining a good woman,' he said to himself" (347). By objectifying Jennie in this manner, by encasing her within the narrowly defined parameters of womanly self-sacrifice, he comes a step closer to leaving her without, however, accepting Letty's judgment uncritically: "Was she as good as Jennie?" (369).[15] He chooses a woman with linguistic weapons whose fortune makes her a "weapon" in her own right, one who can help him to "repay an indifferent, chill, convention-ridden world with some sharp, bitter cuts of the power-whip" (361), whose fortune will be a "club to knock his enemies over the head" (369). By contrast, even the sexuality that paradoxically should mark Jennie as a "fallen," hence silent, woman is rendered harmless by her commonplace language and maternal, self-sacrificing emotions. In marrying Letty, Lester in effect forsakes the representative of the self-sacrificing goodness common to local color fiction for one epitomizing naturalistic force.

Like Jennie, Maggie Johnson of Crane's *Maggie: A Girl of the Streets* (1893) is passive and almost wholly reactive in her use of language. She early adopts a protective silence, first in sheltering her baby brother from their parents' violence, and later in distancing herself as much as possible from her environment. Her gestures of removing herself inevitably fail, as does her attempt at artistic expression, the creation of a lambrequin of "flowered cretonne." Maggie views it and "some faint attempts which she had made with blue ribbon" as an amelioration of the grim surroundings and the "dingy curtain" before which, metaphorically speaking, her life is being played out.[16] Decorating home rather than self marks Maggie as a good woman; however, Pete, her seducer, cannot read such fine distinctions. He gazes only at himself in the mirror when he comes to call, and he then vanishes "without having glanced at the lambrequin" (21), Maggie and mirror alike functioning merely as self-reflective panels for his narcissistic vision of himself as seducer. Similarly, Mrs. Johnson, a failed "good woman" and the symbolic first destroyer of her daughter's innocence, vents "some phase of drunken fury upon the lambrequin."[17] After her fury, the lambrequin is destroyed and "[t]he knots of blue ribbons appeared like violated flowers"(22)—not unlike Maggie herself, who "blossomed in a mud puddle" (17) before her final return, via suicide, to those other dirty waters, the oily surfaces of the river.[18]

Like Jennie, Maggie expresses herself through a combination of gestures, commonplace speech, and authorial descriptions of her feelings. With characteristic phrases like "dis is great" (23), she lacks the exaggeratedly correct grammar and diction of Nell, one of her rivals for Pete's affections: "Oh, it's not of the slightest consequence to me, my dear young man" (49). Her dilemma, like Jennie's, is that the inarticulateness that signifies her sincerity proves to be no match for the glib sophistry of her rival. In his linguistic analysis of *Maggie*, Alan Robert Slotkin comments that Nell's speech "displays an effort on her part to hide her background and to escape from it,"[19] an effort confirmed by Hapke's observation that many prostitutes saw their profession as a means of upward mobility.[20] Maggie's lack of volubility thus doubly condemns her, although for the most part her dialect can be attributed to Crane's representation of lower-class life; most of the characters in *Maggie* speak a language of dialect, oaths, and rampant clichés, over which Crane casts the irony that is his trademark. But the inarticulate quality of her exchanges, like that of Carrie Meeber's, serves also as a reminder of what she is and must be if she is to succeed at her profession: a receptive blank on which the fantasies of others can be played out.

Crane demonstrates this point in his description of "a girl of the painted cohorts" (52), presumably Maggie, walking the streets. After being cursed by her mother and cut off abruptly by Pete, her seducer, Maggie ends by being almost completely without words. Chapter 17 details her stroll through the streets, "giving smiling invitations to those of rural or untaught pattern and usually seeming sedately unconscious of the men with a metropolitan seal upon their faces" (52). During her walk, a polyglot assortment of men stare at her and answer her, though she does not speak: a "belated man in business clothes" tells her, "Brace up, old girl"; a young man with a "mocking smile" asks, "you don't mean to tell me that you sized me up for a farmer?"; a laborer wishes her "a fine evenin'"; a drunken man, more direct than the others, roars, "I ain' ga no money, dammit" (53); a "huge fat man" with "brown, disordered teeth gleaming under a grey, grizzled moustache from which the beer-drops dripped" chuckles and leers as he wordlessly follows her to the silence of the river (53). Each reads upon her face an invitation or a threat that he himself has inscribed there, for her profession operates in a semiotic system that has less to do with words than with the written language of the paint on her face. Quite literally, her body speaks for her. Only once does she actually speak to any of the men, hailing a "man with blotched features" (53). Their exchange—"Ah, there." ... "I've got a date"—demonstrates that her words are not only neutral but irrelevant. Assuming the mantle of silence and blankness, she can express herself only within the constraints of her body and her status as a prostitute. Maggie, in retreating into silence, makes a fatal mistake. She has recreated not only her body but her personality as a surface for inscription and interpretation by others—Pete, her mother, men on the street—and as such her silence is not self-protective, but self-negating.

By contrast, when Carrie Meeber adapts to her surroundings and the men with whom she associates, her behavior is not self-negating but self-defining, as critics have noted. Although she does not sell herself on the streets as Maggie or Susan Lenox do, she operates on the same basic principle of presenting herself as a surface upon which Hurstwood and Drouet can inscribe their fantasies. This process is most evident in their response to her performance in *Under the Gaslight*, when each man invests the words she speaks with a significance that he alone can appreciate: "The manager suffered [her speech] as a personal appeal. It came to him as if they were alone.... Drouet also was beside himself. He was resolving that he would be to Carrie what he had never been before."[21] The part Carrie plays multiplies the layers of concealment. As Laura, a "lissome figure, draped in pearl gray" (190), she is a society woman hiding her past as a juvenile pickpocket; when her past is revealed, she exposes a spiritual nobility through her willingness to sacrifice her own happiness for the sake of others. Like Woolson's Madam Carroll in *For the Major*, Carrie, as the character Laura, enacts the local color virtues of self-denial and self-sacrifice beneath her disguise as a society woman. In her equally fictive incarnation as "Carrie

Madenda," however, Carrie chooses self-interest over self-sacrifice, renouncing generations of local color heroines bound by duty to enfeebled older family members with her curt note to Hurstwood: "I'm going away. I'm not coming back any more" (439). Not surprisingly, Hurstwood fails to note that the "pale face" that charms him is made so by an artificial "touch of blue under the eyes," and that the pearls are "imitation" (190); instead, he and Drouet interpret Laura's story as an emotional gloss on Carrie's own, and they invest Carrie herself with romance. By contrast, Carrie's background, which she does not reveal, is decidedly prosaic. Philip Fisher comments perceptively on this scene and the potent connections it establishes between acting, sex, and commerce:

> The sexualized quality of acting, protected as it is by fantasy and the barrier of the stage that separates the beloved actress from the numerous fantasizing suitors in the audience repeats the paradox mentioned earlier that sheltered within the fiction of her role the actress sells precisely the vitality of her personality.... Acting involves primarily in Dreiser not deception but practice, not insincerity but installment payments on the world of possibility.[22]

Selling herself from a position of relative control, preserving the "fiction of her role," is exactly what the protective conventions implied by the open frame of the proscenium arch allow Carrie to do, thereby avoiding both extremes: the constraints of marriage and the limitless consumption of self implied by prostitution.[23]

A further instance of Carrie's self-protective instincts occurs in one of her later plays. Her wordless frown as the "little Quakeress" evokes a response much like that of Maggie's patrons or Lester Kane: "The portly gentlemen in the front rows began to feel that she was a delicious little morsel. It was the kind of frown they would have loved to force away with kisses" (447). Although this scene appears late in the novel, her appearance as the frowning Quakeress provides a key to her appeal. Her silence, in fact, echoes that of the prostitutes like Madeleine: as a sexualized woman enacting innocence, she projects resistance, not capitulation—the "usual lies men like to hear." "As the Quaker maid, demure and dainty" (459), Carrie is clad once again in gray, the neutral background color for her admirers' fantasies in *Under the Gaslight*, as she recapitulates the "parlor acting" of the prostitute. Further, her Quakeress garb recalls the standardized costumes of lost innocence in houses like Nell Kimball's, emphasizing as it does her status as an unwritten page of innocence upon which the male text of sexuality can be written "with kisses." Too, throughout most of her encounters with Drouet and Hurstwood she maintains a stance of resisting or denying their various claims, a stance that is at once self-protective for her and arousing for the men ("it was the kind of frown they would have loved to force away with kisses"). Like "Madeleine," Carrie allows the men in her life to make up their own version of what her story (and consequently her real self) must be while maintaining a separate version that she never tells. She resists interpretation and saves herself.[24]

Making a virtue of their heroines' verbal passivity, Crane and Dreiser draw their fallen women as figures of dimensions more complex than their utterances would suggest. Both men allow indeterminacy to help shape their characters, trusting to the reader's curiosity about the character, and especially about answering the "question" of her story, to help maintain his engagement with the work. On the other hand, pinning down a character to a few specific dimensions, as David Graham Phillips attempts to do in *Susan Lenox: Her Fall and Rise* (1911; published 1917), risks violating the prostitute's principle of refusing to tell her story. It helps to reduce her to a more simplistic figure, hence one more vulnerable to conventional moral judgments. Born out of wedlock and forced into an arranged marriage, Susan runs away from Cincinnati to New York, where she survives by alternating between what Phillips scornfully calls "honest toil"—making boxes, singing on a showboat and in cheap restaurants, modeling clothes—and prostitution. Like Carrie Meeber, she becomes a successful actress, a profession that translates into respectable terms the lessons in advantageous use of men's imaginations that each had learned as a fallen woman.

In some ways, Susan is a naturalistic test case, within whom heredity, early training, and present environment battle continually:

> One of the strongest factors in Susan's holding herself together ...
> was the nearly seventeen years of early training her Aunt Fanny
> Warham had given her.... Susan Lenox had been trained to order
> and system, and they had become part of her being, beyond the
> power of drink and opium and prostitution to disintegrate them.
> [2:255]

Unlike Dreiser, who insisted that one's inner biological system of "chemisms" such as "catastases" and "metastases" inexorably determined outward behavior, Phillips believed strongly that preserving the outer man or woman through exercise, good food, and even, as in *Old Wives for New* (1908), plastic surgery could stave off both physical and moral decay. By keeping physically healthy, then, Susan demonstrates her steadfast commitment to a higher goal. Her ambitions, as Louis Filler describes them, are "provokingly plain: to do useful work, and to be free to do whatever she liked."[25] But Phillips, despite his seven years of earnest work on the novel, tries to reduce Susan's character to a few simple, and endlessly repeated, traits of behavior: she refuses to explain herself or tell her story; her greatest wish is to be both free and strong; she neither dissembles nor lies, speaking up frequently to her own detriment; like George du Maurier's Trilby, she has beautiful feet and is admired for them; her eyes turn grey when she is businesslike, violet when she is moved emotionally. In spelling out the expressions and interpreting them for the reader, Phillips fails to allow Susan to retain the indeterminate air of wistful melancholy that constitutes Carrie's appeal for her audience—the mouth that appears "about to cry," the "pathetic" shadow about her eyes (*Sister Carrie*, 484). As Ames tells Carrie, "You and I are but mediums, through which something is expressing itself. Now, our duty is to make ourselves ready mediums" (485). In reducing Susan's position as a "ready medium" through his "critical dissection" of her into discrete parts, Phillips breaks the code of her profession and damages the "truth" of his character in the process.

### III

If the naturalists proved sympathetic to fallen women, they heaped heavy scorn upon the convention-bound type of girl whom H. H. Boyesen had damned as the "Iron Madonna," a phrase suggesting both her intransigence and the iconlike status granted to her by worshipers and detractors alike. Cowardice separates this type from the New Women of London and Norris. In Norris's *Vandover and the Brute*, for example, Turner Ravis at first appears to be a courageous New Woman. As Don Graham notes, she is not straitlaced: on the contrary, she joins with Vandover, Ellis, and the others in drinking beer, eating tamales, and playing cards. But Turner shows her true colors when Vandover begins to disintegrate. Instead of attempting to save him, as Norris and his character Vandover believe good women should do, she deserts him after the Ida Wade affair. After Vandover is snubbed at a society dance, Geary explains the real problem: "It's that business with Ida Wade.... It got around somehow that she killed herself on your account."[26] Earlier, Vandover, Geary, and Haight had bemoaned society's unwillingness to chastise its erring members; in getting caught, however, Vandover has transgressed the most important law of all and suffers the consequences that he did not think existed. Meeting him at the library one afternoon, Turner explains that he does not love her enough; girls "really love the man who loves them most" (458), and she believes Vandover incapable of this kind of regard. She ends with a pep talk, telling Vandover to "live up to the best that's in you" (459), and disappears from his life, taking up first with Dolly Haight and then finally, opportunistically, with the amoral but successful Charlie Geary. In other words, she has sold herself. From Norris's perspective, she has deserted Vandover and abnegated one of the highest and noblest functions of a "man's woman": the saving of a weak man through her good influence.

Jack London's *Martin Eden* (1909), a more sustained attack, resembles both Norris's *Blix* (1899) and *Vandover and the Brute* in its broad outlines, including the portrait of a young artist struggling both to find love and to remain true to his art. *Martin Eden* is also a novel of degeneration. Like Vandover, who destroys himself through an excessive love of civilization and its comforts, Martin demands more from his culture than it can possibly provide until, surfeited with its material pleasures and sickened by the absence of spiritual ones, he commits suicide. Through his spiritual malaise and his viewing suicide as an act of self-affirmation, Martin additionally resembles Dick Heldar, the hero of Kipling's artist novel, *The Light That Failed* (1891), as in some ways the conventional Ruth Morse recalls Maisie, Dick's talentless and restrictive foster sister-lover. Beyond these superficial parallels, in *Martin Eden* London launches a wholesale assault on the legend of good women current in his day. From the unlettered Martin's first awestruck visit to the Morse home to his final disdainful departure from it, the novel demonstrates the destructive influence of a feminine culture in which weak men like Arthur, Ruth's brother and pander, survive, while strong, stalwart men like Martin must perish.

The novel's origins are largely autobiographical, as London readily acknowledged. Writing to Anna Strunsky in 1901, London explained his attraction to Mabel Applegarth, his onetime fiancée and the prototype of Ruth Morse:

> It was a great love. But see! Time passed. I grew. I saw immortality fade from her. Saw her only woman.... She was pure, honest, true, sincere, everything. But she was small.... Her culture was a surface smear, her deepest depth a singing shallow.... I awoke, and judged, and my puppy love was over.[27]

The stages of London's disillusionment parallel the experiences of his protagonist, Martin Eden, and in creating Ruth, London initially seems to provide for his readers a conventional love interest for Martin and a wealthy, cultured, feminine figure to contrast with his rough, unlettered hero. Instead, the story pivots on Ruth, who carries within her statically conceived notion of culture the seeds for her own destruction. Martin's increasing discontent with her and with her view of culture parallels and informs that of the reader.

The first chapter of the book establishes the series of antitheses between Martin Eden and the middle-class culture that first ignores, then celebrates, and finally defeats him. The epitome of this culture is Ruth Morse, "a pale, ethereal creature, with wide, spiritual blue eyes and a wealth of golden hair."[28] Her spirituality and "Anglo-Saxon" beauty, so beloved by Norris and London, evoke for Martin visions of the other sorts of women he has known, women darker and more sexual, from "Eurasians ... stamped with degeneracy" and "full-bodied South-Sea-Island women, flower-crowned and brown-skinned" to the "grotesque and terrible nightmare brood" of Whitechapel prostitutes (6–7).[29] Ruth and Martin become aware not only of the contrast that the other represents, but simultaneously of a lack within themselves. They busily invest each other with the missing admirable traits: Martin worships Ruth as "Iseult," heroine of romance and intellectual high priestess, and she speculates on the great strength and vitality (and forbidden sexuality) promised by the phallicism of his "muscular neck, heavy corded, almost bull-like, bronzed by the sun" (11). What each will come to realize, of course, is that the culture and sexuality that each seeks is no route to salvation. Martin's extreme response to Ruth, however, is consistent with his bipolar thinking, and he maintains both physical vigor and intellectual curiosity as long as he oscillates between two points of contrast.[30] Ironically, as long as he struggles to find a place of permanence for himself, his vitality is unimpaired, but, as his beloved Spencer and Darwin would suggest to him, in static "being" rather than in dynamic "becoming" he faces only entropy, disintegration, and death. When the reality and his visions of the ideal coincide near the end of the novel, he ceases to exist.

Throughout the novel, Martin's intellectual maturity can be gauged by the degree of divergence between his view of Ruth and ours. London employs a dual perspective in describing her: the unlettered Martin is initially dazzled by her, although London's narrator and the reader are considerably less easily impressed. When Martin's disdain for her limitations parallels that of the reader and narrator, we understand that he has grown up at last. During her very first meeting with Martin, Ruth disapproves of Swinburne, whom even Martin's unlettered eye can see is "great," because, she says, "he is, well, indelicate. There are many of his poems that should never be read" (10). Her system of social morality determines her standards of literary value. The doubt that London casts over Ruth's understanding of literature coincides with Martin's later judgment (akin to Norris's) that she and her brothers "had been studying about life from the books while he had been busy living life" (25). When Martin reads her his story "The Plot," a story of "the big thing out of life ... not sentence-structure and semicolons" (104), she is "gripped" and "mastered" by it. Her only response is nevertheless wholly consistent with the stuffy views of one who had condemned Swinburne: "Oh! It is degrading! It is not nice! It is nasty! ... Why didn't you select a nice subject? ... We know there are nasty things in the world, but that is no reason—" (105). Ruth believes that art should be divorced from life; moreover, she dislikes literature that masters her, preferring instead to retain the mastery over literature granted by her role as feminine arbiter of culture.

The essence of the relationship between Ruth and Martin is, in fact, a struggle for control, a masochistic reversal of Pygmalion and Galatea in which the statue "kills" first his creator and then himself.[31] Willingly ceding the power of good influence to Ruth, Martin seeks to reestablish himself in her eyes and his own as an ideal man of her class. Her reading of Browning has not taught her that "it was an awkward thing to play with souls" (60), and she works with a vengeance at molding Martin's. Like Letty Pace of *Jennie Gerhardt* and Mrs. Kelcey of *George's Mother*, Ruth turns out to be a woman with weapons. When she plays the piano for him, "[h]er music was a club that swung brutally upon his head; and though it stunned him and crushed him down, it incited him" (20). Similarly, "[h]er purity smote him like a blow" (20). Once Martin is properly bludgeoned into submission, Ruth attempts "to re-thumb the clay of him into a likeness of her father's image, which image she believed to be the finest in the world" (59); her methods, and London's images, grow gentler. She "played to him—no longer at him— and probed him with music that sank to depths beyond her plumb-line" (59) much as Celia Madden, another cultured woman, seduces the ignorant Theron Ware. Here as elsewhere, London's narrator continually undercuts not only Ruth's mastery of culture but Martin's uncritical appreciation of her limited gifts. Though an imperfect interpreter of her culture, she remains a satisfactory vehicle for its transmission, in part because her obvious intellectual limitations render inevitable the moment of his disillusionment with her shallow standards.

Martin's disillusionment with genteel standards progresses through a tightening circle of denunciation scenes; his first occurs when he displaces his considerable wrath at genteel standards onto the magazine editors.

Through his voracious reading, the naive Martin discovers early on that "the immense amount of printed stuff ... was dead" (99) and begins "to doubt that editors were real men. They seemed cogs in a machine" (100). As Martin's passionately cynical friend Brissenden tells him, they favor "wish-wash and slush" (235), not guts, and the "magazine rhymesters" that they publish are effectively "a band of eunuchs" (235). London's worst insults vilify the "dead" literature itself and question the manhood of the editors. They are not rough, virile red-bloods with a taste for real life, like Martin, but pale mollycoddles upholding feminine standards. Discovering that editors match intellectual with fiscal dishonesty, Martin, in a scene reminiscent of one in *The Light That Failed*, tries unsuccessfully to collect payment for an article appearing in the *Transcontinental*. His editors resist until, like Dick Heldar, he threatens them with "red-blood" bodily harm. His friend Russ Brissenden, an intellectual whose cynicism and quest after sensual beauty identify him with the mood of fin de siècle decadence, refuses altogether to allow such riffraff to judge his work, preferring obscurity to their adulation. Fittingly, the worst moment for Martin thus occurs when the editors fawn with "cheapness and vulgarity" (289) over "Ephemera," Brissenden's exquisitely pessimistic poem, which Martin submits for publication after Brissenden commits suicide.

Moving closer to the source of meretricious values, at Ruth's dinner party Martin takes on the social system that allows such tyranny and shoddy dealings. Even though his fierce determination to be published leads him into writing formula fiction from his self-devised "story chart," Martin despises the editorial cabal that forces him into such expedients. The editors, he says, are backed up in their judgments by a man who (like Howells) is "the Dean of American criticism" and one of "the two foremost literary critics in the United States.... Yet I read his stuff, and it seems to me the perfection of the felicitous expression of the inane" (169). Having disposed of his Howells-substitute, Martin next excoriates the "English professors—little, microscopic-minded parrots!" (169). The old literature is dead, entombed and enshrined, and its unjust preservation by Vanderwater and his acolytes constitutes a crime against writers of "real life" like Martin Eden and Jack London.

London uses the image of the dinner party, and indeed food in general, as both a structural device within the novel and a metaphor for Martin's ravenous need for knowledge and approval from the culture that excludes him. Beyond money, Martin wishes to have his own judgment of his literary gift vindicated. He hungers for it, in fact. The dried apricots, rice, and beans that he cooks so excellently well in his room cannot nourish him, as his belief in himself cannot sustain him, without occasional infusions of food/praise from others. Although Martin does not realize it, he commits the same mistake as Mr. Butler, whose entrepreneurial drive Ruth has urged him to emulate: for the sake of a fanatically felt passion, he destroys his appetite for life through intensive privation. Dinner parties function as occasions for Martin to assimilate the ideas, particularly contrasting ideas, that strike him, whether he is gratefully receiving soup from Maria, his landlady, or sharing candy with her children; feeling out of place at a workers' picnic with Lizzie, his lower-class friend; feeding cherries to Ruth; or arguing ideas over a bottle with Brissenden. At his first dinner party at the Morses' residence, for example, he recognizes his own cultural deficiencies, whereas at his final dinner party at their house, he comes to understand that the deficiencies are theirs, not his: "To real literature, real painting, real music, the Morses and their kind, were dead" (213). Like the editors that print dead literature, the Morses are less alive than the soon-to-be suicide, Martin. Later in the novel, surfeited with fame, effort, and life generally, he will decline both adulation and food when he refuses an invitation to the captain's table on the ship, an action that signals his imminent suicide.

As Martin's language of food refers metonymically to spiritual nourishment, so Ruth's language figures economic exchange. Despising the expedients of pawnshops and gas ring cookery that he is driven to by his poverty, Ruth tries to turn Martin variously into a capitalist like Mr. Butler, a lawyer, and a clerk in her father's business. Her entire answer to the problems that Martin encounters in publishing his work is to hold up the popular magazines as correct judges of success: magazine writers, she tells Martin, "sell [their stories], and you—don't" (225). Later, becoming annoyed, she challenges his determination:

> "But why do you persist in writing such things when you know they won't sell?" she went on inexorably. "The reason for your writing is to make a living, isn't it?"
>
> "Yes, that's right; but the miserable story got away with me. I couldn't help writing it. It demanded to be written."
>
> "But that character, that Wiki-Wiki, why do you make him talk so roughly? Surely it will offend your readers, and surely that is why the editors are justified in refusing your work."
>
> "Because the real Wiki-Wiki would have talked that way."
>
> "But it is not good taste." [248]

Martin speaks of literary power, of passion felt and communicated; Ruth counters with "good taste," coded language for the ability to sell, in effect to prostitute, that literary passion. The connection between sex and money becomes explicit when Ruth learns that Martin has passed the Railway Mail civil service exam and still will not get a job. Hitherto she has expressed a healthy physical passion for him in a gesture evocative both of affection and of strangulation: "[S]he reached up and placed both hands upon Martin Eden's sunburnt neck. So exquisite was the pang of love and desire fulfilled that she uttered a low moan, relaxed her hands, and lay half-swooning in his arms" (149–50). Now, however, she proves "a passive sweetheart" when Martin kisses her; the erotic charge of Martin's neck, it seems, owes more to the testimony it provides about his ability to work, to function in the marketplace, than to his own sexual power.

The final chapters of the novel describe Martin's growing emancipation from Ruth and from the dominance of feminine discourse that she represents. The truly terrible corollary of the Iron Madonna's power, London implies, is not just that she deludes herself about the benefits of what she does, but that she creates such havoc under the guise of doing good. Although his determination to educate himself arises from within, Ruth gives Martin his first taste of culture, proffering the apple of the false Tree of Knowledge that ever after makes his old, lower-class existence impossible. Her sincerity does not mitigate the pernicious effects of her destructive influence, and the nihilism in Martin to which she has unwittingly contributed works against her at the last. His final renunciation scene occurs when, tired finally of fame, wealth, and all else he had sought, Martin refuses Ruth when she offers to renew their engagement, recognizing only now that he has never loved her. Ruth then volunteers to come to him "in free love if you will" (330). Martin, however, remains unmoved, for he realizes that the love she offers is anything but "free." Unlike the working-class Lizzie, whose unconditional love for the uncultured Martin critiques Ruth's mercenary ethos, Ruth craves his success and his royalties more than she wants the man himself. Yet as Martin himself realizes, his knowledge of the world of culture has rendered a relationship with Lizzie impossible. Recognizing that he had loved "an idealized Ruth ... an ethereal creature of his own creating" (329), he now can appreciate neither the real lower-class woman whom Lizzie represents nor the real, if mercenary, woman that Ruth has become.

The price of Martin's emancipation from Ruth, then, is cultural anomie and a Pyrrhic victory. Too spiritually depleted to relish the irony in Ruth's humiliation, he nonetheless has exposed the Iron Madonna for what she really is, for Ruth, that bastion of purity who even when she propositions Martin tells him not to swear, has been reduced to a position lower than that of Lizzie and the other girls who equate sex with love. She has agreed, with her family's consent, to barter sex for money, just as Turner Ravis does. The Iron Madonna thus not only forfeits all credibility as a cultural arbiter but becomes in moral terms no better than Maggie Johnson, Susan Lenox, and the other street girls; indeed, in terms of the naturalists' morality, she offers to sell herself with far less excuse than the others, since she need not do so in order to survive. With her much vaunted critical judgment discredited and her claims to idealism and physical purity proven to be a sham, Ruth, and by implication the Iron Madonna, has nothing left. By revealing the shallowness and limitations of her values, by reducing, reinventing, and parodying her, London destroys the Iron Madonna's image of herself, and with that image her power.

IV

Stephen Crane's short novel *George's Mother* (1896) explores further limitations of the "good woman" and her weapons. Like *Vandover and the Brute*, it is the story of a weak man's reaction, or lack of reaction, to the external and internal forces that cause his degeneration.[32] In his introduction to the Virginia edition, James B. Colvert speculates that *George's Mother* "was conceived as a response to Crane's 'literary fathers,'" since it is "a study in the psychology of moral deprivation, more subdued than *Maggie* and less conspicuously concentrated in execution.... in short, the kind of realistic novel Howells or Garland might write."[33] One might add that, with its emphasis on moral deprivation, its depiction of ordinary life for a mother and son only three years removed from a small town, and its unsparing look at the effects of an excess of unexamined virtues, the novel also indirectly recalls the local color tradition that Howells approved and Garland defended. In *George's Mother* Crane does not side with the meliorists of that tradition; he resembles rather those who, like Mary Wilkins Freeman and Rose Terry Cooke, cast a critical eye on either the motives or the good sense of those who represent traditional Christianity and conventional virtues. For the most part, however, the novel stands as Crane's ironic commentary on the destructive power of a good woman's saving influence. With unassailable virtue and the best of intentions, Mrs. Kelcey unwittingly drives George from comparative respectability into the pointless existence of a street drifter.

Within the first few chapters Crane presents the opposing choices open to George Kelcey: saloon and street corner, home and church. Also introduced is the repeated pattern of rejection and helpless entanglement that characterizes George's relationship with his mother. Hailed by the men at the "little smiling saloon," George stays past suppertime drinking beer; his mother, sensing a change in him, asks him to "come t'prayermeetin'" with her.[34] George, annoyed by the request, uneasily excuses himself ("it wouldn't do me no good t'go if I didn't wanta go" [124]) and heads once again for the saloon. This pattern of mild misbehavior-confrontation-worse misbehavior recurs throughout the novel. The cycle establishes George's life as following the classic naturalistic downward spiral into degradation and thus forms a basic structural element.

Although Crane had originally entitled the novel "A Woman without Weapons," Mrs. Kelcey in fact has several in her arsenal: fanatical housekeeping, right beliefs, and a sharp tongue. Pointing her broom "lance-wise, at dust demons," she raises her voice "in a long cry, a strange war chant, a shout of battle and defiance" (120) as she cleans the house. Other weapons include Mrs. Kelcey's misplaced confidence in George and herself. She believes that "she must be a model mother to have such a son" (133), a son who "was going to become a white and looming king among men" (135). To control George, she tries various methods, including coaxing "him with caresses" (124), giving him a "martyr-like glance" (125), nagging at him about swearing and drinking (as Ruth Morse does with Martin Eden), and finally, on her deathbed when her mind regresses in time, failing to recognize him at all, presumably because he has fallen so far from the "Georgie" whom she tries to call in from the fields.

Weapons or no, Mrs. Kelcey begins to lose the battle right from the start, as George slips away from the feminine realm of stability and virtue to the masculine world of the saloon. If Mrs. Kelcey's weapons and beliefs allude to medieval romance, as Brennan suggests, surely George's thoughts refer equally strongly to classical epic, or rather mock-epic tradition. The saloon scenes, with their focus on drinking, stories, and the camaraderie of men, provide the most direct classical allusions. On his first visit, for example, George meets Bleecker, who, sensing the boy's admiration, extends himself: "Directly, then, he launched forth into a tale of by-gone days, when the world was better. He had known all the great men of that age.... He rejoiced at the glory of the world of dead spirits. He grieved at the youth and flippancy of the present one" (126–27). The tales of great men in a mythic golden age, the allusion to an (under)world of dead spirits, the *ubi sunt* tone of the whole—all these suggest epic tradition, even if, as here, the tradition is parodied through its association with a group of drunks in a Bowery saloon. The men seek consolation from a "grinding world filled with men who were harsh," and they find it in the "chorus of violent sympathy" (128) with which they greet each other's stories. Like George, they believe that "they were fitted for a tree-shaded land, where everything was peace" (129), recalling perhaps Odysseus's lotus-eaters on Circe's island. Such a belief conflicts directly with the aims of women like Mrs. Kelcey, whose creaking hymn and "war-chant" addresses the same rhetorical question:

> "Should I be car-reed tew th' skies
> O-on flow'ry be-eds of ee-ease,
> While others fought tew win th' prize
> An' sailed through blood-ee seas." [119]

Her answer, and the church's answer, is of course a resounding "no." Battling to win the prize of salvation, not "ease," is the purpose of life on earth.

George's initiation into the world of men occurs during the feast at Bleecker's lodgings. In analyzing initiation rites from what an 1897 *North American Review* article called "the Golden Age of Fraternity," Mark Carnes provides a framework for interpreting George's initiation. Carnes found the rituals' models of "liminality," "extended allegor[ies] involving personal development," and "emotionally charged psychodrama[s] centering on family relations" to have a specific function in their practitioners' re-creation of a primitive past:

> Restated in gender-role terms, the dilemma for boys in Victorian America was not simply that their fathers were absent ... but that adult gender roles were invariant and narrowly defined, and that boys were mostly taught the sensibilities and moral values associated with the adult female role.... As young men, they were drawn to the male secret orders, where they repeatedly practiced rituals that effaced the religious values and emotional ties associated with women.[35]

George's initiation follows a similar pattern, and Crane again evokes the world of ancient epic as a means of heightening its ritualistic qualities. The "feast" of beer, whiskey, and pipes is carefully laid out upon a table resembling a "primitive bar" (142) so that the feast becomes an exalted version of their nightly rendezvous at the saloon. The audience listens raptly when, "in rapid singsong" like that of traditional bards (144), the symbolically named Zeusentell recites his ridiculous saga "Patrick Clancy's Pig." After the recitation, the members hurl the drunken George into a corner "and pile chairs and tables upon him" (149), suggesting the symbolic executions common to fraternal initiation rituals, after which the epic games commence with ritual wrestling, degraded here to a "great old mill" between

Zeusentell and O'Connor (151). The religious quality of their meeting is reinforced by the image of "lazy cloud-banks" (143) of tobacco smoke "from which the laughter arose like incense. He knew that old sentiment of brotherly regard for those about him.... He was capable of heroisms" (146). Having undergone a ritual initiation into the world of men, George deludes himself that he has found a heroic brotherhood that will provide an escape from his mother's demands.

By contrast, the church meeting he attends with his mother offers ritual with no feeling of brotherhood. When Kelcey enters the comfortably dim saloon, he is greeted by a sympathetic brotherhood of men; but the "riot of lights" in the church highlight the judgmental "multitudinous pairs of eyes that turned toward him ... implacable in their cool valuations" (156). The "indefinable presence" that pervades the altar makes him brood as the "portentous black figure" of the beer keg in the saloon never does, although the latter is more to blame for his downfall. The minister preaches a sermon, and the churchgoers, like the men at the saloon, tell stories, "little tales of religious faith" (157), but Kelcey, "not familiar with their types," chooses to understand only that he is damned. The saloon, by cementing brotherhood and fostering heroic action, replaces the church in George's mind. With his fallible judgment, George ironically never perceives his total inability to sustain this brotherhood or to act heroically.

His initiation into the saloon world of "heroic" men tips the balance of his descent into degeneration. When George loses his job and is thereby barred from the men's world of the saloon, he finds an acceptable substitute in the company of street toughs led by Fidsey Corcoran and his gang. The forms are less courtly, but the message is the same: drink and its ritual sharing, consisting of standing the others to rounds of drinks at the saloon, or taking turns ("smokes") at a pail of beer in the vacant lot, differentiates the men's world from the women's. The distinction between "real men" and "Willieboys" that so occupied Gelett Burgess, Theodore Roosevelt, and the naturalists is never more evident than in this slum setting. Passing the vacant lot, George refuses Fidsey's repeated offers to share a pail of beer:

> Kelcey turned dejectedly homeward. "Oh, I guess not, this roun'."
>
> "What's d' matter wi'che?" said Fidsey. "Yer gittin t' be a reg'lar willie. Come ahn, I tell ye!" [172]

When the others drink too much, Fidsey again condemns them with what is apparently a dreaded epithet: "'Look what yeh lef'us! Ah, say, youse

was a dandy! What 'a yeh tink we ah? Willies?'" (173). Clearly, effeminate
Willieboys don't drink the way real men do, and Fidsey repeats the term in
its shortened form—"Wille"—as though it is a favored and deadly insult
needing no explanation. Requiring no further impetus, Kelcey drinks his
share. The boastful heroism of the saloon reasserts itself, and when Blue
Billie demands, "Did youse say yeh could do me?" Kelcey, newly rebaptized
"Kel," growls, "Well, what if I did?" (174). The fight is postponed because
George's mother calls for him on her deathbed, a temporary retreat into the
woman's world of his mother's ordered flat. From the world of epic grandeur
and brotherhood evoked by the saloon habitués, George has sunk to a
narrowly averted fight with Blue Billie and the other street toughs. Only
guilt remains of his mother's teachings, a legacy that leaves him singularly
unfit to survive.

Crane's use of mock epic obscures but does not conceal a very real
concern with the place of courage and right action in such a world. Mrs.
Kelcey *is* courageous. She battles unceasingly for the welfare of herself and
her son, calling into play those virtues—cleanliness, family loyalty, self-
sacrifice—that should secure for her a degree of success in the small-town
world from whence she moved to the city. Yet these virtues do not work for
her in a naturalistic environment. Her cleanliness becomes a pointless
exercise, her faith in George a delusion, her self-sacrifice a snare to prevent
his leaving her and to delay the necessary process of his individuation. Local
color virtues cannot save a woman who, like Wharton's Bunner sisters, fails
to see the truth of the naturalistic world surrounding her.[36] Not only has her
limited arsenal of virtues failed, but the environment conspires to deprive her
of her ability to dominate George. In unfilial revolt, George blurts out the
true state of affairs between them when Mrs. Kelcey admonishes him for
swearing: "Whatter ye goin' t' do 'bout it?" (167). The fact of her economic
dependence thus brought home, she "threw out her hands in the gesture of
an impotent one ... as if she had survived a massacre in which all that she
loved had been torn from her by the brutality of savages" (167). George,
whose brutishness, like Vandover's, results from his drinking, has thus
"massacred" her illusion that virtue counts. Set adrift by a world of
transience and inverted values, one physically as well as symbolically
dominated by the "machine of mighty strength" (120) that is the brewery,
George's mother learns that all along she has been a woman without
weapons. Like her blowzy, drunken neighbor Mrs. Johnson of *Maggie: A Girl
of the Streets*, she is helpless to control her child. Even Mrs. Kelcey's death
does not ensure her victory, since the final vision is of George, staring at the
wallpaper with his "nerveless arms [allowing] his fingers to sweep the floor"

(177) in one of naturalism's characteristic trance scenes. Rather than attempting to integrate elements of the men's world with his mother's, George settles for the dichotomy of moral absolutes and ends up a failure both in his mother's terms (the church) and his own (the spurious heroism of the saloon). Attempting to be independent, he has degenerated into a street tough; attempting to save him and recognizing her defeat, she dies. In a world that values neither her efforts nor his, both are failures.

Nor does the irrelevance of a good woman's virtues render George's choices any easier. George faces a different problem from that of his mother: her impossible task was to impose a set of prescribed moral values on an actively hostile environment. George, on the other hand, confronts a shifting and uncertain world with few absolutes save those based on opposition to his mother. Following the code of the street and saloon, he becomes for his mother a bad provider and a "wild son"; yet he prefers those consequences to the far more dreadful fate of having the men on the street question his manhood and condemn him as a "Willie." Only one force can efface the "good woman's" moral apothegms: the swaggering linguistic fearlessness of the Jimmie Johnsons, Blue Billies, and, in the future, George Kelceys of Hester Street. As a gesture not of hopelessness but of nihilistic defiance, "Wot de hell!" infuses *Maggie* and *George's Mother* with a kind of anarchic energy. The phrase functions also as a charm, an incantation against the literary world's supercilious and too-proper ways. Crane uses it in his fiction as if he relished its power to deflate pretenses, as if the victory belongs not just to his characters but to himself. Through language, a self-described "frail boy" like Crane (or George) can escape the world of Willieboys and participate in the masculine pursuits of "real life."

## V

According to Eric Solomon, "In Stephen Crane's own judgment, *The Monster* was his best novel."[37] Solomon places it in the tradition of unsentimental small-town satires begun by Edward Eggleston's *Hoosier Schoolmaster* (1871), E. W. Howe's *Story of a Country Town* (1883), and Joseph Kirkland's *Zury: The Meanest Man in Spring County* (1887), a tradition continued by such writers as Edwin Arlington Robinson, Sherwood Anderson, and Sinclair Lewis (178–79). The story tells of two outcasts: Henry Johnson, an African-American hostler horribly disfigured when he rescues his employer's son from a fire; and Dr. Trescott, who, grateful for Henry's action, undertakes to protect him against the town's outrage at his mutilated presence. In one sense, *The Monster* combines a broad message of alienation and an attack on hypocrisy, for, as Thomas Gullason points out, "the monster is society, and it becomes the anti-heroic central character only after Henry's tragedy."[38]

Like *George's Mother*, *The Monster* demonstrates that "the prescribed virtues of honesty, good intentions, and a sense of obligation"[39] are insufficient protection against the fluctuating, violent, naturalistic world of the New York slums, but Crane's readers would have anticipated the absence, not the presence, of virtues in such surroundings. Within the conventions of each genre, the slum literature of naturalism could present the grotesque and horrifying because it promised its readers the safety of economic distance, just as local color fiction, through its use of village life and a nostalgic recent past, assured its public that outrageous or violent human behavior was beyond its geographic and symbolic scope of representation. *The Monster* shocks precisely because Crane, by intermingling them, undercuts the safety implied by both genres. Two years before *The Monster* was published, Frank Norris wrote of the essential element in naturalistic fiction:

> Terrible things must happen to the characters of the naturalistic tale. They must be twisted from the ordinary, wrenched out from the quiet, uneventful round of every-day life, and flung into the throes of a vast and terrible drama that works itself out in unleashed passions, in blood, and in sudden death ... no teacup tragedies here.[40]

The mutilated Henry Johnson ("a thing, a dreadful thing") functions as a destabilizing influence cast into the seemingly secure but actually fragile social structure of the town.[41] His presence, together with Dr. Trescott's obstinate and heroic defense of him, simultaneously wrenches the townspeople from their "quiet, uneventful round of everyday life" and reveals the inadequacy of their moral systems. Like Henry Johnson, Crane outrages convention by dragging an alien form—naturalism—into the serenity of the local color tale.

Until chapter II, *The Monster* promotes the myth of the orderly, almost idyllic small town. Local color elements abound, including the small-town atmosphere, the ritual gatherings, the place of gossip and storytelling, and, perhaps most importantly, the theme of the outsider. The sense of order is established in chapter I. Critics have generally agreed that the first chapter, virtually a prologue, establishes the themes of the whole. As he will later figure in Henry's destruction, Jimmie Trescott, playing at being a mechanical "engine number 36," destroys part of the natural world, a peony. He tries to prop it upright but fails to do so. Just as Jimmie must accept punishment for being unable to fix what is broken, his father must suffer the town's punishment for the opposite reason: he transgresses natural law when he heals Henry Johnson, who in Judge Hagenthorpe's opinion "ought to die" (31), and he is ostracized as a result. Eric Solomon reads this passage as a warning unheeded: "Dr. Trescott 'could make nothing of it.' ... The lesson is lost on him, and he will later challenge this law of nature."[42] Later the same day, the rituals continue undisturbed: amid "tremendous civilities" (16) Henry courts Miss Bella Farragut; the barbershop habitués, who function as a chorus for the perspective of the town's men, exchange gossip and stare at Henry; people wait for their out-of-town mail and stroll to the band concert.

The first intimations of disorder, provided by the "great hoarse roar of a factory whistle" (18) that signals a fire, reach all simultaneously. It is a measure of Whilomville cohesiveness that everyone, right down to the child Willie, who wants to see the fire, understands instantly its significance, for they are educated in interpreting what concerns their town. So confident of success and well versed in interpretation are the town's boys that, rather than fearing the fire, they wish for even more excitement, contrasting the new chief's slow style unfavorably with that of his predecessor, the dramatic "old Sykes Huntington [who] ... used to bellow continually like a bull and gesticulate in a sort of delirium" (27). The last to hear of the calamity is the person most directly involved. Driving home from a case, Dr. Trescott enjoys the sense of control that he has over life because "this last case was now in complete obedience to him" (25). It is an instance of control that he will not enjoy again after the news of the fire reaches him.

The fire allows the town to do what it likes to do best: indulge its penchant for mythmaking. Henry plunges into the burning house, rescues Jimmie, and, stymied by the "delicate, trembling sapphire shape like a fairy lady" that blocks his path, falls prey to the "ruby-red snakelike thing" that destroys his face (24).[43] He enters the house "the biggest dude in town" (15) and leaves it "a thing ... laid on the grass" (26). The story of the fire travels through several versions as the townspeople refine it to fit their prejudices. The first version, that of "[t]he man who had information," blames Henry:

> "That was the kid's room—in the corner there. He had measles or somethin', and this coon—Johnson—was a settin' up with 'im, and Johnson got sleepy or somethin' and upset the lamp, and the doctor he was down in his office, and he came running up, and they all got burned together till they dragged 'em out." [28]

It is a story of duty neglected rather than heroism performed, wrong on every point. Wrong, too, is the man "preserved for the deliverance of the final judgment," who decrees abruptly that "they'll die sure. Burned to flinders. No chance. Hull lot of'em. Anybody can see" (18).[44] In true local color fashion, the disturbing element has been rendered harmless by being placed in the recent past. Certain that Henry "could not live ... [because] he now had no face" (29), the town congratulates itself on its tolerance; now that Henry will die, the customary social sanctions and color bar can briefly be suspended.

In one way or another, Henry has been a "thing" for the townspeople his whole life: as a second-class citizen in a white man's world, as a being whose realm is in the stable with the horses, as the parodic cynosure of the mocking eyes in Reifsnyder's Barber Shop, as the "thing" that had been a man. Now, however, he becomes a hero when the town's official voice, the morning paper, continues the mythmaking process by wrongly printing a laudatory obituary of Henry. To bask in the reflected glory of Henry's apotheosis, Bella Farragut also contributes to the misinformation with a false story of her own, namely "that she had been engaged to marry Mr. Henry Johnson" (30). Even the children sense Henry's change in stature. Because his name "became suddenly the title of a saint," they try to bury the "odious couplet" that ironically fulfills itself: "Nigger, nigger, never die, / Black face and shiny eye" (30). James Halfley suggests that the townspeople treat the veiled Henry as God;[45] further, like God, he keeps his "shiny eye" on the town's actions: watching Judge Hagenthorpe suggest uneasily that Henry be allowed to die, witnessing the cowardice of Bella and her mother, and peering into the real lives of the white ruling class as they are symbolized by Theresa Page's party. And like God, Henry disconcertingly refuses to go away. Although his madness prevents him from judging them, his gaze, the reproachful reflection of their racism, rests on a society indicting itself.

Confident of their ability as interpreters, the townspeople feel that they understand the conventions governing this local drama—first fire, then rescue, then death—well enough to know that Henry must die, an expectation that becomes for them an imperative. Having elevated him from object of gossip to subject of myth, they can relax as he becomes literally yesterday's news. They are in essence rewriting not only Henry's life but Henry's body, inscribing his race as a manageable discourse within the narrative they create. At least one part of their fury at Henry's survival is sheer frustration: like the characters of local color villages, the residents of Whilomville want to control their version of the story. Denied that possibility, they vent their hostility on those who, like Henry and Dr. Trescott, disrupt or otherwise transform the conventions of their genre. The story cannot have closure or any kind of satisfactory ending, and it is this quality of uncertainty that dominates the town's reactions to the situation. Deprived of a coherent myth to render him harmless, the group must destroy Henry.

The middle sections of the story describe this process of destruction, and along with it the deterioration of the town's moral certitude. In the first of three parallel discussions that exemplify the town's viewpoint, Alek Williams, the black man who boards Henry, complains to the judge that his family is disrupted and is gradually being ostracized, a foreshadowing of Dr. Trescott's fate. The embarrassingly facetious scene that follows his complaint ends with Alek's accepting six dollars a week rather than five, the extra dollar apparently compensating for the social inconvenience. The money alone is not enough, since Alek tries to compel the judge's respect: "'Well, if I bo'd Hennery Johnson fer six dollehs er week, I uhns it! I uhns it!' cried Williams, wildly" (39). However burlesqued the portrait of Alek may be, Crane does make a serious point, juxtaposing Alek's willingness to sell his principles against Dr. Trescott's refusal to do so. Further, just as Crane has Henry's exaggerated manners mimic those of the town's white society, Alek's exaggerated complaints and his frantic attempts at self-justification both parody and foreshadow those later made by the townspeople, thus undercutting any possible moral legitimacy of their claims.

The setting for the second scene of discussion is that perennial smalltown men's club, the local barbershop. As they had earlier discussed Henry's lavender trousers, now the barbershop patrons discuss his mutilated face, taking opposing sides on the question of Dr. Trescott's action. The unusually garrulous barber, Reifsnyder, begins by defending Dr. Trescott, using virtually the doctor's own words to Judge Hagenthorpe: "How can you let a man die?" (40). But Bainbridge the engineer indirectly threatens Reifsnyder—"You'd better shave some people"—reminding Reifsnyder that, after all, his livelihood depends on his customers and not on defending Dr. Trescott. His opposition wavering, Reifsnyder significantly then joins the others in singing a bit of doggerel: "'He has no face in the front of his head, / In the place where his face ought to grow'" (40). Summing up the town's new attitude, this "story" fragment replaces both the "odious couplet" and the official myth of Henry as saint. Reifsnyder, who has been putting himself in Trescott's place, now projects himself imaginatively into Henry's: "'I wonder how it feels to be without any face?'" (41). The cycle begins anew as a man repeats Reifsnyder's initial argument that if a man had saved your son, "'you'd do anything on earth for him'" (41). Reifsnyder, meanwhile, can no longer attest to the rightness of the doctor's decision, saying that the doctor "may be sorry he made him live" (41). The chapter ends with the two alternating ideas being repeated. There is no answer or solution, Crane suggests: to delve, like Reifsnyder, into the ethics of the situation leads not to certainty but to moral ambiguity.

In contrast with the indecisive men at the barbershop, the women and their fixed prejudices emerge as the most important force in the final third of the story. Crane devotes much of chapter 19 to an extended character sketch of Martha Goodwin, whose secure position and immense power are unmistakable despite her being the "mausoleum of a dead passion" (51). Martha is, in fact, a sharp-tongued spinster of the New England local color school, dominating her meek married sister and bullying the other women until they ally themselves "in secret revolt" against her (50). While the men in the barbershop dither pointlessly over ethics, and Dr. Trescott's one overt antagonist, Jake Winter, yelps angrily after the doctor "like a little dog" (59), Martha fearlessly pronounces judgment like Atropos herself: "'Serves him right if he was to lose all his patients,' she said suddenly, in bloodthirsty tones. She nipped her words out as if her lips were scissors" (52). She functions as the town's voice of prophecy, and as its executioner.

Left as the vengeful Fury-Fate she is in chapter 19, Martha would be nothing more than an emblem of all that is wrong with the town, a straw woman for Crane to demolish. But Crane makes of Martha much more than a mere stereotype. She is vengeful, but she also has a moral sense similar to, but more developed than, that of her male counterpart, Reifsnyder, the voice of the town's men as she is of the women. By chapter 22 she has become one of Dr. Trescott's defenders—one of the last people, in fact, to defend him and his vision of truth against the distortions put forth by the town. Martha's instinct for gossip is matched by an equally keen desire to get at the facts. When her sister Kate and Carrie Dungen exaggerate gossip about the illness of Sadie Winter, the little girl Henry had frightened at Theresa Page's party, Martha, a good woman with weapons, sets the record straight: "Martha wheeled from the sink. She held an iron spoon, and it seemed as if she was going to attack them. 'Sadie Winter has passed here many a morning since then carrying her school-bag. Where was she going? To a wedding?'" (60). Told that "you can't go against the whole town" (60), Martha will still not be denied: "I'd like to know what you call 'the whole town.' Do you call these silly people who are scared of Henry Johnson 'the whole town'?" (60). In setting herself against the town, she resembles indomitable women like Mrs. Flint of Rose Terry Cooke's "Mrs. Flint's Married Experience" and such Mary E. Wilkins Freeman heroines as Hetty Fifield ("A Church Mouse"), Sarah Penn ("The Revolt of Mother"), and Candace Whitcomb ("A Village

Singer"). For a brief moment, she lives up to the kind of courage and moral sense that local color literature tried to promote, virtues represented in Whilomville only by Dr. Trescott.

In addition to her respect for truth, Martha tries to live up to the inclusivity characteristic of local color communities. However grotesque Henry's appearance may be, however stiff-necked and peculiar Dr. Trescott's refusal to give Henry up may seem, Martha resists consigning them to the status of outcasts, arguing instead for their inclusion.[46] Like Mrs. Todd, who finds for poor Joanna a place in the human community after the legalistically minded minister gives her up, Martha recognizes that the town is a human community greater than the influence of one faction of "silly people." Ironically, this is apparently the only time when her opinion has no impact on the people of Whilomville. Recognizing that gossip is the source of her power as the barbershop is Reifsnyder's, she is readily distracted by fresh news and leaves the outcasts to their fate. Like the literary tradition from which she springs, she has been sheltered from direct knowledge of the "real life" that naturalism describes and that Henry Johnson symbolizes, and her failure to meet this test of inclusivity marks equally the failure of the local color community.

The final chapters suggest initially the triumph of respectability and the town's women. In the penultimate chapter, the rich grocer, John Twelve, and his cohorts try one last time to persuade Dr. Trescott to give Henry up. To justify their actions, some speak of concern for Trescott, but one excuse reverberates throughout: "It's the women" (63).[47] And indeed it is the women who administer the coup de grâce. Returning to his house in the final chapter, Dr. Trescott sees his wife weeping among the untouched teacups and, recognizing that she shares his ostracism, distractedly finds "himself occasionally trying to count the cups" (65). The monstertown becomes, at least in the men's retelling, a female monster-town, one that destroys both accidental victims like Henry and principled heroes like Dr. Trescott. From the naturalists' point of view, the ending becomes another ghastly triumph for the conventional good woman with weapons. Yet naturalism has struck some telling blows of its own. Like Twain's Hadleyville, the town and its perceptions of order, its virtue, and its storytelling abilities have been destroyed. Whilomville is no longer any place for Dr. Trescott to be, but neither is it the cohesive social unit it was at the beginning. It cannot regain the lost image of its own perfection.

*The Monster* in one sense combines the conventions of local color and naturalism, most notably in its themes of exclusion and the outsider, a local color staple. Central to stories by Mary E. Wilkins Freeman, Rose Terry

Cooke, Mary N. Murfree, Sarah Orne Jewett, and Constance Fenimore Woolson, the problem of the outsider is typically one of inclusion: how to incorporate the outsider into the life of the community without disrupting its rituals or its inhabitants. *The Monster*, however, provides instead a story of the almost violent exclusion of two men who should be firmly fixed within the structure of the community. A mirrored pair encompassing the polarities of rich/poor, educated/superstitious, black/white, socially entrenched/socially tolerated, the two men together represent a form of otherness that the town fears even as it studies them. The stories of two dissimilar outsiders are each so extreme that they help to explode the form as Henry's and Dr. Trescott's inevitable ostracism from the town provides a frightening tale of virtue wronged. As Levenson remarks in his introduction to the University of Virginia edition, it is the story of "how Dr. Trescott, firmly set in the established order and prompted only by motives of which his society approved, acted to bring on himself a relentless process of exclusion and alienation."[48] The town thrusts him out ruthlessly because he is a turncoat. Talking with Judge Hagenthorpe midway through the novel, Dr. Trescott chooses right action over the town's storytelling when he declines any longer to interpret their language "correctly":

> "Well, I don't want you to think I would say anything to—It was only that I thought that I might be able to suggest to you that—perhaps—the affair was a little dubious."
> With an appearance of suddenly disclosing his real mental perturbation, the doctor said: "Well, what would you do? Would you kill him?" he asked, abruptly and sternly.
> "Trescott, you fool," said the old man, gently. [33]

Trescott is a fool because he cuts directly to the point of the Judge's evasive, hesitant language. He speaks the unspeakable—"Would you kill him?"—and ushers in the age of truth and discord. If, as Jewett's narrator claims, "tact is a kind of mind-reading" that facilitates community understanding, Trescott refuses to participate. When he removes himself from participation in the community's discourse, he inexorably removes himself from the community.

The tale of Henry Johnson is quite another kind of ultimate outsider story, so extreme that it reads as a kind of invasion myth. It is an invasion story of the most terrifying kind, for the "monster" comes from within the town's psyche, generated by its fears of social instability, its prejudices about appearance (including racism), and its all-consuming passion for gossip and drama. Dr. Trescott, the one man free from such illusions, ironically becomes in the town's eyes a captive to the "monster," first to "the monster" Henry Johnson, to whom he owes his son's life, and then to "the monster" of the town and its attitudes. None of the townspeople want to look at him, for to look "real life" in the face, so to speak, involves recognition that it can be unimaginably grotesque. In his preface to *The Picture of Dorian Gray*, Oscar Wilde writes, "The nineteenth-century dislike of Realism is the rage of Caliban seeing his own face in a glass."[49] Because of his Caliban-like qualities, which are actually projected onto him by the town's fantasies, the people initially see Henry as the monster. What Henry does, however, is within his own visage hold up that mirror to the Calibantown, exposing fraudulent harmony and corrupt virtue.

Read symbolically, Henry represents both naturalism and the naturalists' idea of "real life." As he makes his way through the town, recognizing no social distinctions and following no decorum, Henry becomes a force sweeping "from high to low," much like the personified Romance (naturalism) of Norris's metaphor. Also, in his degenerated physical state, he resembles other naturalistic "things" that had been men, among them Wolf Larsen at the end of *The Sea-Wolf*, the gibbering Vandover at the end of *Vandover and the Brute*, and the crusader in Norris's "Lauth," who becomes a spineless puddle of protoplasm by the end of the story. The naturalistic version of "real life" has no neat story; "real life" does not adapt well to mythmaking, closure, or safety. Bereft of their first comfortable myths of Henry, the townspeople still cannot escape because Dr. Trescott, the principled man of science, like the "scientific" naturalists, refuses to allow them to look away, to return to their idealized town and forget about Henry and the unpleasant reality he represents. They create new, darker myths, this time not laudatory ones but tales of Henry-the-monster and, by association, Trescott-the-monster. "If you're sick and nervous, Doctor Trescott would scare the life out of you, wouldn't he?" says Carrie Dungen (52). By interweaving elements of local color and naturalism, Crane has also accomplished another seemingly impossible feat. In his discussions of Zola, of Howells, and of naturalism, Frank Norris had several times spoken contemptuously about "teacup tragedies" as if the term were an oxymoron. Blending the terrible with the ordinary, Crane ends *The Monster* with just such a seemingly conventional scene: Mrs. Trescott, realizing the finality of her ostracism by the town, cries among the unused teacups set out for her party as Dr. Trescott pointlessly begins to count them.[50] But the horror of Henry's plight, and the tragedy of Dr. Trescott's destruction for the sake of principle, renders the ordinary scene extraordinary. As if taking up the gauntlet that Norris had flung down, Crane makes *The Monster* a "teacup tragedy."

VI

The conflict being waged in these works is clearly the one against what these authors perceived as the excessive feminine discourse controlling masculine literature in particular and male lives in general. The reader sees within the first chapter of *Martin Eden* that Ruth is an Iron Madonna, and that she is limited, shallow, and unworthy of Martin, yet the narrative voice hammers away at these points chapter after chapter, contrasting always Martin's eagerness for real life and fresh experience with Ruth's preference for the canned variety. Mrs. Kelcey, Ruth, and the other highly conventional good women wreak havoc despite the kindest of intentions. In one sense, the legends of good women here are all tales of resisting female influence and of monster creation: Ruth tries mightily to remake Martin into what London clearly sees as a mere effigy of a man; Mrs. Kelcey tries to recreate a dutiful son on her own terms and instead spawns Kel the street tough; and the woman-dominated society of Whilomville creates Henry and Dr. Trescott as monsters by its rigid insistence on conventional behavior. Small wonder that the naturalists identified themselves rather with those other persecuted victims of too much respectability, the fallen women.

Interestingly, by telling the prostitutes' stories, the naturalists achieve what George's mother and the other good women cannot: the naturalists "rescue" the fallen women as fit subjects for fiction, but George's mother, despite her virtues, cannot save George from the streets. The point is not merely that by joining the world of convention and professed virtue the men would be stifled. It is that they would be becoming adjunct women— "Willieboys." In *George's Mother,* Mrs. Kelcey perceives George as a mythic St. George fighting "green dragons," never realizing that the dragon he must fight is herself. As guilt is her weapon, so words become George's in his ongoing struggle to differentiate himself from his mother and her feminine values. Through language, Crane and the naturalists, like the street tough, can render her not only harmless but defenseless—a woman without weapons.

## NOTES

1. June Howard demonstrates that within some of these novels the theme of proletarianization, or the fear that one may descend as well as ascend the socioeconomic scale, prevents the reader from assuming that a safe distance exists between himself and the characters being studied: "The gesture of exclusion reinforces the antinomy between human and brute without rendering the image of the brute any less potent, and the assertion of superiority always inscribes a doubt: 'that isn't me (is it?)—that couldn't happen to me (could it?)'" (*Form and History in American Literary Naturalism,* 101).

2. Norris, "Frank Norris' Weekly Letter," *Chicago American*, 3 August 1901; reprinted in *Literary Criticism of Frank Norris*, 75.

3. "A Plea for Romantic Fiction," 77. Norris considered naturalism to be a form of Romance, and he frequently used the terms interchangeably.

4. See, for example, Elaine Showalter, "Syphilis, Sexuality, and the Fiction of the Fin de Siècle" in Ruth Bernard Yeazell, *Sex, Politics, and Science in the Nineteenth-Century Novel* (Baltimore: Johns Hopkins University Press, 1986).

5. Laura Hapke, *Girls Who Went Wrong: Prostitutes in American Fiction, 1885–1917* (Bowling Green, Ohio: Bowling Green State University Press, 1989), 20.

6. Carol Hurd Green, "Stephen Crane and the Fallen Women," in *American Novelists Revisited: Essays in Feminist Criticism*, ed. Fritz Fleischmann (Boston: G. K. Hall, 1982), 234.

7. Wai-Chee Dimock, "'Debasing Exchange': Edith Wharton's *The House of Mirth*," *PMLA* 100 (October 1985): 783–92; reprinted in Harold Bloom, *Edith Wharton*, Modern Critical Views (New York: Chelsea House, 1986), 124.

8. Nell Kimball and "Madeleine" both comment on their customers' interest in this question. Another such source is a collection of letters from a former prostitute, edited and collected by Ruth Rosen and Sue Davidson as *The Maimie Papers* (Old Westbury, N.Y.: Feminist Press, 1977).

9. According to Barbara Meil Hobson's *Uneasy Virtue: The Politics of Prostitution and the American Reform Tradition* (New York: Basic Books, 1987), "One estimate ... has set the published material on prostitution at one billion pages during this period" (140). In *The Response to Prostitution in the Progressive Era* (Chapel Hill: University of North Carolina Press, 1980), Mark Connelly describes the basic plot of the white slave narrative: "Typically, a chaste and comely native American country girl would forsake her idyllic country home and family for the promise of the city. On the way, or shortly after arrival, she would fall victim to one of the swarm of panders.... Using one of his vast array of tricks—a promise of marriage, an offer to assist in securing lodging, or, if these were to no avail, the chloroformed cloth, the hypodermic needle, or the drugged drink—the insidious white slaver would brutally seduce the girl and install her in a brothel, where she became an enslaved prostitute" (116). Describing the narratives as fulfilling a psychological need much as the Indian captivity narratives had done, Connelly sees the movement as embodying the nation's "ethnocentrism" and nativist fears, its "conspiratorial mentality," and the "illogic ... and authoritarianism of the Prohibitionist crusade" (134). In *The Lost Sisterhood: Prostitution in America, 1900–1918* (Baltimore: Johns Hopkins University Press, 1982), Ruth Rosen gives much greater credence to the threat posed by the white slave trade. For an examination of these themes in fiction, see Laura Hapke's *Girls Who Went Wrong*.

10. *Madeleine: An Autobiography*, (1919; reprint, New York: Persea Books, 1986), 45; italics in original. The "dissection" of the female body resonates in texts of the period. In "Statistical Persons" (*Diacritics* 17 [1987]: 83–98), Mark Seltzer comments that the realist project of embodiment "of turning the body inside out for inspection, takes a virtually *obstetrical* form in realist discourse" (84; italics Seltzer's) and finds the "body of the monstrously productive mother" a central figure for the slums that becomes "a visual and corporeal model of the social" (87). See also chapter 3 ("A Woman's Case") of *Sexual Anarchy*, in which Elaine Showalter argues that men "open up a woman as a substitute for self-knowledge, both maintaining the illusion of their own invulnerability and destroying the terrifying female reminder of their impotence and uncertainty" (134).

11. David Graham Phillips, *Susan Lenox: Her Fall and Rise* (1917; reprint, 2 vols., Upper Saddle River, N.J.: Gregg Press, 1968), 2:260. Subsequent references will be cited

in the text. The one-volume edition published by Southern Illinois Press in 1977 does not reproduce the full unexpurgated text.

12. The phrase is Nell Kimball's, from *Nell Kimball: Her Life as an American Madam,* ed. Stephen Longstreet (New York: Berkeley, 1970), 138.

13. *Theodore Dreiser, Jennie Gerhardt,* ed. James L. West III (New York: Penguin, 1992), 146; italics are Dreiser's. Subsequent references are to this edition and will be cited parenthetically within the text.

14. Carol Schwartz, "*Jennie Gerhardt:* Fairy Tale as Social Criticism," *American Literary Realism* 19.2 (Winter 1987): 17.

15. In his reading of *Jennie Gerhardt* in "Dreiser and the Naturalistic Drama of Consciousness" (*The Theory and Practice of American Literary Naturalism: Selected Essays and Reviews* [Carbondale: Southern Illinois University Press, 1993]), Donald Pizer demonstrates the ways in which Dreiser uses subtle shifts in perspective "as metaphorical reflections of distinctive states of mind, as moments in the drama of a consciousness rather than in generalized philosophical observations" (77). Dreiser's repetition, with variations, of the "good woman" idea suggests a similarly subtle representation of Lester's state of mind.

16. Stephen Crane, *Maggie: A Girl of the Streets,* ed. Thomas Gullason, Norton Critical Edition (New York: Norton, 1979), 20. Subsequent references are to this edition and will be cited parenthetically in the text.

17. Ibid., 21. Chester Wolford in *The Anger of Stephen Crane: Fiction and the Epic Tradition* (Lincoln: University of Nebraska Press, 1983) likens this scene to one of a perverse Ceres destroying the earth after Proserpina's loss (82).

18. Brander Matthews's "Before the Break of Day" (*Harper's New Monthly Magazine* 89 [July 1894]: 222–27), one of his "Vignettes of Manhattan," provides an interesting glimpse into a different possibility for Maggie Johnson. His heroine, Maggie O'Donnell, is also born in the Bowery; suffers beatings at the hands of her drunken parents; takes up with a petty criminal (Jim McDermott) and is consequently locked out despite her innocence; and is subsequently seduced and abandoned by him. Later married to saloon owner Terry O'Donnell, she exacts retribution when McDermott tries to rob the bar. When McDermott pulls a gun, she tells him to "shoot and be damned," and he does. Matthews allows the full drama of this moment to stand before adding that Maggie has received only a flesh wound in the arm.

19. Alan Robert Slotkin, *The Language of Stephen Crane's* Bowery Tales: *Developing Mastery of Character Diction* (New York: Garland, 1993), 44.

20. Hapke, *Girls Who Went Wrong,* 158.

21. Theodore Dreiser, *Sister Carrie,* ed. John C. Berkey, Alice M. Winters, James L. W. West III, and Neda M. Westlake (New York: Penguin, 1981), 192. Subsequent references to this edition will be made in the text.

22. Fisher, *Hard Facts,* 166–67. See also Barbara Hochman on Carrie's acting in "A Portrait of the Artist as a Young Actress: The Rewards of Representation in *Sister Carrie,*" in *New Essays on* Sister Carrie, ed. Donald Pizer (Cambridge: Cambridge University Press, 1991). Hochman uses Walter Benjamin's figure of the storyteller to analyze the reciprocal nature of Carrie's (and Dreiser's) exchanges with the audience, finding that "Dreiser's process of composition, especially his involvement with others throughout, partially restored the rewards of the oral storyteller to the work of the latter-day novelist" (58).

23. As Walter Benn Michaels points out, "Selling 'sex attraction' to thousands instead of just one, Carrie leaves the restricted economy of the marriage market for the general economy of show business" ("The Contracted Heart," *New Literary History* 21 [Spring 1990]: 500).

24. The validity of Dreiser's account receives confirmation from an unexpected source. Speaking first of Paul Dreiser, Nell Kimball remarks: "He had a brother who became a writer too, under another name. In New Orleans 1912 some guest gave me one of the brother's books, *Sister Carry* [*sic*], and it was a dandy. The girl was real, for a man writer anyway.... I knew men like the saloon manager in the book, who ran off with the safe's money. And I could have been the girl, if I weren't a whore" (*Nell Kimball*, 113).

25. Louis Filler, *Voice of the Democracy: A Critical Biography of David Graham Phillips, Journalist, Novelist, Progressive* (University Park: Pennsylvania State University Press, 1978), 174.

26. Frank Norris, *Vandover and the Brute*, 455. Subsequent references will be cited parenthetically in the text.

27. London, *Letters of Jack London*, 1:263.

28. Jack London, *Martin Eden* (New York: Bantam, 1986), 6. Subsequent references are to this edition and will be cited parenthetically within the text.

29. Like Norris and others of his time, London viewed the Anglo-Saxon "race" as exemplifying the highest product of evolutionary perfection, as he explained to Cloudsley Johns in July 1899:

> [W]e are blind puppets at the play of great, unreasoning forces.... These forces generated the altruistic in man; the race with the highest altruism will endure—the highest altruism considered from the standpoint of merciless natural law.... The lesser breeds cannot endure. The Indian is an example, as is the black man of the Austrailian [*sic*] Bush, the South Sea Islander, the inhabitant of the Sub-Arctics, etc. [*Letters of Jack London*, 1:92]

The mixing of races (i.e., London's "Eurasian") was seen as often harmful in itself, especially when the stock of "lesser" races was improved at the expense of "superior" ones. "Lesser" meant "hot-blooded" races given to passion rather than, so the theory went, to reason like the altruistic, temperate Anglo-Saxons. Maria Macapa of *McTeague* is one such "degenerate" product, as is the vicious mixed-blood Spanish woman in Norris's "Case for Lombroso." An interest in "scientific" studies of physiognomy and in genetics gave rise to books like *Our Country: Its Possible Future and Its Present Crisis* (1885), in which the Reverend Josiah Strong "argued that native stock would be adversely affected if the genetic and moral effects of the foreign horde were not stopped in time" (Martha Banta, *Imaging American Women: Idea and Ideals in Cultural History* [New York: Columbia University Press, 1987], 117). Other works, including Joseph Simms's *Physiognomy Illustrated* (1891), V. G. Rocine's *Heads, Faces, Types, Races* (1910), and Henry Dwight Sedgwick's *New American Type and Other Essays* (1908), purported to demonstrate the superior beauty and intelligence of "Aryans."

30. In "Divided Self and World in *Martin Eden*," *Jack London Newsletter* 9 (September-December 1976): 118–26, George Spangler identifies a series of "binary pairs" that inform Martin's view of the world, a view that includes "Martin's tendency ... to step back from himself, to observe from a corner of his mind some past, present or future image of self, i.e., to divide the self" (123).

31. The submission subplot here reverses Norris's in *Moran of the* Lady Letty. The "Viking goddess" Moran gives up her prodigious strength when Ross Wilbur wrestles her to a draw. Recognizing her love for him, she submits and becomes weak, thus setting the stage for her failure to fight back against the Chinese pirates that kill her. Writing to Cloudsley Johns on 30 April 1899, London approved of *Moran of the* Lady Letty, saying, "It's well done" (*Letters of Jack London*, 1:72).

32. The conflict within the novel has been interpreted variously. Maxwell Geismar sees the tension between George and his mother a "tragic-comic oedipal love relationship" resulting in George's self-destruction (*Rebels and Ancestors: The American Novel, 1890–1915* [Boston: Houghton Mifflin, 1953], 94), whereas Agnes Moreland Jackson finds the real source of conflict to be the battle Mrs. Kelcey wages and George loses against alcohol ("Stephen Crane's Imagery of Conflict in *George's Mother,*" *American Quarterly* 25 [Winter 1969]: 313–18). Joseph X. Brennan defines the conflict more broadly, with George and his mother representing "larger opposed forces—the Church versus the city of Mammon, the old morality and conformity versus modern license and amorality"; he additionally shows how the pervasive battle imagery is really a "parody of medieval romance literature," specifically recalling the myth of St. George and the dragon ("The Imagery and Art of *George's Mother,*" *CLA Journal* 4 [December 1960]: 106–15; reprinted in Wertheim, *The Merrill Studies in* Maggie *and* George's Mother [Columbus, Ohio: Merrill, 1970], 126, 127). In terms of literary sources, Eric Solomon reads *George's Mother* as a parody of temperance tracts, such as those Crane's father wrote, and of Horatio Alger stories (*Stephen Crane: From Parody to Realism* [Cambridge, Mass.: Harvard University Press, 1966]). Finding a source within the text itself, Brenda Murphy identifies the Isaac Watts hymn "Holy Fortitude; or, The Christian Soldier" that Mrs. Kelcey sings in chapter 2 as a commentary on the action of the story. Murphy's thesis depends on an acceptance of Watts's line "Thy saints, in all this glorious war, / Shall conquer, though they die" as confirmation of Mrs. Kelcey's victory over George ("A Woman with Weapons: The Victor in *George's Mother,*" *Modern Language Studies* 11.2 [Spring 1981]: 88–93).

33. James B. Colvert, introduction to *George's Mother,* by Stephen Crane, in *Bowery Tales: Maggie/George's Mother,* ed. Fredson Bowers (Charlottesville: University of Virginia Press, 1969), 103, 104.

34. Stephen Crane, *George's Mother* in *Bowery Tales: Maggie/George's Mother,* ed. Fredson Bowers (Charlottesville: University of Virginia Press, 1969), 128, 124. Subsequent references are to this edition and will be cited parenthetically in the text.

35. Mark C. Carnes, "Middle-Class Men and the Solace of Fraternal Ritual," in *Meanings for Manhood: Constructions of Masculinity in Victorian America,* ed. Mark C. Carnes and Clyde Griffen (Chicago: University of Chicago Press, 1990), 38, 42, 43, 45, 47–48.

36. In his unsympathetic interpretation of Mrs. Kelcey in *A Reading of Stephen Crane* (Oxford: Clarendon Press, 1971), Marston La France argues that "for George and his mother the saloon and church represent futile retreats from reality ... [and] Mrs. Kelcey is as personally dishonest, as wilful in her withdrawal from reality, as George is. She deliberately refuses to accept what her eyes reveal to her because she knows that her vain and lazy son is no king among men, that if her dreams of his greatness were 'worded, they would be ridiculous.' ... She refuses to see what everyone else in the tenement sees, that she has 'a wild son'" (91).

37. Solomon, *Stephen Crane,* 177.

38. Thomas Gullason, "The Symbolic Unity of 'The Monster,'" *Modern Language Notes* 75 (December 1960): 663.

39. J. C. Levenson, introduction to "The Monster," in *Tales of Whilomville,* ed. Fredson Bowers, vol. 7 of *The Works of Stephen Crane* (Charlottesville: University of Virginia Press, 1969), xv.

40. Frank Norris, "Zola as a Romantic Writer," *Wave* 15 (27 June 1896); reprinted in *The Literary Criticism of Frank Norris,* 72.

41. Stephen Crane, "The Monster" in *Tales of Whilomville,* ed. Fredson Bowers, vol. 7

of *The Works of Stephen Crane* (Charlottesville: University of Virginia Press, 1969), 7–67. Subsequent references are to this edition and will be cited parenthetically within the text.

42. Solomon, *Stephen Crane*, 183.

43. See especially Michael Fried's careful if controversial reading of this section in *Realism, Writing, Disfiguration: On Thomas Eakins and Stephen Crane* (Chicago: University of Chicago Press, 1987).

44. The brusque, telegraphic language here recalls that of the doctor in *George's Mother*, another man whose "knowledgeable" advice is worthless: "'Can't tell,' he said. 'She's wonderful woman! Got more vitality than you and I together! Can't tell! May—may not! Good-day! Back in two hours!'" (176).

45. James Halfley, "'The Monster' and the Art of Stephen Crane," *Accent* 19 (Summer 1959): 159–65; reprinted in Thomas A. Gullason, *Stephen Crane's Career: Perspectives and Evaluations* (New York: New York University Press, 1972), 444.

46. In "Face, Race, and Disfiguration in Stephen Crane's *The Monster*" (*Critical Inquiry* 17.1 [Fall 1990]: 174–92), Lee Clark Mitchell observes that Martha's sympathy stems from "the dream of her pockmarked face of her dead fiancé. The psychology thereby revealed significantly links truth with disfigurement, morality with prosopopoeia, narrative with absence, all in a paradoxical convergence that constitutes the story's plot" (191).

47. Blaming the women for the men's own cowardly evasions rings a prophetic note. Beer reports that when Crane tried to publish "The Monster," Richard Watson Gilder turned it down for the *Century*, saying, "We couldn't publish that thing with half the expectant mothers in America on our subscription list" (Beer, *Stephen Crane*, 164).

48. Levenson, introduction to "The Monster," xv.

49. Oscar Wilde, *The Picture of Dorian Gray* (1891; reprint, Harmondsworth, England: Penguin, 1949), 5.

50. Fried sees this action as a figure for the reader's own impotence at the end, whereas Ronald K. Giles, in "Responding to Crane's 'The Monster'" (*South Atlantic Review* 57.2 [May 1992]: 45–55), views it as an affirmative analogue of Dr. Trescott's "exacting moral vision" (53).

# Chronology

| | |
|---|---|
| 1880 | Emile Zola: *Le Roman expérimental*. Henry Adams: *Democracy*. Death of George Eliot. |
| 1881 | President James A. Garfield is assasinated; succeeded by Chester A. Arthur. Tuskegee Institute founded by Booker T. Washington. Joel Chandler Harris: *Uncle Remus*. Henry James: *The Portrait of a Lady* and *Washington Square*. |
| 1882 | Deaths of Ralph Waldo Emerson and Henry Wadsworth Longfellow. |
| 1883 | Northern Pacific transcontinental railroad completed. Mark Twain: *Life on the Mississippi*. Brooklyn Bridge opens. Robert Louis Stevenson: *Treasure Island*. |
| 1884 | Mark Twain: *Adventures of Huckleberry Finn*. |
| 1885 | Internal combustion engine patented. Walter Pater: *Marius the Epicurean*. William Dean Howells: *The Rise of Silas Lapham*. |
| 1886 | Haymarket riot in Chicago. First appearance in English of Karl Marx's *Das Kapital*. Henry James: *The Bostonians*. Thomas Hardy: *The Mayor of Castorbridge*. |
| 1887 | Interstate Commerce Act passed. First electric streetcars are used. Thomas Hardy: *The Woodlanders*. |
| 1888 | Box camera perfected by George Eastman. Rudyard Kipling: *Plain Tales from the Hills*. Henry James: *The Aspern Papers*. |

| 1889 | Benjamin Harrison elected president. Arthur Conan Doyle: *The Sign of Four*. Leo Tolstoy: *The Kreutzer Sonata*. |
| 1890 | Henrik Ibsen: *Hedda Gabler*. Emily Dickinson: *Poems*. Sherman Anti-Trust Act passed. William James: *The Principles of Psychology*. Jacob Riis: *How the Other Half Lives*. William Morris: *News from Nowhere*. |
| 1891 | Deaths of James Russell Lowell and Herman Melville. Thomas Hardy: *Tess of the D'Urbervilles*. First International Copyright Law established. Mary Wilkins Freeman: *A New England Nun and Other Stories*. Hamlin Garland: *Main-Travelled Roads*. Arthur Conan Doyle begins to publish Sherlock Holmes stories in *Strand* magazine. |
| 1892 | Strikers riot at Carnegie Steel Company. Formation of the People's party. Deaths of Walt Whitman and John Greenleaf Whittier. Charlotte Perkins Gilman: "The Yellow Wallpaper." |
| 1893 | Grover Cleveland elected president. Onset of economic depression following Wall Street Panic. Stephen Crane: *Maggie: A Girl of the Streets*. Frederick Jackson Turner: "The Significance of the Frontier in American History." Chicago hosts the World's Fair. |
| 1894 | First motion picture shows in New York. Hamlin Garland: *Crumbling Idols*. George Bernard Shaw: *Arms and the Man*. Dreyfus convicted for treason. |
| 1895 | Stephen Crane: *The Red Badge of Courage*. Hamlin Garland: *Rose of Dutcher's Coolly*. Joseph Conrad: *Almayer's Folly*. Radio telegraphy invented. Oscar Wilde: *The Importance of Being Earnest*. |
| 1896 | Klondike Gold Rush begins. Death of Harriet Beecher Stowe. Nobel Prizes established. Sarah Orne Jewett: *The Country of the Pointed Firs*. Abraham Cahan: *Yekl: A Tale of the New York Ghetto*. |
| 1897 | William McKinley elected president. Rudyard Kipling: *Captains Courageous*. Henry James: *The Spoils of Poynton*. |
| 1898 | Stephen Crane: *The Open Boat and Other Tales of Adventure*. Spanish American War begins April 25, ends August 12, following the defeat of Spanish forces at Manila Bay, Cuba, and in Puerto Rico. H.G. Wells: *The War of the Worlds*. |

| 1899 | Boer War begins in South Africa. Charles W. Chestnutt: *The Conjure Woman*. Kate Chopin: *The Awakening*. Stephen Crane: *The Monster and Other Stories*. Frank Norris: *McTeague*. Thorstein Veblen: *The Theory of the Leisure Class*. |
|------|------|
| 1900 | Sigmund Freud: *The Interpretation of Dreams*. Death of Stephen Crane. Jack London: *The Son of the Wolf*. Joseph Conrad: *Lord Jim*. Boxer Rebellion takes place in China. British Labor Party founded. Theodore Dreiser: *Sister Carrie*. |
| 1901 | William McKinley reelected, but is assassinated; succeeded by Theodore Roosevelt. J.P. Morgan organizes United States Steel Corporation. Frank Norris: *The Octopus*. Booker T. Washington: *Up from Slavery*. Death of Queen Victoria. |
| 1902 | Deaths of Frank Norris and Emile Zola. Ellen Glasgow: *The Battle-Ground*. Henry James: *The Wings of the Dove*. William James: *The Varieties of Religious Experience*. |
| 1903 | Wright Brothers' first successful flight. Jack London: *The Call of the Wild*. Death of Herbert Spencer. Ford Motor Company founded. W.E.B. DuBois: *The Souls of Black Folk*. Women's Social and Political Union founded by Emmeline Pankhurst. Frank Norris: *The Pit*. |
| 1904 | Death of Kate Chopin. Russo-Japanese War begins. American Academy of Arts and Letters founded. Jack London: *The Sea Wolf*. Ellen Glasgow: *The Deliverance*. Ida Tarbell: *The History of the Standard Oil Company*. |
| 1905 | International Workers of the World founded. Edith Wharton: *The House of Mirth*. Special theory of relativity formulated by Albert Einstein. Sigmund Freud: *Three Essays on the Theory of Sexuality*. Robert Herrick: *The Memoirs of an American Citizen*. |
| 1906 | Jack London: *White Fang*. Upton Sinclair: *The Jungle*. Earthquake devastates San Francisco. O. Henry: *The Four Million*. |
| 1907 | Henry Adams: *The Education of Henry Adams*. Henry James: *The American Scene*. Financial Panic causes economic upheaval. William James: *Pragmatism*. Pablo Picasso: *Les Demoiselles d'Avignon*. |

| | |
|---|---|
| 1908 | E.M. Forster: *A Room with a View*. Jack London: *The Iron Heel*. |
| 1909 | William Howard Taft elected president. Jack London: *Martin Eden*. Ford begins mass production of Model T. Ezra Pound: *Personae*. Gertrude Stein: *Three Lives*. Gustav Mahler: *Symphony No. 9*. |
| 1910 | Death of King Edward VII of England; George V takes the throne. Edwin Arlington Robinson: *The Town Down the River*. Deaths of William James, Leo Tolstoy, Florence Nightengale, and Mark Twain. Igor Stravinsky: *The Firebird*. |
| 1911 | Standard Oil Company and the American Tobacco Company ordered to dissolve by the Supreme Court. Theodore Dreiser: *Jennie Gerhardt*. |
| 1912 | Woodrow Wilson elected president. Titanic sinks on its maiden voyage. James Weldon Johnson: *The Autobiography of an Ex-Colored Man*. Theodore Dreiser: *The Financier*. *Poetry* magazine started in Chicago. Marcel Duchamp: *Nude Descending a Staircase*. Sarah Bernhardt stars in *Queen Elizabeth*. |
| 1913 | Federal Income Tax authorized by Sixteenth Amendment. Edith Wharton: *The Custom of the Country*. Robert Frost: *A Boy's Will*. Willa Cather: *O Pioneers!* D.H. Lawrence: *Sons and Lovers*. Thomas Mann: *Death in Venice*. Marcel Proust: *Swann's Way*. |
| 1914 | World War I begins. Theodore Dreiser: *The Titan*. Robert Frost: *North of Boston*. Panama Canal opens. James Joyce: *Dubliners*. Joseph Conrad: *Chance*. |
| 1915 | Willa Cather: *The Song of the Lark*. Somerset Maugham: *Of Human Bondage*. D.H. Lawrence: *The Rainbow*. |
| 1916 | Carl Sandburg: *Chicago Poems*. Amy Lowell: *Men, Women, and Ghosts*. Deaths of Henry James and Jack London. Woodrow Wilson reelected. Workman's Compensation Act passed. James Joyce: *A Portrait of the Artist as a Young Man*. |
| 1917 | Selective Service Act passed. Hamlin Garland: *A Son of the Middle Border*. T.S. Eliot: *Prufrock and Other Observations*. The United States enters World War I; the first U.S. troops arrive in France in October. Edith Wharton: *Summer*. Russian Revolution takes place. |

| 1918 | Willa Cather: *My Antonia*. Influenza epidemic hits, killing over twenty million worldwide in one year. Germany signs armistice treaty. Lytton Strachey: *Eminent Victorians*. |
|------|------|
| 1919 | Communist Party is formed in Chicago. Sherwood Anderson: *Winesburg, Ohio*. Versailles Treaty is signed. Robert Weine: *The Cabinet of Dr. Caligari*. |
| 1920 | Prohibition law goes into effect. 19th Amendment allows women to vote. Nicola Sacco and Bartolomeo Vanzetti arrested. Edith Wharton: *The Age of Innocence*. F. Scott Fitzgerald: *This Side of Paradise*. Death of William Dean Howells. Warren G. Harding elected president. Henri Matisse: *L'Odalisque*. D.H. Lawrence: *Women in Love*. |
| 1921 | Albert Einstein lectures in New York. John Dos Passos: *Three Soldiers*. Emergency Quota Act passed, restricting immigration. Charles Chaplin: *The Kid*. |
| 1922 | T.S. Eliot: *The Waste Land*. Sinclair Lewis: *Babbitt*. Anzia Yezierska: *Salome of the Tenements*. Eugene O'Neill: *The Hairy Ape*. James Joyce: *Ulysses*. British Broadcasting Company founded. Friedrich Murnau: *Nasferatu*. |
| 1923 | President Harding dies after suffering poisoning and pneumonia; Calvin Coolidge sworn into office. Wallace Stevens: *Harmonium*. William Carlos Williams: *Spring and All*. Jean Toomer: *Cane*. U.S. Steel implements the eight-hour workday. |
| 1924 | Japanese immigration suspended. Coolidge elected president. Edith Wharton: *Old New York*. E. M. Forster: *A Passage to India*. Pablo Neruda: *Twenty Love Poems and a Song of Despair*. |
| 1925 | F. Scott Fitzgerald: *The Great Gatsby*. Ernest Hemingway: *In Our Time*. Theodore Dreiser: *An American Tragedy*. John Dos Passos: *Manhattan Transfer*. Harold Ross founds *The New Yorker*. Scopes Trial begins as John Scopes is arrested for teaching Darwin's theory of evolution in Tennessee. Sergei Eisenstein: *Battleship Potemkin*. Virginia Woolf: *Mrs. Dalloway*. Charles Chaplin: *The Gold Rush*. Adolf Hitler: *Mein Kampf*. |
| 1926 | Army Air Corps established. Ernest Hemingway: *The Sun* |

*Also Rises*. Hart Crane: *White Buildings*. Langston Hughes: *The Weary Blues*. William Faulkner: *Soldier's Pay*.

| | |
|---|---|
| 1927 | Ernest Hemingway: *Men without Women*. Virginia Woolf: *To the Lighthouse*. Willa Cather: *Death Comes for the Archbishop*. Charles Lindbergh flies *The Spirit of St. Louis* from New York to Paris. |
| 1928 | W.B. Yeats: *The Tower*. D.H. Lawrence: *Lady Chatterly's Lover*. Nella Larsen: *Quicksand*. Herbert Hoover elected president. Sergei Eisenstein: *October*. Penicillin discovered. |
| 1929 | William Faulkner: *The Sound and the Fury*. Ernest Hemingway: *A Farewell to Arms*. Nella Larsen: *Passing*. Stock market crash initiates the Great Depression. Virginia Woolf: *A Room of One's Own*. Museum of Modern Art opens in New York. |
| 1930 | Hart Crane: *The Bridge*. Sigmund Freud: *Civilization and its Discontents*. William Faulkner: *As I Lay Dying*. F.R. Leavis: *Mass Civilization and Minority Culture*. Empire State Building erected in New York City. |
| 1931 | Eugene O'Neill: *Mourning Becomes Electra*. Charles Chaplin: *City Lights*. Henri Matisse: *The Dance*. Virginia Woolf: *The Waves*. |
| 1932 | Aldous Huxley: *Brave New World*. Franklin D. Roosevelt elected president. William Faulkner: *Light in August*. Ernest Hemingway: *Death in the Afternoon*. |
| 1933 | Gertrude Stein: *The Autobiography of Alice B. Toklas*. André Malraux: *La Condition humaine*. Carl Jung: *Modern Man in Search of a Soul*. |
| 1934 | F. Scott Fitzgerald: *Tender Is the Night*. Henry Miller: *Tropic of Cancer*. |
| 1935 | T.S. Eliot: *Murder in the Cathedral*. Salvador Dali: *Giraffe on Fire*. Clifford Odets: *Waiting for Lefty*. Ernest Hemingway: *The Green Hills of Africa*. |
| 1936 | Dylan Thomas: *Twenty-five Poems*. Piet Mondrian: *Composition in Red and Blue*. Charles Chaplin: *Modern Times*. William Faulkner: *Absalom, Absalom!* Spanish Civil War begins. |
| 1937 | Ernest Hemingway: *To Have and Have Not*. Virginia Woolf: *The Years*. First jet engine constructed. Japanese invade |

China. John Steinbeck: *Of Mice and Men*. Pablo Picasso: *Guernica*.

1938    Elizabeth Bowen: *The Death of the Heart*. Jean Cocteau: *Les Parents terribles*. Lewis Mumford: *The Culture of the Cities*. Samuel Beckett: *Murphy*. E.E. Cummings: *Collected Poems*. Adolf Hitler assumes command of German army. John Dos Passos: *U.S.A.*

1939    James Joyce: *Finnegan's Wake*. Outbreak of World War II. John Steinbeck: *The Grapes of Wrath*. Henry Miller: *Tropic of Capricorn*.

1940    Ernest Hemingway: *For Whom the Bell Tolls*. Graham Greene: *The Power and the Glory*. Paris occupied by the Germans. Richard Wright: *Native Son*.

1941    Japanese attack Pearl Harbor. Germany invades U.S.S.R. Orson Welles: *Citizen Kane*. Edward Hopper: *Nighthawks*. Deaths of James Joyce and Virginia Woolf.

1942    Albert Camus: *The Stranger*. *Casablanca* premieres in theaters. Napalm invented. Walter De La Mare: *Collected Poems*.

1943    Jean Paul Sartre: *Being and Nothingness*. Allies invade Italy.

1944    T.S Eliot: *Four Quartets*. Roosevelt elected for fourth term as U.S. president. Saul Bellow: *Dangling Man*.

1945    Atomic bomb dropped on Hiroshima. World War II ends. John Steinbeck: *Cannery Row*. George Orwell: *Animal Farm*. Microwave oven invented. Richard Wright: *Black Boy*. Death of Theodore Dreiser.

1946    Erich Auerbach: *Mimesis*. Eugene O'Neill: *The Iceman Cometh*. Robert Penn Warren: *All the King's Men*. Bertrand Russell: *History of Western Philosophy*.

1947    Thomas Mann: *Doktor Faustus*. John Steinbeck: *The Pearl*. Tennessee Williams: *A Streetcar Named Desire*.

1948    Norman Mailer: *The Naked and the Dead*. South Africa adopts *apartheid* as official policy. Foundation of Israel. Gandhi assassinated.

1949    NATO founded. Arthur Miller: *Death of a Salesman*. Alejo Carpentier: *The Kingdom of the World*. Simone de Beauvoir: *The Second Sex*. George Orwell: *Nineteen Eighty-Four*.

1950        McCarthy Era begins. The United States attacks Korea. India declares itself a republic. Jackson Pollock: *Lavendar Mist*. Ernest Hemingway: *Across the River and into the Trees*.

1951        Samuel Beckett: *Molloy* and *Malone Dies*. First nuclear power plant built. Julio Cortázar: *Bestiario*. First color television appears. Graham Greene: *The End of the Affair*. J. D. Salinger: *Catcher in the Rye*. John Huston: *The African Queen*.

1952        Ralph Ellison: *Invisible Man*. Dwight Eisenhower elected president. John Steinbeck: *East of Eden*. Willem de Kooning: *Woman and Bicycle*. Ernest Hemingway: *The Old Man and the Sea*. John Huston: *The Red Badge of Courage*.

1953        Conquest of Mt. Everest. James Baldwin: *Go Tell It on the Mountain*. DNA discovered. Arthur Miller: *The Crucible*. Tennessee Williams: *Camino Real*.

1954        Ernest Hemingway wins the Nobel Prize for Literature. Supreme Court rules to end segregation in public schools. William Golding: *Lord of the Flies*. Wallace Stevens: *Collected Poems*. William Carlos Williams: *The Desert Music*. Death of Henri Matisse.

1955        Vladimir Nabokov: *Lolita*. Samuel Beckett: *Waiting for Godot*. Allen Ginsberg: *Howl*. J.R.R. Tolkien: *Lord of the Rings*. Jasper Johns: *Flag*. Deaths of Albert Einstein and Charlie Parker.

1956        Albert Camus: *The Fall*. Eisenhower reelected president. Stanley Kubrick: *The Killing*. Deaths of Jackson Pollock, Art Tatum, and H.L. Mencken. Eugene O'Neill: *Long Day's Journey into Night*.

1957        Samuel Beckett: *Endgame*. David Lean: *The Bridge on the River Kwai*. Ayn Rand: *Atlas Shrugged*. Jack Kerouac: *On the Road*. Death of Wallace Stevens.

1958        U.S. launches its first satellite. Alfred Hitchcock: *Vertigo*. Stanley Kramer: *The Defiant Ones*. Chinua Achebe: *Things Fall Apart*. Harold Pinter: *The Birthday Party*.

1959        Alaska and Hawaii become 49th and 50th states in the union. Philip Roth: *Goodbye, Columbus*. William Burroughs: *Naked Lunch*. Saul Bellow: *Henderson the Rain King*. Deaths of Frank Lloyd Wright and Billie Holiday.

| 1960 | Alfred Hitchcock: *Psycho*. U. S. begins embargo on Cuba. John F. Kennedy elected president. Frederico Fellini: *La Dolce Vita*. John Updike: *Rabbit, Run*. John Barth: *The Sot Weed Factor*. Flannery O'Connor: *The Violent Bear It Away*. Harper Lee: *To Kill a Mockingbird*. Death of Richard Wright. |
|------|------|
| 1961 | U.S.S.R. makes first manned space flight. Bay of Pigs invasion fails. Joseph Heller: *Catch-22*. V. S. Naipaul: *A House for Mister Biswas*. James Baldwin: *Nobody Knows My Name*. Berlin Wall erected in Germany. Death of Ernest Hemingway. |
| 1962 | John Steinbeck wins the Nobel Prize. U. S. sends troops to Vietnam. Rachel Carson: *Silent Spring*. Ken Kesey: *One Flew Over the Cuckoo's Nest*. William Faulkner: *The Reivers*. Anthony Burgess: *A Clockwork Orange*. James Baldwin: *Another Country*. John Frankenheimer: *The Manchurian Candidate*. Deaths of William Faulkner and Robinson Jeffers. |
| 1963 | John F. Kennedy assassinated; Lyndon B. Johnson is sworn in as president. Julio Cortázar: *Hopscotch*. Kurt Vonnegut: *Cat's Cradle*. Thomas Pynchon: *V.* Alfred Hitchcock: *The Birds*. Deaths of Sylvia Plath, Robert Frost, and William Carlos Williams. |
| 1964 | Nikita Khruschev removed from power in the Soviet Union; replaced by Leonid Brezhnev. Lyndon Johnson elected president. Saul Bellow: *Herzog*. Gore Vidal: *Julian*. Vietnam War begins. Ernest Hemingway: *A Moveable Feast*. |
| 1965 | Malcolm X assassinated. Truman Capote: *In Cold Blood*. Deaths of Shirley Jackson and Randall Jarrell. Harold Pinter: *The Homecoming*. |
| 1966 | Seamus Heaney: *Death of a Naturalist*. Race riots spread through Chicago, Cleveland, and Atlanta. Bernard Malamud: *The Fixer*. Thomas Pynchon: *The Crying of Lot 49*. Jean Rhys: *Wide Sargasso Sea*. |
| 1967 | William Styron: *The Confessions of Nat Turner*. Gabriel García Márquez: *One Hundred Years of Solitude*. Stuart Rosenberg: *Cool Hand Luke*. Tom Stoppard: *Rosencrantz and Guildenstern Are Dead*. Death of Langston Hughes. |

1968        Martin Luther King assassinated. Richard Nixon elected
            president. Norman Mailer: *Armies of the Night*. Joan
            Didion: *Slouching Toward Bethlehem*. Joyce Carol Oates:
            *Expensive People*. Deaths of John Steinbeck and Upton
            Sinclair. First manned landing on the moon.

1969        Joyce Carol Oates: *them*. Dennis Hopper: *Easy Rider*.
            Philip Roth: *Portnoy's Complaint*. Woodstock music festival
            draws over 300,000 fans. Deaths of Jack Kerouac and
            Theodore Adorno.

1970        U. S. military invades Cambodia and Laos. Four student
            demonstrators are killed by the National Guard at Kent
            State University. Deaths of John Dos Passos, Janis Joplin,
            Jimi Hendrix, and John O'Hara. Environmental Protection
            Agency created. Studs Terkel: *Hard Times*. The Beatles: *Let
            It Be*.

1971        President Nixon initiates the Christmas Bombings in
            Vietnam. Iris Murdoch: *An Accidental Man*. Deaths of Jim
            Morrison and Louis Armstrong.

1972        Drought causes Soviet Union to purchase a quarter of the
            U.S. wheat crop in the "Russian Wheat Deal." Nixon
            reelected president. John Boorman: *Deliverance*. Francis
            Ford Coppola: *The Godfather*. William Peter Blattey: *The
            Exorcist*. Deaths of Ezra Pound, Marianne Moore, and
            Edmund Wilson.

1973        Abortion legalized in the U.S. International energy crisis
            brought about by Arab restrictions on oil production.
            Thomas Pynchon: *Gravity's Rainbow*. Erica Jong: *Fear of
            Flying*. Kurt Vonnegut: *Breakfast of Champions*. Deaths of
            Pablo Picasso and W.H. Auden.

1974        Impeachment and resignation of President Richard Nixon;
            Gerald Ford sworn in. Nadine Gordimer: *The
            Conservationist*. Robert Stone: *Dog Soldiers*. Iris Murdoch:
            *The Sacred and Profane Love*. Philip Larkin: *High Windows*.

1975        Saul Bellow: *Humboldt's Gift*. E.L. Doctorow: *Ragtime*. V.S.
            Naipaul: *Guerillas*. Vietnam War ends. Teamster boss
            Jimmy Hoffa disappears and is never found again.
            Microsoft founded. James Salter: *Light Years*.

| | |
|---|---|
| 1976 | Jimmy Carter elected president. Saul Bellow is awarded the Nobel Prize. Alex Haley: *Roots*. Iris Murdoch: *Henry and Cato*. Michael Harrington: *The Twilight of Capitalism*. Death of Martin Heidgger. Raymond Carver: *Will You Please Be Quiet, Please?* |
| 1977 | Department of Energy created in the wake of the energy crisis. Woody Allen: *Annie Hall*. George Lucas: *Star Wars*. Joan Didion: *A Book of Common Prayer*. Deaths of Elvis Presley, Charles Chaplin, and Groucho Marx. |
| 1978 | John Updike: *The Coup*. John Irving: *The World According to Garp*. Death of Norman Rockwell. A.S. Byatt: *The Virgin in the Garden*. Don DeLillo: *Running Dog*. |
| 1979 | Margaret Thatcher elected first woman Prime Minister in United Kingdom. Francis Ford Coppola: *Apocalypse Now*. Partial meltdown releases radioactive material on Three Mile Island. William Styron: *Sophie's Choice*. Norman Mailer: *The Executioner's Song*. Death of John Wayne. |
| 1980 | Outbreak of Iran-Iraq war. Ronald Reagan elected president. John Lennon shot in New York City. Raymond Carver: *What We Talk About When We Talk About Love*. Anthony Burgess: *Earthly Powers*. |
| 1981 | First reports of AIDS are made. John Updike: *Rabbit Is Rich*. Salman Rushdie: *Midnight's Children*. Tobias Wolff: *In the Garden of North American Martyrs*. Philip Roth: *Zuckerman Unbound*. |
| 1982 | Gabriel García Márquez is awarded the Nobel Prize for Literature. Paul Theroux: *Mosquito Cost*. Peter Ackroyd: *The Great Fire of London*. Don DeLillo: *The Names*. |
| 1983 | William Golding, author of *Lord of the Flies*, wins the Nobel Prize for Literature. J.M. Coetzee: *The Life and Times of Michael K*. Death of Tennessee Williams. Raymond Carver: *Cathedral*. |
| 1984 | U.S.S.R. boycotts Los Angeles Olympics. Gore Vidal: *Lincoln*. Norman Mailer: *Tough Guys Don't Dance*. Martin Amis: *Money*. John Updike: *The Witches of Eastwick*. Thomas Pynchon: *Slow Learner*. David Mamet: *Glengarry Glen Ross*. |
| 1985 | Death of Philip Larkin. Anthony Burgess: *The Kingdom of* |

*the Wicked*. Peter Ackroyd: *Hawksmor*. Cormac McCarthy: *Blood Meridian*. Truman Capote: *Three*. Don DeLillo: *White Noise*.

1986        Chernobyl nuclear disaster takes place. Death of Simone de Beauvoir. Donald Barthelme: *Paradise*. Kingsley Amis: *The Old Devils*.

1987        Toni Morrison: *Beloved*. V.S. Naipaul: *The Enigma of Arrival*. Iran attacks United States tanker in Persian Gulf. Joyce Carol Oates: *You Must Remember This*.

1988        Raymond Carver: *Where I'm Calling From*. George Bush elected president. Don DeLillo: *Libra*. James Salter: *Dusk and Other Stories*.

1989        Ayatollah Khomeini issues fatwa on Salman Rushdie after publication of *Satanic Verses*. Oscar Hijuelos: *The Mambo Kings Play Songs of Love*. Kazuo Ishiguro: *The Remains of the Day*. Death of Samuel Beckett.

1990        Nelson Mandela freed after twenty-seven years in jail. Reunification of Germany. Iraq invades Kuwait. J.M. Coetzee: *Age of Iron*. John Updike: *Rabbit at Rest*.

# Contributors

HAROLD BLOOM is Sterling Professor of the Humanities at Yale University. He is the author of over 20 books, including *Shelley's Mythmaking* (1959), *The Visionary Company* (1961), *Blake's Apocalypse* (1963), *Yeats* (1970), *A Map of Misreading* (1975), *Kabbalah and Criticism* (1975), *Agon: Toward a Theory of Revisionism* (1982), *The American Religion* (1992), *The Western Canon* (1994), and *Omens of Millennium: The Gnosis of Angels, Dreams, and Resurrection* (1996). *The Anxiety of Influence* (1973) sets forth Professor Bloom's provocative theory of the literary relationships between the great writers and their predecessors. His most recent books include *Shakespeare: The Invention of the Human* (1998), a 1998 National Book Award finalist, *How to Read and Why* (2000), *Genius: A Mosaic of One Hundred Exemplary Creative Minds* (2002), and *Hamlet: Poem Unlimited* (2003). In 1999, Professor Bloom received the prestigious American Academy of Arts and Letters Gold Medal for Criticism, and in 2002 he received the Catalonia International Prize.

FRANK NORRIS (1870–1902) is considered, along with Stephen Crane, Theodore Dreiser, James Farrell, and John Dos Passos, one of the central figures of American literary naturalism. His works include *McTeague*, *The Octopus*, and *The Pit*.

LIONEL TRILLING (1905–1975) taught at Columbia University, Hunter College, and the University of Wisconsin over the course of a fifty-year academic career. He is the author of a novel, *The Middle of the Journey*, but is more well-known as an essayist interested in culture and ethics. His books include *The Liberal Imagination*, a classic collection of essays, *Beyond Culture*, and *Mind in the Modern World*.

PHILIP RAHV (1908–1973) is known chiefly as the founder and editor of the *Partisan Review*, an influential liberal literary and political journal. He taught at Brandeis University. His books include *Modern Occasions, Image and Idea*, and *Literature and the Sixth Sense*.

MALCOLM COWLEY (1898–1989) served as literary editor of *The New Republic* and edited the *Portable Hemingway, Faulkner*, and *Hawthorne* volumes for Viking. His books include *Exile's Return, Fitzgerald and the Jazz Age*, and *Lesson of the Masters*.

DONALD PIZER is Pierce Butler Professor of English at Tulane University. An eloquent and prolific critic of the American Naturalist tradition, he has published studies of Frank Norris, Theodore Dreiser, and John Dos Passos's *U. S. A.*, as well as several books on the naturalist movement, including *Realism and Naturalism in Nineteenth-Century American Literature, Twentieth-Century American Literary Naturalism: An Interpretation*, and *The Theory and Practice of American Literary Naturalism*.

RICHARD POIRIER is Distinguished Professor of English, Emeritus at Rutgers University and is the Editor-in-Chief of *Raritan*. He is the author of an acclaimed study of Robert Frost, *Robert Frost: The Work of Knowing*, as well as *The Performing Self* and *Trying It Out in America*.

ANN DOUGLAS has taught American studies at Harvard and Princeton Universities and is now Professor of English and Comparative Literature at Columbia University. She is the author of *The Feminization of American Culture* and a highly regarded history of New York City, *Terrible Honesty: Mongrel Manhattan in the 1920's*.

HAROLD KAPLAN is Emeritus Professor of English and American Literature at Northwestern University. He has written *Power and Order: Henry Adams and the Naturalist Tradition in American Fiction* and *Conscience and Memory*.

RICHARD LEHAN is Professor English at UCLA and is the author of *Theodore Dreiser: His World and His Novels*, *A Dangerous Crossing: French Literary Existentialism and the Modern American Novel*, *The Great Gatsby: The Limits of Wonder* and *The City in Literature*.

MICHEL FABRE teaches at the University of Paris. He has written several books on Richard Wright and Chester Himes as well as *From Harlem to Paris: Black American Writers in France, 1840–1980*.

PHILIP FISHER teaches English and American literature at Harvard University. He is the author of *Wonder, The Rainbow, and the Aesthetics of Rare Experiences*, *Making and Effacing Modern Art*, and *The Vehement Passions*.

MICHAEL DAVITT BELL was the J. Leland Miller Professor of American History, Literature, and Eloquence, and the chair of the Department of English at Williams College. His works include *Hawthorne and the Historical Romance of New England*, *The Development of American Romance: The Sacrifice of Relation*, and *The Problem of American Realism: Studies in the Cultural History of a Literary Idea*.

BARBARA HOCHMAN is Lecturer in English at Tel Aviv University. She has written a book-length study of Frank Norris, as well as essays on Edith Wharton and Theodore Dreiser.

DONNA M. CAMPBELL is Associate Professor of English at Gonzaga University. She is the author of *Resisting Regionalism: Gender and Naturalism in American Fiction, 1885–1915* and maintains a website devoted to American Literature and its backgrounds at <http://guweb2.gonzaga.edu/faculty/campbell/enl413/natural.htm>

# Bibliography

Ahnebrink, Lars. *The Beginnings of Naturalism in American Fiction 1891–1903*. Cambridge: Harvard University Press, 1950.

Auerbach, Erich. *Mimesis: The Representation of Reality in Western Literature*. Princeton: Princeton University Press, 1953.

Baguley, David. *Naturalist Fiction: The Entropic Vision*. Cambridge: Cambridge University Press, 1990.

Becker, George J., ed. *Documents of Modern Literary Realism*. Princeton: Princeton University Press, 1963.

Bell, Michael Davitt. "African-American Writing, 'Protest,' and the Burden of Naturalism: The Case of *Native Son*" in *Culture, Genre, and Literary Vocation: Selected Essays on American Literature*. Chicago: University of Chicago Press, 2001.

———. *The Problem of American Realism: Studies in the Cultural History of a Literary Idea*. Chicago: University of Chicago Press, 1993.

Berthoff, Warner. *The Ferment of Realism: American Literature, 1884–1919*. New York: Free Press, 1965.

Block, Haskell M. *Naturalistic Triptych: The Fictive and the Real in Zola, Mann, and Dreiser*. New York: Random House, 1970.

Bloom, Harold, ed. *Modern Critical Interpretations: Theodore Dreiser's* An American Tragedy. New York: Chelsea House, 1988.

———, ed. *Modern Critical Views: John Steinbeck*. New York: Chelsea House, 1987.

———, ed. *Modern Critical Views: Stephen Crane.* New York: Chelsea House, 1987.

———, ed. *Modern Critical Views: Edith Wharton.* New York: Chelsea House, 1986.

———, ed. *Modern Critical Views: Norman Mailer.* New York: Chelsea House, 1986.

Borus, Daniel H. *Writing Realism: Howells, James, and Norris in the Mass Market.* Chapel Hill: University of North Carolina Press, 1989.

Branch, Edgar M. *James T. Farrell.* New York: Twayne, 1971.

Cady, Edwin H. *The Light of Common Day: Realism in American Fiction.* Bloomington: Indiana University Press, 1971.

Campbell, Donna M. *Resisting Regionalism: Gender and Naturalism in American Fiction, 1885–1915.* Athens: Ohio University Press, 1997.

Cassuto, Leonard and Jeanne Campbell Reesman, eds. *Rereading Jack London.* Stanford: Stanford University Press, 1996.

Chase, Richard. *The American Novel and Its Tradition.* Garden City: Doubleday Anchor, 1957.

Civello, Paul. *American Literary Naturalism and Its Twentieth-Century Transformations.* Athens: University of Georgia Press, 1994.

Conder, John J. *Naturalism in American Fiction: The Classic Phase.* Lexington: University Press of Kentucky, 1984.

Cowley, Malcolm. "'Not Men': A Natural History of American Naturalism." *Kenyon Review* 9 (1947): 414–35.

Douglas, Ann. "*Studs Lonigan* and the Failure of History in Mass Society: A Study in Claustrophobia." *American Quarterly* 29, no. 5 (Winter 1977): 487–505.

Fabre, Michel. *The World of Richard Wright.* Jackson: University Press of Mississippi, 1985.

Farrell, James T. "Some Observations on Naturalism, So Called, in Fiction" in *Reflections at Fifty.* New York: Vanguard, 1950.

Figg, Robert M. "Naturalism as a Literary Form." *Georgia Review* 18 (1964): 308–16.

Fisher, Philip. *Hard Facts: Setting and Form in the American Novel.* New York: Oxford University Press, 1985.

Frierson, William C., and Herbert Edwards. "Impact of French Naturalism on American Critical Opinion, 1877–1892." *PMLA* 63 (1948): 1007–16.

Furst, Lilian R., and Peter N. Skrine. *Naturalism*. London: Methuen, 1971.

Gair, Christopher. *Complicity and Resistance in Jack London's Novels*. Lewiston: Edwin Mellen Press, 1997.

Geismar, Maxwell. *Rebels and Ancestors: The American Novel, 1890-1915*. Boston: Houghton Mifflin, 1953.

Giles, James R. *The Naturalistic Inner-City Novel in America: Encounters with the Fat Man*. Columbia: University of South Carolina Press, 1995.

Graham, Don, ed. *Critical Essays on Frank Norris*. Boston: G. K. Hall, 1980.

————. *The Fiction of Frank Norris: The Aesthetic Context*. Columbia: University of Missouri Press, 1978.

Graham, Philip. "Naturalism in America: A Status Report." *Studies in American Fiction* 10 (1982): 1–16.

Habegger, Alfred. *Gender, Fantasy, and Realism in American Literature*. New York: Columbia University Press, 1982.

Hakutani, Yoshinobu, and Lewis Fried, eds. *American Literary Naturalism: A Reassessment*. Heidelberg: Carl Winter, 1975.

Hayles, N. Katherine. *Chaos Bound: Orderly Disorder in Contemporary Literature and Science*. Ithaca: Cornell University Press, 1990.

Hicks, Granville. *The Great Tradition: An Interpretation of American Literature Since the Civil War*. New York: Macmillan, 1933.

Hochman, Barbara. *The Art of Frank Norris, Storyteller*. Columbia: University of Missouri Press, 1988.

Howard, June. *Form and History in American Literary Naturalism*. Chapel Hill: University of North Carolina Press, 1985.

Kaplan, Amy. *The Social Construction of American Realism*. Chicago: University of Chicago Press, 1981.

Kaplan, Harold. *Power and Order: Henry Adams and the Naturalist Tradition in American Fiction*. Chicago: University of Chicago Press, 1981.

Lawlor, Mary. *Recalling the Wild: Naturalism and the Closing of the American West*. New Brunswick: Rutgers University Press, 2000.

LeClair, Tom. *In the Loop: Don DeLillo and the Systems Novel*. Urbana: University of Illinois Press, 1987.

Lehan, Richard. "American Literary Naturalism: The French Connection." *Nineteenth-Century Fiction* 38, no. 4 (1984): 529–557.

————. *Theodore Dreiser: His World and His Novels*. Carbondale: Southern Illinois University Press, 1969.

Lukács, Georg. "Narrate or Describe? A Preliminary Discussion of Naturalism and Formalism" in *Writer and Critic and Other Essays*, ed. Arthur D. Kahn. London: Martin Press, 1970.

McElrath, Joseph R., Jr. *Frank Norris Revisited*. New York: Twayne Publishers, 1992.

Martin, Jay. *Harvests of Change: American Literature, 1865–1914*. Englewood Cliffs: Prentice-Hall, 1967.

Martin, Ronald E. *American Literature and the Universe of Force*. Durham: Duke University Press, 1981.

Michaels, Walter Benn. *The Gold Standard and the Logic of Naturalism*. Berkeley: University of California Press, 1987.

Mitchell, Lee Clark. *Determined Fictions: American Literary Naturalism*. New York: Columbia University Press, 1989.

Nadeau, Robert. *Readings from the New Book on Nature: Physics and Metaphysics in the Modern Novel*. Amherst: University of Massachusetts Press, 1987.

Nuernberg, Susan M., ed. *Critical Response to Jack London*. Westport: Greenwood Press, 1995.

Perosa, Sergio. *American Theories of the Novel, 1793–1903*. New York: New York University Press, 1983

Pizer, Donald, ed. *The Cambridge Companion to American Realism and Naturalism: Howells to London*. New York: Cambridge University Press, 1995.

———. *The Theory and Practice of American Literary Naturalism: Selected Essays and Reviews*. Carbondale: Southern Illinois University Press, 1993.

———. *Passos's U. S. A.: A Critical Study*. Charlottesville: University Press of Virginia, 1988.

———. *Twentieth-Century American Literary Naturalism: An Interpretation*. Carbondale: Southern Illinois University Press, 1982.

———. *Realism and Naturalism in Nineteenth-Century American Literature*. Carbondale: Southern Illinois University Press, 1966

———, ed. *The Literary Criticism of Frank Norris*. Austin: University of Texas Press, 1964.

Poirier, Richard. *A World Elsewhere: The Place of Style in American Literature*. New York: Oxford University Press, 1966.

Rahv, Philip. *Image and Idea*. Norfolk: New Directions, 1949.

Seaman, Roger. "Naturalist Narratives and Their Ideational Context: A Theory of American Naturalist Fiction." *Canadian Review of American Studies* 19 (1988): 47–64.

Seltzer, Mark. "The Naturalist Machine" in *Sex, Politics, and Science in the Nineteenth-Century Novel*, ed. Ruth Bernard Yeazell. Baltimore: Johns Hopkins University Press, 1986.

Shi, David. *Facing Facts: Realism in American Thought and Culture, 1850–1920*. New York: Oxford University Press, 1995.

Spanier, Sandra Whipple. "Catherine Barkley and the Hemingway Code: Ritual and Survival in *A Farewell to Arms*" in *Modern Critical Interpretations: Ernest Hemingway's* A Farewell to Arms, ed. Harold Bloom. New York: Chelsea House, 1987.

Spilka, Mark. "The Death of Love in *The Sun Also Rises*" in *Modern Critical Interpretations: Hemingway's* The Sun Also Rises, ed. Harold Bloom. New York: Chelsea House, 1987.

Stromberg, Roland N. *Realism, Naturalism, and Symbolism: Modes of Thought and Expression in Europe*. New York: Walker: 1968.

Sundquist, Eric J., ed. *American Realism: New Essays*. Baltimore: Johns Hopkins University Press, 1982.

Tandt, Christophe Den. *The Urban Sublime in American Literary Naturalism*. Urbana: University of Illinois Press, 1998.

Tanner, Tony. "On the Parapet: A Study of the Novels of Norman Mailer." *The Critical Quarterly* 12, no. 2 (Summer 1970): 153–176.

Taylor, Gordon O. *The Passages of Thought: Psychological Representation in the American Novel, 1870–1900*. New York: Oxford University Press, 1969.

Thorp, Willard. *American Writing in the Twentieth Century*. Cambridge: Harvard University Press, 1960.

Trachtenberg, Alan. *The Incorporation of America: Culture and Society in the Gilded Age*. New York: Hill and Wang, 1982.

Trilling, Lionel. *The Liberal Imagination*. New York: Viking, 1950.

Walcutt, Charles Child. *American Literary Naturalism: A Divided Stream*. Minneapolis: University of Minnesota Press, 1956.

Ziff, Larzer. *The American 1890's*. New York: Viking, 1966.

# Acknowledgments

"Zola as a Romantic Writer" by Frank Norris. From *The Literary Criticism of Frank Norris*, ed. Donald Pizer. © 1964 by Donald Pizer. Reprinted by permission.

"Reality in America" by Lionel Trilling. From *The Liberal Imagination*. © 1940, 1941, 1943, 1945, 1946, 1947, 1948, 1949, 1950 by Lionel Trilling, first published in *The Liberal Imagination*, reprinted with the permission of the Wylie Agency, Inc., 1952.

"Notes on the Decline of Naturalism" by Philip Rahv. From *Image and Idea: Fourteen Essays on Literary Themes*. © 1949 by Philip Rahv. Used by permission of New Directions Publishing Corporation.

"Naturalism in American Literature" by Malcolm Cowley. From *Evolutionary Thought in America*, ed. Stow Persons. © 1950 by Yale University Press. Reprinted by permission.

"Late Nineteenth-Century American Naturalism" by Donald Pizer. From *Realism and Naturalism in Nineteenth-Century American Literature*. © 1966 by Donald Pizer. Reprinted by permission.

"Panoramic Environment and the Anonymity of the Self" by Richard Poirier. From *A World Elsewhere: The Place of Style in American Literature*. © 1966 by Richard Poirier. Reprinted by permission.

361

"*Studs Lonigan* and the Failure of History in Mass Society: A Study in Claustrophobia" by Ann Douglas. From *American Quarterly* 29, no. 5 (Winter 1977): 487–505. © 1977 by the American Studies Association. Reprinted with permission of the Johns Hopkins University Press.

"Naturalist Fiction and Political Allegory" by Harold Kaplan. From *Power and Order: Henry Adams and the Naturalist Tradition in American Fiction*. © 1981 by the University of Chicago. Reprinted by permission.

"American Literary Naturalism: The French Connection" by Richard Lehan. From *Nineteenth-Century Fiction* 38, no. 4 (March 1984): 529–557. © 1984 by the Regents of the University of California. Reprinted by permission.

"Beyond Naturalism?" by Michel Fabre. From *The World of Richard Wright*. © 1985 by Michel Fabre. Reprinted by permission of the author.

"The Naturalist Novel and the City: Temporary Worlds" by Philip Fisher. From *Hard Facts: Setting and Form in the American Novel*. © 1985 by Oxford University Press, Inc. Reprinted by permission.

"The Revolt Against Style: Frank Norris" by Michael Davitt Bell. From *The Problem of American Realism: Studies in the Cultural History of a Literary Idea*. © 1993 by The University of Chicago. Reprinted by permission.

"Contemporary Literary Naturalism," by Donald Pizer. From *The Theory and Practice of American Literary Naturalism*. © 1993 by the Board of Trustees, Southern Illinois University. Reprinted by permission.

"*The Awakening* and *The House of Mirth*: Plotting Experience and Experiencing Plot" by Barbara Hochman. From *The Cambridge Companion to American Realism and Naturalism*, ed. Donald Pizer. © 1995 by Cambridge University Press. Reprinted by permission.

"Dreiser, London, Crane, and the Iron Madonna" by Donna M. Campbell. From *Resisting Regionalism: Gender and Naturalism in American Fiction, 1885–1915*. © 1997 by Donna M. Campbell. Published by Ohio University Press. Reprinted by permission.

# Index